Democracy
in the United States

Democracy

in the United States

SECOND EDITION

William H. Riker

Professor of Political Science
The University of Rochester

THE MACMILLAN COMPANY, NEW YORK
COLLIER–MACMILLAN LIMITED, LONDON

TO MY *Mother and Father*

Second Printing, 1965

Earlier edition, entitled *Democracy in the United States,* copyright 1953 by The Macmillan Company.

Library of Congress catalog card number: 65–15173

THE MACMILLAN COMPANY, New York
COLLIER–MACMILLAN CANADA, LTD., Toronto, Ontario

PRINTED IN THE UNITED STATES OF AMERICA

Preface to the Second Edition

In this revision I have tried to preserve completely the flavor of the argument of the first edition. This argument was, I believe, the main merit of the book and the chief ingredient of its usefulness in the classroom. At the same time, I have tried to bring it up to date by the substitution and addition of recent illustrations of the principles discussed.

WILLIAM H. RIKER

Preface to
the First Edition

In this book I have endeavored to interpret our political institutions on the basis of an internally consistent theory of the democratic ideal. My version of the ideal, which serves as my standard of judgment, is set forth at length in Chapter 1. But the argument of the book also rests on certain presuppositions about method, presuppositions which in all fairness ought to be explained to the reader.

My fundamental assumption about method is that fact and value are inseparably intertwined. More precisely stated, this is the proposition that all knowledge about society is constructed and has its meaning in terms only of an ideology or a moral philosophy. The social reality exists even when people do not think about it; but it exists without meaning; it acquires meaning only when it is understood by a moralizing human mind. As the words I have used indicate, I have adapted this assumption from A. N. Whitehead and Karl Mannheim; and I refer the reader to their works for two elaborate, yet very different, justifications of it.[1] Aristotle meant the same thing, I believe, when he defined politics as a branch of ethics, as indeed the highest and ultimate moral science. He contrasted the science of politics with natural science, saying that the latter starts with things and

---

[1] See Karl Mannheim, *Ideology and Utopia: An Introduction to the Sociology of Knowledge* (New York, Harcourt, Brace, second edition, 1949). While Whitehead's comments on this subject are scattered throughout most of his later writing, the most convenient source is probably *Modes of Thought* (New York, Macmillan, 1938).

searches for their causes, while the former starts with a goal and searches for a way to attain it. Both kinds of science occasionally use the approach of the other, but the political scientist should never forget that his main interest is in achieving an ideal, not in the analysis of causes.

Having assumed that politics is a moral science, it follows that the first duty of the scientist must be the rationalization of an ideology, the working out of a coherent value system. Following that, the scientific question is: "What institutions will encourage the chosen morality?" Description and the analysis of causes (or perhaps more accurately, the analysis of occasions) are necessary for answering this question; but description and analysis are always subordinate to a greater issue, which is the determination of the moral significance of reality.

This is the procedure I have tried to follow here. In the first chapter, I have tried to work out a coherent political ideal and in the succeeding chapters I have analyzed our political institutions, asking always how they can be made to realize it. The reader ought not to infer that I have attempted any more than this. He ought always to be aware that, unless he accepts in its entirety the ideal set forth in Chapter 1, he need not accept the analysis of institutions that follows, except insofar as it fits in with his own moral philosophy. Even if some readers cannot accept my value system, which like all political theories is an unprovable given, they will, I hope, find it a worth-while exercise in the procedure of this science to follow an analysis such as this all the way through.

*

Many people have helped to write this book and I want to thank them all. It grew originally out of discussions with my teachers, my students and others of my friends. Since the area it covers is so vast, I am, of course, deeply indebted to many writers—those to whom I feel the greatest obligation

I have listed in the "Suggestions for Further Reading." I owe much to the careful critical comment of Professors Merle Fainsod and Charles Cherington of Harvard University and Erwin Bard of Brooklyn College. Two of my colleagues at Lawrence College, Professors Craig Thompson who read carefully through the whole manuscript and Maurice Cunningham who read several chapters, not only removed many infelicities of style but also in many ways sharpened the argument. To Miss Sylvia Godschalx, who typed the manuscript, I owe much for her willingness to do extra work and for her ability to decipher. I acknowledge my deepest obligation to my father not only for his judicious comments on this book but also for his constant inspiration in life and scholarship.

WILLIAM H. RIKER

Lawrence College
January 1, 1953

Contents

3.

THE TECHNIQUES OF DEMOCRACY: POLITICAL PARTIES AND CIVIL LIBERTIES 84

4.

THE CONSTITUTION AND THE THEORY OF THE SEPARATION OF POWERS 121

5.

THE CONGRESS 150

6.

THE PRESIDENT   185

7.

THE SUPREME COURT   235

1.

The Meaning of Democracy

> Legislators and would-be founders of any constitution . . . will find that the work of construction is not their only or principal business. The maintenance of a constitution is the thing which really matters.
>
> —ARISTOTLE, *Politics,* 1319b [1]

INTRODUCTION: SELF-KNOWLEDGE FOR SELF-CONTROL

Few men ever really understand their own institutions. Even the most civilized often live like the Trobriand Islanders, unaware, that is, of the neat dovetail of their trading system until an anthropologist from outside, a Malinowski, observes it for them. And then the Islanders' surprise at his revelations signifies simply their (and mankind's) persistent incredulity in the face of reason. The supposedly civilized, moreover, have so often said "natural law" (or "ideals," or an "unseen hand," or a "god") manipulates mundane things that it seems they have despaired of comprehending their own rituals and forms.

Such despair—or perhaps indifference—is in the long run the mask which smothers even the greatest and most beloved institutions. The penalty for not understanding is unforeseen change—change which, in fact, seems to the unsophisticated ghostly and unpredictable. Western believers in the "unseen hand" theory of economics, for example, are still bewildered and frightened by the disappearance of the nineteenth century "free market." Man's institutions, whether governmental, familial, or economic, are the one part of his environment which he can control for better or worse. To climate and geography man can

---

[1] All quotations from the *Politics* are from the translation by Ernest Barker, *The Politics of Aristotle,* 1946. Reprinted by permission of the Clarendon Press, Oxford.

only adapt; but what he himself has made he can conceivably make over. Unfortunately, this self-command, however existent *a priori,* is in fact seldom possible *because* men do not understand their own creations. Difficult as the understanding is, however, it is essential to the preservation and intelligent operation of society's forms.

One of the first and greatest problems which every society must face is, therefore, the gathering and organizing of enough self-knowledge for its self-control. This book is intended as a small contribution to the American effort at self-knowledge.

American democracy is dearly loved by us but less dearly preserved. In an age of competing systems that would destroy it, this form of life must carefully review its defenses. Even more than guns and bombs, the defenses are knowledge of its real operation and faith in its ideal.

The necessity of defense is real enough, considering the presence of antidemocratic totalitarians to the right and left. Let us hope that the American Republic does not suffer the same fate as the Weimar Republic in Germany or the Third Republic in France. And even more, let us hope that the democracy all over the world does not disappear as abruptly and as permanently as the independent Greek city states in the fourth century before Christ. At the very time Aristotle, in the words quoted at the head of this chapter, first attempted to acquire the necessary self-knowledge, they were being absorbed into the Alexandrine empire and the despotism of the Epigoni.

"A Conceptual Gladstone Bag"

We proudly call our government a democracy; yet ordinarily we have but a vague idea of what the word means. Among both scholars and the general citizenry, the more frequent its use, the less uniform is its sense.

Unfortunate as this confusion may be, it is certainly understandable. In the twenty-five centuries since the word first came into common speech, it has been used to describe a great array of institutions, many of which resemble each other far less than they differ. It was applied first to the governments of some Aegean cities; but it has since come to name also governments as widely dissimilar as those in certain medieval friaries and those of contemporary Leviathans. With even more garbling results, it has been used to convey a variety of abstract ideas drawn from different philosophies, based on different premises, and existing in different cultures. Among the Greeks, the word soon came to mean a way of life as well as government, a way of life both despised and admired. In subsequent cultures its spiritual reference has been equally ambivalent. Both supporters and opponents have at once, for example, claimed it for and attacked it in the name of such contrasting philosophies as idealism and materialism. Each new application to institutions or ideas has left a mark upon its meaning so that today its real sense is almost completely covered up.

In addition to these usually legitimate extensions in the past, "democracy" is frequently used in the contemporary world without justification either in logic or in observation. It has, that is, become a stock and abused slogan in the vocabulary of propagandists for almost every system of government.

It was not always so. During most periods of history, only a small minority (or none at all) could be named "democrat." In medieval and early modern times, "democracy" was just one word on a list of known, but unpracticed, sins. And as recently as the middle of the nineteenth century, both the name and practice of democracy were anathema to respectable people. For bourgeois minds the word identified both Jacobin terror and Jacksonian vulgarity.

Early in the twentieth century, however, "democracy" began to achieve its present status as a universally approved stereotype. The three largest states calling themselves democracies were almost the masters of the earth. From Downing Street and the City, from the Quai d'Orsay and the Bourse, from the White House and Wall Street emanated orders ultimately controlling every continent of the world except (before 1918) the German part of Europe and (after 1917) Russia. In the careless logic of propagandists, democracy was itself credited for the imperial ascendancy of its practitioners. Coexistence was mistaken for cause; and the worldly success of democracies lent approval to the democratic ideal.

At the same time "democracy" received this unlooked for legacy from imperialism, the antagonism of its enemies was largely diverted to communism, which was to them a more ominous threat to the stability of ownership. Hence, democracy ceased to be the main slogan of the far left and the main bogey of the far right. By these two events, perhaps more than coincidentally related, the word "democracy" was relieved from serious attack and praised for its very being. It has become a mild enough slogan to thrive on universal acclaim.

In consequence, the word has now far more popularity than meaning. Its confusion of sense, complicated enough from mere age, is now compounded many times over by the deliberate distortion of some who mouth it constantly. Thus, for example, patriotic, but unscientific, anthropologists have found "democracy" among all sorts of primitives, ancient and modern. And the systems which most nineteenth century critics would surely have called the feudal despotism of Falangist Spain, the military despotisms of certain Balkan and Latin American republics, and the party despotism of the Soviet Union are described by their unblushing propagandists as "democracies."

Consequently, some contemporary writers, disgusted with the apparently increasing complications of the word, have suggested that it be abandoned altogether. Consider, for example, this comment by T. S. Eliot: [2]

When a term has become so universally sanctified as "democracy" now is, I begin to wonder whether it means anything, in meaning too many things: it has arrived perhaps at the position of a Merovingian Emperor, and wherever it is invoked, one begins to look for the Major of the Palace.

To find a hidden equivalent (as Eliot does in the equally vague "Liberalism") is an obscurantist device. And complete abandonment of the word would be an admission of the inutility of language and the impotence of abstract thought. This is too great a price simply for an arid and pedantic precision. So, if the word be indispensable, yet its meaning confused, the first task of its users is its definition. Definition is indeed the more reasonable path, even though it is at the outset recognized that, as Carl Becker so neatly suggests, the word is "a kind of conceptual Gladstone bag which, with a little manipulation, can be made to accommodate almost any collection of social facts we may wish to carry about in it." [3]

Yet definition is a difficult matter. It is no great exaggeration to say that the definition of words like "democracy," words of indefinite reference which describe the relations of men, is the most persistent and difficult problem of philosophy. As in the science of mathematics, such definitions must be internally consistent in order to avoid sophism. By

[2] T. S. Eliot, *The Idea of a Christian Society* (New York, Harcourt, Brace and Co., 1940), pp. 11–12.
[3] Carl Becker, *Modern Democracy* (New Haven, Yale University Press, 1941), p. 4.

comparison, however, mathematical definitions, even though they are the central issues of the science, are easy because they are by *fiat*. Definitions of words about society must be more than internally consistent; they must also be in accord with the intuitive logic of the past which has adapted meaning to experience. Even if one wished to do so, that logic cannot be denied. The multiplicity of meanings a word today inherits is based upon many centuries of empirical observation, observation of relations between new phenomena and old words. In defining these words tradition has authority, not because of age, but because the tradition is itself the very treasury of knowledge which passes from generation to generation and from culture to culture. While men may inventory the storehouse in order to differentiate the pure metal from the fool's gold hoarded by unwitting predecessors, they dare not in a fit of cynicism throw away the treasury altogether.

So the problem of definition comes to this: the central thread must be untangled out of a knot of confused meanings. Once the essentials are picked out, the hidden logic which tangled them and which knotted on the short strands of side-issues will be apparent enough for all to see. But how shall the essentials be distinguished?

There is only one method available. If some of the most important examples of the idea of "democracy" are set side by side, then the definition-maker can perhaps discern the essential meaning. He can select those elements that recurrently seem indispensable and that are implicit in all of them. He can discard those faddish ideas which are sometimes parasitically attached. He can perhaps observe, if the examples are arranged chronologically, the line of descent of the central theme and even note the occasion for the attachment of side-issues. If, further, the examples well typify the main democratic movements, he can be somewhat confident that his definition is accurate. It will be accurate at least to the degree that democrats have understood what they believed in.

The crucial step in this method of definition is, manifestly, the selection of examples. By what standards can they be chosen for comparison? The first standard is certainly that each one be a type, that is, be admitted by the society in which it arose as an adequate statement of its ideal. For the most part, therefore, the examples will be documents prepared by and for a group of representative men, documents, for example, like the *Declaration of Independence*. They will seldom be products of individual writers, except for unusual cases like the *Gettys-*

burg Address in which the society has with remarkable unanimity seized upon one man's ideals for its own. A second standard is that the examples be chosen from what most men would agree are major democratic movements. The modern form of the idea of democracy is probably not much older than three hundred years; but at least one ancient society, the Athenian, must be represented inasmuch as the institution and ideal of democracy originated there (or in some lesser city like it). While thoroughness would require a choice of at least one document from every modern democratic society, so many examples would be unmanageable. To combine brevity with accuracy, the several examples ought to be selected from the great democratic crises which have affected the whole world.

On the basis of these standards, this set of five documents offers most promise for a definition: Pericles' *Funeral Oration,* the *Agreement of the People,* the *Declaration of Independence,* the *Declaration of the Rights of Man and Citizen,* and Lincoln's *Gettysburg Address.*

FIVE DOCUMENTS IN THE DEMOCRATIC TRADITION

Each of the five documents is customarily called an exposition of democratic ideals, though only the first one actually uses the word democracy. Each of them is usually regarded as an epitome of the ideals of the society which produced it. Among them they represent most of the major democratic movements of the world.[4]

Pericles delivered the *Funeral Oration* to an angry and shaken people —a people which had, in the two generations since Marathon, nourished its youth on a sense of destiny; a people which had, in the self-confidence of its leadership, created an empire for the practice of commerce and the ideals of liberty; a people which had, in the knowledge of its glory, surpassed even itself in arts and letters and science and learning; a people which had, in the maturity of its spirit, constructed a government appropriate to its creativity; and yet, with all this, a people which had, in the exigencies of war, just been forced to submit to a summer of siege. It was the first winter of the Peloponnesian War; and Athenians, who thought themselves the freest and strongest of Greeks, had been cooped up by Spartans through the harvest season,

---

[4] See Appendix A for the texts of these documents.

unable to retaliate for the destruction of their crops and orchards except by a small naval expedition against a few of Sparta's weakest allies. If the between-the-lines impression from the *Funeral Oration* is correct, this event produced two moods among the prisoners. One was a shaken self-confidence. The other was a will to victory both for revenge and for renewed self-esteem. The *Oration* was delivered to dissipate the doubt and solidify the determination.

Though the Athenians faced a crisis, they had not yet suffered enough to be afraid. Hence it was both possible and imperative for the leader of the people to compose this noble declaration of their ideals. And, no matter whether Thucydides' report is even partially in Pericles' own words, the *Funeral Oration* is indeed noble. Although it is of course a funeral oration, it is more than the usual eulogy of the dead; it is also and especially a loving eulogy of the city for which they died, of its people, its ideals, and its freedom. In both the ancient and modern world, it has usually been accepted as the classic description of all that was good in Athenian democracy and even in democracy everywhere.

The *Funeral Oration* was produced in a practicing democracy; the *Agreement of the People* originated in anarchy and hope. In the 1640's England was disordered. For the one hundred and fifty years past new commerce, new religion, new industry, new learning, new agriculture, and a new dynasty had exerted increasingly insupportable pressure upon the medieval structure of life and thought. Finally, in ten years of rebellion, the columns and beams of that settled structure collapsed irreparably. The decade was an era of constitution writing simply because no old constitution was still usable. Even royalists like Hobbes were in the constitutionalizing business.

The most active and persistent of the constitution writers were, however, the Independents in the Army. Elevated by a sincere faith, driven by the first conscious humanitarianism of the modern world, they realized more clearly than the rest the need for a better foundation for society. Presbyterians in Parliament may have forced the rebellion; but the Independents (i.e. assorted sects, mostly Baptist) won the war. What made the New Model Army indeed new and really a model was not so much its somewhat regular pay and sterner discipline but rather more the sprinkling of inspired volunteers from Cromwell on down who fought for their vision of a better world. Yet at the end the Independents found "New Presbyter is but Old Priest writ large" in politics as well as cult; in fact it seemed to them that they had exchanged the tyranny of episcopal king for the tyranny of Presbyterian Parliament. They could no more accept the government that was than the government which had been.

The Army was not, however, agreed within itself upon the constitution it should write. During six months, for example, Cromwell veered from supporting a plan of constitutional monarchy to forcing tyrannicide. Varied as Cromwell's views were, he represented only a small part of Army opinion. Civil strife and the collapse of effective censorship encouraged a jungle lushness of new political ideas. And the failure of the king's men impressed ineradicably the conviction that monarchy was not the only form of government.

So the democratic idea sprouted here for the first time in the modern world; it has not since been ever wholly absent. There were good reasons for its rise then: Part of the war was an ideological conflict for the loyalty of the common soldier, who in both his civil and military form is always the center of democratic thought. And the preaching colonels, being aggressive congregationalists and Christians, often found the politics of democracy quite reasonable and appropriate. But, whatever the causes of rebirth, the idea was incorporated into the doctrine of the Levellers whose leader, when Parliament or Protector did not have him in the Tower, was John Lilburne.

During the constitutional crisis of 1647–1648 when the Army was finally forced to decide who should rule, a majority of the elected regimental representatives, the Agitators of the Army, were Lilburne's followers—and possibly also were a majority of the soldiers themselves. The Agitators drew up the *Agreement of the People* as a solution to the governmental problem, a consciously democratic solution. (It was one of them, Colonel Rainsborough, who made that classic statement of the democratic dogma: "For really I think that the poorest he that is in England hath a life to live, as the greatest he.") Though it was debated at length in the Army Council and the purged Parliament, the *Agreement* was, of course, not adopted, even in a modified form. It contained perhaps too reasonable and too startling an idea; and Cromwell, now almost a dictator, was so much the country squire that he could not abandon property qualifications for voting.

The *Agreement* was forgotten, even though it was brief and just, the first and best description of modern democratic ideas. But the ideals generated by the Levellers lived in practice, not so much in England as in America; and they waxed great again in both countries toward the end of the eighteenth century.

The *Declaration of Independence* was then the clear and stirring signal for the rebirth of democratic politics. It was clear, for it was the herald of what was soon evidently the first successful democratic revolution. It was stirring, for it was composed by Thomas Jefferson, the most realistic of propagandists and most devoted of democrats. And it was a signal, for in the century which followed nearly every country of the Western world experienced some armed revolt for democracy.

After the end of the Commonwealth, there was no place in consciously oligarchic England for democratic ideas. Even in America, most of the colonies were, in government at least, small scale replicas of the class tyranny at home. But here and there in America, thanks to England's "salutary neglect," the ideals of the common soldier of the Ironsides were kept alive and smouldering in political practice as well as political thought. The Revolution was a bellows to blow them to flame.

The New England merchants and Piedmont planters who financed and agitated what was eventually to be revolution were probably not interested in promoting democracy. A quick break without the social upheaval of revolution would have suited them well. It would have remedied their financial grievances without in the least imperiling their financial security. But, in a time of real warfare, disorder initiates changes the end of which no man can foresee. In this case the major unforeseen change was the price which the back-country farmer demanded to finish the war.

The price was democracy, unquestionably the highest wage yet paid for common infantry. Small farmers, who were the main body of soldiers, were attracted and retained in the Continental army only by special inducements. Though poor, they were not so poor that they wanted to serve as mercenaries like European peasants. Though subjects, neither government which claimed their allegiance could exact it by force. By condition equalitarian, the orders of a social superior influenced only a few of them. By circumstance free, Platonic theories of civic duty impressed them not at all. The desertion rate in the Continental army was high. Unable to enlist men wholly by force or gold or hypocritical words, the Revolutionary leaders necessarily relied on genuine inducements: nationalism and especially democracy (which are, in part at least, two sides of one medal).

For evidence of this often overlooked fact one need go no further than the *Declaration* itself. Other evidence indeed exists: the great expansion of the suffrage during the years of war, the state bills of rights, the expulsion and expropriation of the most ardent Tory twelfth of the colonists, the gradual abolition of entail, etc. The *Declaration* was, however, almost the first of the democratic actions. Superficially examined, the *Declaration* is no more than a formal statute of separation. But it contains more than the formalities; it is an explanation of the reasons for rebellion. As there set forth, these are not only immediate grievances but also a political theory, one which without much twisting is wholly democratic.

The first reverberation from the wave of democracy in America was the *Declaration of the Rights of Man and Citizen* in France. Of the documents here compared, it is no doubt the least satisfying; it is too hesitant, too patently a compromise. Even though its democratic voice speaks loudly while its aristo-monarchic voice whispers, the very presence of the whisper unfortunately suggests the democratic speaker has his fingers crossed. Even so, the hopes of '89 and the *Declaration* which verbalized them have dominated French politics for the 160 years since. By only a little bit of premeditated deafness, the contemporary democrat can still receive through the voice of the National Assembly a fierce and profound inspiration.

It is not very strange that the *Declaration* is a compromise; what is truly surprising is that the voice of privilege is so muted. The *Declaration* is in its origin a paradox: a democratic charter composed by monarchists. Not only was the Assembly then monarchist in spirit; but, of those who proposed drafts, Mounier went into aristocratic emigration, Lafayette persisted in devotion to constitutional monarchy, and Sieyès, though no monarchist, had afterward an odd career for a democrat. The *rapporteurs* of the two committees on the *Declaration* were the conservative Archbishop of Bordeaux and that strange and reluctant republican, Mirabeau, who remained until his death secretly in the king's pay. Yet, disregarding the *Declaration's* authors, it cannot be denied that it is essentially democratic. How is this paradox to be explained?

The answer is chiefly that these men were obliged, regardless of conviction, to abandon the past. The *ancien regime* had failed; the symbol of its failure was the very summons which had brought them together. Louis XVI, divinely appointed but unable to raise money for current living, had decided to ask the Estates-General to finance him. In so doing he threw his class on the mercy of the Third Estate, a mercy which soon became euthanasia. Within three months after the Estates met the old order was destroyed in this sequence of events: the Third Estate absorbed the clergy and nobility to become the National Assembly; Parisians symbolically liberated themselves by opening the Bastille; the Jacquerie all over France during the weeks of the Great Fear dispossessed privileged people; and, under the impact of this epidemic violence, the Assembly, almost unanimously, nobles with commoners, formally abolished feudalism.

The old society demolished, it was necessary for the Assembly to rebuild. But there were no architects' plans to guide it. So, before it made a constitution, it listed the principles to be followed in the *Declaration of the Rights of Man and Citizen.*

As might be expected from this origin, the list is a hodge-podge of ideas—a hodge-podge upon which the members could at that time agree. Insofar as they had before them the example of America, it was democratic; since it was a list of principles rather than practices, it was much more democratic than it might otherwise have been. Insofar as they were steeped in eighteenth century rationalism, it was liberal and paternal. But insofar as they were the heirs of the French past, it was equivocal, unwilling to repeat boldly the lessons of America or the maxims of Rousseau.

Lincoln, like Pericles, spoke to a nation in arms. The *Gettysburg Address,* like the *Funeral Oration,* is a eulogy of brave men and of the government for which they fought and died. In similar situations, both statesmen avoided the obvious platitudes in order that they might evoke from the sorrow at the funeral an even greater sacrifice at home and on the field.

Gettysburg was a time of most genuine crisis for the American democracy. During the generation past, the democratic and aristocratic elements in American life had separated geographically. Hence, two nations, based on irreconcilable philosophies and folkways, had matured within one scheme of government. They maneuvered against each other for a decade; the aristocratic society, finding itself outvoted, withdrew; and so precipitated a civil war to determine whether slave-owning "aristocracy" might continue to exist and whether democracy could control the dissidents who would destroy it.

Gettysburg was a crisis also for democracy everywhere. The United States government, in American and European eyes alike, was the model of nineteenth century democracy. As the great experiment with universal suffrage, its success determined the repute of democracy everywhere. The present world-wide ascendancy of democratic theory is in no small part a consequence of the fact that American democracy survived its civil war.

This war was difficult. It was ideological and amateur—both attributes which increase ferocity; it was godfather to the new and horrible tactics of attrition, mass maneuvers, and destruction of war supplies. Most Americans, or rather most Northerners, have today forgotten their grandfathers' intense partisanship; but they have acquired out of the history books, as a substitute and less fruitful bias, a belief that the Confederacy could not possibly have won. Yet in 1863 Northerners had not this easy self-confidence of hindsight. Both sides had in the beginning anticipated easy victory; as the war dragged inconclusively on, however, defeatism spread in South and North alike.

The moral of Gettysburg for the North, a moral which was abundantly clear four months later when Lincoln spoke at the battle-ground, was that only Southern defeatism was justified. The best Confederate effort had failed; Lee's only major invasion army had been repulsed (though not routed). To the North the battle therefore suggested: "Though the South is not yet defeated, it cannot win; but you can—if you have great determination." Lincoln sought to instill that determination in the people.

His "brief remarks" are the classic statement of nineteenth century democracy. In a few epigrammatic clauses, the ideals and methods of the democratic life are expounded with inspired and sympathetic clarity. It is not strange that this speech became the classic form of the democratic dogma, not only in his own country but all over the world.

THE DEMOCRATIC IDEAL

Such were the origins of the five documents here to be analyzed. Viewed historically, they have nothing in common except their roots in Western civilization. Considered in content, however, there are two ideas discernible in a comparable form in all of them. One is an ideal; the other is a means of realizing it.

What is the ideal? The five statements are various; but they have all the same basic sense. They are like five proofs of the same geometric theorem: they proceed by a variety of routes, some devious, some direct; but since they are really proofs, they all end up in the same place.

None of them straightforwardly defines its ideal, democracy. As might be expected in papers prepared by men of action, each emphasizes immediate problems of practice and policy. All of them do, however, make comments on democratic theory and list attributes of the democratic ideal. To find, then, a reasonable statement of the ideal itself, it is only necessary, following the procedure set forth previously, to compare the attributes listed in all documents.

To begin with, all agree that democracy is a government operated by a vague entity called the people, which is to be contrasted with governments operated by an elite. Operation by the people may in fact mean no more than operation by elites responsible not to themselves alone but in some direct way to the larger society. Democracy is, therefore, a government directed by the popular will rather than by the will of an assumed few. This is the sense of Lincoln's aphorism: ". . . government of the people, by the people, for the people . . ." Pericles said the same thing almost as concisely: "Our constitution is named a democracy, because it is in the hands not of the few but of the many." Less trenchant, but no less certain, the *Agreement of the People* suggested in its very title the popular basis of the government it proposed. And, to make its position definite, it called for universal suffrage and even defined "good" laws as those ". . . not . . . destructive to the . . . well-being of the people." Two of the famous self-evident truths set forth at the beginning of the *Declaration of Independence* are government by and for the people: "To secure these rights [i.e. Life, Liberty, and the pursuit of Happiness, presumably for everybody] Governments are instituted among Men, deriving their just powers from the consent of the governed." Finally, the *Declaration of the Rights of Man* (popular enough by its very title) contains these two unconditional assertions: "The source of all sovereignty is essentially in the nation . . ." and "Law is the expression of the general will. All citizens have the right to take part . . . in its formation." All five documents agree, therefore, that government by the people and in their own interest must be an essential part of the ideal of democracy.

But it is not all of the ideal. In addition, all the documents repeatedly insist on the paramount importance of what they call "liberty" or "freedom." Lincoln called the United States ". . . a new

nation, conceived in liberty . . ." The other papers, much more detailed than the *Gettysburg Address,* enumerate particular liberties at
length. Unfortunately, they do not agree on what the liberties are.
Pericles, though he lacked the modern theory of natural rights, still
evidently believed that in a democracy men were "free." Thus, for
example, in comparing Spartan and Athenian war-potential, he pointed
to the Athenian advantage of a free education (i.e. education controlled by custom and family rather than by city):

They toil from early boyhood in a laborious pursuit after courage, while
we, free to live and wander as we please, march out nonetheless to face
the self-same dangers.

Although the *Agreement* proposed a sovereign legislature, the Levellers
valued certain liberties so highly that they prohibited legislative interference with them. Thus the *Agreement* forbade an established church,
a draft law, any retribution for the "late public disturbances," legal
special privileges, or "bad" laws. Aside from the rights of free worship
and equal protection of law, these prohibitions were either too particular or too vague to be continued in the eighteenth century bills of
rights, bills which nonetheless catalogued rights at great length. The
Declaration of Independence, for example, asserted first generally:
". . . [all men] are endowed . . . with certain inalienable rights;
. . . among these are Life, Liberty and the pursuit of Happiness . . ."
Then, in a list of supposed violations by George III, it implied a
claim to specific rights such as: to revolt, to have legislatures, to
receive fair and equal justice, to consent to taxes and the quartering of
troops, to be tried by a jury, to live under "English laws," etc. While
the *Declaration of Independence* defined freedom indirectly, noting
rights by grievances, the *Declaration of Rights* tabulated in a final
register all the liberal, democratic, constitutional, and humanitarian
thought of the previous 150 years. Starting with a general and inclusive
pronouncement on natural rights, it lists as essential rights self-
government, fair legal procedure, free speech and opinion, responsible
government, and private property.

Very clearly, all five documents connect democracy closely with
"liberty," "freedom," and "rights." The affinity is certain; but the form
and reason of the relation is obscured altogether, perhaps because
there is so little agreement on what liberty really is.

Similarly, all five commend "equality," although not always in the

same sense. In two of them, "equality" means merely the equal operation of laws. Thus Pericles boasted: ". . . our laws secure equal justice
for all in their private disputes"; and one of the limits the *Agreement*
sought to impose on Parliament was:

That in all laws made or to be made every person may be bound alike,
and that no tenure, estate, charter, degree, birth, or place do confer any
exemption from the ordinary course of legal proceedings whereunto others
are subjected.

Influenced by the natural rights idea, the remaining three proclaimed
a much broader equality. Beyond the equal operation of the laws,
they insisted as well on the equality of the laws' subjects. The
Declaration of Independence avows: "We hold these truths to be self-
evident: that all men are created equal . . ." and Lincoln, echoing
this grandeur, spoke of ". . . a new nation . . . dedicated to the
proposition that all men are created equal . . ." The *Declaration of
Rights* seems to extol both sorts of equality, for the first article strongly
asserts: "Men are born and remain free and equal in rights"; while
the sixth more mildly says: "[law] must be the same for all, whether it
protects or punishes." Democrats have never doubted that democracy
requires equality; but evidently they cannot decide what kind.

Several of the documents rather tentatively parallel democracy and
tolerance. Pericles rejoiced that in Athenian democracy:

We have no black looks or angry words for our neighbor if he enjoys himself in his own way, and we abstain from the little acts of churlishness
which, though they leave no mark, yet cause annoyance to whoso notes
them . . .

—an exemplary ideal, even if it is hard to believe that he spoke the
exact truth. On a more theoretical level, the *Declaration of Rights*
sets forth the same ideal by emphasizing that one man's rights are
limited by the same grant to everybody else. In a much more specific
and ephemeral form, the *Agreement* too stressed tolerance. It was
the only proposed solution to the Civil Wars which included both
religious toleration and a general amnesty.

Several other similarities are evident among the five. In all, for
example, deference (usually perfunctory) is displayed for the pre-
vailing religion; in all, likewise, one finds a mild (but somewhat less
perfunctory) nationalism. But only one other consciously advocated

doctrine is significant in at least several of them. This is an implied connection between democracy and a willing obedience to law. Lincoln alone did not mention the matter; and in the *Gettysburg Address* there is no reason to. Two documents, the *Funeral Oration* and the *Declaration of Rights,* emphasize the connection. The former asserted: ". . . we are obedient to whomsoever is set in authority, and to the laws; . . ." while the latter pronounced in the seventh article that:

. . . every citizen summoned or seized in virtue of the law ought to render instant obedience; he makes himself guilty by resistance.

The *Declaration of Independence* suggested a little of the same idea by stressing the hesitance of the colonists to revolt. Even the *Agreement* indirectly makes obedience a democratic virtue by saying: ". . . in all laws made . . . every person may be bound alike . . ." To many contemporaries the relation between democracy and submission to law may seem trivial, hardly deserving inclusion among the great democratic principles. Yet it is a connection insisted upon in two documents and clearly implied in two more. To neglect its meaning for democracy would destroy whatever value this method of definition has.

Thus far, the investigation has shown that democracy is defined by a combination of Popularness, Liberty, Equality, Tolerance, and Obedience. Thus far also, not only is the definition ambiguous and abstract, but worse it explains neither what democracy is nor why men love it. These characteristics by themselves hardly seem ideals to fight for. How desirable, for example, is a liberty that depraves or an equality that stultifies? What purpose has popular government that votes itself into despotism? Cannot one obey as well and easily the edicts of a tyrant as the laws of a democracy? Is not tolerance more necessary and more realizable in an anarchy than under any government? And what great evil is a government catering to the most vile of the people's interests!

Apart from some play on words, these questions are absurd because no one of the discovered democratic attributes is an ultimate value. They are means to ends, not ends in themselves. No system of morals, for example, values liberty because of a Viking-complex or equality because of a Samson-complex. Piratical aggrandizement or equality of destruction may often be objectives for the corrupt. But for the democrat, as for the Christian, equality and liberty are good because of the good they bring, because they contribute to the construction of a good man.

Behind all of the characteristics is an ethical judgment, a judgment of what constitutes a good life. Democrats value each of them because they think each can help produce it. What is this democratic vision?

Democracy is self-respect for everybody. Within this simple phrase is all that is and ought to be the democratic ideal. Man's self-respect is an understanding of his dignity. It is the value he sets on his own full development, the condition and result of his self-realization. It is his recognition, with neither pride nor groveling, of his indispensability to society and his insignificance in the universe. Most of all, within the limits society allows, it is a function of his self-direction and self-control, of the choice and living of the life he thinks best.

If self-respect is the democratic good, then all things that prevent its attainment are democratic evils. Servility, which is the essence of self-contempt, and the subordination which engenders it are, therefore, the ultimate evils in the democratic scheme. Servility and pride—for pride feeds on the servility of the humble and is nought but servility expressed in the person who exacts it from others—are the antithesis of democratic self-respect. By them men devalue their persons and disfigure their souls.

Provisionally, self-respect may be called the democratic good and servility (or pride) the democratic evil. The accuracy of this statement of the democratic vision can be tested by the coherence it gives to the five discovered characteristics. If the democratic good is really self-respect and if the democratic evil is really servility (or pride), then each of the five characteristics ought to encourage the one and discourage the other.

Popular government, government by and for the people, is obviously the essential encouragement because self-respect is a function of self-direction. No doubt this world is unreliable and irrational; but some men, it is true, do make plans and carry them out. Some men do control the controllable of their environment. Those who can thus direct themselves, within the range allowed by nature and society, can in just that degree be self-respecting. If the function of man is to live, the sense of realized manhood must develop out of such full living. Since all the controllable environment is ultimately maneuvered by government, only those who participate in it can be in the highest degree self-directing. Of course, even in a despotism, if rulers are weak, the power to maneuver reverts to whoever can usurp it. Witness the rise of the bourgeoisie while the power of the feudal oligarchy, unprepared for modern life, lapsed. Such self-direction is at best accidental and temporary, however. If the ideal is to maintain self-respect for everybody permanently, everybody must help govern: The knowledge of self-direction is acquired in no other way than the having of it in the important affairs of life.

All five documents, therefore, emphasize popular government. There is no substitute for it in a democracy.

But popular government is not the only encouragement for self-respect. The wider the area of self-direction, the more easily self-respect can be developed. The reason democrats have been persistently enamoured of words like "liberty," "freedom," and "natural right" is simply that all of them in one sense or another imply a very wide area for personal self-direction.

But "liberty," "freedom," and "natural right" are possibly even more confusing words than "democracy" itself; their life as slogans has been longer. Although they designate a wide area of self-direction, they do not at all designate for whom. Hence, "liberty" and "freedom" have much of their significance outside of democratic thought. Both were first used by Englishmen to mean "special privilege"; they were, as in the Magna Charta, names for the exemptions enjoyed by a favored few from the laws which governed everybody else. Even as late as the nineteenth century "liberty" often meant no more than much self-direction for an absurdly small number of merchants and manufacturers to exploit the rest of society. And still there are propagandists on the extreme right who identify a free society with a free market by which they apparently mean a market in which the rich are free to fleece the poor. "Liberty" and "freedom" have thus often been class-linked words meaning the irresponsibility of a ruling class. With them the class expressed its self-righteous exultation and pride. Even natural right, a phrase peculiarly associated with democratic thought, originated in the bourgeois and Protestant revolts against medieval politics and religion. The rights which were natural, therefore, were those of the Protestant theocrats and the bourgeoisie—both classes as small minorities as those they sought to displace.

Still, "liberty" and "freedom" and "natural right" all have a democratic sense. As democrats have tried to generalize special privilege, they have generalized also the words which name it. And, of course, they have thus also increased the verbal confusion.

Jack-strawed as all the meanings of the words may be, when each word is considered as a means to the democratic ideal, its practical content is clear enough. "Liberty," for example, in the democratic sense means a wide area of self-direction for the whole citizenry. It consists of privileges which all can exercise without narrowing the self-direction of anyone (except those who have special privileges of which in democratic theory they ought to be deprived). It is freedom of speech, for example, or the election of those who tax. It is not, however, freedom for the industrialist to mulct the worker; nor freedom for the worker to refuse to give an honest day's work; it is not the right of the Nazi's so-called racial people to dispossess "inferior races"; indeed, it is not any right or freedom which systematically deprives other people of their self-respect.

It is in this sense that the eighteenth century obsession with natural rights is to be understood. If democrats today overlook the Enlightenment's wish to generalize privilege, they will find this obsession inexplicable, even when they know that "natural rights" are really moral ideals masquerading as statements of fact or history. The unfortunate results of guaranteeing all rights by natural law, when some of them are mutually exclusive, are today all too clear. It does democracy no service, for example, to call property a "sacred and inviolable right." So long as it is not a means to subordinate others, private property has an indispensable moral value. When, however, it is a right beyond social control, it is more a deprivation than an aid of self-direction. Many contemporaries have wondered why the eighteenth century was unaware of the antinomy. No doubt part of the reason for its lack of hindsight's perception was that it did not have our example of great agglomerations of wealth. It did have, however, a sharply defined class-structure. And still, it was not aware of the antinomy; it was blinded by its eagerness to extend the area of self-direction for as many people as it might. It seized, therefore, on the best expedient it knew. Its best expedient may seem crude indeed for a century cultivating abstract "reason," but there is a very satisfying reassurance in basing everybody's chance for self-respect on immutable, universal law. And since the eighteenth century believed that natural rights inhere in all humans, it could use them not only to guarantee self-direction but also generalize special privileges to everyone.

If these remarks on liberty be granted, then the democratic significance of equality follows clearly. Equality is simply insistence that liberty be democratic, not the privilege of a class. Equality is incompatible with special favor: Among people infused with the ideal of equality neither the pride-swollen nor the servile exist. Democrats have, therefore, always emphasized equality.

It does not make much difference whether equality be equal laws or equal people. For equality to serve as a way to pull down pride, it is only essential that some doctrine of equality exist. Whether it be mild or extreme is less important than that it be appropriate to the nation and generation.

Today the most important form of the equalitarian principle is economic. No document of twentieth century democracy has been here compared because it is too early to select one which epitomizes our time. But had one been analyzed, the only important variation it would show in democratic theory is a new form of equality. Sensitized by depression, by Marxist competition, and by capitalist self-interest, present-day democrats have become increasingly aware that the excessive wealth of a few is the privilege currently most curtailing self-respect. Quite justifiably, therefore, they have expanded equality to mean equal economic opportunity.

Equality is one democratizer of liberty; tolerance is another. Both deny special privilege. The equalitarian democrat opposes the rise of privilege in law or wealth or rank. The tolerant democrat restrains the kind of bigotry that grows into established churches, censored publishing, or superior races. He who wishes self-direction must prove his worthiness by abstaining from interference with others who do not interfere with him. He who lives must know how to let live. This is the meaning of the French revolutionary word "fraternité." It is essential if democracy is to perpetuate itself. Without tolerance, then pride of race, class, nation, wealth, or religion can easily cancel freedom as it did in Hitler's Germany or Franco's Spain.

Obedience, the remaining characteristic, seems at first to contribute less to self-respect than any other one. Indeed, political theory which envirtues obedience usually is produced in most thoroughgoing despotisms. But there is more than one kind of obedience. Despots, seeking to promote servility, extol automatic goosestepping; democrats, seeking to promote self-respect, praise compliance with law as a form of equality. The freedom to disobey laws is a privilege intolerable to democracy. Moreover, since democratic laws are the expression of democratic equality, a willing obedience to them is a way to make democracy work. But note that it is law, the consensus of some sort of general will in custom or legislation, which is democratically obeyed; it is not edict, the order of a particular will. In short, while inordinate respect for powerful persons is a democratic vice, obedience to law is a democratic virtue.

All five of the characteristics discovered in the documents, Popularness, Liberty, Equality, Tolerance, and Obedience, are now seen to be means to one and a greater end. It can therefore be said with more than conditional assurance that democracy is indeed self-respect for everybody.

But let it not be assumed that nations which appropriate the name really practice the doctrine. The ideal is clear enough from the documents; and it is there clearly an ideal. It is quite to be expected, therefore, that all modern democracies contain much special privilege. They have, for the most part, a minimum of the democratic virtues— just enough to permit their claim to the democratic title. Their merit is their adoption of the ideal in spite of strong opposition from the specially privileged within them. Unfortunately, they have not got far toward the practicing of it.

SELF-RESPECT: ONE PERSISTENT IDEAL OF MANKIND

Democracy has, however, no monopoly on this objective. The hope for human dignity, for self-respect, has motivated men in all time. Christianity, for example, exhibits in part the same aspiration. Much of the literature of peasant revolt is beautiful because it breathes the same fire. And nationalism, vicious as its consequences often are, is tolerable only because it generates a bastard self-respect. Indeed, the ideal which sometimes wears the dress of democracy is one of the presistent ideals of mankind.

Christianity, though it is named first in the preceding paragraph, is not the best example of another system of thought inspired by the ideal of universal self-respect. Christianity is a religion, although it produces a social philosophy: And in its religious function it has other ideals besides self-respect. Since the religious aspect is paramount, Christianity is not even primarily impelled by the vision of human dignity. Rather it recompenses for the fear and insecurity of this uncertain world; and its central doctrine is the atonement. But Christianity is in some part also an ethical system; and in this character it is moved by the same spirit as democracy. Thus the sayings of Jesus speak best to a democratic society. And part of the reason men have for so long cherished the promise of the millennium is simply that, in a world of subordination, it stands as one hope for human dignity, after death if not before.

Throughout the New Testament, therefore, one finds as compass points of Christian ethics many of the virtues characteristic of democracy. Jesus said: "And as ye would that men should do unto you, do ye also to them likewise"; and "Thou shalt love thy neighbor as thyself." (Luke 6, 31; Mark 12, 31.) Are not these precepts the democratic spirit of tolerance carried to an ultimate morality? Does not Paul's statement of equality foreshadow Jefferson?

> Now there are diversities of gifts, but the same Spirit. And there are differences of administration, but the same Lord. And there are diversities of operation, but it is the same God which worketh all in all.
>
> I Corinth. 12, 4–6

Did not Jesus reiterate a quasi-democratic criticism of pride, as for example in Luke 20, 46?

> Beware of the scribes, which desire to walk in long robes, and love greetings in the markets, and the highest seats in the synagogues, and chief rooms at feasts.

May there not even be a hint of the ideal of government for the people in Mark 10, 43–44?

> . . . whosoever will be great among you, shall be your minister: And whosoever of you will be the chiefest, shall be the servant of all.

Some may object that these mundane virtues have only religious significance. But the apothegms quoted concern the life of this world and the living of it. The only ideal that can give them coherence is one of universal self-respect. Unfortunately, in the history of Christian institutions, Jesus' social teachings have been only too rarely practiced.

One of the classics of peasant revolt, a classic which displays clearly the human yearning for self-respect, is the ballads of Robin Hood. While they are in part simply medieval romances, they typify chiefly the outlook of the yeomen who sang them at fairs and firesides. Though Robin is proud, courteous, and devout, he is especially a peasants' hero, free, merry, and "a good outlaw, that dyde pore men much good." The quintessential political stanzas of *A Lytell Geste of Robyn Hode* are those in which Robin instructs Little John in the moral principles of highway robbery: [5]

> But loke ye do no housbonde harme
> That tylleth with his plough;
> No more ye shall no good yemàn
> That walketh by grene wode shawe,
> Ne no knyght, ne no squyèr,
> That wolde be a good felawe.

> These byshoppes and thyse archebysshoppes
> Ye shall them bete and bynde;
> The hye sheryfe of Notynghame
> Hym holde in your mynde.

The moral is clear: Men of the highest class are never good fellows; presumably they are inevitably infected with the pride of station. Men of the lowest class are always good; presumably they have no chance to be prideful. Men of the middling class are sometimes good fellows, sometimes bad, sometimes humble, sometimes swaggering.

Robin hated men of power, but not all authority. He hated fat bishops; but he said three masses before each meal and held all women sacred because of the Virgin. He seized and robbed the haughty sheriff and killed the king's deer; but when the king himself came unarmed to meet and marvel at this bold outlaw, Robin knelt to ask for mercy. The contrast is obvious. Robin respected the authority which recognized his manhood. He hated authority which in its pride demanded his servility. He was an outlaw because he hated the unequal law, the law which reversed the democratic ideal to make pride a virtue and servility a merit. Although twisted by the bitterness of a Jacquerie, the ideal of self-respect is still the basis of this myth. Unfortunately, the violence of outlaws, whether in song or in fact, does not realize any ideal for many people or for very long.

[5] F. J. Child, *English and Scottish Ballads* (Boston, Little, Brown, 6 vols., 1859, et seq.), V, pp. 44–123, lines 51–60 of Fytte I.

Marxian communism is in many respects an urbanized form of peasant protest. It displays the same intense resentment of a society that violates human dignity. It was not simply the workers' poverty, degrading though it was, which inspired the *Communist Manifesto;* it was rather the servility of the workers' life. Marx' and Engel's central complaint against the capitalist oligarchies of the mid-nineteenth century was that they deprived the workingman of self-direction:

Masses of laborers, crowded into the factory, are organized like soldiers. As privates of the industrial army they are placed under the command of a perfect hierarchy of officers and sergeants. Not only are they slaves of the bourgeois class, and of the bourgeois state; they are daily and hourly enslaved by the machine, by the overlooker, and, above all, by the individual bourgeois manufacturer himself. The more openly this despotism proclaims gain to be its end and aim, the more petty, the more hateful and the more embittering it is.

The particular proposals made in the *Manifesto* to change society are all aimed at removing what its authors thought were the main barriers to self-respect for everybody. Thus bourgeois property is to be abolished because it is "based on the exploitation of the many by the few." The bourgeois family is to be abolished in order to "do away with the status of women as mere instruments of production." And national states are to be abolished because "the workingmen have no country." Communism, at least the Marxian sort, is more urbane than the Robin Hood ballads, but it is infused with the same spirit. Although it looks much farther than most peasant programs to a point beyond revolt, its method is the permanent enthronement of the revolutionary leaders so that it in fact gets only a very little nearer to evoking human dignity. The chief difference is that the ballad is dramatic catharsis while the *Manifesto* ends: "Workingmen of all countries, unite."

Even forms of nationalism serve to develop self-respect for everybody. Quite often, of course, nationalism is the antithesis of democracy. Instead of diffusing and generalizing liberty, it diffuses and generalizes pride. The racial people lording and the white men strutting with their burden are among the most repulsive of human types. But nationalism also sometimes helps oppressed people to create their own self-respect. And when it is simply compensation for oppression, it serves the same ideal as democracy. Unfortunately, however, the nationalism of the oppressed too easily becomes the nationalism of the oppressor. The nationalism which saved France and the Revolution in 1793 very soon gave Europe Napoleon. Today the once-noble Indian nationalism is an excuse to murder its own noblest hero and to en-slave Hindu and Muslim alike. Yet it remains true that in each case the nationalism was at first a means of self-respect for most Frenchmen and most Indians, no matter what happened later.

The city of God, the outlaw pillage, the proletarian dictatorship, the balkanized world, and finally democracy itself—is it not strange to group such diverse practices as these? Yet the category is in one sense reasonable enough. In spite of the immense differences among the in-stitutions which embody them, all these social movements and others like them are at least partially inspired by the same quest for human dignity.

This identity of ideal is easy enough to observe. Indeed, perhaps too easy. Zealots can, too easily because of this coincidence, equate one movement with another. Thus, in the United States, for example, it has been common enough to make democracy synonymous with Christianity and nationalism. In the Soviet Union, for another example, communism and democracy are customarily identified. And there lately nationalism and Christianity (at least in the Orthodoxy of Moscow, the Third Rome) have been officially superimposed upon the other two.

These identifications, though they all have a plausible base in the sameness of ideal, are patently nonsense. Something is missing from the definition of democracy if it can on paper be equated with in-stitutions which rudimentary common sense insists are different. What is it that distinguishes democracy from other movements with the same ideal? Why is democracy democracy and not something else?

The Democratic Method

The five documents contain the answer. Democracy is more than an ideal; it is also a method. Democracy may hold its ideal jointly; its method it has alone. The method is government responsible to the people. Hence, the essential democratic institution is the ballot box and all that goes with it.

All the documents place electoral responsibility at the very center of the democratic system.

The *Agreement of the People,* the only formal constitution among the five, is the most definite on this subject. Its major proposal was to establish a sovereign legislature responsible to the people:

We declare . . . that the people do, of course, choose themselves a Parliament once in two years . . . [and] that the power of . . . Representatives of this Nation, is inferior only to theirs who choose them . . .

Even though the *Declaration of Rights* was written as a preface to a constitution rather than as a constitution itself, it is almost as specific as the *Agreement*. The first element of the idea of responsible government was laid down in the third article, which along with the first and second is regarded as the heart of the *Declaration:*

The source of all sovereignty is essentially in the nation; no body, no individual can exercise authority that does not proceed from it in plain terms.

More significantly, however, the sixth, twelfth, thirteenth, fourteenth, fifteenth and sixteenth articles (or more than one-third of the text) explain the institutions by which government is to be made truly responsible to the people.

The *Declaration of Independence*, written as a justification of revolution can hardly be expected to set forth in detail the construction of democratic government. One can, however, infer from the grievances listed the type of government Continental Congressmen approved. And indeed, the inference is easy. Fully half the specific "facts . . . submitted to a candid world" concern George the Third's denial of responsible government. Besides the famous complaint about taxation without representation, he is said to have, for example, "dissolved Representative Houses," refused to "cause others to be elected," "called together legislative bodies at places unusual, uncomfortable and distant from the depository of their public Records," badgered the colonists into relinquishing "the right of representation in the legislature," neglected and refused to pass laws, kept standing armies in time of peace "without the consent of our legislatures," and "combined with others to subject us to a jurisdiction foreign to our constitution and unacknowledged by our laws, giving his Assent to their Acts of pretended Legislation." If such interference is what annoyed the colonials, then surely they wanted responsible government of the democratic sort.

The *Funeral Oration*, being a speech rather than a treatise, does not describe minutely the institutions it defends. When Pericles said "Our constitution is named a democracy, because it is in the hands not of the few but of the many," his hearers had a clear picture of the institutions the "many" used. If this picture is re-created from other sources, it is evident that Pericles meant responsible government. In Athens the essential policy-makers were elected by and responsible to the assembly of citizens. Minor officials, though selected by lot, were responsible to the very large juries. To Athenians the rule of the many —which Pericles placed at the center of his definition of democracy —meant the election of officials and the jury method of control.

It is futile to argue long over the precise reference of each preposition in Lincoln's phrase "government of . . . by . . . for the people." "For" almost certainly here means "in the interest of." "By" almost as certainly means "with the participation of." But what does "of" mean? Very possibly Lincoln's only purpose was stylistic. If, however, "of" has any significance of its own, it must mean "responsible to." Not only is this a reasonable observation about the institutions over which Lincoln presided; it is also a complement to "by" and "for" in democratic practice generally. No matter, though, what each preposition by itself means; the phrase in sum refers to the American government existent then. And that, so all observers thought, was characterized chiefly by an intent to make the rulers responsible to the ruled.

All the documents do indeed place electoral responsibility at the very center of the democratic system. And for good reason. It is a method by which society can simultaneously encourage self-respect and eliminate pride and servility.

The democratic assumption is that the most despicable pride is caused by tyranny. The despot exacts more servility than any other prideful man because he controls not only action but speech, not only speech but opinion. Sometimes, in an expanding despotism, rulers and ruled aim at the same goals so that even court flatterers can dignify their occupation with an ideal. In Tudor England or the Soviet Union, for example, most men hoped to begin a better world. But Tudors gave way to Stuarts and Old Bolsheviks to New: Once expansion slows down, the ideal fades and subjects achieve dignity only in death. In the phrase exact, turned by Lord Acton, "Power tends to corrupt and absolute power corrupts absolutely." [6] And it corrupts not only the holders of it but absolutely the whole society.

Democracy hopes to be and often is a means to prevent such corruption, partial or absolute. Its technique is to grant power provisionally.

[6] Letter to Mandell Creighton, April 5, 1887, printed in *Essays on Freedom and Power*, edited by Gertrude Himmelfarb (Boston, Beacon Press, 1948), p. 364.

Rulers rule as agents of the popular will. Since their power depends on frequent electoral redelegations, neither the despot's pride nor the subjects' servility is likely to exist for long. Provisional power seldom corrupts.[7]

Robert Sherwood, in *Roosevelt and Hopkins*, marveled that Roosevelt was ennobled by power rather than corrupted. He therefore concluded that Lord Acton's phrase "is one of those pontifical pronouncements which do not bear analysis."[8] But may it not be that public service ennobled, as in this case Sherwood thought it did, simply because such power as Roosevelt had was granted quadrennially and was never a certain possession? Stephen Spender, in that remarkable collection of renunciations of the Communist party, *The God That Failed*, says this:[9]

Although I never have agreed with the view . . . that all power corrupts, I think that power is only saved from corruption if it is humanized with humility. Without humility, power is turned to persecutions and executions and public lies.

It is that humility which democracy hopes to instill as it periodically confronts the rulers with the ruled.

Were democracy's purpose simply to forestall the servility of despotism, it would have little more to recommend it than has systematic tyrannicide. It would deserve in full the sneers it receives from elitists of the right and left. Would it not be indeed stupid to praise democratic morality if its sole contribution to the making of the good man were the prevention of only one evil?

Democracy intends, however, far more than that. It is as well a method of living the good life, of encouraging self-respect for everybody. Electoral responsibility generates in some way each of the attributes of the democratic ideal.

First, it promotes self-direction through participation in making public policy. The ballot and the system of political parties are the means and the assurance of that participation. They are the means

---

[7] See, Arnold Rogow and Harold Lasswell, *Power, Corruption, and Rectitude* (Englewood Cliffs, N.J., Prentice-Hall, 1963), *passim*.

[8] Robert Sherwood, *Roosevelt and Hopkins: An Intimate History* (New York, Harper & Brothers, 1948), p. 122.

[9] Richard Crossman, editor, *The God That Failed* (New York, Harper & Brothers, 1949), pp. 254–55.

because, however much the process of voting may be obscured, the basic decision on policy is always the choice of the policy-makers. They are the assurance because all the paraphernalia of participation (campaigning, petitioning, canvassing, propagandizing, etc.) is the one essential way to compel rulers to respond to pressure from the ruled.

Second, electoral responsibility promotes democratic liberty. The politics of democracy eventually produces legislators who favor generalized freedom in private spheres as well as public. Consider the case of democracy's response to *laissez-faire* economics. Democrats did not often object to the early growth of economic liberalism since it seemed at first a democratic freedom. They realized increasingly during the nineteenth century, however, that the syndicalist anarchy of *laissez-faire* benefited only a few. Transfer of the power of government to those private persons who could seize it created a society in which, as Marx said, the laborer brings "his own hide to market and has nothing to expect but—a hiding." During the twentieth century democracy all over the world has, therefore, endeavored to rectify this accident. It has increased democratic liberty by abandoning the practice and philosophy of *laissez-faire*, by equalizing incomes through social services, and by fostering labor unions. Reparation for the loss of liberty under liberalism is still far from complete. But it has gone far enough to demonstrate, in spite of Communist disbelief, that the long-run tendency of democratic politics is toward democratic freedom.

Third, electoral responsibility, assuming an equal vote, promotes in time some equality of manhood. Equality springs from the ballot box in about the same way as liberty. He who comes to feel himself, as Aristotle might have said, both equal and unequally treated votes to enforce equality. It is thus no accident that Negroes in Northern cities have in this generation increasingly exacted formally equal treatment. They have ceased voting perfunctorily for the party of the Great Emancipator and traded their votes to whichever party they thought offered them the most real equality.

Fourth, electoral responsibility promotes a measure of tolerance. Politicians in democracy discover in the not-too-long run that intolerance of any very large minority of voters presently creates a dangerously implacable enemy. Hence, in the North, where victims of the intolerance of the Ku Klux Klan were voters, its success was brief and its discredit certain. In the South, where the victims of intolerance have not had a vote that counts, the KKK has been active intermittently for ninety-five years.

Fifth, electoral responsibility, as the early modern democrats repeatedly proclaimed, promotes obedience. Obedience to edict is servility; but obedience to law made by the obeyers' responsible agents involves no loss of self-respect. The actual process of democratic consent is, of course, not so simple as this proposition implies; but still the indispensable ingredient of consent and obedience is responsibility of the governors to governed. Taxes with representation are unpleasant enough and often evaded; but taxes without representation are an incitement to rebellion.

Such is the rationale of electoral responsibility. In each of the foregoing ways it is supposed to give practical effect to elements of the democratic ideal of self-respect. Of course, in this imperfect world, no institutions function in fact as they seem to function in words. So many details of procedure affect the operation of the electoral system that it is impossible, in a changing society, to maintain a combination which enforces the highest degree of rulers' responsibility. The number and kind of political parties, the form of election districts, the way of voting and of counting votes, the nature of the institutions with sovereignty, etc.—all these are variables which must be combined perfectly for perfect electoral responsibility. Thus, for example, though obviously electoral responsibility can encourage self-respect only in the electorate, very few democracies have permitted every adult to vote. Each of the five documents implies universal suffrage; but no one of the five societies had it. Probably at least one-third of fifth century Athens consisted of slaves or metics; the *Agreement* proposed a universal male suffrage in England which was not adopted there until 1919; that "all men" of the *Declaration of Independence* in most colonies meant "some" or those who owned a specified number of acres; the *Declaration of Rights* asserted that everyone should help make law—but not everyone was permitted to, except during the short-lived Jacobin dominance; and the ultimate occasion of the *Gettysburg Address* was the slavery of Negroes (many of whom cannot yet vote in the United States). Still, in spite of institutional imperfections, democratic theory assumes that the democratic method of responsible rulers will effect the democratic ideal of self-respect. It is understood, of course, that the amount of self-respect engendered is in some rough way related to the degree of responsibility of the rulers to the ruled.

The Meaning of Democracy

And now, having determined what the method of democracy is and how it is related to the democratic ideal, it is possible to define "democracy" itself, which was the task set for this chapter. And the defining can be done thus shortly: Democracy is a form of government in which the rulers are fully responsible to the ruled in order to realize self-respect for everybody. It is a sublime purpose and a system worthy of it. How unfortunate that, even in the so-called democracies of the Western world, rulers' responsibility is so indistinct. How unfortunate that the practice of democracy everywhere is so partial, so hesitant, and so incomplete.

How Shall What Is Become What Ought to Be?

All that has been heretofore said about the meaning of democracy is wholly unaffected by the ultimate truth or falsity of the theory of democracy. Although this chapter has so far sketched a picture of the ideal form of democracy, it is not intended to imply, like Plato and a host of metaphysicians after him, that a form is self-justifying because it is an ideal. In this definition, democracy assumes too many "unprovables" for it to pass unchallenged by philosophers. It assumes, for example, a relativistic and pragmatic epistemology, which places "truth" (not ultimate truth, with which it is not concerned, but such truth as man can know) in the hands of the majority or a series of majorities. It assumes also a rationalist axiology, i.e. the belief that men are able to know their own interests and act to achieve them. It assumes the psychological theory that men have both social and anti-social propensities or, in theological terms, that men are fashioned in the image of God as well as endowed with original sin. In ethics, it assumes a particular goal of conduct (universal self-respect). These assumptions, however moot, will not be argued over here. Whether or not they are "really" right or "really" good, it is enough to know that they have been accepted into the democratic heritage and that many men have chosen them with democracy to guide their lives. The concern here is with the more pressing questions: How can the democratic ideal be realized? How can the democratic method be made to work? It is, of course, foolish to expect a millennium; but, since democrats are sure that democracy can mean a better life for all, it is worth while to consider this less exalted, less philosophical question: How can democracy be? To consider this in the space of one book, it is necessary to accept provisionally the philosophical implications of the democratic faith. Only thus can one come to grips with the democratic problem. And the democratic problem is this: Democracy attempts what is, perhaps, impossible—and therein lies the condition of both its beauty and its failure. It tries to transform government, which has through most history been an agent of tyranny, into a means of self-respect. It tries to engraft a good morality rather than an evil one onto the institution which controls force. And it tries to do so in the face of age-old and almost universal acclaim of the evil.

Considered ideally, government is simply an instrument to channel social effort. But considered historically, it has almost always been also the chain by which few enslave many.

Nor is this dual nature surprising. In any government (except democracy sometimes) power acquired for a legitimate purpose can as easily be used for an illegitimate one. In the Soviet Union, to cite a contemporary example, power to create a prosperous and equalitarian society presently became also power to perpetuate the privilege of a ruling clique. Those who persuaded the country to accept them as its stewards soon forced it to accept them as its masters. If power created for good be not hemmed in with real sanctions on its misuse, the love of pride which pervades mankind is certain to pervert it.

Government probably originated from aggrandizement by the strongest; but it continued even after several slaves together became stronger than he who enslaved them. Men have loyally endured perpetual subordination the better to conquer and kill. Most people comprehend that some objects of life can be got only through the joint action that government organizes. Thus, almost everywhere and almost always, men have accepted exploitation for the sake of social order. Even when authority is as arbitrary and malignant as Caligula's or Hitler's, one part is loyal for it shares in the plunder and the rest is loyal because it lacks an alternative civilizing organization.

Acceptance of government has throughout history been accompanied, however, by some effort (often indirect) to reduce its exploitation. Men have not, it is true, commonly sought to make government wholly good. The custom of servility has been too thoroughly engrained even for insubordinate men to discern more than rarely that the institutions of cooperation might produce self-respect as easily as pride. But, even when lacking this democratic vision, men have sought to restrain the most vicious of special privileges. The greater portion of political philosophizing from Plato's day to our own attempts such restraint. Most of the great world religions try (unsuccessfully, to be sure) to establish minimum standards of decency for rulers. In both Oriental and European absolutism, systematic tyrannicide has at times had a temporarily salutary effect on princes. But all such restraints, whether by pen or dagger, only curb the illegitimate power; they do not exorcize the evil spirit which produces it.

Democracy, on the other hand, does try to exorcize. It seeks to control power by transforming it into a servant of universal self-respect. Or, in the phrase Rousseau suggested, it seeks to make the chains which bind men in society entirely legitimate. Unlike other methods of restraining rulers, it seeks to make them responsible to the ruled by means of a sanction which (unlike custom) is observable and physical, which (unlike religion) is mundane and certain, and which (unlike any incoherent revolt from tyrannicide to Communist dictatorship) is permanent and pervasive.

Democracy's task is immense. "If men were angels . . ."—but Madison, who used the subjunctive, knew that they are not. Most men have rather what we call the *normal* human weaknesses: greed, selfishness, and pride. Even to the leaders of democracy themselves, special privilege often seems a finer fruit than their fellows' self-respect. Why else, for example, the apt invention of the word "plutocracy" (literally: the rule of rich men) as a scornful synonym for the modern democratic state? And, what magnifies democracy's task manyfold more, the propensity to pride increases in rough proportion to the facilities for gratifying it. The more power men have, the more likely they are to abuse it pridefully. Such at least is the testimony of sensitive spirits from Ptahhotep's time to our own. Of course, then, democracy's task is immense: it is to control the ineradicable anti-sociality of men.

The pride which democracy would control is hydra-headed, Loki-shaped. Its manifestations are far more numerous than the inventions of democracy to subdue it. Forceful subordination and special privilege, being rooted in the unvariable portion of man's nature, are humanly ineradicable. Whether or not they are controllable depends upon the resilience of democracy in meeting their challenge. And so far democracy, despite its promise, has shown itself neither so strong as Heracles nor so wise as Odin.

The real problem of democracy, therefore, in America as well as in every other nation, is the difference between democratic promise and democratic performance. Its task is to narrow the gap between the real and the ideal, to make the picture for our eyes as pretty as the picture in our heads. It is, no doubt, impossible in this imperfect world to identify the *is* with the *ought*; but democracy must scheme always to superimpose them—else it is untrue to its nature and function.

The process of superimposition is the content of democratic politics. Democratic statesmen ought always to try to make government democratic in fact as well as name. It is a difficult mission. Only the most intense devotion and the most persistent effort carry men forward in it at all. And what makes the task of superimposition almost unmanageable is that the forms of the political problem change with every generation and often with every year.

2.

Suffrage in the United States

These considerations prove . . . that the name of citizen is particularly applicable to those who share in the offices and honours of the state. Homer accordingly speaks in the *Iliad* of a man being treated "like an alien man, *without honour*"; and it is true that those who do not share in the offices and honours of the state are just like resident aliens.

—Aristotle, *Politics,* 1278a

What we have to define is the citizen in the strict and unqualified sense, who has no defect that has to be made good before he can bear the name—no defect such as youth or age, or such as those attaching to disfranchised or exiled citizens. . . . The citizen in this strict sense is best defined by the one criterion, "a man who shares in the administration of justice and in the holding of office. . . ." It may possibly be contended that judges in the courts and members of the assembly are not holders of "office". . . . But it would be ridiculous to exclude from the category of holders of office those who actually hold the most sovereign position in the state.

—Aristotle, *Politics,* 1274b

The American Achievement in Suffrage

The basic instrument of democracy is popular voting, for by it rulers are held responsible. The first care of the democratic conscience ought therefore to be the widest possible extension of the suffrage.

Herein America has been the model for the democratic world. In the United States by the decade of the 1830's nearly universal white male suffrage had been established. This was a score of years before the Second French Republic tried to enfranchise all men and two score before the Third Republic actually did it. It was a half-century ahead of England and almost a full century ahead of Italy, Germany, Russia, and Scandinavia. To all these the American experiment proved the practicality of popular government. And this experimental proof was and is the United States' great contribution to the theory and practice of democracy.

It was, moreover, a contribution not easily made. When the Constitution was adopted, all thirteen states had some kind of financial requirement for voting. Although the people's insistence on sharing in the government they had fought to make impelled seven states to lower the qualifications, still in 1788 Pennsylvania (the most democratic government) permitted only taxpayers to vote. All other states required in addition that voters own various amounts of property in land or houses.[1] The constitutional fathers failed to establish a property qualification only because they could not agree upon one which would fit the diverse electoral laws and economic conditions of thirteen states.[2] But practically the Constitution did not need to set forth property qualifications: Between one-fifth and one-third of the adult white males were already disfranchised by state law. And many more had not yet learned the value of their suffrage, for no more than twenty-five percent of them voted on the ratification of the Constitution.[3]

During the next fifty years there was a remarkable change. In 1835 for a hostile and aristocratic Europe, De Tocqueville epitomized American government as "equality of conditions" and "universal suffrage." Although the universality he divined did not yet really exist, this presumed democracy was (often through the influence of his book itself) imitated in Europe for fifty years thereafter.[4] This government had been transformed in less than two generations from a semi-oligarchic to a semi-democratic type. Of course, such very great reversal, personified in the succession from Hamilton to Jackson, was accomplished only after persistent struggle. While manhood suffrage was never the central question of national politics, it was probably debated over a longer time and in sum more voluminously than any

[1] Kirk H. Porter, *A History of Suffrage in the United States* (Chicago, University of Chicago Press, 1918), ch. 1.

[2] Max Farrand, *The Records of the Federal Convention of 1787* (New Haven, Yale University Press, 1911, 3 vols.), II, pp. 201–5, 248–49 (hereafter cited as Farrand, *Records*).

[3] Charles A. Beard, *An Economic Interpretation of the Constitution of the United States* (New York, Macmillan, 1913), pp. 242, 250.

[4] Alexis De Tocqueville, *Democracy in America*, edited by Phillips Bradley (New York, Knopf, 2 vols., 1945), I, pp. 3, 173, xxxix, xlix–li.

other constitutional problem of the new Republic. In at least twenty state conventions held between 1790 and 1840, it was either a major issue or even the only important one.

And with good reason—for therein is involved not only the vested interests of property but the vested interests of politicians as well. In representative governments a particular form of suffrage always pre-conditions a particular balance among political parties. A revision of suffrage, which involves a revision of the rules of competition and the eligible competitors, is bound to change the fortunes of each com-peting party. Thus the Federalist party was gradually eclipsed after 1800 by expansion of the electorate—most new members of which voted for the Jeffersonian Republicans. And similarly, after 1870 the Republican party was excluded from the South by suffrage contrac-tion.

These facts suggest a paradox: If changes in suffrage upset the balance of parties and thus endangered the jobs of office holders, the rational and self-interested politicians of the majority party ought never to change the pattern of suffrage; yet in fact they have done so—repeatedly in the United States. This paradox requires an explanation.

One possible explanation is, of course, that office holders are not self-interested, that they are altruistically devoted to achieving demo-cratic ideals. But this is too easy. Considering the intensity of the strug-gles against vested interests to establish democratic institutions, it seems unlikely that majorities of office holders from time to time suddenly become altruists. We need a better explanation, one that does not require us to posit such surprising qualities for large bodies of politicians. The kind of explanation we are looking for is one that explains why office holders selfishly interested in continuing in office should oc-casionally find it to their advantage to upset the pattern of suffrage.

This consideration leads us to a general theory of changes in suffrage: Politicians, we assume, seek to establish institutions which will keep them in control of government. In some instances the per-petuation of their control involves extension of the suffrage; in other instances, contraction. When a majority of a government or legislature believes that bringing new voters into the system of suffrage will perpetuate their control, they expand. When, however, they believe that the exclusion of some of the presently voting citizens will per-petuate their control, they contract. The ground on which they might believe expansion profitable is the supposition that the majority of the potentially included voters would, if permitted, vote for them. Similarly, the ground on which they might believe contraction profitable is the supposition that a majority of the potentially excluded voters regularly vote for their opponents.

The great practical difficulty with suffrage extension is that the politicians of the majority party must be persuaded of its feasibility. This means they must be persuaded that the greater part of the new participants will help to turn their present majority into a future one. Difficult as such persuasion may be, this was apparently what influenced the Anti-federalist majorities in the frontier states of the 1790's (Vermont, New Hampshire, and Kentucky) to establish manhood suffrage while conservative values and Federalist politicians were yet weak. It seemed also to have influenced Jacksonian Democrats in New York and New England to fight so persistently for a free vote. In some few cases, for example in Rhode Island after Dorr's War, the poor were enfranchised by conservatives in order to get their votes, just as Disraeli "dished the Whigs" by the Reform Bill of 1867. Typically in the United States, however, universal white male suffrage was established by the party of radicalism trying to maintain its majority for all the foreseeable future. Naturally, therefore, the conservative parties have sadly envisioned for themselves (however inaccurately) a future of permanent minorities. Is it surprising, then, that they fought to preserve their privilege with a dogged bitterness?

But in spite of them, by the time of the Civil War only five states had any kind of financial qualification. All these were small poll taxes; Massachusetts and North Carolina abandoned them before 1865 and Pennsylvania, Delaware, and Rhode Island abandoned theirs by 1900. All the new states either had been admitted with white male suffrage or had achieved it under the impetus of Jacksonian radicalism. It was this generalization of the franchise which so impressed the rest of the world throughout the nineteenth century. The subsequent adoption of the Fifteenth and Nineteenth Amendments merely confirmed the impression in both American and European minds.

THE MORAL SIGNIFICANCE OF VOTING:
NORTHERN NEGROES

It is too easy today to overlook the significance of suffrage extension. This movement was the nineteenth century effort to institutionalize the democratic ideals inherited from the eighteenth. It was based on the sure insight that suffrage and self-respect are related intimately. But now that democracy has been the political ideal and "universal suffrage" the political method for over one hundred years, votes are almost as routine as taxes. Thoughtless habit obscures the benefit of both.

The democratic theory that suffrage promotes self-respect was set forth in Chapter 1. But a much more vivid reminder of the connection can be got by surveying the history of any newly enfranchised class. In our century there are two such: women and Northern Negroes, most of whom have become voters only in the last two generations. In each case suffrage extension coincides with an obvious increment of self-respect for people in the class. Such repeated coincidence can hardly be accidental.

The current agitation over racial discrimination and Negro disfranchisement obscures one important fact: The condition of Negro people has improved since the Civil War, especially in the last decade. For example, Negroes do go to integrated schools and colleges in most states, even most Southern states. (Of course, *de facto* segregation exists, but it is not legally enforced and the determined Negro can rise above it.) There are now many Negro professional and business men as against almost none in 1870, which demonstrates the existence of at least some class mobility and economic opportunity for Negroes. While indeed the plantation cabin has usually been succeeded by the cropper's shack or the urban slum, for some Negroes, especially in the North, it has been replaced by a substantial house or apartment. The most significant change of all, however, is in white attitudes toward Negroes. The white majority is today more willing than it was two generations ago to concede to Negroes a human and citizen status. Indeed, recent public opinion polls show that approximately three-fourths of the Northern whites are willing to concede full citizen and human status to Negroes, at least in the abstract propositions of the polls. This is a recent phenomenon entirely dependent on agitation for civil rights. Thus, one contemporary Negro sociologist concluded a survey of Negroes in America with this striking observation: [5]

. . . the categoric picture of the Negro as given in our culture has changed. The Negro who is presented, for example, in the advertisement of a popular brand of whiskey today is a kindly, dignified human being, entirely different from the grotesque apelike caricature . . . that was used thirty or forty years ago to advertise shoe polish.

[5] E. Franklin Frazier, *The Negro in the United States* (New York, Macmillan, 1949), p. 690.

Frazier wrote these words in 1949. So accelerated has been the rate of white acceptance and sympathy for Negroes in the intervening time that it has now become embarrassing to depict Negroes in a servile position at all, no matter how dignified. And one might add evidence from the words "Uncle Tom." For a long time after 1852 they meant to most Northern whites the highest possible Negro virtue: unwavering loyalty in spite of mistreatment. Today the reference for many Northern whites is the same as for many Negroes: regrettable and self-effacing servility. Thus far have American Negroes come from the day of Harriet Beecher Stowe, an advance formally recognized in the Civil Rights Act of 1964, which aims at guaranteeing that in public accommodations, job opportunities, and civil rights Negroes are to be treated as full citizens.

The first and no doubt greatest advance was Emancipation, even though both the Proclamation and the Thirteenth Amendment were perhaps aimed more at winning the war and restricting the ambitions of the planter oligarchy than at facilitating Negro development. Thereafter, however, the greater portion of Negro improvement has been made only in recent years. Yet Negro slavery was abolished a century ago. Whence came the lag? Why did not formal freedom soon bring genuine material and political improvement? It is true that some effort was made to help Negroes at the beginning of their freedom; but the Abolitionists' fervor cooled off as the South proved unable and the North proved unwilling to pay the necessary bills. Southern whites were reinstated in national politics and the agitation for democratic inclusion of Negroes died down, not to be heard again until the third decade of this century. Again, whence came the lag? While no historian dare state a "cause," is it not significant that the lag in improvement coincides roughly with the lag in agitation? Is it not important also that both these coincide in turn with the trend of Negro suffrage? May it not be that suffrage has been a precondition of both an improved status and a widespread agitation for it? The coincidence deserves close examination.

Only in the last generation have Negroes been permitted an effective franchise. While free Negroes could vote throughout the nineteenth century in a few Northern states (New York and New England where, indeed, few Negroes lived) all the rest of the states, North as well as South, specifically excluded them. It has often been noted that Northerners, however much they abhorred the plantation agriculture, were reluctant abolitionists. No better evidence exists of their lack of sympathy with Negroes than the thoroughness with which Northern election codes disfranchised them. The Fifteenth Amendment was partly the product of abolitionist idealism; but it was also clearly a Radical device to produce pliant Southern Congressmen and thus to perpetuate Radical control of Congress. It served, therefore, to protect all Negroes' votes only so long as Reconstruction lasted. After Radicals lost control of the Republican party and Reconstruction was abandoned, Negroes were systematically disfranchised by violence and deceit in judicially condoned disobedience of the Fifteenth Amendment. Yet the amendment did achieve one permanent reform: It voided those provisions in Northern state constitutions and codes that decitizenized Negroes. How paradoxical it is that this amendment, which victorious Northerners forced on the South, actually reformed the Northern electorate more than the Southern.[6] So Northern Negroes could indeed vote; but, until well into the twentieth century, they were too few to be effective.

They became effective only in the 1920's and 1930's after many Negroes migrated Northward. The industrial boom in the twenties created new jobs for the unskilled, while the immigration restrictions limited cheap white competition. So in such cities as Pittsburgh, Detroit, Chicago, Cleveland, and Philadelphia, little Harlems sprang up and spilled over the restrictive covenants with each Negro influx. At first the new votes, absorbed into Republican city machines, operated chiefly to obtain public jobs for Negroes. When, in 1928, Oscar De Priest was elected Representative as a Republican from Chicago, he was, as the successor of the last Southern Negro Republican (defeated in 1900), both the symbol and the highest achievement of the newly effective Negro votes. In the 1930's Negro votes became much more remunerative, not only because there were more of them, but also because they were now a marginal bloc for which both parties had to bid. A Democratic President provided that Negroes receive about the same federal bounty and relief as whites and his *wife* had no objection to being photographed with Negroes. Is it not quite natural that Roosevelt

[6] There is some evidence that such was the intention of Republicans like Charles Sumner. See Stephen Weeks, "History of Negro Suffrage in the South," *Political Science Quarterly*, IX (1894), pp. 671–703, 683, where Sumner is quoted as writing apropos the amendment and the 1868 election: "Let them [i.e. Negroes] vote in Pennsylvania, and you will give more than 20,000 votes to the Republican Cause."

attracted many Negro voters away from the party of Emancipation and Reconstruction? Since these votes thus polevaulted from the very core of the Republican party to the periphery of the Democratic, is it not quite natural also that the parties should have maneuvered excitedly for Negro allegiance throughout the 1940's, 1950's and 1960's? The Democrats have, of course, had the best of the bartering, for they have offered such prizes as integration in poor relief (under Roosevelt), integration in the armed services (under Truman), and continual litigation and executive action to improve civil rights for Negroes (under Kennedy). Republicans under Eisenhower offered something of the same, of course, although apparently with a little reluctance. Comparing the determination and self-assurance of President Kennedy in enforcing court decisions about Negro enrollments in Southern state universities (especially in Mississippi) with President Eisenhower's vacillation and negotiation in enforcing court decisions about Little Rock schools, it is clear that Democrats have been willing to offer more. This partisan conflict is reflected in the career of Adam Clayton Powell, who has represented a Harlem district since 1944. Powell has always been elected as a Democrat, but he supported Eisenhower for re-election in 1956 and has had several dramatic conflicts in primaries with the New York City Democratic organization. There is no doubt that Powell speaks for Harlem Negroes, that he has found the Democratic party slightly more congenial than the Republican, but that he can and will cross party lines if Republicans make good promises. Hence, though, as illustrated by Powell's career, the Democrats have offered the best bargains, the Republicans have not and need not despair of ever getting the Negro vote back. Indeed, there are such severe strains in the Democratic alliance, with its attempt to appeal simultaneously to Southern whites and Negroes and Northern whites and Negroes, that one may expect continued Republican efforts to regain the allegiance of Negroes, at least in Northern states. It is true that the national Republican party in its 1964 candidate, Barry Goldwater, and its 1964 platform turned its back on Negro votes in an attempt to win the South away from the Democratic party. But it is unlikely that this policy will be permanent, for even in the South Negroes are now voters and the parties may be expected in the long run to compete for their votes. So the partisan maneuvering continues. And, incidentally, the Negro suffrage movement, at first confined to the North, presently infiltrated the Supreme Court, from which it was redirected also to the South.

The effective franchise of the Northern Negro has already encouraged a new environment for Negro life. Material conditions more closely approach those of whites—the urban slum, while shocking, is still better than the sharecropper's shack, and most urban renewal projects are completely integrated. Spiritual conditions, e.g., the concern that large numbers of whites feel for the condition of Negroes, permit Negroes to acquire self-respect. And most important, there has been for the two decades past a high intensity of agitation for political equality, from the march on Washington in 1941 led by Philip Randolph, the Negro leader of the AFL, to the great civil rights demonstration in Washington in August, 1963, led by so many distinguished Negroes that it would be invidious to name only a few.

Ever since the Civil War there have been two strands of Negro thought and action about adjustment to whites. One strand demands full citizen equality and self-respect. It is represented by the succession from Frederick Douglass to W. E. B. DuBois and then to such diverse contemporaries as Richard Wright, Adam Powell, Ralph Bunche, Thurgood Marshall and James Farmer. The other seeks the security of a protected status, however lowly. Its foremost representative was Booker T. Washington, followed latterly by George Washington Carver. In the diversity of American life and in the Negro people's long struggle upward, both strands of thought have been necessary. Each has made a valuable contribution to American life. Still, is it not a great democratic advance that Booker T. Washington's approach, once so dominant in Negro life, should now have been generally supplanted with Douglass' and DuBois' and Farmer's? And does not the evidence here assembled suggest that the precondition of the shift in standards was effective suffrage for Northern Negroes?

THE MORAL SIGNIFICANCE OF VOTING: WOMEN

In the four and a half decades since the Nineteenth Amendment, it has become fashionable to devalue and debunk the suffragettes' achievement. Many textbook writers imply, if they do not actually assert, that woman suffrage was an unimportant reform. They point out that until the 1952 election not as many women have voted as men, that not many women are active politicians, and that women's votes have not materially altered the balance between political parties. And so they conclude that the three generations' crusade was to a minor purpose.

But they are wrong. The place of women in society has been revolutionized in the two generations past. Whether that revolution caused, or was caused by, or simply accompanied the spread of woman suffrage is more than any historian dare say. But that the revolution in manners and voting occurred about the same time is an undeniable fact. The Western European family system, which was thus transvalued, has through most history postulated a master-servant relationship between husband and wife. Both the classical and Christian traditions subordinated women to men: Aristotle, for example, compared the husband's authority to the slaveowner's and quoted from Homer, "a modest silence is a woman's crown." [7] St. Paul, whose strictures on women are so often footnoted, compared the family to the Church: The husband, he said, is "the head of the wife, even as Christ is the head of the church." [8] In urging that husbands use their authority as lovingly as Christ, he overlooked the difference between husbands and Jesus. Thereby he provided in the very heart of Christian literature a persistent justification of women's subordination. European social institutions and legal systems for the two thousand years since have with varying degrees of virtue embodied these virile opinions. Modifications have indeed been made in the direction of equality, as happened during the high middle ages when chivalric ideals created a new role (albeit a passive one) for women. But modifications have also been made in the direction of the purdah, as happened in the twilight of the ancient world when the dark ages of barbarism settled over the Mediterranean. In the last century in North America and Western Europe, however, changes in the status of women have been more than modifications: the family has been transvalued by abandoning the master-servant ideal, by replacing it with an ideal of cooperation between equals.

One valuable index of the equalization of women's status—valuable because it permits specific and statistical comparisons—is the change in divorce laws and customs. When, as during most of Western civilization, marriage is a contract between unequals, divorce is the ultimate protection of the weaker party. It is for this reason that the earliest advocates of women's rights in America (such people as Robert Dale

[7] *Politics*, I, 13 (1260a).
[8] Ephesians 5, 23.

Owen and Elizabeth Cady Stanton) emphasized the need for easier divorce laws.[9] So thorough had been women's subordination up to the mid-nineteenth century that usually they had been denied even this defense for their human dignity. While divorce (which is intended to protect both sexes) was castigated as license, the "double-standard" (which releases men from supposedly indissoluble union) was tacitly and even sometimes openly approved. When divorce became easy against this background, the sexes began to be equal. At worst this equalization leveled downward toward the male half of the Victorian duality. In its best form, however, equalization leveled upward from a family based on hierarchy to a family based on mutual respect and self-respect. If divorce be thus interpreted as an equalizer of the heretofore unequal, the rising divorce rate, bad as one aspect of it is, does demonstrate a very real change in family values and the status of women. In the United States in the last eighty years the rise has been continuous and tremendous. In 1876 three-tenths of a divorce was granted for every 1000 persons; in 1900, seven-tenths for every thousand; in 1920, one and six-tenths; in 1947, three and three-tenths; and in 1959, two and two-tenths.[10] While this increase may reflect an increase in license, it also reflects women's search for equal treatment. And the decrease since the postwar years suggests that the over-all increase is less a reflection of license than it is a search for equal treatment. Women do not yet, of course, have an equal status in the family—if they did, divorce would be less frequently necessary. But clearly they are learning to use the method which will obtain it.

This remarkable transvaluation probably appeared first in the economic sphere: In the New World the rigidity of the European family system broke down, under the stress of frontier conditions and the scarcity of women, in the way described in Willa Cather's novels, *O Pioneers* and *My Antonia*. And wherever the industrial revolution occurred the extreme subordination of women proved incompatible with factory labor. But almost simultaneously the transvaluation started in other departments of life, for example, in education, in law and in citizen status.

[9] Elizabeth C. Stanton, Susan B. Anthony and M. J. Gage, *History of Woman Suffrage* (Rochester, National American Woman Suffrage Association, 1900–1920, 6 vols.), I, pp. 717 ff.

[10] U. S. Department of Commerce, Bureau of the Census, *Vital Statistics of the United States, 1959*, Vol. I, *Introductory Text and General Tables* (Washington, Government Printing Office, 1961), pp. 2–17.

Women could not vote in 1800 (except in New Jersey and there the privilege was lost in 1807).[11] During the course of the nineteenth century, however, women in increasing numbers claimed civic rights. As early as 1869 the territory of Wyoming unconditionally permitted women to vote. By 1900 they could vote for President in Wyoming, Colorado, Idaho, and Utah and for school board officials in twenty-one other states.[12] Before the first World War, more than half the women in the country could vote for President, a situation that was nationalized by the Nineteenth Amendment. Since that time women have voted in increasing numbers, though not yet as frequently as men.

The economic, social, marital, and political position of women has indeed changed greatly in the last century. Our society has formally, although not always operationally, abandoned the ancient premise that women are inferior. While it is improper to single out one specific cause for this increment in human dignity, it is clear that the new status in family and society soon expressed itself in citizenship. The franchise has in turn reinforced, protected, and expanded the marital and economic emancipation.

It is on this level, then, that one can truly understand the Nineteenth Amendment. Voting—an act in a vacuum—is nothing; the right to vote—as an "operating ideal" of the society—is the guarantee of emancipation. The suffragettes ensured some permanence for the trend toward equal status, a trend of which they themselves were both the product and the cause. Ida Husted Harper, in the first flush of victory, prophesised that: [13]

Women will find . . . that in the home, in club life and in all lines of religious, philanthropic, educational and civic work the possession of a vote has increased their influence and power beyond measure.

Who can doubt that her prophecy was right? Social restrictions on the employment of women have speedily declined since women have voted (compare the "lady street car conductor" of the first World War with the women welders of the second). The proportion of women employed in the labor force increased from thirteen percent in 1940 to twenty-

---

[11] Harold Gosnell, *Democracy: The Threshold of Freedom* (New York, Ronald Press, 1948), p. 51.
[12] Stanton, Anthony, Gage, *op. cit.*, IV, p. 461.
[13] *Ibid.*, VI, p. iv.

three percent in 1960, largely because of the employment of married women. Although much of this increase is simply in the same kinds of jobs women held in the nineteenth century (e.g., grade school teaching and clerical and food handling jobs), still it has become possible and in some industries common for women to hold executive and supervisory positions. Women have acquired some formal position in politics —for example, in both parties the national committee consists of one man and one woman from each state. In recent Congresses there have been about a dozen women Representatives and two women Senators. President Eisenhower appointed Mrs. Hobby to the Cabinet (Secretary of Health, Education, and Welfare) and President Johnson systematically appointed women to high-level administrative posts. President Johnson apparently perceived that it is women who now do a large portion of the precinct work in politics, and evidently he wished to provide incentives in the form of high political office. Quite clearly, the idea that women have a value equal to men has been more frequently accepted in everyday living (as distinct from political theory) since the Nineteenth Amendment.

Such is the democratic significance of suffrage as it appears in the experience of the newly enfranchised. Considering its ramifications in nearly all the spiritual and material conditions of life, suffrage extension is surely no mean achievement.

Is Voting Rational?

In spite of this apparent relationship in two instances between enfranchisement and increments in self-respect, many recent students of voting behavior insist that such a relationship cannot exist because individual decisions on voting are "irrational." Thus, Berelson, Lazarsfeld, and McPhee, in the conclusion of their elaborate study of voting in Elmira, New York, point out that political preferences seem to be akin to cultural tastes, are based on sentiment rather than reasoned choice, and are "characterized more by faith than conviction." [14] Presumably, if voting decisions are based on mere sentiment rather than calculations of advantage, then it is hardly possible for the newly enfranchised to gain self-respect from suffrage. Similarly, while they carefully eschew comments on the "rationality" of voting, the authors

[14] Bernard R. Berelson, Paul F. Lazarsfeld, and William N. McPhee, *Voting* (Chicago, University of Chicago Press, 1954).

of *The American Voter,* that magnificent summary of the work of the
Survey Research Center of the University of Michigan, nevertheless
imply many of the same judgments as the authors of *Voting.*[15] In *The
American Voter* "causes" of the voting decision are found in such
variables as socio-economic status, education, parental party preference,
and the like. The implied conclusion is that factors such as these rather
than rational calculations of advantage are what bring about choices
in voting. Again, if supposedly relevant features of social position are
what "cause" decisions in voting, then it can hardly be expected that
the newly enfranchised gain self-respect from suffrage. Thus there
appears to be a clear contradiction between the inferences from the
microcosmic study of voting decisions and the inferences from the
macrocosmic study of large social movements. The contradiction seems
so sharp that it can be reconciled only by a definite choice of one interpretation over the other.

Initially, the choice between the two seems to favor the inferences
from the microcosmic studies, for their authors have delved deeply and
carefully into the actual process of decision by voters. One is restrained
from agreement with them only by the fact that such agreement implies
a complete rejection of the traditional rationale of democracy. Indeed,
to accept the inferences from the voting studies is to reject the purposes
and aspirations of all those politicians who created the system of democratic suffrage.

Fortunately such a rejection is not necessary. If it can be shown
that a significant body of voters do make rational calculations of advantage, then the anti-democratic implications of the microcosmic studies
cannot stand. And such is in fact the case, based on evidence from the
microcosmic studies themselves. One example will suffice: In 1960
American voters were, for only the second time, faced with the choice
between Catholic and Protestant candidates for President. The choice
was poignant, for on the previous occasion the Catholic had lost, partially, it is said, because of his Catholicism. In 1960 the Catholic won,
but not without significant protest. According to the report of the Survey Research Center of the University of Michigan, about forty percent of the Democrats (identified as those persons who voted or would
have voted for Stevenson in 1956) who were also self-proclaimed regular attendants at Protestant church services voted for the Republican

15 Angus Campbell, Philip E. Converse, Warren E. Miller, and Donald E.
Stokes, *The American Voter* (New York, John Wiley and Sons, 1960).

Protestant rather than the Catholic Democrat.[16] Furthermore, as the frequency of church attendance declined, so also did the frequency of voting for Nixon decline, which seems particularly impressive evidence that the choice was inspired by a resolution of the politico-religious conflict in favor of the religious value. If the sample on which this estimate is based is at all representative—and the Center is notable for its methodological rigor in selecting samples—this means that approximately three million deeply convinced Democrats voted Republican because of a calculation about the religious affiliation of the Democratic candidate. Apparently also a similarly large number of Catholic Republicans voted for the Catholic Democrat, so that probably no net gain accrued to either candidate on account of his religion. What this survey research result indicates is that a very large number of voters, when faced with a real conflict of values (i.e., party affiliation against religious affiliation), thought deeply about the conflict and made some sort of rational calculation of which affiliation was more important for them.

It is not often, of course, that voters are forced to such fundamental re-evaluations of their political preferences. And the infrequency of the re-evaluations is probably what accounts for the interpretation based on studies of individual decisions that voters are irrational. All that is required for the democratic assumption to be valid is that voters be able to re-evaluate when required by conflicts of value to do so. The fact that voters can, when faced with conflict, resolve it is amply demonstrated by the data on Protestant voting in 1960—however much one might deplore the crude prejudice involved in that particular decision.

Granted then that voting is rational, that it provides a means for rational self-control in the larger society, the American Democrat should be pleased with achievement of his ancestors in providing closer and closer approximations of universal suffrage.

The Status of Suffrage in the United States

The American democrat ought not to hoodwink himself, however, with the magnitude of his ancestors' achievement. Aged and respectable as American democracy is, it is not, as crude propagandists sometimes

---

[16] Philip Converse, Angus Campbell, Warren E. Miller, Donald E. Stokes, "Stability and Change in 1960: A Reinstating Election," *American Political Science Review*, LV (1961), pp. 269–80.

suggest, the complete embodiment of the democratic ideal. Much special privilege still hides in the suffrage system, unfortunately both undetected and undecried.

Each generation of Americans has enlarged the body of voters; but the progress has been uneven. Enfranchisement of some has been partially offset by disfranchisement of others. Yet most Americans, mesmerized by their preconceptions, seem unaware of the retreat. They assume, quite rightly, that democracy and universal suffrage are roughly equivalent; and since they use the word "democracy" to describe the United States government, they assume further that universal suffrage is its basis. Thereby they confuse the ideal they imagine with the reality they do not observe; and thereby also they too often fall into a smug self-satisfaction, unjustified and stultifying.

Though the American democracy was once the beacon for the whole world, it is now surpassed in democratic suffrage by many other countries. In England, for example, since 1928 universal suffrage has been almost a reality. Only felons, lunatics, aliens, peers, and royalty cannot vote—and the latter two nominally participate personally in legislation. In France since 1945 all adults may vote (except again felons, lunatics and aliens). The same pattern of suffrage is found in most other North European democracies: the Low Countries, Scandinavia, and latterly Western Germany. And even in Canada, New Zealand and Australia—where voting by aborigines and orientals is limited—a higher proportion of the population may vote than in the United States.

As against this close approximation to universal suffrage in the rest of the democratic world, the United States today absolutely disfranchises a substantial minority of the adults within its borders. Like all other democracies most states exclude felons, lunatics and aliens. But in addition, many Negroes of the deep South cannot vote even though they are by any reasonable standard capable. Democracy can justifiably except certain people from the rule of universal suffrage: felons, lunatics, aliens, and children under twenty-one. Such people are for various reasons temporarily incapable of the full human dignity and self-respect that the democratic method can procure. But beyond these listed exceptions disfranchisement is a democratic sin. Unfortunately, the United States commits it all too often.

But we are conscious of this sin, especially so in the last decade. And we are making strenuous efforts to eliminate it, as indicated by the newest amendments to the Constitution: The Twenty-Third (adopted in 1961), which enfranchises the residents of the District of Columbia for at least Presidential elections, and the Twenty-Fourth (adopted in 1964), which prohibits poll taxes. Still much remains to be done. And to sustain the momentum of the present drive for universal suffrage, the best morale builder is simply a review of the lapses from universality today. If this review helps us sustain the attack, we can hope that in this generation special privilege will be eliminated from the suffrage system.

THE DISFRANCHISEMENT OF SOUTHERN NEGROES

The most serious of these lapses is the systematic disfranchisement of Negroes through most of the South, the more distressing because it directly contavenes the provision of the Fifteenth Amendment that "the right of citizens of the United States to vote shall not be denied or abridged by the United States or by any State on account of race, color, or previous condition of servitude."

How came this disfranchisement to be?

Negro suffrage after the Civil War was, as has already been intimated, primarily a system for Radical control of Congress. The war had been fought, at least in part, to destroy the disproportionate political power of the planter class. Yet if Negroes had not been enfranchised, the planters' dominance in ten states would have disturbed national politics as much in 1866 as it had in 1860. As it was, Negro votes supplied enough carpetbagger Congressmen for ten years' Reconstruction. Republican Radicals (with a surer sense of politics than the historians who have lately reviled them) realized that Copperheads and Confederates would surely outvote them as the Democratic inter-sectional coalition revived. The prospect was the more ominous because President Andrew Johnson, an ex-Democrat from Tennessee, seemed eager to midwife the regenerated coalition. Republicans therefore devised a system to neutralize Confederate votes: Planter interests were to be balanced immediately and arbitrarily by military "Reconstruction" and permanently and democratically by Negro voters' majorities.

Naturally this kind of Negro suffrage was insecure. It rested on planter-Negro equality, though planters believed themselves superior; it directly opposed sectionalism and racism, though these ideologies had inspired the Confederate cause; and most important of all, it required the encouragement of the national army, though the Commander-in-Chief was increasingly reluctant. Had the army stayed for another decade, Negro suffrage might have become a reality. But Northern Republicans gradually lost incentive to protect the Southern Negroes' vote. Between 1858 and 1876, seven new Northern states and two Congressional reapportionments added a net gain of fourteen Senators and thirty-one Representatives to the Northern majority. In 1872 the Democratic party was so disorganized it had to nominate the "Liberal Republican" Horace Greeley. Small wonder that Northern Republicans, disgusted with sectional strife, enthusiastic for capitalist and agrarian expansion, and, above all, assured that cotton imperialism would no longer block their path, abandoned the Reconstruction effort. In most of the states of the deep South federal troops were removed and Negro majorities evaporated, until Hayes finally terminated Reconstruction. In 1890, after Republicans had somewhat revived abolitionist idealism and had been mildly frightened by Cleveland's first term, the House passed a "Force Bill" to protect Negro suffrage. It died in the Senate under the threat of a Southern filibuster, and thereafter for a very long time the federal government did not "interfere" with the South except for tacit Congressional approval and overt judicial approval of Negro disfranchisement.

Left to themselves, Southern whites gradually put an end to Negro voting. In the 1870's, however, before they had recovered from the war, they did not often practice the crude intimidation which was so prevalent later. At least after the Ku Klux Klan Act of 1871 (which strengthened the law against conspiracy) Southern whites customarily regained control of state governments by methods copied from the most unsavory of Northern urban machines.[17] That is, they stuffed ballot boxes, bribed Negroes, doctored returns. Once again in control, however, the whites not only perpetrated such illegalities more easily, but also, with revived confidence, brandished the physical threat. The votes of all but the most courageous Negroes simply were not cast.

The generation of Southern whites which remembered Reconstruction hesitated, however, to rely on lynch law alone. Physical intimidation and the custom of servility which it enforced were indeed then and still are today the basis of Negro disfranchisement.[18] But Southern

---

[17] W. A. Dunning, "The Undoing of Reconstruction," *Atlantic Monthly*, LXXXVIII (1901), 437–49.

[18] Numerous authorities attest this statement. For the nineteenth century see Paul Lewinson, *Race, Class and Party* (New York, Oxford, 1932), ch. IV; For the contemporary period see John Dollard, *Caste and Class in a Southern Town* (New York, Harper, 1949, 2nd ed.), pp. 314–15 and *passim*; and V. O. Key, *Southern Politics in State and Nation* (New York, Knopf, 1949), pp. 555 and *passim*.

whites of the eighties and nineties seemed also under some guilt-inspired compulsion to devise legal methods of evading the Fifteenth Amendment. They were also under some political obligation to provide the Supreme Court, which had in *United States* v. *Reece* (1876) indicated its sympathy, with legislation which it could use to justify disfranchisement.[19] During the eighties, therefore, Southern legislatures enacted extremely intricate registration and election laws, residence requirements, etc., expecting that whites would find their way through the maze with greater facility than Negroes. And in 1890 the Mississippi constitutional convention established what soon became the most famous of these disfranchising devices. It provided for a poll tax, against which their ancestors had fought so arduously, and for a literacy test, which was copied from Massachusetts and Connecticut, from the Know-Nothing disfranchisement of naturalized immigrants. The Mississippi version, adapted to local circumstances, required that electors be able to read from the state constitution *or* to understand it *or* to interpret it reasonably. The alternatives were, of course, intended to allow registration of wholly illiterate whites while the test itself was to be administered to exclude all Negroes, whether literate or not. Other state conventions of the nineties improved the Mississippi invention. The test was changed from "reading" to "reading and understanding" to give greater scope for administrative refusal to register literate Negroes. "Good character," property ownership, and the "grandfather clause" (i.e. the requirement that voters possess ancestors who voted or could have voted before Reconstruction) were variously designated as alternatives to literacy, alternatives of course available only to illiterate whites. The other half of the Mississippi invention, the poll tax, had been authorized in several states already; but it was from the Mississippi use that it became popular through the South. Since the voting fee bore equally on the poor of both races, however, it is moot whether racism or class antagonism inspired the device.

Although Negroes were at first disfranchised by violence, these suffrage qualifications and later the white primary regularized the exclusion and in a sense softened it. The South had to constitutionalize the unconstitutional, for surely the Supreme Court would never have sanctioned either perpetual violence or outright disfranchisement. But once Southern statesmen had provided some basis for the argument that Negroes were treated the same as whites in full compliance with the

[19] 92 U.S. 214.

Fifteenth Amendment, the Court could overlook the actual disfranchising effect of the laws. Thus, in *Williams* v. *Mississippi* the Court condoned the literacy test, even in spite of the fact that Mr. Justice McKenna's opinion actually cited an admission by the Mississippi Supreme Court that the laws discriminated against Negroes.[20] Although in the "grandfather clause" case the Court did look deep enough into one of the alternatives to the literacy test to find it unconstitutional, the clause had by that time ceased to be important.[21] No Negroes were enfranchised by the decision. Not until 1949, when the Court refused to review the action of a lower court in voiding a "literacy—good character—employment" requirement, did the Court ever really question the sophistry of the literacy test.[22]

Though these technicalities were in the nineties and are still now useful for white supremacy, they were soon eclipsed by the white primary. The fault of literacy tests, poll taxes, etc. was that they did not fully prohibit Negro voting. Some Negroes, if wise enough to obey all the election laws, if literate enough to read the state constitution, if prosperous enough to pay the poll tax, and if, above all, courageous enough to risk violence, could still vote in spite of all the barriers. Their number was larger than is generally imagined, for this was the generation of Negroes which had learned to vote under Reconstruction. As late as 1896 North and South Carolina each sent a Negro Representative to Congress. But Negro voting almost entirely disappeared once the white primary was established.

The disfranchising effect of the white primary depended upon two political conditions: a concentration of whites in one party and a contraction of the Negro electorate. The first was assured when the Democrats absorbed the Populists (in and after 1896); the second resulted from thirty years of intimidation and "legal" exclusion. Since most Negroes who could vote were Republican, it was quite easy for local Democratic parties to adopt rules excluding Negroes from their primaries. And, because most whites were Democrats, the real political decision was made in the Democratic primary. Thus Negroes were finally and almost wholly separated from the political life of the South.

Undemocratic as was the disenfranchisement of Negroes for two generations, today democracy is growing in the South. Northern politi-

[20] 170 U.S. 203 (1898).
[21] *Guinn* v. *United States*, 238 U.S. 347 (1915).
[22] *Davis* v. *Schnell*, 81 F. Supp. 872 (1949), 69 S. Ct. 749 (1949).

cians and publicists, aroused by the struggle over Northern Negro votes, have repeatedly reproached the South and realerted the democratic conscience. This new attitude—based on both the Democratic party's interest in Negro votes in the North and a revived humanitarianism toward Negro people—has been impressed deeply upon the Supreme Court; and the Justices have for the past two decades attempted to atone for their predecessors' injustice. Of course, judicial reappraisal has opened up the whole suffrage controversy again. Very probably this time the democratic rather than racist institutions will triumph.

The major incident of the atonement is the case of *Smith v. Allwright* (1944).[23] Here, after five earlier cases covering twenty years of litigation, the Court finally struck down white primaries in language sufficiently broad to forestall any evasion. For seventy-five years the Court had reasoned about the South with averted eyes and ingenious quibbles; but in *Smith v. Allwright* it finally looked at the realities of Southern politics.

The case electrified the South. It forced Southerners to re-examine their position. As already emphasized, Negro disfranchisement had been perpetuated by rope and faggot, though these were masked with the white primary and other devices. By holding the white primary unconstitutional, this decision tore off the mask and the South was required to acknowledge its violence. As might have been expected, whites of the black belt consciously embraced physical intimidation; but in white majority areas violence often seemed wrong or distasteful or useless to many whites. Hence, sometimes out of conviction and sometimes by default they allowed Negroes to vote. In 1946, 1948, 1950, and 1952, for the first times since 1876, Negroes voted in large numbers. Negro disfranchisement had never, of course, been entirely complete. Paul Lewinson found in 1930 that as many as 30,000 Negroes could vote in municipal elections and a few Democratic primaries, especially in the border states.[24] After the *Smith v. Allwright* decision, however, about 75,000 Negroes voted in Texas alone in 1946. In six urban counties Negro poll tax collectors were deputized or Negroes were elected to minor offices in the Democratic party. And politicians like Wright Patman and Beauford Jester, formerly advocates of white supremacy, openly solicited Negro votes.[25] This is, of course, only ten or twelve

[23] 321 U.S. 649.
[24] Lewinson, *op. cit.*, pp. 134–60.
[25] Donald S. Strong, "The Rise of Negro Voting in Texas," *American Political Science Review*, XLII (1948), pp. 510–22.

percent of the adult Southern Negroes; but it is a remarkable increase over 1930. In the nearly two decades since *Smith* v. *Allwright* Negro voting in the South has continued to expand. Today an increase in Negro registration is the main item on the action program of most civil rights groups in the South. In 1960, nearly 30 percent of Southern Negro adults were registered,[26] and it is not fanciful to expect that, in the eleven Southern states, nearly forty percent of the five million adult Southern Negroes will soon be eligible to vote. In marginal states like Tennessee, in the spring of 1964, at least sixty-five percent of the adult Negroes were actually registered. Of course, it is not merely *Smith* v. *Allwright* that enfranchised them. It was rather the new spirit of participation that the political significance of the Negro vote implied that encouraged Northern (and some Southern) white support for it. Numerous specific steps have included registration by the Civil Rights Division in the Department of Justice, acting primarily under the Civil Rights Acts of 1957 and 1960, and the consistent protection of voting privileges in the Supreme Court.

Genuine citizenship for Southern Negroes seems possible today for the first time since the Civil War. Two circumstances are, however, necessary to realize the possibility: (a) continued action and agitation for democracy and (b) genuine Southern effort to relieve the growing race tensions in a civilized manner. The first is the essential requirement. Both times in history that the Southern Negro has voted, democratic agitators have in their own self-interest obtained his suffrage for him. In the 1870's, however, democratic agitators lost interest. What is the likelihood that they will not today? In the 1870's Negro votes lost value in national politics. Today and for so long as Northern Negroes are divided and undecided in their party affiliation, democratic politicians dare not lose interest in Negro votes anywhere. Political interest in Negro voting is therefore assured for the foreseeable future.

What of the Southern reaction? How determined is the South to uproot the seedlings of democracy? Some elements—heretofore dominant in Southern life—are, of course, pledged to maintain white supremacy. But many other Southerners are sick of Jim Crow politics. The latter have often exhibited a tolerance not usually included in the popular stereotype of a Southerner. In the 1880's for example, most Populists

[26] Donald R. Matthews and James Prothro, "Social and Economic Factors and Negro Voter Registration in the South," *American Political Science Review*, LVII (1963), pp. 24–44.

allied with Negroes against the rich and well-born, though later some like Ben Tillman cavorted as furious Negro-haters. The disfranchising acts of the 1890's were everywhere strongly opposed by minorities among the whites. Their motives were mixed: some feared the loss of political allies, others feared for their own suffrage, still others were appalled by the democratic retreat. But whatever their purpose, they did defend democracy. And in the last decade the same split has reappeared among Southern whites. Only where the Dixiecrats flourished in 1948 and where Goldwater won in 1964 have whites insisted upon Negro submissiveness. Elsewhere some have exhibited true willingness to let go their monopoly for a new pattern of race relations. Matthews and Prothro report that political toleration, as exhibited in legal toleration of Negro political groups, is an important factor in Negro registration and that such toleration is built into the legal system of most Southern states. Furthermore, they report that the social and economic factors associated with high Negro registration (e.g. greater income for both whites and Negroes, a greater proportion of white-collar workers, etc.) are increasing rapidly for the South as a whole, while the factors associated with antipathy to Negro registration (e.g., high degree of farm tenancy) are declining.[27] Hence follows a white willingness— however slow-moving and mild—to accept Negro voting, and this augurs well for American democracy.

RESIDENCE REQUIREMENTS

Jim Crow laws can be justified only by outright denial of democratic values. With a little prodding, then, the democratic conscience can recognize their iniquity. Most of the other obstacles to suffrage, however, are not so patently undemocratic and hence do not occasion democratic crusades. They obstruct suffrage, therefore, systematically, surreptitiously and without protest.

Consider the case of residence requirements which make a year's or two years' residence in the state a prerequisite for voting. Unknown to the common law, they are probably a watered-down version of the "forty-shilling freehold." Certainly, at least, they were invented toward the end of the eighteenth century, when universal suffrage seemed

[27] Ibid.; and Donald R. Matthews and James Prothro, "Political Factors and Negro Voter Registration in the South," American Political Science Review, LVII (1963), pp. 355–67.

imminent, to substitute for land ownership as proof of an "interest" in the election of local officials.[28] No matter how anti-democratic their ancestry, however, they can be justified today as an educational qualification, which is neutral enough to democratic eyes. Of course, no democrat would admit that formal education increases the claim to self-respect; the moral value of each personality is independent of the money spent to educate it. Still, even the most radical democrat can admit that a rational knowledge of the voters' own interest necessitates familiarity with local politics and custom. The simplest test of familiarity is residence, for it does not permit partisan administration. In this sense, therefore, residence requirements are necessary and desirable in a system of democratic suffrage.

But sometimes they operate undemocratically. In the South, where the residence requirement is usually two years in the state and one year in the voting district, it is a part of the legal network to disfranchise Negroes. The lengthy residence requirement exploits the popular belief that Negroes change jobs and homes oftener than whites. Of course, it disfranchises migratory whites too. Outside the South residence requirements are usually one year in the state and ten days to six months in the voting district. To a sedentary citizen one year does not perhaps seem excessive. But wherever agriculture is based on migratory labor, one year is enough to deprive farm hands of citizen rights. Thus, for example, the migrating Okies could not vote to protect themselves from the exploitation and terrorism of the corporate ranch owners. The distant humanitarianism of the LaFollette Committee, which published numerous exposés of the Associated Farmers and similar combines of ranchers, was no substitute at all for suffrage.[29] Similarly, during the migration which dislocated urban life from 1940 to 1945, residence requirements deprived the chief victims of a voice in adjusting their environment. Though without a Steinbeck to memorialize them, many a family of migratory factory workers found themselves as trapped by circumstance as the Joads and equally unable to extricate themselves through the democratic method.

[28] Porter, *op. cit.*, p. 37.
[29] Senate Committee on Education and Labor, *Violations of Free Speech and the Rights of Labor,* "Employers' Associations and Collective Bargaining in California," Senate Report #1150; part 4, 77th Congress, 2nd Session, pp. 407–696, and Senate Report #398, part 4, 78th Congress, 2nd Session, pp. 1129–1640.

REGISTRATION

Consider also the case of registration systems. If residence requirements, even the fairest ones, are enforced at all, there must necessarily be a register of qualified voters. And in cities, where the neighbors of a precinct are seldom known to one another and where so many electoral frauds are possible, voters must be identified in some way. Registration is, therefore, a positive necessity for honest elections; and in most states, especially those with permanent registration systems, it has been used only for this one essential purpose: protecting the purity of the ballot.

In a few places, however, it has been distorted to serve the interest of corrupt machines which want only their reliables to vote and of reactionary cliques which want a minimum of popular participation in politics. Almost as soon as registration was invented, these interests discovered that a perversion of registration can make voting difficult, especially for the urban poor. If registration is required for every election or during the usual working hours or at a downtown center difficult to reach or many months ahead of the campaign, urban voting can be remarkably reduced. If, further, the system is disorganized by conscious maladministration, even more otherwise eligible voters can be disfranchised.

LITERACY TESTS

Finally, consider the case of the literacy test. So disarming is its rationale that its real purpose and effect are commonly misunderstood. Its defense runs thus: Voters should be able to participate rationally in politics if democracy is to promote self-respect; the best test of rationality is literacy; voters should therefore be literate. The democrat is often misled by this fallacious logic, possibly because it is verbally similar to the democratic reason for disfranchising felons and lunatics. The catch in the argument would, of course, be obvious in any but this literate century. Literacy is a test of school attendance, not at all a test of rationality. The public school should not blind democrats to the rights and reason of those who for one cause or another have not been able to take advantage of it. The real political purpose, so artfully concealed, is to deprive of citizen rights certain minorities believed to have a low literacy rate. Eighteen states have adopted the test, seven to disfranchise Negroes, five to disfranchise Indians and Mexicans and Orientals, and six to disfranchise European immigrants.

The most widely publicized of literacy tests, if they can be dignified by that name, are those used in the South to disfranchise Negroes, even Negro college graduates. Tests of this sort do not, of course, have any particular relation to either literacy or testing, especially when administered by white registrars who are often themselves not fully literate. Even when the literacy test is procedurally fair, however, it significantly stunts the democratic ideal. In New York, for example, although administered impartially by school authorities, it disfranchised each year during the 1920's almost twenty percent of the people who took it, most of whom were presumably rational.[30] Since many of the failures were repeaters, much less than that proportion of the total electorate was disfranchised. While its incidence is lower now that immigration has declined,[31] its true significance, however, lies in its origin: it was a hotly contested party issue intended, as all politicians at the time (1921 and after) understood, to disfranchise foreign-born citizens.[32] Elsewhere as in New York, the test roots in nativist resentments or in (what is often the same) a conservative fear of the whole people.

In the British general election of 1959 seventy-seven percent of the adults voted.[33] The United States could not possibly equal this record. In England, however, no minority is systematically intimidated; the register of voters is carefully maintained; the residence requirements are brief; and there are no obstacles such as literacy tests, poll taxes and the like. Manifestly, the American democracy can regain its democratic leadership only by unblocking the road to universal suffrage. Yet, considering the gravity of our problem, is it not both sad and ludicrous that one of the chief suffrage questions now debated in the public press is lowering the minimum voting age from twenty-one to eighteen?

[30] F. G. Crawford, "Observation of the Literacy Test for Voters in New York," *American Political Science Review,* XXV (1931), pp. 342–45.
[31] Even in 1944, however, 36,000 or about fifteen percent of those who took the test failed. See Secretary of State Thomas J. Curran, *Manual for the Use of the Legislature of New York, 1945* (Albany, 1945), p. 832.
[32] Arthur Bromage, "Literacy and the Electorate," *American Political Science Review,* XXIV (1930), pp. 946–66.
[33] D. E. Butler and Richard Rose, *The British General Election of 1959* (London, Macmillan, 1960), p. 232.

"One Man, One Vote"

The democratic method of universal suffrage means first of all that every person vote. But it means also and equally that every vote weighs the same. This is the nineteenth century slogan, "one man, one vote." It would indeed be absurd to attack special privilege with votes, if, at the same time, special privilege imbedded itself in the system of voting. The democratic method ought not to contain its own negation.

Yet almost all democratic constitutions do contain some special privilege in their voting systems. The classic instance is plural voting, as, for example, that which as recently as 1948 existed in Great Britain. Owners of business property could vote twice, once in the place of residence and once in the place of business. University graduates could vote both at home and in a university constituency.

While the United States has fortunately escaped this particular democratic deformity, at least since colonial times, it does not follow that we have really institutionalized the principle "one man, one vote." Like all other representative governments, we are plagued with dishonesty and violence and intimidation in elections, simply because government policy depends upon their results. Crude disturbances, such as intimidation, less gravely endanger the principle "one man, one vote," however, than provisions for weighing votes differently. The United States has happily been spared an aristocratic house in the legislature such as the House of Lords in Great Britain, which before 1911 was an institutional embodiment of "one peer, one vote; one commoner, one twenty-thousandth vote." We have, all the same, real inequality in weighing votes. Perhaps because our case is not as extreme as elsewhere, Americans have seldom been conscious of their lapse.

Intimidation and Corruption

Earlier in this chapter it was suggested that American democrats need to reawaken their democratic conscience. The first step toward the extirpation of special privilege is an alert insight into its disguise. It is here appropriate, therefore, to set forth the major violations of "one man, one vote."

Considering first the crude and illegal violations, it should be noted that they are an endemic disease in all democracies with an incidence almost as high as the common cold. The most virulent form is outright intimidation which not only nullifies the victims' votes but actually adds them to the opposition tally.

Fortunately intimidation has been rare in the United States, aside from the mistreatment of Negroes. After the expulsion of the colonial aristocracy and under the militant democratic leadership of Jefferson and Jackson, Americans seldom diagnosed or fretted about the disease. It was either unknown or, in some areas, too usual to appear abnormal. Rather suddenly in the 1870's and 1880's however, intimidation appeared to be a great democratic problem. Southerners attempted to evade Reconstruction by intimidating Negroes. Radical Republicans in turn attempted (rather ineffectually) to police the Ku Klux Klan and its allies. Southerners, stung by the charge of illegality, retaliated with *tu quoque:* a famous investigation conducted by Senate Democrats found many examples of "civilized bulldozing" in the North. For example: [34]

It was shown that in the tenth ward of Providence, at the Presidential election of 1876, the time-keeper employed by The Corliss Steam Engine Company was at the polls with his book, and as every man working for his establishment would cast his ballot he would check his name or write his name down upon the book. [Sc: since voting involved a request for the ballot of one party or the other, the implication is that the timekeeper recorded the employés choice between parties]. . . . The ward was largely Democratic and this action produced disturbance on the part of citizens who sought to have the time-keeper removed because the employés of the Corliss Steam Engine Company were afraid if they voted their principles they would be discharged from the works. . . .

It is greatly to the credit of American democracy that, when the epidemic of intimidation was recognized, the secret ballot was so promptly adopted. It was imported from Australia—whence the name "Australian Ballot"—and adopted for Wisconsin cities in 1887 and for all Kentucky in 1888.[35] By 1900 thirty-eight states had followed this lead.[36] In 1960 only one state (South Carolina) still openly permitted intimidation of voters.

And so it happens that in this century voters have been intimidated

---

[34] Select Committee to Inquire into Alleged Frauds in the Late Elections, *Report,* #497, U.S. Senate, 46th Congress, 2nd Session, April 19, 1880, p. 10.
[35] E. C. Evans, *A History of the Australian Ballot System in the United States* (Chicago, University of Chicago Library, 1917), p. 19.
[36] *Ibid.,* p. 27.

much less frequently. Aside from the mistreatment of Negroes in the South, the most effective and arrogant intimidation has been in company towns, for the most part inhabited by two sorts of people: recent immigrants, unaware of the moral value of suffrage, as in the steel and coal towns of Pennsylvania, and Southern poor whites and mountaineers cut off by several generations' disfranchisement or geographic remoteness from the main stream of American democracy, as in textile towns and mine villages of the Southern Appalachians.

The New Deal awakened political interest in many half-feudal places, and Roosevelt, almost in person, instructed many of the submerged and intimidated in the process of self-direction. Labor unions, nurtured by the Wagner Act, kept the new consciousness alert and extended the instruction to places even Roosevelt could not reach. For example, in the steel towns of western Pennsylvania, where company managers long dominated political life and where men seldom dared vote for any candidate but the Republican, the New Deal and the Steelworkers Organizing Committee together canceled out this domination. The measure of the change is seen in Aliquippa (population 27,116 in 1930) which had only eight registered Democrats in 1933 but which elected a Democratic city government in 1937.[37] So it was elsewhere; and during the three decades past this kind of political intimidation has diminished remarkably.

So far as the white population is concerned, therefore, the United States has taken vigorous action to preclude the kind of intimidation which was so rampant in, for example, the Third French Republic that after almost every election numerous deputies were unseated because their constituents had been forced to support them. The menace against Southern Negroes remains, then, the only kind of intimidation of really grave proportions. Even it has abated on the fringes of the South and, if democrats continue to insist, it too may be minimized in our time.

Corrupt practices in elections have been much more prevalent than intimidation. Their total effect is fully as evil. They have taken a multitude of shapes; the variety itself testifies to the frequency of fraud, to the persistence of reform, and above all to the ingenuity of the depraved. The most enervating corruption for democracy is, of course, outright bribery, for it persuades the voter to value his vote and himself at no more than the few dollars actually paid. Only slightly less demoralizing

[37] *New York Times*, Nov. 1, 1937, p. 9.

is the payment of the voter's poll tax—a practice probably much more common today than direct bribery itself. Fortunately, bribery of both kinds is uneconomic when on a really large scale and sometimes even corrupt bosses themselves have taken the initiative in minimizing it. Usually today, therefore, the worst frauds are behind the scenes, either in voting or in counting the votes. Until good registration systems put them partially out of business, *repeaters* and *substitutes* were common techniques. For corrupt machines really in control of their bailiwicks, however, none of these crude methods is necessary. All that is required is full control of the count. Then ballot boxes can be stuffed with impunity, or for that matter, votes need not be counted at all. Whatever form corrupt practices take, however, they substitute for the will of the whole people the lust of a depraved coterie, befouling thus the democratic ideal.

The necessary dual conditions of corruption are these: a people who have lost the democratic vision (or perhaps have never seen it) and an insolent clique, contemptuous of the vision and the people as well. The latter condition is forever present because, as this very listing of derelictions suggests, criminal types are inevitable in this imperfect world. Much discusssion of corrupt politicians loses relevance from overlooking this obvious fact. In seeking motivations for bossdom outside the bosses themselves, hesitant democrats like Lord Bryce, blame "the ignorance and recklessness of the humbler classes.[38] Radical democrats, like Lincoln Steffens, blame the wealthy: "In all my time, J. P. Morgan sat on the American throne as *boss of bosses,* as the ultimate American sovereign." [39] Both explanations omit the thing explained, the corrupt boss himself. No doubt people are sometimes misled by demagogues and no doubt the rich have purchased privilege from every local Tammany; but the boss, like the vulture, is natural and inevitable: he circles wherever the people's ideals are dead. If men are willing to sell their votes, if they are willing to have them counted wrongly, then there is certain to appear from somewhere the depraved agent of bribery and fraud.

Since the potential agents of evil are a constant, it is thus the people themselves who are the variable factor in corruption. Citizens may use

[38] Viscount Bryce, *The American Commonwealth* (New York, Macmillan, 1923, 2 vols., revised), II, p. 175.
[39] Lincoln Steffens, *Autobiography* (New York, Harcourt Brace, 1931), p. 590, emphasis added.

the ballot with greater or less understanding of its real meaning. When the people are uninstructed in democracy, when they do not see its vision, corruption appears. It is not enough, however, in the American case to accuse poor understanding of the democratic method. Why should the United States, with the oldest and most famous democratic heritage, the country which first attempted to institutionalize the vision, be also discredited by so many world-known, infamous scandals? Other democracies, of course, have had as many. French scandals are almost as notorious as our own and have had an even more determining influence on national politics. The Panama Canal debacle, the Dreyfus affair, and the Stavisky pawnshops are more than a match for Credit Mobilier, Teapot Dome, and the recent rash of suspected influence peddling, from Sherman Adams to Bobby Baker.[40] So in part our reputation derives from an honest public laundering of dirty clothes. But still the question recurs: Why so many scandals in America?

While it is impossible to isolate one sufficient cause, still one important condition seems to be that not all Americans have been taught to value democracy. Some immigrants, for example, escaping from European oligarchies where they could not learn the democratic truth, enrolled all unaware in the ranks of a hundred Tammanies—the only organizations available for achieving the self-respect they craved. Negroes, systematically brutalized by slavery, of course could not appreciate fully the Reconstruction ballot. The wonder is not that they were bribed, but that they produced as many good democrats as they did; one would have expected them to be fully as venal as Southern apologists assert. Negroes, escaping from quasi-peonage to urban centers North and South, have quite understandably swelled the vote of a Big Bill Thompson and a Boss Kelly in Chicago or a Boss Crump in Memphis.

If this analysis be correct, if indeed corruption spores when the democratic vision fades, only the brightness of a true democracy can really desiccate the rot. This is, in fact, the lesson of our history. Corrupt politics has preyed upon the distressed until great democratic leaders have instructed them in the democratic way. The depraved flourish because they perform some service for the voters. Their service is indeed petty, acceptable only when voters do not realize the true

---

[40] D. W. Brogan, *France Under the Republic: The Development of Modern France (1870–1939)*, (New York, Harper & Brothers, 1940), pp. 268–85, 329–90, 427, 661–69 and *passim*.

value of their vote, but it is nonetheless real. Martin Lomasney, boss of Boston's ward eight, once justified himself in these now famous words: [41]

I think there's got to be in every ward somebody that any bloke can come to—no matter what he's done, and get help. Help, you understand; none of your law and justice, but help.

His kind of help, alms and protection, is not enough, however, when citizens realize the self-respect and the material self-control obtainable through democracy. In this century, with the growth of public social services, election scandals are certainly rarer than they once were. Conscious governmental direction of the economy, sponsored by Theodore Roosevelt, Woodrow Wilson, and Franklin Roosevelt, has created the kind of government that makes voting worth while. And by the teaching of these hero Presidents, the real value of suffrage has been impressed on each generation.

Reform movements have also helped. But it is true that, except where corruption is not deeply inbedded, they have been seldom effective. "Good government" reformers—the kind Tammany wardheelers called "goo-goos"—have often, even usually, been more interested in cheap government than in effective government. Unlike the democratic heroes, they have wanted to abolish graft more because it raises taxes than because it is used to buy votes and defraud democracy. They have, therefore, failed to inspire the voters with a new faith. In consequence, democratic leaders rather than reformers (insofar as they are distinct types) are the ones who have really carried through reform.

The case of New York City is instructive. Ever since the Tweed ring of the early seventies, reformers have sporadically dislodged corrupt machines. But none could permanently disturb the dominion of thieves until Mayor La Guardia bounced upon the scene. He taught New Yorkers what no one else had yet tried to teach: that democratic government gave them better schools, better social services, better parks, better houses, better trade unions, and what is more important, a better sense of their own worth than the alms-giving oligarchy of ward bosses. Some sensitive citizens deplored as vulgar and demagogic his flair for publicity, his ubiquitous speechmaking, his firefighting regalia, and his eloquent and exuberant sponsorship of a thousand cornerstones. Yet these were

[41] Steffens, *op. cit.*, p. 618.

his teaching methods; however unorthodox, they awoke in many a new sense of the democratic ideal. Corruption survives in spite of his twelve years of demonic activity; but few would deny that New Yorkers are better citizens because he was there. Certainly no machine is able to control unless it has popular support, and the last of the old-time Tammany leaders, Carmine de Sapio, found he could not himself be reelected in the face of popular reformist opposition. What is true of New York is true elsewhere. Though the New Deal relied on and gave patronage to many corrupt machines, paradoxically and in a sense unintentionally, it also undermined them by inspiring a new respect for the ballot's purpose. And in recent years some of the places most deeply touched by the democratic spirit of the New Deal have minimized, at least, the frauds on democracy (e.g., Chicago, Philadelphia, and Jersey City as well as New York). The moral seems clear: citizens who understand democracy do not tolerate corrupt elections. Two quotations summarize this point. Even in the eighties Bryce recognized that: [42]

When there is a real issue before the voters, bribery diminishes. In the mayoralty contest of 1886, in New York, the usually venal classes went straight for the Labour candidate, and would not be bought.

On the eve of the New Deal, another English visitor noted after an exhaustive study of corruption in American politics: [43]

Where politics are cleanest in the United States is where real political issues are fostered and in modern times such issues must be economic, must be open to the danagers of demagogy and give a chance to "radicalism," that nightmare of the believers in the divine rights of business men.

Gerrymanders and Rotten Districts

Vicious and prevalent as intimidation and corruption are, they do not, at least in recent years, vitiate the principle of "one man, one vote" nearly so much as legal methods of miscalculating the popular will.

Between the citizens and public policy stand the representatives. They transmute the popular will into law or action—and therein lies

---

[42] Bryce, *op. cit.*, II, p. 151, note.
[43] D. W. Brogan, *Government of the People* (New York, Harper & Brothers, 1933), p. 294.

much chance of error. The chance is not so much that they honestly misinterpret, because the next election always decides that question. The real danger is that they not truly represent, that they be not truly responsible to the whole people. When this happens, misinterpretation can never be tested at the polls.

Even if everyone can vote, it does not follow that everyone will be truly represented. Politicians long ago discovered how to construct systems of representation for the permanent advantage of their faction. The ideal system (probably unrealizable) is one which all factions agree is fair. But constitution makers, who are expected to be as selfless and omniscient as Rousseau's great Legislator, are only politicians momentarily exalted. A few may be humbled by their responsibility, but most bother little with ideals. They concentrate instead on manipulating their two variables of representation: (a) the method of selection and (b) the arrangement of constituencies. By clever combinations of these alternatives they can influence future elections and hence future public policy, perhaps even for generations.

Our constitutional fathers devised three methods of selecting public officers. One was the direct popular election of Representatives. The other two inserted intermediary bodies (state legislatures and an *ad hoc* college) between the voters and the Senators and President. The purpose of indirect elections was, as Hamilton phrased it, "to afford as little opportunity as possible to tumult and disorder." [44] Experience taught, however, that the intermediaries moderated tumult far less than they distorted popular intent. Direct popular election seemed to succeeding generations most democratic. Hence the other two methods were abandoned in favor of it.

The electoral college, originally elected by state legislatures, was intended to act without responsibility to anyone in choosing a President. Very early in our history, however, electors were bound by party instructions and eventually they were elected by popular vote. Although the collegiate form survives, these changes substantially abolished the intermediaries.[45] Similarly, Senators were originally elected

[44] *Federalist*, No. 68.

[45] The survival of the form is, however, of some importance. It threatens always to frustrate popular intent. As occasional defiance suggests, electors may possibly disobey instructions. And in 1948 and again in 1964 the collegiate form permitted Alabama Dixiecrats to deprive the Democratic candidate of the Democratic party label and hence of Alabama Democratic electors. Furthermore, the President's constituency is not really the whole nation because the college injects a slight bias in favor of the less populous states. These defects have only once

by state legislatures; but after a half-century of democratic agitation, the Seventeenth Amendment (1913) substituted direct election. At present, therefore, the method of election is substantially the same for all national officers. The constituencies do vary in size from subdivisions of states to the whole nation; but in each constituency the method of choice is similar. The bias once imparted by the alternative methods of voting has thus been corrected.

Today, then, the only variations of significance are in electoral districts. Even when districts are of equal population, alternative sets of boundaries produce different kinds of representation. The Constitution suggests that state legislatures construct the congressional districts and they have fulfilled the trust with gerrymandering.[46]

A gerrymander requires only that one party control the state government. The controlling party can then draw district lines to increase its own control. It may divide the opposition votes among several districts in which the controlling party is sure to win by small but safe majorities; thus few opposition candidates can be elected. Or it may concentrate the opposition vote in a few districts in which opposition candidates will always be elected by tremendous margins, while candidates of the controlling party will win in the rest of the districts by safe, but smaller, majorities. Usually both kinds of gerrymander exist side by side. Although the worst features of the gerrymander have been curbed by Congress's requirement (first applied in 1814) that districts be contiguous, the map of at least ten states is mute evidence that the gerrymander is very important today.

A typical example is displayed in Charts I and II. The New York districts there displayed are cited simply to show the technique of the

---

prevented the choice of a candidate with a popular plurality—Cleveland in 1888 had a plurality of 95,913 in over eleven million votes but lost in the electoral college. [Though Tilden lost with what seemed a popular plurality in 1876, there was so much fraud that no one knows what the popular vote really was. See Paul L. Haworth, *The Hayes-Tilden Disputed Election of 1876* (Cleveland, Burrows Bros., 1906).] So long as the college exists disobedience or distortion may again occur.

[46] The word derives from Elbridge Gerry, Governor of Massachusetts and a member of the Federal Convention of 1787; but he did not invent the practice. Adjusting constituency lines to prejudice elections is as old as elections themselves. Gerry's name connotes infamy only because as Governor he helped redistrict the General Court in 1811–1812 in the interest of the Republican party. One new district had a vaguely reptilian shape; and an inspired Federalist journalist coined the name from *Gerry* and *salamander*. See Elmer C. Griffith, *The Rise and Development of the Gerrymander* (Chicago, Scott, Foresman and Co., 1907), p. 18.

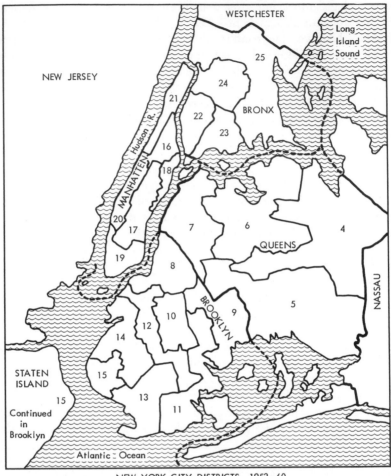

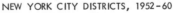

NEW YORK CITY DISTRICTS, 1952-60

CHART I

gerrymander. The significance of the gerrymander is, however, the result, not the technique. And in New York, even with the gerrymander that failed in Brooklyn, Republicans gained about three seats by means of judicious use of the technique. Although the New York districts are approximately equal in population—inasmuch as only twelve districts out of forty-one vary by more than ten percent from the average

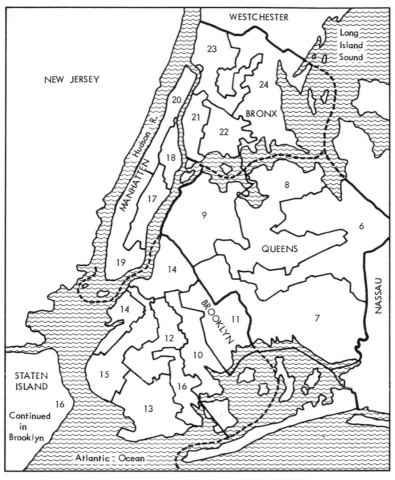

NEW YORK CITY DISTRICTS, 1962 TO PRESENT

CHART II

size and no districts vary more than fifteen percent—still they are highly inequitable, as a glance at the charts indicates. The convoluted boundaries of numerous districts suggest that some sort of skulduggery was involved in drawing the district lines, as was indeed the situation. In Brooklyn, the northern and southern parts of the present fourteenth district are connected only by an uninhabited strip of wharves and streets. The fifteenth, on the other hand, looks something like the salamander for which gerrymanders are named and so indeed does that portion of the sixteenth which is in Brooklyn. In the Bronx the twenty-fourth district looks even more like the classic beast, and in Queens the sixth, seventh, and eighth are almost as curious in shape. These misshapen districts are sufficient mute evidence of the intent to gerrymander.

The rationale of these curious shapes is completely partisan. Consider the most obvious case of Brooklyn, where the crux of the explanation is that the Republican state legislature was trying to preserve two Republican districts. Under the 1952–60 districting, six of Brooklyn's eight districts went consistently Democratic while two usually went Republican. These two were composed thus:

15. The southwest section of the present fifteenth district and Staten Island.
12. A narrow, worm-shaped district starting with what is now the northwest section of the present fifteenth district and proceeding in a southeasterly direction and in a narrow strip almost to Jamaica Bay, taking in at the southeast end most of what is now the Brooklyn part of the sixteenth district.

This was an effective gerrymander, one of the classics of the type. Unfortunately for admirers of the art, this could not stand, for, under the 1960 census, Brooklyn was reduced to seven districts. Republican state legislators, perhaps too greedily for their own good, sought to preserve two of these seven for themselves—and thereby lost everything, at least in 1962 and 1964, though in a Republican year they might regain what they lost. The crucial problem for Republican gerrymanderers was to force three Democratic districts into two. This they did by dividing the old fourteenth up into northern and southern halves, giving the northern half to the former eighth and the southern half to the former tenth. The new combinations resulted in two districts:

14. A district the northern half of which was the old eighth and the southern half of which was the northern half of the old fourteenth.
12. The core of the old tenth plus the southern half of the old fourteenth.

The trouble with this combination, from a technical point of view, was that the new twelfth district had to cut through the old twelfth district, that narrow worm running from the East River to Jamaica Bay, in order to connect up with its addition from the old fourteenth. No amount of topological sophistication could avoid this result, so two new presumably Republican districts had to be devised. These were, of course, created out of the old Republican districts.

15. The new fifteenth consisted of the Brooklyn part of the old fifteenth, the northwestern part of the old twelfth and a small connecting band (part of the old fourteenth) between the southern halves of the new fifteenth and the new twelfth. In taking on this connecting band the security of the fifteenth was severely endangered, however.

16. The new sixteenth consisted of the southeastern half of the old twelfth and, moving westward thirty miles through the waters of Jamaica Bay and the Atlantic (not inhabited by humans), Staten Island.

Thus except for a portion of the old fourteenth in the new fifteenth, the new fifteenth and sixteenth considered largely of the old twelfth and fifteenth.

Once these adjustments had been made, it was not necessary to revise the remaining three districts significantly. The old ninth became the new eleventh; the old eleventh became the new tenth (although some of the old eleventh had to go to the new sixteenth to connect it with Jamaica Bay so that it could be contiguous—over water—with Staten Island, a transfer which made the new sixteenth much less Republican than the old twelfth had been); and the old thirteenth became substantially the new thirteenth.

The Republicans failed in Brooklyn, but elsewhere in the city they improved the gerrymander. In the Bronx the twenty-fourth (old twenty-fifth) was made to look like a dragon in order to strengthen the Republican hold on that district, so that Republicans retained their one-fourth control of that borough. In Manhattan as in Brooklyn the number of seats declined, but by judicious maintenance of an earlier gerrymander Republicans (who had had one seat in six) came to have one seat in four. In Queens the gerrymander of 1951 was substantially repeated in 1961. Each of the four districts stuck fingers from the Republican edges down into the Democratic core. In the good Democratic year of 1962 this gerrymander was not enough and the Republican proportion slipped from two out of four to one out of four, but in a good Republican year the former proportion might again be attained.

State legislatures do worse than gerrymander, however, when they tolerate rotten boroughs. The principle "one man, one vote" can extend to policy-making only if representatives have reasonably equal constituencies. If district boundaries are not periodically revised, some soon become "rotten," i.e. they have far fewer voters than the average. The voter in the rotten borough then has relatively much more influence than his neighbor in a larger district. But redistricting is peculiarly difficult. It upsets, often radically, the balance of party power. In England, for example, where the phrase "rotton borough" originated, Locke described and condemned them as early as 1690: [47]

Things of this world are in so constant a flux that nothing remains long in the same state. Thus people, riches, trade, power change their stations; flourishing mighty cities come to ruin, and prove in time neglected desolate corners, whilst other unfrequented places grow into populous countries filled with wealth and inhabitants. . . . [I]t often comes to pass . . . that in tract of time . . . representation becomes very unequal and disproportionate to the reasons it was at first established upon. To what gross absurdities the following of custom when reason has left it may lead, we may be satisfied when we see the bare name of a town, of which there remains not so much as the ruins, where scarce so much housing as a sheepcote, or more inhabitants than a shepherd is to be found, send as many representatives to the grand assembly of law-makers as a whole county numerous in people and powerful in riches. This strangers stand amazed at, and everyone must confess needs a remedy; though most think it hard to find one. . . .

Locke's pessimism was justified: Even the worst rotten boroughs were not abolished until 1832.

In the United States the allocation of Representatives to states—a problem much disputed during the nineteenth century by politicians who fancied themselves mathematicians and mathematicians who fancied themselves politicians—was satisfactorily settled by the Permanent Apportionment Act of 1929 which placed the burden of the work on the relatively non-political Census Bureau.[48] Since then each state has had a fair share of seats. The real problem of rotten boroughs

[47] John Locke, *Of Civil Government*, sec. 157.
[48] Lawrence Schmeckebier, *Congressional Apportionment* (Washington, Brookings Institution, 1941), pp. 107–26.

is, therefore, within the states. According to the 1960 census, Representatives should be chosen for, on the average, each 412,000 people. But this standard cannot always be met. In a state with, for example, one million people and two Representatives, some districts must be oversized. In a heavily populated state, however, it is possible to divide the districts so that they approximate 412,000. Very few do. State legislatures in fact protect rotten boroughs by every conceivable parliamentary tactic. Thus the Illinois legislature did not redistrict from 1901 to 1947, despite tremendous population shifts. At present there are five districts larger than 700,000 in population: the district of Atlanta, Georgia (823,000), of Dayton, Ohio (726,000), Dearborn, Michigan (802,000), Dallas, Texas (951,000), and the northern Baltimore area (711,000); fourteen more are between 600,000 and 700,-000.

It is difficult to measure the degree of rottenness. The most frequently used method, however, is a calculation of the percentage by which each district differs from the ideal size for the state. (The ideal size is the population of the state divided by the number of districts, a figure which for most populous states is by the 1960 census between 400,000 and 420,000.) Most authorities would agree that districts ought not to exceed or fall short of the ideal by more than twenty percent.[49] On this basis, thirty-four states have rotten districts. All together, sixty-four districts are more than twenty percent oversized and fifty-six are over twenty percent undersized. Thus over one-fourth of the members of Congress represent malapportioned districts.

Schubert and Press have devised a much more sophisticated measure of apportionment which takes into account the variance in size of districts, the ratio of number of persons residing in significantly oversized districts to the number in significantly undersized districts, and the distribution of undersized and oversized districts.[50] On the basis of this technique, they graded the legislatures of the fifty states and the United States, as of the population of 1960 and apportionment of 1962. The five states with the best apportionment were Massachusetts, Oregon, Ohio, Nebraska, and Maine. The five states with the worst apportionment were Indiana, Georgia, Minnesota, Iowa, and Oklahoma. The United States Congress stood in thirty-fourth place.

Gerrymandering and rotten districts are really alternative methods

[49] *Ibid.*, p. 130.
[50] Glendon Schubert and Charles Press, "Measuring Malapportionment," *American Political Science Review*, LVIII (1964), pp. 302–27.

of misrepresentation. Most state legislatures accomplish their purpose simply by constructing or tolerating unequal districts, the so-called "silent gerrymander." The gerrymander itself, a much more difficult technique, is feasible on a large scale only when redistricting is forced by national reapportionment. But taking both alternatives together, the people of most states which have more than one representative (44 in all) are misrepresented in Congress.

Gerrymandering and the perpetuation of rotten boroughs could perhaps be endured if, over the country as a whole, the distortions canceled each other out. But they do not. With one or two exceptions (e.g. southern Missouri and eastern Tennessee) these twin evils consistently underrepresent metropolitan areas and thereby give rural and small-town dwellers an excessively large voice in national affairs. In Michigan, for example, when urban and suburban districts are compared with rural and small-town districts, it is found that the latter average only about sixty percent as many people as the former. In effect urban and suburban voters lose two districts. Similarly, rural and small-town districts in Texas average only sixty percent of the urban ones, thus transferring four seats to rural voters.

TABLE I. Michigan Congressional Districts

	Urban	Rural–Small Town
Republican	4 districts	7 districts
	average size: 566,000	average size: 318,000
Democratic	7 districts	
	average size: 495,000	—
Total	11 districts	7 districts
	average size: 508,000	average size: 318,000

Whence comes this consistent underrepresentation of cities? The immediate cause is that they are even more flagrantly underrepresented in state legislatures. Most large cities and suburban areas are partially disfranchised by one or both of two effective devices: (1) one branch of the state legislature is constitutionally constructed to represent areas (on the analogy of the United States Senate), and (2) rotten districting is allowed to occur even more flagrantly in state legislatures than in the House of Representatives. The first device is used in thirty-two states; but the analogy between States in the Senate and subordinate political units (like towns and counties) in the state legislatures is perversely false. As the Supreme Court has repeatedly pointed out in the recent cases on apportionment (*Baker* v. *Carr, Gray* v. *Sanders, Reynolds* v. *Sims,* on which see the discussion below), in the constitutional theory of federalism states are sovereign entities which must themselves be represented, while towns and counties are mere creatures of the state with no rights other than those granted by the states. Yet in most New England states, one house of the state legislature represents towns, so that, in Vermont for example, Burlington with 30,000 people and Stratton with fifty each have one representative. The second device, while usually not enshrined in state constitutions, is probably just as significant for perpetuating rural control of state governments. In a number of states, redistricting of the state legislatures has not been undertaken for one or even two generations, despite the vast population shifts that have occurred in this time. In Tennessee, where the notable case of *Baker* v. *Carr* arose, the state legislature had not been redistricted from 1901 to 1961—and doubtless the inaction would have continued had not the Court intervened. This resulted in such inequities as a vote in one county having nineteen times the weight of a vote in another county. Legislative bodies as distorted as this are the ones which draw the district lines for the House of Representatives. No wonder this body is itself distorted.

Even the consistent rural bias in the House of Representatives might be forgiven, however, if rural and urban areas were equally divided between parties and factions in parties. But they are not. In the North, rural and suburban districts tend to be Republican, while wholly urban districts tend to be Democratic. In the South, rural districts usually produce the more conservative kind of Democrats, while urban districts often produce the New Deal sort. The net effect of the gerrymanders and rotten borough on the partisan and ideological composition of the whole House is difficult to calculate, but the information in Table I suggests a partial answer. Although Michigan is perhaps an extreme example, the table indicates that Republicans gain representation in undersized rural districts and lose it in oversized urban ones, thus balancing out. The Democrats, without rural districts lose consistently.

How much Northern Democrats lose in this way is indeterminate, but it seems likely that they lose all together about twenty seats. In the South rural conservatives probably gain ten seats at the expense of urban liberals. Ideologically speaking, this means a shift of about thirty seats from left to right.

Such is misrepresentation in the House; but what shall one say of the Senate? Is it not even more flagrantly unrepresentative? The thirty-six Senators from the eighteen smallest states represent fewer people than New York's two. Twenty-two Senators represent one half the people; seventy-eight Senators represent the other half. The rotten counties of the House pale beside the rotten states of the Senate.

The quasi-gerrymander of the Senate was in 1787 the only institutional compromise which would reconcile the smaller states to the federal constitution. And indeed, when the central government was perhaps regarded as a federation of sovereign states, there was good reason for the inequity. Even then, however, the writers of the *Federalist Papers* tolerated and justified it only as a "lesser evil" in comparison with the weak government under the Articles: [51]

If indeed it be right, that among a people thoroughly incorporated into one nation, every district ought to have a *proportional* share in the government, and that among independent and sovereign States, bound together by a simple league, the parties, however unequal in size, ought to have an *equal* share in the common councils, it does not appear to be without some reason that in a compound republic, partaking both of the national and federal character, the government ought to be founded on a mixture of the principles of proportional and equal representation.

But the eighteenth century danger of weak government is in the twentieth century a historical phantom. And the Civil War certainly settled that these states were "incorporated into one nation." We have the evidence of the Gettysburg Address and judicial confirmation in *Texas* v. *White*.[52]

Now that we have indeed become one nation, the danger is not, as in 1787, that government be weak, but that government be wrong. If, by reason of the Senate's misrepresentation, social changes desired by the vast majority should be prevented, then there is real danger of that ultimate horror, civil war. Democracy assumes majority rule; and, while it must protect minority rights, it dare not let minority will dominate. The democratic method is an alternative to brute force in government, but it is no alternative at all if minorities twist it to control the majority. Such is the lesson of the Civil War. Had the Southern minority, ensconced in the Senate, not been able to thwart Northern majorities all through the 1850's, very likely the Southern civilization

[51] *Federalist*, No. 62
[52] 7 Wall. 700 (1869).

would have been adapted to Northern standards without four years of horror and devastation. Men have now forgotten that one vital condition of the war was the constitutional rottenness of the Senate. But in the 1850's the point was clear enough; and as long as sectional and rural interests control the Senate, minorities may again occasion civil strife.

Which of the two legislative houses today more startlingly misrepresents is a moot question. Unrepresentative as the Senate is, even Senators from rural states do face some urban voters. Relatively few states are wholly rural, in sharp contrast to a large number of House districts. Paradoxically, it now seems possible that the intentionally unrepresentative Senate is actually more representative of the whole people than the supposedly and nominally representative House. It is, of course, impossible to calculate the comparative misrepresentation; but the testimony of one Congressman is instructive. In committee hearings on the Taft-Hartley bill, Representative Gwinn, an upstate New York Republican, told a lobbyist of the Farm Bureau Federation: [53]

Mr. O'Neal, the ten recommendations [i.e. for legislation regulating labor unions] you make here have been made over and over again, and the evidence is overwhelmingly in favor of these recommendations.

A great many men sitting here on this committee are farmers, or come from rural areas. Just speaking personally, I do not think this legislation is going to have any difficulty in the House, because we are in favor of maintaining freedom, order, and justice in this country of ours for all.

But the farmer's trouble is going to be in the Senate, because the Senators represent the big cities. That makes them more skittish about bold laws for freedom.

I wonder if the farmers couldn't write to their Senators more than they do and keep telling them what they think is right. . . .

What can be done about this legislative distortion of "one man, one vote?" The Senate's districting is protected by the Constitution, supposedly even from the amending process. Article V, dealing with amendments, provides that "no state, without its consent, shall be deprived of its equal suffrage in the Senate." And it is unlikely that any state, especially a small one, would relinquish voluntarily its claim to eminence. W. Y. Elliott has suggested that this provision could be

---

[53] Committee on Education and Labor, *Hearings on Amendments to the National Labor Relations Act,* House of Representatives, 80th Congress, 1st Session, III, pp. 1817–18.

evaded by packing the Senate with Senators chosen from regions larger than states; and this would indeed go far to democratize American government.[54] It would be just as easy, however, to amend Article I (on the structure of the Senate) and V together, even though one clause of Article V is supposedly unamendable. Whether a constitution with an amending process is in fact partially unamendable is a nice point, more appropriate to the controversies of the Renaissance lawyers than to a contemporary jurisprudence. It is only important here to note that probably for a long time the Senate cannot change. Only a great national crisis of the proportions of the slavery issue is likely to occasion reform; but that one will eventually arise seems inherent in the present structure of the Senate.

The House of Representatives is another matter. It is only constitutional suggestion and long-standing habit which lodges ultimate control over districts in state legislatures. The Constitution does say that: "The times, places and manner of holding election for senators and representatives shall be prescribed in each state by the legislature thereof . . . ," but it immediately adds: "Congress may at any time by law make or alter such regulations," which suggests the priority of the federal right to control the composition of the House. Recently the Supreme Court has attempted to exercise this right on its own initiative and, if the attempt turns out to be effective, much of the present distortion in the composition of the House will disappear. The Court has for nearly a century supervised voting in federal elections, policing corrupt practices and subterfuges to evade the Fourteenth and Fifteenth Amendments. But until very recently the Court refused to supervise the construction of districts in which voting takes place. Indeed, in *Colegrove* v. *Green* (1946) the Court specifically held that the apportionment of the Illinois House of Representatives was a "political question" which the courts could not decide.[55] In the case of *Baker* v. *Carr* (1962), however, the Court held that the rotten districting in the Tennessee legislatures violated the equal protection clause of the Fourteenth Amendment.[56] The relief granted was to return the suit to the lower federal court for the adjudication of fair boundaries. *Baker* v. *Carr* has resulted in numerous challenges to

[54] William Y. Elliott, *The Need for Constitutional Reform* (New York, Whittlesey House, 1935), pp. 196–98.
[55] 328 U.S. 549.
[56] 369 U.S. 186

present districting and one may expect that before long the rotten districts of state legislatures will be removed.

Once *Baker* v. *Carr* opened up the avenue for federal regulation of voting districts, it was not long before the rotten districts of the House itself became a legal controversy. And in *Wesberry* v. *Sanders* (1964) the Court held that the districting in Georgia also violated the equal protection clause. Presumably this case will have a direct effect on House districting in numerous states and the grossest rotten districts will be removed in the next few years.

The Court made it abundantly clear in the recent case of *Reynolds* v. *Sims* (1964) and related cases that it intends to hold states to a strict standard of equality of representation, or "one man, one vote." [57] In these cases it held that state legislative apportionment in New York (which stood eighth highest on Schubert and Press' list as one of the best apportioned states—among, of course, a set of fifty states that, with the single exception of Massachusetts, are all badly apportioned), in Colorado (which stood at twenty-third place or just about midway, but which had just approved by popular referendum a state constitutional amendment providing that the upper house be apportioned on the basis of area as well as population), and in Alabama (which stood forty-third on the list) was inadequate and required that the states redistrict. If the Court's standard of equality is maintained, then it is quite possible that within a few years the inequalities here described will be eliminated. On the other hand, it is also possible that a constitutional amendment eliminating the Court's jurisdiction in matters of state legislative apportionment could be adopted.

Regardless of the outcome of the current agitation for a constitutional amendment on apportionment, however, all this recent reform affects only rotten districts and does not affect gerrymanders. One consequence may well be, therefore, that what was formerly accomplished by rotten districts will now be accomplished by gerrymanders. This will be an improvement, of course, for gerrymanders are less certain in their results and, furthermore, as rotten districts in the state legislatures are removed, the determination to gerrymander may also decline. Nevertheless gerrymanders are certain to remain with us and for this also there is a specific remedy. Clearly Congress could, for

[57] 377 U.S. 533.

example, follow the newly instituted British practice of a Parliamentary constituencies commission, i.e. a bipartisan group of respected citizens charged with drawing district boundaries for the whole country. It is too much to expect that all petty partisanship be excluded from district making, but certainly the grosser evils could be extirpated. Whether they will be or not depends largely on the amount of democratic action.

THE FUTURE OF AMERICAN SUFFRAGE

After close to two centuries of intermittent agitation, democratic ideologists have firmly established the democratic principle of universal, equal suffrage as an article of the American faith. And further, democratic politicians have actually embodied much of that ideal in institutional practice. It is no mean praise of the achievement of seven generations that this chapter on suffrage in American democracy could concentrate so much on the *lapses* from the ideal. That very emphasis itself suggests that Americans need not be convinced of the value of voting and that the basic steps toward realization of the ideal have been taken. We are well over half-way on our road to the operational goal of democratic theory.

Important as some of the derelictions from the ideal of "one-man, one-vote" still are, we can take hope from the fact that the democratic conscience is now quite aroused. Great changes in the fundamental outline of American democracy have occurred in the last five years. As a result of persistent agitation and federal protection of civil rights, large numbers of Negroes are voting in the South. In 1961 the voters of the District of Columbia were given three electoral votes by the Twenty-third Amendment. In 1962 *Baker* v. *Carr* and in 1964 *Wesberry* v. *Sanders* launched attacks on rotten districting. In 1964, the Twenty-fourth Amendment prohibiting poll taxes was finally passed. All over the country registration is now being made easier. In short, some of the main reforms in recent years have been aimed at improving the suffrage system. So one may ask: Will reform continue until universal suffrage is obtained?

Great as the difficulties are, other democracies have substantially done so. As the first section of this chapter indicated, however, each of the American advances during the nineteenth and twentieth centuries were made only after persistent struggle. The propertyless, Negroes, women did not get the vote merely by asking for it. Only their own and others' long-continued agitation made them full citizens. And so it is today. The condition of success is, of course, that their votes be needed by a temporarily dominant party seeking its own perpetuation. Such was the case with each previously enfranchised class. The propertyless, for example, were successfully politicized only because the radical parties in the states during the 1780's, the Anti-federalist-Jeffersonian Republicans, and finally the Jacksonian Democrats needed their votes. Negroes, for another example, have been partially politicized only because Radical Republicans in the 1860's and New Deal Democrats in the 1930's likewise thought that their votes would provide the margin of victory. But this condition for the success of democratic agitation can never long be lacking in America where social movements like Jeffersonian Republicanism, Jacksonian Democracy, Radical Republicanism, Populism, Theodore Roosevelt's Progressivism and latterly New Dealism are recurrent phenomena. The condition of success is, therefore, almost certain to be present, at least on the crest of waves of popular political excitement. And so again the emphasis of this chapter: the expansion of democracy depends upon democratic agitation.

3.

The Techniques of Democracy: Political Parties and Civil Liberties

Democrats [say] that justice consists in the will of a majority of persons.

—ARISTOTLE, *Politics,* 1318b

"IN EVERY FREE AND DELIBERATING SOCIETY, THERE MUST . . . BE OPPOSITE PARTIES . . ."

The simple act of voting is the first step on the democratic road to self-respect. Without it, no man can hope to travel the road at all. This is why all true democrats have so persistently agitated for universal suffrage. But one step is not a journey and voting will not carry one the whole way. Responsible government, self-direction, and ultimately self-respect do not automatically ensue from casual trips to the polling place. Human dignity is too precious a thing to be got simply by the performance of the democratic ritual, for, as Spinoza truly said, "all things excellent are as difficult as they are rare."

If the democratic method is to fulfill its promise, voting must be more than a mechanical act. It must take place in a coherent, rational context. The democratic method proposes to instill in public officers a perpetual sense of responsibility to all voters, to all groups, to the whole people. Elections are the necessary condition of this sense; but it cannot be fully conscious, nor always consulted, unless all the political institutions surrounding elections are designed to develop it. The rulers' sense of responsibility may be, and often is, indifferent, intermittent, and only half-realized. Truly responsible government is only possible when elections are so conducted that a choice of men is a decision on policy, that a decision on policy is soon transformed into action, and that action taken is popularly supervised. And for all this, elections must be rationally and coherently organized.

Without an institutional context to impart coherence, voting and universal suffrage are unsubstantial forms, serving chiefly as the convincing detail that embellishes deceit. Consider, for example, plebiscites in the Soviet Union. As Soviet propagandists boast with amusing frequency and even more amusing complacency, Soviet elections are based on universal suffrage. Yet under Stalin the Soviet Union was by Khrushchev's own subsequent admission a complete dictatorship. In the Stalin era, in this complete dictatorship, Soviet citizens did vote. "Never in a single country did the people manifest such activity in elections as did the Soviet people. Never has any capitalist country known, nor can it know, such a high percentage of those participating in voting as did the USSR," said Vyshinsky, speaking of the 1937 elections.[1] And, overlooking the specious comparison, he was right. By the 1936 constitution all persons over eighteen years old, except criminals and lunatics, are entitled to vote. Every effort was made to see that they did. "Agitators," appointed by the party for every twenty to thirty voters, conducted intensive person-to-person campaigns.[2] On election day even ships at sea were included in constituencies and passengers on long-distance trains descended at noon for lunch and ballot marking.[3] In 1937, ninety-nine million people (96.8 percent of those eligible) voted and in 1946 this amazing participation increased to one hundred-one million (99.7 percent of the eligibles).[4] This universal suffrage and almost universal participation was, however, only superficial and sophistical evidence of responsible government. As Stalin himself forthrightly said, ". . . they who rule, not they who elect and vote, have the power."[5] The popular will was not really consulted; and the people, however avidly they voted, indeed did not rule. Elections were a facade for oligarchy because the structure of government did not permit elections to influence policy making.

[1] Andrei Y. Vyshinsky, *The Law of the Soviet State*, translated by Hugh W. Babb (New York, Macmillan, 1948), p. 724.
[2] Julian Towster, *Political Power in the USSR* (New York, Oxford University Press, 1948), p. 195.
[3] *Ibid.*, p. 191.
[4] *Ibid.*, p. 197.
[5] Quoted in Vyshinsky, *op. cit.*, p. 664 from Stalin, *Articles and Speeches on the Ukraine* (1936), p. 38.

Although the unanimity displayed in Soviet elections is possibly useful for foreign and domestic propaganda, it is useless for responsible government: Unanimous votes decide nothing which is not already decided. Such elections are at best plebiscites, i.e. displays of popular approval of the basic constitution. The approval is, of course, mild because no reasonable alternative is apparent to most citizens; and, in the absence of open revolution, the approval is assumed to exist anyway.

Clearly, then, government responsible to the people requires more than universal suffrage. In the halcyon confidence of the nineteenth century, universal suffrage seemed to lead directly to the millennium; in the turbulent doubt of the twentieth, we have realized that universal suffrage is not enough. Millennium there may be, though even that we doubt; one thing we know, however, is that one isolated institution will not project us into it.

Responsible popular government requires also, next to universal suffrage itself, the clarifying hand of faction. Factions, organized into political parties, define issues and ideologies for elections by means of their incessant controversy. Without parties to state the case, to educate and arouse voters, there would be nothing to vote about—as in the case of the Soviet citizen. Moreover, factions, by organizing a governing majority, carry election results into law and policy. With an insight uncommon in his day Bagehot observed of English government in the nineteenth century that "party government is the vital principle of representative government." [6] Without parties to direct the chosen governors, elections would be mere popularity contests, as they often are now in the United States in areas where one party has uncontested control. But where parties do compete, they organize hundreds of representatives in applying the electoral will and thus they make representative democracy possible. Rousseau, writing before much democratic practice could be observed, and foreseeing the problem of organizing representatives, was unable to conceive of a democratic, representative government. He thought representatives would necessarily be elected despots and, in words so often quoted, said of England, ". . . it is free only during the election of members of Parliament." [7] Had the party system remained as rudimentary as it was in his day— when Burke could announce to the electors of Bristol his intention to

---

[6] Walter Bagehot, *The English Constitution* (World's Classics ed., London, Oxford University Press, 1928), p. 126.
[7] J. J. Rousseau, *The Social Contract*, Bk. III, ch. 15.

be irresponsible—Rousseau's assertion would still be true today. But the democratic spirit could not be deterred by what is at bottom only a technical problem. So it developed party government—the vital principle so clear to Bagehot a hundred years later—to obviate Rousseau's difficulty. And, once developed, parties proved efficient for one more thing: the supervision of government in action. While voters supervise their elected agents only sporadically and infrequently, parties can supervise them every day, systematically and minutely, as a part of their perpetual contest for office. This Jefferson saw in the infancy of our Republic and, unlike most men of his time was not unduly frightened by it: [8]

In every free and deliberating society, there must, from the nature of man, be opposite parties, and violent dissensions and discords; and one of these, for the most part, must prevail. . . . Perhaps this party division is necessary to induce each to watch and relate to the people the proceedings of the other.

Thus are ideals and interests, incoherent in the mass, elicited, organized, and made effectual. Behind and above the whole process stands the system of party conflict, rationalizing the popular will, carrying election results into law and action. So essential are parties to the democratic method that one contemporary writer has observed: [9]

The parties created democracy, or perhaps more accurately, modern democracy is a by-product of party competition.

To say that democracy is bred in faction is to say that democracy is a series of tolerated disagreements. Unanimity, on the other hand, is essential to every type of absolutism. In absolutisms the will of the rulers must be the will of all, in theory as well as fact. If it is not in theory, then the rulers' moral right to dominion evaporates, as every alert apologist for oppression from Plato to Marx has clearly seen. If the rulers' will is not the will of all in fact, then their dominion itself is insecure, which is the emphasis of more realistic strategists of absolutism like Machiavelli, Hobbes and Lenin. Thus it is that the literature of authoritarianism, whether justifying monarchy, oligarchy,

[8] *Thomas Jefferson on Democracy,* edited by S. K. Padover (New York, New American Library, 1946), pp. 42–43.
[9] E. E. Schattschneider, *Party Government* (New York, Farrar and Rinehart, 1942), p. 4.

dictatorship, or theocracy, has elevated unanimity, however forced, as the capstone of virtue.

Democracy, as the converse of absolutism, cannot tolerate unanimity. The whim of the autocrat, the pleasure of the aristocrat, the dogma of the hierarch, are equally unendurable. It has become customary to express the democratic position as simply an "agreement to disagree." By this formula is meant a conscious determination to govern by a series of temporary coalitions in spite of disagreement about fundamental nationalisms, religious beliefs, and class ideologies. To agree on fundamentals like these is to establish unanimity on at least one basic political policy. Such partial unanimity of course prevents the free play of faction; it sets certain areas of policy beyond the playing field. But, if democracy is really to develop self-respect, no area of policy can be out-of-bounds for party politics. In the out-of-bounds area special privilege erects an absolutism. Democratic politics must, therefore, eschew all forms of unanimity on policy, either partial or complete. The only version of unanimity which democracy can permit—and in fact this it requires—is substantial agreement on the democratic method itself, a pattern of behavior which observes the rules, wherever the game is played. This is the "agreement to disagree"; in the slogan of the French Revolution, it is *fraternité*.

RESPONSIBLE PARTIES AND DEMOCRATIC SELF-RESPECT

Political parties, which give meaning to suffrage and are themselves the expression of tolerated disagreement, are thus an essential instrument of the democratic method of self-respect. Yet they are imperfect because they work by indirection. However much parties serve an exalted purpose, the men who operate them seldom are conscious, except verbally on patriotic holidays, of any exaltation. In the large, parties are indeed the agency of self-respect; but to the working politician they are an agency for the petty rewards of office and privilege. Pendleton Herring defines the problem thus: [10]

The task of democratic politics is to evolve and execute a policy reflecting the desires of the community and capable of meeting current demands for

[10] Pendleton Herring, *The Politics of Democracy* (New York, Farrar and Rinehart, 1940), p. 24.

security and prosperity. This must be accomplished through a system of free partisan struggle, wherein office seeking is often put before considerations of public policy.

Therein lies the central problem of the practice of democracy: Politicians who operate parties are inspired not with a sense of democratic stewardship but with hope of personal reward and partisan conquest. How can the personal and immediate ends of parties and politicians be made to serve the democratic end of government responsible to the people? What institutional arrangements can we construct which will transmute private ambition into a servant of the public weal? How, briefly, can parties as well as elected officials be made responsible to the people? It is this question to which this chapter, and indeed the rest of this book, will be devoted.[11]

This question, it ought to be noted, is not new. It has been asked repeatedly ever since students of politics have recognized the real role of political parties in a democracy. Woodrow Wilson in 1885 put the question of party responsibility at the very center of his pioneer study of congressional government: [12]

I know that it has been proposed by enthusiastic, but not too practical reformers to do away with parties by some legerdemain of governmental reconstruction, accompanied by and supplemented by some rehabilitation, devoutly to be wished, of the virtues least commonly controlling in fallen human nature; but it seems to me that it would be more difficult and less desirable than these amiable persons suppose to conduct a government of the many by means of any other device than party organization, and that the great need is, not to get rid of parties, but to find and use some expedient by which they can be managed and made amenable from day to day to public opinion.

In another epoch-making study of American government, Frank Goodnow's *Politics and Administration*, written in 1900, this same question is again set forth as the central theme: [13]

It has been shown that the American political party is not as responsible to the people as it should be if the governmental system is to be popular

---

[11] For an interesting and wholly theoretical inquiry into this question, see Anthony Downs, *An Economic Theory of Democracy* (New York, Harper and Brothers, 1957), *passim*.

[12] Woodrow Wilson, *Congressional Government*. (Fifteenth edition, Boston, Houghton Mifflin, 1900), pp. 97–98.

[13] Frank Goodnow, *Politics and Administration* (New York, Macmillan, 1900), p. 199.

in character, and that the American party leader, as a result, is hardly amenable to popular control. It has also been shown that in order that the party leader shall be made amenable the party must become responsible. The question now naturally presents itself, How can this be accomplished?

Today the question seems even more pressing, and indeed many contemporary writers, of whom one of the best has already been quoted, place it in the foreground of their study. But urgent as it is today, it has been the central problem of the Republic from the beginning. In fact, the first great study of American institutions, De Tocqueville's *Democracy in America,* can be interpreted as an attempt to formulate this question two generations before less empirical minds grasped it.

De Tocqueville, at the end of the second volume of *Democracy in America,* discussed the prospect of a new kind of oppression which, he feared, might arise in America. He could give no name to what seemed to him so novel, but the content of his mightmare was a powerful, benevolent bureaucracy doing so much for citizens that they would lack the power to act against it: [14]

Our contemporaries are constantly excited by two conflicting passions: they want to be led, and they wish to remain free. As they cannot destroy either one or the other of these contrary propensities, they strive to satisfy them both at once. They devise a sole, tutelary, and all-powerful form of government, but elected by the people. . . .

By this system the people shake off their state of dependence just long enough to select their master and then relapse into it again.

He continued with the observation that, while many were satisfied with this "compromise between administrative despotism and sovereignty of the people," he himself was not. To this problem of popular control, so reminiscent of Rousseau's distrust of representative government, De Tocqueville then saw no solution. But in his first volume, written five years earlier when his empirical observation was fresh in his mind, he was more sanguine. The second part of that volume is devoted to the question: "How it can be strictly said that the people govern in the United States." His answer was, first, that "the people elect their representatives *directly* . . . in order to assure their dependence," and, second, that "they are surrounded by the incessant agitation of parties, who attempt to gain their cooperation and support." [15] De

[14] Alexis De Tocqueville, *Democracy in America,* edited by Phillips Bradley (New York, Knopf, 2 vols., 1945), II, p. 319.
[15] *Ibid.,* I, p. 173.

Tocqueville, like most men of his time, was only half-conscious of the function of party politics; but, as a careful observer, he could not avoid placing them at the very center of the democratic process. Lacking a theoretical apparatus to appreciate parties, he was unable to connect the problem he set forth in Volume II with the institutions he described in Volume I. But he did foresee the possibility of a failure in popular control and he did describe the only available means by which "the people govern." Today we have got only this much further than De Tocqueville: We know that the failure of popular control can be averted only by the improvement of party responsibility, of the institutions by which "the people govern."

Thus clearly the institutional question of responsible government has been often posed and often answered from De Tocqueville's time to our own. This repeated discussion need not deter us, however, from contemporary analysis. Just as every generation must write its own history, even more each generation must redefine, reanalyze and re-direct its own institutions. And so the rest of this chapter will be devoted to a discussion of the several essential conditions of responsible party government.

"LIBERTY IS TO FACTION WHAT AIR IS TO FIRE": THE CASE OF FREE SPEECH

"Liberty is to faction what air is to fire" said Madison in the tenth *Federalist*; and a national atmosphere of the traditional democratic liberties is indeed the only condition in which faction will blaze up. In our own day the ideals of the eighteenth century bills of rights have become ends-in-themselves. Freedom of religion and expression, fair criminal procedures and the like seem now to be no small part of the self-direction and self-respect we hope democracy can give us. We often forget, therefore, that they have an institutional significance also. Their original purpose was, in fact, not so much to dignify mankind as to foster faction and distribute dissent. And so long as these liberties operate, faction is indeed inevitable because the interests of neighbors vary. Without them factions can only be conspiracies: Unscrupulous placemen will drive all opposition underground.

Let us examine briefly, in light of the needs of faction, the traditional democratic liberties set forth in the Constitution and the Bill of Rights. Would political parties be possible if they did not exist?

Probably the most essential liberties are the congressional privileges of Article I: representatives' immunity from arrest, the exemption of their legislative utterances from libel and sedition laws, and each house's right to judge its membership and to establish its order of business. In the sixteenth and seventeenth centuries these privileges protected Parliamentmen in their contest with the English monarchy. The Commoners' struggles for them prefaced the Civil Wars, both as first skirmishes and as the food which, once got, nourished Parliamentary opposition to the Crown. But while they originally shielded the legislature from outside interference, they soon acquired and have today a broader application.[16] They guaranteed at least in part the free play of faction in the legislature, where sit the party leaders and where strife is hottest.

Next to Congressional privilege, which encourages factional strife at its center, stand the freedoms partially protected by the First Amendment, which encourage factional strife on its periphery. Both logically and historically they are a generalization of the privileges of legislators. Free discussion, a feeble seedling in Tudor Parliaments, matured during the English Civil Wars to include non-parliamentary pamphlets and harangues. The relation is obvious: really free discussion in the legislature must be fed by really free discussion outside.

Religious toleration and liberty of speech, press, assembly, and petition serve two purposes, which are often confused. They are, of course, a part of the democratic ideal of self-respect. Each involves one kind of self-direction. But they were originally and are today first of all a method. They encourage faction. The idea of religious liberty, for example, was directly fashioned by and has now become the keystone supporting the oldest kind of factionalism in Western Europe. "The only influence capable of resisting the feudal hierarchy was the ecclesiastical hierarchy," said Lord Acton; "To that conflict of four hundred years we owe the rise of civil liberty." [17] These beginnings of liberty were nourished also by the division of Christendom in the Reformation; and they finally matured in the uneasy tolerance which emerged out of the Reformation settlement. When men decided in the sixteenth, seventeenth, and eighteenth centuries not to kill each other to silence heretical tongues, tolerance of one kind of faction, tolerance

---

[16] Mary Patterson Clarke, *Parliamentary Privilege in the American Colonies* (New Haven, Yale University Press, 1943), p. 269.

[17] Lord Acton, *op. cit.*, p. 62.

of the right to disagree, became a truly operative ideal. It is, therefore, appropriate that the first clause of our Bill of Rights should forbid both government support of a church and government interference with the exercise of any religion. Thus, negatively at least, religious toleration is thereby ensured. Similarly, the freedom to assemble, that is, to form parties and lesser political groups, is a fundamental requirement of disagreement over economic and social questions. And the freedom to agitate by talk and writing is the easiest means by which factions of all sorts can make those disagreements politically intelligible. If denied these freedoms of the First Amendment, factions could develop only with a great difficulty and as conspiracies.

Such is the purpose also of the procedural protections in the Constitution and the Bill of Rights. Consider, for example, the definition of treason and the guarantee of the writ of habeas corpus. It is difficult to imagine tolerance of political dissent when treason is defined as opposition to the sovereign as it was in treason statutes from Edward III to the Stuarts or as it is now in the Soviet Union. And open faction is inconceivable if opposition leaders may be permanently imprisoned, arbitrarily and without trial. The founding fathers, therefore, looking back on English experience from the Petition of Right in 1629 to the Revolutionary settlement in 1689 and recalling their own experience from 1765 to 1775, copied English protections of dissent. Treason was precisely defined in Article III as levying war against the United States or "adhering to their enemies, giving them aid and comfort." To forestall more surely still the use of treason charges to suppress political opposition, "two witnesses to the same overt act" or "confession in open court" were required for conviction. And, following the English Habeas Corpus Act of 1679, they provided in Article I that the privilege of this writ, the use of which prevents imprisonment without charges or trial, "shall not be suspended, unless when in cases of rebellion or invasion the public safety may require it."

Other procedural protections, such as the prohibitions of unreasonable search and seizure, indictment without grand jury, double jeopardy, self-incrimination, etc., in Amendments IV, V, VI, VII, are today less obviously related to the protection of faction. They are now usually invoked in non-political cases; and we have, therefore, come to regard them as democratic recognition of the dignity of all people, even possible criminals. But in their origin, and less obviously but just as surely today, they safeguard minorities. They protect minority leaders from the kind of search and seizure which during the 1760's in England silenced Wilkes and *The North Briton* and in America led to the conviction of politico-smugglers of the Bay State. Even the system of trial by jury, the origins of which are shrouded in medieval mystery, owes its present popularity and its guarantee in Article III to the frequent refusals of sixteenth century juries to convict political opponents of the sovereign. Because of that, men like Coke and Selden and later Blackstone, the lawyers, that is, whose work the founding fathers read, idealized the jury process and called it the crux of English liberty in the common law. Even as late as 1830, when juries had lost an active political function and had become simply a judicial technique, De Tocqueville could still interpret them as essential to the democratic method, having a significance equal to that of elections.

That most of these constitutional liberties have their origin and first purpose in the protection of faction there can be little doubt. What is more important is that they be perpetuated, for factions' sake as well as our own. But mere prohibitions in constitutions are not self-enforcing. It is necessary also that they be, as Rousseau required, engraved on the hearts of the people.

It is the enduring merit of American life that in no small part these liberties and prohibitions are really there engraved. One can find many exceptions, of course, such as the mass hysteria which occasionally silences free speech. But on the whole these essentials have been maintained, perhaps largely because the system of party struggle is self-perpetuating. Despite some observable exceptions, it is possible to say with the President's Committee on Civil Rights: [18]

No fair minded student of American history, or of world history, will deny to the United States a position of leadership in enlarging the range of human liberties and rights, in recognizing and stating the ideals of freedom and equality, and in steadily and loyally working to make those ideals a reality.

Consider, for example, how well we have kept freedom of speech and press. "Give me," said Milton in *Areopagitica*, "the liberty to know, to utter, and to argue freely according to conscience above all liberties." It was a sure insight, for in the democratic method free expression is the first occasion of the free development of faction. For the philosopher in quest of truth, free speech is the freedom of questing.

[18] President's Committee on Civil Rights, *op. cit.*, p. ix.

But for the users of whatever truth there is, for the people, that is, who make public policy, free speech has another, equally important meaning. Truths and even partial truths have no significance in this world unless men acquiesce in them. And free speech is the only means by which new truth is spread. As Mill remarked in his essay *On Liberty*: "Persecution has always succeeded, save where the heretics were too strong a party to be effectually persecuted." Free expression is the instrument, therefore, not only of new truth for new times but also of new majorities for new issues. It amplifies and broadcasts everywhere the din of party conflict. With an understanding based on experience of the two-fold value of free speech and press, the state ratifying conventions of 1787–1788 insisted on their formal guarantee. So the First Amendment protects them from one sinister threat: government abridgement. It is based on the democratic understanding that, when the people get from faction their power to hold rulers responsible, they cannot keep it long if one faction temporarily in control can regulate, suppress, or monopolize the institutions of factional life.

The prohibitions of the First Amendment have to a rather remarkable degree been maintained in practice.[19] After the popular repudiation of the Alien and Sedition Acts and the Federalist party in the election of 1800, no national crisis of the nineteenth century occasioned government control of speech or press. Desperate as was the condition of the country during the Civil War, for example, Copperheads in the North were not silenced. Although the most notorious Copperhead of all, Vallandigham of Ohio, was imprisoned perhaps unjustly, Lincoln allowed him to escape to the South. And, more important still, the fishwifely vituperation in opposition newspapers, which seems so crude to present taste, was never forbidden.

Not until the twentieth century did the federal government again seriously restrict freedom of speech. During the first World War, newspapers suffered political as well as military censorship prior to publication. And from 1917 to 1921 the federal government tried over 2,000 people for printing and saying things which were believed to have a "bad tendency," even though their words did no actual damage to public order.

In reaction to this abuse, the Supreme Court gradually reinterpreted the words of the amendment more precisely. Mr. Justice Holmes in-

---

[19] This and the several following paragraphs are based on Z. Chaffee, *Free Speech in the United States* (Cambridge, Harvard University Press, 1941).

vented the "clear and present danger" doctrine, i.e. that all words not creating a "clear and present danger" to public order cannot be prohibited nor their authors punished.[20] During the two succeeding decades this doctrine, when used to interpret the First and Fourteenth Amendments, greatly enhanced the privilege of minority free speech when it has been endangered by states and administrators (but not when endangered by Congress). In the second World War, therefore, the abuses of the first were avoided. Newspapers, it is true, accepted censorship of military news voluntarily; but there was no dearth of political criticism and no pro-Nazis were sentenced for their writings. Americans of Japanese ancestry on the West Coast were deprived of free speech when they were imprisoned, for dubious military reasons, in what Mr. Justice Roberts called "concentration camps." But, however unjust their detention, public discussion of it was not curtailed. Currently there is considerable agitation for abridgement of Communists' right to speak out—an agitation aimed, it seems, not so much at Communists, who notoriously work by indirection, as at outspoken democrats of the left. And it is possible that, as the fear of the Soviet Union obsesses us entirely, the First Amendment will again be violated. But as yet the record is fairly clear: *The Daily Worker* is regularly published.

Insofar as it is protected by the First Amendment, therefore, free expression is an operative ideal. It can fairly be said that, in spite of some lapses, laws have not often nor for long abridged this freedom.

There are other threats to free expression, however, besides government regulation or monopoly. While the First Amendment has so far been an effective enough guide in avoiding this one danger, it does nothing to protect free speech from others equally serious. Therein lies the chief danger today.

Along with governmental suppression of free speech there is the danger of private suppression, which is especially acute when the media of communication are privately owned and operated. Today the tone of politics is tolerant and mild so that this danger seems remote, but even in the relatively recent past the concentration of ownership of newspapers (e.g. the development of one-newspaper towns) in the hands of proprietors who for the most part were personally allied with the Republican party seemed to indicate that private privilege might

[20] *Schenk* v. *United States,* 249 U.S. 47 (1919).

suppress free discussion. Fortunately, that eventuality has not come about, partly because of competition from television but more, I believe, because newspaper owners gradually recognized the public service feature of their business and therefore moderated their personal biases. Nevertheless, so long as the main channels of communication are privately and monopolistically controlled, the threat to free speech remains potential.

Nevertheless our traditions of free expression are strong and when threatened, even by non-governmental sources, we have found ways to protect them. Such is the lesson indeed in one recent experience with the right of peaceable assembly. Although Congress and state legislatures have not in recent decades placed unreasonable restrictions on the formation of private societies, still the right of assembly was until the middle 1930's effactually denied to most people who wanted to join labor unions. Large business organizations had sufficient economic power to suppress opposing groups. The situation was analogous to the threat contained in private monopoly in communications. That is, the First Amendment protected the right only from government abridgement, while the real threat to the ideal grew out of private action. But, at a time when labor unions seemed almost destroyed, Congress positively and consciously attempted to revive them in light of the ideal expressed in the First Amendment. Because, as the Wagner Act says, employees did not "possess full freedom of association," Congress established a method of determining whether or not men wished to join unions and forbade employers to use certain unfair labor practices which negate "the right to self-organization." In some respects the Wagner Act went too far, even curtailing, in certain circumstances, employers' right to free discussion of the issue of unionization; but this defect was certainly removed by the Taft-Hartly Act. And although this seemed unduly repressive to union leaders, it did not repeal the basic protection of unionization. Over fourteen million union members in 1960—as against less than three million in 1933—testify adequately that the Wagner Act, even as amended by the Taft-Hartley Act, engendered real freedom of assembly. Let us hope that, should freedom of expression be similarly curtailed, an equally imaginative way would be found to protect it.

Further surveys of the condition of other faction-fostering freedoms in the Constitution and the Bill of Rights would lead to much the same conclusion as this one brief study of freedom of expression: that we do possess enough liberty for faction to flourish. In this one case, as in most others, the formal prohibition of the Bill of Rights has generally been observed. And if the special privilege which democracy must forever fight has discovered a new way to taint the ideal, it lies yet in our power to blot out the taint. We have about us, therefore, the liberty and liberties which are the first condition of the free play of faction, though they are not always in as pure a form as we desire.

The Ideal Structure of a Responsible Party System

Freedom for factions to organize and agitate does not, however, automatically produce governments responsible to the people. If democratic liberties are genuine, open factions are, of course, inevitable; but party institutions are not necessarily effective simply because they are free. The degree to which parties do respond to popular direction depends in addition upon the particular structure of the party system. Even when the democratic liberties are assured, parties can operate either as agents of governments responsible to the popular will or as cliques of the specially privileged manipulating the many in the interest of the few. Whether they be democratic or oligarchic depends on a variety of institutional habits, such as the location of the power to govern (or what used to be called sovereignty), the method of conducting elections, the internal structure of parties themselves, and so forth.

The problem—which is by no means simple—is, therefore, to determine what institutions are necessary to democratic parties and the democratic method. Since parties perfectly responsible to the people do exist only as ideals, no one can describe the specific visible institutions which generate them. It is only possible to describe such parties inferentially from an analysis of the idea of responsibility.

In the most exact sense, responsible government means that public officers submit themselves in elections to the judgment of the people. Institutionally, this general responsibility requires regular elections and universal suffrage on the basis of "one man, one vote"—which was discussed in Chapter 2. But in addition it requires that voters have a clear sense of their power of selection or at least of their power of choice. How else can they hold officers responsible unless they are aware that voting does some good, that it is clearly related to their own personal circumstances? On the other hand, in the officials themselves this general responsibility requires a continuing consciousness of the popular, electoral sanction. Every political decision ought to rest both on the pertinent technical considerations and on this question: "How will the action affect myself (and my party) in the next election?" It has often been fashionable to deride the democratic politician's habit of looking for this home truth. Antagonists of democracy like Burke resent, of course, the dependence on the people thus implied. Even good democrats have sometimes thought that asking this question precluded creative leadership, although, as will be shown in detail later, creative leadership is itself the highest and most adroit way of using this standard.

Government responsible to the people means, therefore, three things: first, a sanction; second, the voters' knowledge of it; and third, the governors' respect for it. This kind of responsible government ought not be confused with other kinds of responsibility which are sometimes equated with it. It is not responsibility to the nation, for the nation is a non-human abstraction that has neither a sanction nor a means of using it. Nor is it responsibility to "higher law," for higher law varies with interpreters and cannot possibly be enforced.

The first element of responsible government, the sanction itself, was discussed in Chapter 2. But, as noted at the beginning of this chapter, universal and equal suffrage is not enough. If government is to be fully responsible, parties must make the electoral sanction operate with maximum effectiveness for both the rulers and the ruled. Each group ought to be constantly aware of the use and meaning of elections; and party functioning should make them so—in these three ways:

First, parties ought to create majorities, however artificial. A true majority, achieved when one overwhelming question agitates the entire nation and when over half the voters take exactly the same position on it, is probably impossible. How can we expect it in a society as complex as ours? No issue, not even war and peace, can submerge all others, as was so clearly demonstrated between 1941 and 1945 when domestic economic controversies sometimes overshadowed war issues in our politics. Furthermore, most real political questions have too many facets for a majority of voters to have exactly the same opinion on them. Referring again to the early forties, it is evident that most people were not entirely for or entirely against the activity of the Office of Price Administration. Some were, of course; but much the larger number approved in part and disapproved in part, either because they wished to expand the OPA's operations or because they wished to curtail them. And concerning the specific areas of expansion and curtailment, there were no doubt as many different combinations of opinions as there were people who held them.

While a true majority is thus impossible, some kind of artificial majority is necessary for responsible government. If there is no majority, no observable group of voters who have used the electoral sanction, then rulers have nothing to be responsible to. And if no group of voters can use the sanction, the democratic understanding of *all voters* becomes atrophied. Hence, if there is no majority out of elections, the electoral sanction just does not work.

The significance of a majority, however artificial, can best be grasped abstractly by a consideration of the so-called paradox of voting, which is the fact that in some circumstances voting does not lead to a definitive social choice.[21] Suppose there are three voters (1, 2, and 3) and three alternatives (*a*, *b*, and *c*). Suppose further that the voters order their preferences thus:

1 prefers *a* to *b*, *b* to *c*, and *a* to *c*
2 prefers *b* to *c*, *c* to *a*, and *b* to *a*
3 prefers *c* to *a*, *a* to *b*, and *c* to *b*

Then two voters prefer *a* to *b* (1 and 3), but two voters prefer *c* to *a* (2 and 3). Similarly two voters prefer *b* to *c* (1 and 2), but two prefer *a* to *b*. Finally two voters prefer *c* to *a*, but two also prefer *b* to *c*. Thus no alternative can beat both the others. Kenneth Arrow has shown that voting systems such as those used in committees, legislatures, and elections cannot eliminate this indecisive feature of voting. Indeed the only way in which indecision can be eliminated is by reducing the alternatives to exactly two, which is what parties in a two-party system actually do.

It may seem to some that this emphasis on an artificial majority is mere word play. It may seem indeed that democratic theorists, having abstracted the idea of a sanction out of the electoral process, have then

---

[21] See Duncan Black, *The Theory of Committees and Elections* (Cambridge, Cambridge University Press, 1958); Kenneth Arrow, *Social Choice and Individual Values* (New York, John Wiley and Sons, 2nd edition, 1963); and William H. Riker, "Voting and the Summation of Preferences," *American Political Science Review*, LV (1961), pp. 900–11.

invented an equally abstract and unreal agent, the majority, to wield the sanction, just as mathematicians, having abstracted the idea of a square root out of a series of real numbers, have invented an imaginary number to be the square root of a negative. But there is much more than semantic fancy involved. One has only to observe governments without majorities, such as the Soviet Union or the Weimar Republic in Germany, to discover that majorities are necessary to responsible government in fact as well as words. In the one case, formal unanimity is substituted for a majority and Soviet rulers are thus responsible to everyone. But rulers responsible to presumably unanimous abstractions like nation, class, race, or ideal are in fact not responsible to any one at all. Rulers responsible to a majority, however, have some real, enumerable, and observable people as their masters. In the Weimer Republic, on the other hand, majorities were seldom in any way created so that government was always formally a collection of minorities. Party leaders were responsible to party members, perhaps, but no ruler was either responsible to a majority or equipped with a majority by which to govern. Policy making became then a series of insoluble deadlocks because there was no majority to give rulers a mandate for action. The deadlocks were reconciled only when a despotism destroyed the Republic. In both formal unanimity and formal minorityism, therefore, responsible government cannot exist.

Second, parties ought to make majorities meaningful. Rational decisions on public policy ought to result from electoral decisions. The process of government can be controlled by citizens only when elections are a transmission belt of ideas and decisions from the voters to the rulers. If elections have no relevance to public policy, then the policy makers need not respect the electoral sanction. What need then is there for them to ask: "How will this act affect the next election?" And, of course, if rulers need not so question, voters can only regard elections as an elaborate and expensive game, no more exciting than a World Series, and no more significant. Certainly they cannot conceive of them as a great part of their self-direction and self-respect.

Of course, if elections make majorities, some kind of decision inevitably follows. The very process of dividing men this way decides something, if only which set of leaders will get the spoils. But the significance of majorities for public policy varies with the structure of the party system. Elections can simply be popularity contests between two sets of baby-kissing, back-slapping, would-be placemen. In such cases, the rulers are responsible to the ruled only on the rather low level of personal favors and pleasantries. Or elections can be the ultimate control of the whole social and economic environment. Rulers are then really agents of citizens' self-direction; they are responsible to the ruled on the much higher plane of policy and ideology.

We have both kinds of elections in the United States. Witness, on the one hand, many local elections in which the winner differs from the loser only by greater endurance in hand-shaking and a larger number of club memberships. Witness, on the other hand, such decisive popular judgments as the presidential elections of 1896 or 1964. Our problem is to determine what institutions make the difference between them so that we can make all majorities meaningful.

Third, parties ought to make majorities effective. If the rulers, chosen by electoral majorities do not have the power to govern, then responsible government is as impossible as if there were no majority at all. The idea of a sanction is simply praise and blame leading to rewards and punishments. Yet praise and blame cannot be rationally assigned unless rulers have in fact the power to carry out the majority will. If rulers have not the power to govern, how can they be fairly blamed for failure to enact electoral decisions? Though in their failure they mock the electoral sanction, they can at most be blamed for promising the electorate too much. And, when affairs go well, how can impotent rulers be honestly praised for what is to them adventitious success?

Consider what happens when citizens cannot assign praise or blame because their rulers have not full power to govern. Throughout American history it has been customary, at the peak of the business cycle, to praise the party in office for prosperity and, in the trough, to blame it for depression. Yet, although the national government now seems to be acquiring it, no government so far has really had the power to manipulate the economy enough to control the business cycle. Thus, in this one quite central political problem, the process of rewards and punishments has been rendered at least partly irrational by lack of the power to govern. What has happened? In hard times the rulers have evaded the electoral sanction by crying "it was not my fault, but circumstance." In good times, however, no party or politician has long hesitated to take credit for what he has not done. The voters, misled by the dishonest claim and then confused by the equally dishonest excuse, know not where to turn. Sometimes, when frustrated by the escape of the obvious victim, they blame scapegoats, the most popular of which have been foreigners, Wall Street, and labor. And so we have had a series of aggressions against minorities, from the Know-Nothing party to the White Citizens' Council and the John Birch society. Though later most people are ashamed, the aggressor's regret does not repair the minorities' loss of self-respect. Sometimes, also, citizens lose faith in democracy itself, accepting failure in bitter resignation or following the standards of undemocratic demagogues like Huey Long. Most often, however, voters have merely praised or blamed the party in office. Every major depression has been followed by a change in the party holding the presidency—except in 1876, and then Tilden, the candidate of the party out of office, almost certainly received more popular votes than Hayes, who was, however, declared the winner. How many millions of cracker-barrel arguments, how many millions of campaign promises, how many millions of presumably thought-out votes, have been rendered largely irrelevant by failure of the electoral sanction? And what makes this party irresponsibility even more regrettable is that it came about largely by accident rather than by design.

The effectiveness of the electoral sanction can thus be said to depend upon the ability of parties to create effective, meaningful majorities. Government truly responsible to the people cannot exist on less. Such is the result of the analysis of the idea of responsibility which was undertaken a few pages back in order to describe the institutions necessary for an effective party system. And now these institutions can be summarily listed.

Of the several methods devised by democrats to make majorities, none is more effective than the two-party system. If there are only two contestants in elections, then a majority is inevitable. This is in sharp contrast to the multi-party system in which, since elections do not make them, majorities are formed only by haphazard compromise in the legislature. Whether the majorities be meaningful or not depends largely on the structure of the two parties. Only parties with leadership strong enough to unify them are capable of taking a stand on public policy in elections. When parties are largely unorganized and ideologically heterogeneous, the majority they create means different things at different times and places, if in fact such majorities mean anything at all. And finally, the effectiveness of majorities depends largely upon whether or not parties in office have plenary power to govern. If they do not have it, all the meaningful majorities they may produce are utterly useless.

The essential institutions of responsible government are, therefore, a system of two parties, each with strong leadership, and one (as decided in elections) with the full power to govern. In the United States, we do have the two-party system, though whether or not we have the other two essentials is far from certain. The rest of this chapter will, therefore, be devoted to a brief appraisal of our two-party system, leaving the rest of the book to consider our party structure and the power of parties to govern.

THE TWO-PARTY SYSTEM AND THE INSTITUTIONS THAT ENCOURAGE IT

Just why we are fortunate enough to have a two-party system is not entirely clear. Certainly no one planned it; most early democratic theorists, like Rousseau and Madison, would have preferred either many parties or none at all. Yet spontaneous factionalism did harden into a stable two-party pattern, an accident which many scholars attribute to our method of holding elections. Single-member districts and popularly elected executives do indeed favor a political duopoly. But political theorists who give these forms entire credit for the two-party system are simplifying far too inaccurately. In concentrating on an easy explanation, they omit those less identifiable historical forces which brought about the two-party division in the first place.

It is true, however, that, once a two-party division exists, elections by single-member districts will tend to preserve it indefinitely. The influence comes about thus: When there is only one job to be filled from the election district, whether it be a senator from a state, or an alderman from a ward, it is folly for more than two candidates to run. If there should be three, one may win with as low as thirty-four percent of the vote. Then the losers, each with thirty-three percent, can only reflect bitterly that they might have compromised on a candidate and won with a clear majority. Even in less extreme cases, when the winner has a forty or forty-five percent vote, the reflection and disgust are still inescapable. In a single-member district election, therefore, the third, fourth, fifth, etc., parties are sorely inefficient.[22] This explains why third parties soon lose most of their adherents, even if, like the Bull

[22] See E. E. Schattschneider, *op. cit.*, for a detailed exposition of this cause of the two-party system, pp. 69–98. See also: Maurice Duverger, *Political Parties*, trans. by Barbara and Robert North (London, Methuen and Co., 1954).

Moose Progressives in 1912, they have a great hero to lead them. Both voters and candidates lose heart at the prospect of perpetual defeat. Furthermore, they both also soon regret the help they indirectly give to the candidate they like the least, as the Bull Moosers regretted their help to Wilson when he won with forty-two percent of the vote. Discontented politicians have many times formed third parties, hoping to displace one of the duopolists. But only one third party, the Republican in 1856, has ever been able to do it. Even this case is not clear, however, for one can say that the Republicans were never a third party but simply a regrouping of the already disorganized Whigs. Most adherents of third parties, having learned the hopelessness and folly of their position in single-member district elections, straggle back to a major party, leaving a few zealous but impractical propagandists to conduct the funeral ceremonies.

How much the single-member district contributes to the two-party system can be estimated through comparison with the party systems fostered by multi-member districts. Compare, for example, the fractionalization of politics accomplished by proportional representation in the German Republic. The Republic adopted proportional representation in 1919 to maintain a balance among the several parties inherited from the Empire, not anticipating that P.R. would splinter these up even more. In 1919 in the first P.R. election, six parties polled a million or more votes. The Social Democrats accounted for about one-third of the poll and with the two center parties it could make a strong majority. There were very few splinter groups masquerading as parties. In 1930, however, in the sixth P.R. election, *ten* parties polled over a million votes. Since the Social Democrats had declined to less than one-fourth the poll, no party was clearly dominant. And besides the ten major parties, there were over fifteen more splinter parties scattered over the country. The details are set forth in Table II which displays vividly the ten years' atomization. The election system which generated this array of minorities was based on thirty-five constituencies, averaging over one million voters. Each sixty thousand votes elected a deputy so that the size of the Reichstag varied with the size of the poll. In such large constituencies, at least five or six parties could expect to elect deputies. To make matters worse, parties were permitted to run the same list in several constituencies so that, if they could not get 60,000 votes in one, they might in several together. No wonder that large parties were weakened by the sniping of small ones and that

TABLE II.* Elections in the Weimer Republic

Parties Receiving over 100,000 Votes in Reichstag Elections, 1919, 1930
(in thousands)

Parties Formed After 1919 Are in Italics

Party	1919	1930
Right		
Nazis	....	6,410
Nationalists	3,121	2,458
Peoples Party	1,346	1,578
Württenberg Farmers' & Vineyardists' League	....	194
German-Hanoverian Party	....	144
German Country People	....	1,109
Conservative People's Party	....	313
Center		
Democrats	5,642	1,322
Center	5,980	4,128
Bavarian People's Party	....	1,059
Bavarian Farmer's League	275	....
German Middle Class Party	....	1,363
German Farmers' Party	....	340
People's Rights Party	....	271
Christian Social People's Service	....	868
Left		
Social Democrats	11,509	8,578
Independent Socialists	2,317	....
Communists	....	4,592
Minor parties less than 100,000 votes each	210	244
Total	30,400	34,971

* Based on S. L. W. Mellen, "The German People and the Post-War World,"
American Political Science Review, XXXVII (1943) pp. 612–13.

eventually it became impossible to form a stable majority even by
adroit parliamentary maneuvers.[23]

Proportional representation with its multi-member districts may not

[23] F. A. Hermens, Democracy or Anarchy (Notre Dame, Ind., University of
Notre Dame Press, 1941), p. 222. This book is a systematic and impressive
analysis and indictment of P.R. See especially pp. 244–46, 253, 293–300.

be entirely responsible for a multi-party system. Usually, in fact, P.R. is adopted because more than two strong parties already exist. But there can be no doubt that, once adopted, it does lead to even greater fractionalization than existed before. Consider the case of New York City.[24] Proportional representation for the city council was adopted in 1936. At that time only the two major parties were widely organized, although La Guardia's reform group, the City Fusion Party, united many Republicans, anti-Tammany Democrats, and assorted reformers in campaigns for city offices. There were, of course, several minor parties (Socialist, Industrial Government, Communist, etc.) which never had elected any candidates. For them, campaigns were only an opportunity to distribute propaganda and to collect funds, not a serious drive for political power. In the ensuing decade, however, minor parties multiplied and even succeeded in filling a number of offices. Besides Democrats and Republicans, there were on the City Council at one time or another Fusionists, American Laborites, Liberals, Communists, and Independents; and at least seven more parties presented lists. Not all this splintering can, however, be blamed on P.R. In part it resulted from cross filing, that curious practice by which two or more parties nominate the same man. By this means, minor parties can show their strength and thereby make occasional deals to elect their leaders in single-member districts. But cross filing had been permitted for a long time before 1937; so one may conclude that it was P.R. which generated so many parties and gave "a lion's roar to irresponsible fleas." At least, New Yorkers thought so, for they abolished it in 1947. The Liberal party, the only one of the minor parties generated by P.R. to survive it, has presumably been kept alive by multiple nominations and by the close-knit labor union which dominates it, but since it is now rarely able to place its leaders in office, its future seems rather dismal. Nevertheless, it has survived, and recently has been joined by the Conservative party at the opposite extreme of the ideological spectrum—which facts suggest that although P.R. is a potent force in the multiplication of parties, other devices like cross filing can generate minor parties also.

---

[24] Belle Zeller and Hugh A. Bone, "The Repeal of P.R. in New York City—Ten Years in Retrospect," *American Political Science Review*, XLII (1948), pp. 1127–48. G. M. McCaffrey, "Proportional Representation in New York City," *American Political Science Review*, XXXIII (1939), pp. 841–52. Hugh A. Bone, "Political Parties in New York City," *American Political Science Review*, XL (1946), pp. 272–82. All of these articles are by P.R. supporters and gloss over the party fractionalization promoted by P.R.

As this evidence suggests, the two-party system cannot be attributed entirely to single-member districts. Parliamentary elections in England have, with minor exceptions, always been based on them. Yet since 1845 England has had a series of strong third parties: Peelite, Radical, Irish National, Labour, and recently Liberal. For about one-fifth of this last hundred and twenty years third parties have held the balance of power, in spite of the fact that English politics is said to be the prototype of all two-party systems.[25] Two generations ago even this amazing thing happened: The Labour party actually displaced the well-organized, powerful Liberal party to become itself the majority. The Labour party's feat could probably not be duplicated here nor can our third parties even influence policy the way the Irish Nationalists, for example, did. Wherein lies the difference? Why is our two-party system so much more stable than the British, even though we both have single-member districts?

In Britain the executive is chosen by the legislature; but here the President and governors are elected popularly and separately. Consequently, the British third party, once established in the legislature, can expect to have some real governing power. But the American third party cannot—single-member district elections prevent its control of the executive. Since most legislative districts are relatively small, a third party can hope to succeed in them, especially when, as is so often the case, the second major party is disorganized and disheartened. Capitalizing on new issues or great popular discontent, a third party can become one of the two parties in local politics. And, indeed, most temporarily successful third parties have dominated politics in their home area. Thus it was with Know-Nothings in Massachusetts and Connecticut, Populists in many Southern and Western states, the La-Follette Progressives in Wisconsin, the Farmer-Labor party in Minnesota, etc. In Britain, the Labour party could maintain itself as a strong third party in Parliament from the 1890's to 1924 because in South Wales and Lanarkshire it was the major party. But while a third party may keep a toehold on the legislature with local strength, it cannot hope to accomplish its goals or even get jobs for its workers unless it also influences the election of the executive. The great difference between the two-party system in the United States and Britain lies in this: In Britain, once a third party has a secure territorial base like

[25] W. I. Jennings, *Cabinet Government* (Cambridge, Cambridge University Press, 1936), pp. 26–27 and 368.

Labour's control in mining areas, it can always bargain over policy and even over the Prime Ministership when the other parties are closely divided. And with this power to feed on, it can even, again like the Labour party, grow into a major party. In the United States, on the other hand, a third party probably can never influence the choice of the President because he is chosen in a single-member district of the whole nation (or rather in forty-eight single-member districts) in which, for the reasons previously set forth, third parties are ineffective. In other words, third parties probably can succeed in the United States only by becoming one of the two major parties. This they have done in areas as small as states, electing governors as well as legislators. A third party could succeed nationally, however, only in a political crisis of civil war proportions. Even then it is likely that one of the major parties would absorb it for presidential elections, as the Democrats absorbed the Populists in 1896. It is the separate election of the President, therefore, which makes the American two-party system so much more rigid than the British system from which it grew. As Arthur MacMahon summarizes in the *Encyclopaedia of the Social Sciences:* "The centripetalism generated by this office more than any other factor discouraged the development of the multiplicity of parties anticipated by the founders of the constitution." [26]

". . . OF GREAT REVOLUTIONS AND
GREAT PARTIES . . . OF SMALL PARTIES AND
INTRIGUE . . ."

Single-member districts and popularly elected executives are reason enough for the two-party system to keep going. They cannot be said to cause it, however, because many governments based on them simply do not have two stable parties. In the South, for example, where there are about the same constitutional forms as elsewhere in the United States, one party is almost wholly dominant. But inside this one dominant party are many factions so that most Southern states really have a kind of multi-party system. In some of them the factionalism even exceeds the worst splintering of P.R. and is the more confusing because it is not formally organized. However beautiful, then, the theory which derives political duopoly from electoral mechanisms, it

[26] Arthur W. MacMahon, "Political Parties" (United States), *Encyclopaedia of the Social Sciences* (New York, Macmillan, 1931), XI, p. 596.

is destroyed by these inescapable facts. We must look more deeply into political history, therefore, if we hope to discover the cause of the two-party system.

V. O. Key, after his thorough survey of Southern politics, concluded that a sort of two-faction system developed within the Democratic party in two Southern situations.[27] When there was a small but effective Republican opposition entrenched in a section of the state, a strong majority faction organized the Democratic party and dissident Democrats perforce formed a minority faction. This was the case in Virginia, North Carolina and Tennessee, in all of which there were pockets of Republican highlanders. Even more stable two-faction systems have developed, however, in states which have been racked by great political issues. This was the case in Louisiana (where the issue was Huey Long) and Georgia (where the issue was Eugene Talmadge); and it was the case two generations previously in South Carolina, Georgia, and Mississippi (where Populism directed by men like Ben Tillman, Tom Watson, and Cole Blease left its strongest imprint). In states like Arkansas and South Carolina or Mississippi a decade ago, which at the time Key wrote were not troubled by Republican minorities and which had not recently experienced any great political issue, there were so many temporary, personal factions that politics was almost completely incoherent.

Since Key wrote there has been in the South both a revival of Republicanism (especially in the cities) and the kindling of a great political issue (segregation versus compliance with national policy). The Goldwater movement in the South has channeled this issue into the center of party politics. Hence a two-party South now seems to be certain for the foreseeable future. And this two-party system is clearly the product of a new great issue.

Much can be learned about the roots of the two-party system from this observation about contemporary Southern politics. The main source of the dual division is, it appears, great political issues; and the greater the issue the sharper the division. But this generalization seems true for the whole course of American party history.

Each great issue in American politics has produced or intensified the political duality. The Revolutionary ferment, of course, drove all men into either the Whig or Tory camp, for in war there can only be

---

[27] V. O. Key, *Southern Politics in State and Nation* (New York, Knopf, 1949), pp. 298–302 and ch. II–XIV, *passim*.

two sides. While the Tory party was destoyed by American victory, the depression which followed in peace soon split moderate and radical Whig factions into two well-organized parties in almost all the thirteen states.[28] These state parties quite naturally grew into national ones as the Constitutional Convention provided a new national issue. In a sense it can be said that the Federalist party even antedates the Constitution, for the Convention itself was the result of a union of a series of conservative parties mostly out of power in the states.[29] Once the Federalist party existed, the Anti-Federalists were not slow to organize on a national basis. In the struggle between them, in the struggle which eventually came to center around Jefferson's person, the Anti-Federalists became Republicans and the two-party pattern of national politics was firmly established. Unfortunately, the Federalist party was destroyed by its unpatriotic attitude toward the War of 1812 and for fifteen years after the Hartford Convention, the all-inclusive Republican party was dominant. A system of multi-factionalism appeared within it; but on the surface the nation seemed so united in one party that later historians called that time the "era of good feeling." De Tocqueville visiting America in the middle of the Jackson administration was impressed that "great parties" (Federalist and Republican) by which "the nation was divided into two opinions" had disappeared and that in their place stood "minor parties" so that the United States "swarms with lesser controversies." [30] Even as he wrote, however, the multi-factionalism which he observed was hardening again into a rigid two-party division over the personality and program of Andrew Jackson. While the contemporary Democratic party can find its roots in Jeffersonian Republicanism and, earlier still, in Virginia Qo'hees, Pennsylvania Constitutionalists, Clintonians in New York, and the Hancock faction in Massachusetts, its present form is nevertheless the creation of Andrew Jackson.[31] And by its very existence it forced opposition elements to collect together in revitalized Whiggism.

A dualism created around the person of one hero leader could not long outlast his life. Hence during the 1850's American parties were

[28] Allan Nevins, *The American States* (New York, Macmillan, 1924), pp. 210, 245, 323–24, 358.

[29] Charles Beard, *Economic Interpretation of the Constitution of the United States,* pp. 52–63.

[30] De Tocqueville, *op. cit.,* I, pp. 175–77.

[31] Charles Beard, *The American Party Battle* (New York, Macmillan, 1928), pp. 61–63.

splintered up, as they had been after the War of 1812.[32] Neither one was well enough organized nationally to withstand the intense sectionalism of the slavery issue. Early in the course of the irrepressible conflict, Whigs disappeared entirely, only to be reincarnated as Republicans, having sloughed off their Southern members and revitalized with many Northern Democrats. The Democratic party with an older tradition and an electoral majority disintegrated slowly; but by 1860 it too split into three parts. During the 1850's, therefore, the United States, for all practical purposes, had a multi-party system.

Civil war again dualized parties. Wars, and especially civil wars, are the most emotion-concentrating forces in all politics. With soldiers, as with priests, "he that is not with me is against me; and he that gathereth not with me scattereth." The Civil War ended, but it left an unrenounceable estate. The controversies over which men had killed each other remained the controversies over which they hated long after the killing stopped. The war-defined sectionalism of parties continued for a generation thereafter and even now that the war itself is in good part forgotten the partisan sectionalism remains. The great popular issues centering around Bryan, Theodore Roosevelt, Wilson, and Franklin Roosevelt have refashioned alignments somewhat. But mostly those issues have simply reinforced the duality of our politics within the pattern laid down by the Civil War.

The first cause of the two-party system thus seems to be, as De Tocqueville suggested, great issues: [33]

At certain periods a nation may be oppressed by such insupportable evils as to conceive the design of effecting a total change in its political constitution; at other times, the mischief lies still deeper and the existence of society itself is endangered. Such are the times of great revolutions and of great parties. But between these epochs of misery and confusion there are periods during which human society seems to rest and mankind to take breath. . . . These are the times of small parties and of intrigue.

Great revolutions demand, nay force, two sides. This is demonstrably the case in America; and it is true in England also, where a century-long conflict between Stuart kings and Parliaments cemented a variety of loose factions into two enduring parties. Once two parties have been made, single-member district elections and in the United States the

---

[32] A. M. Schlesinger, Jr., *The Age of Jackson* (Boston, Little, Brown, 1945), pp. 488–90.

[33] De Tocqueville, *op. cit.*, I, pp. 174–75.

struggle for the Presidency have perpetuated them even long after the original impetus has been worn out.

Two Parties, but Innumerable Factions

And so our politics is played within the rigid limits of two parties; Anti-Masonic, Know-Nothings, Populists, Bull-Moose, have never been able to disturb the duopoly. To the degree that the duopoly prevails, therefore, our institutions provide the first requisite of government responsible to the people. But underneath this formal dualism hides another contradictory reality. Only in the constituency of the President, only in the nation considered as a whole, do the two giants face and grapple. In no other kind of election can we be certain to find a stable two-party system.

In almost eighty percent of the congressional districts, for example, one party is so overwhelmingly the majority that it always wins elections. As Table III shows, 342 districts out of 435 have been represented by members of the same party from 1952 to 1960—which period includes the notable Republican victory of 1952 and the notable Democratic victories of 1958 and 1960. Note also from the table that, contrary

Table III.* One-Party Congressional Districts
Congressional Districts Won by the Same Party
In Every Election, 1952–1960 Inclusive

Party	North	Border	South	Far West	Total
Republican	110	3	5	21	139
Democratic	64	25	98	16	203
Total	174	28	103	37	342
Total Number of Seats in Area	234	38	106	57	435
Percent of Seats One-Party	74%	74%	97%	65%	79%

* Source: Compiled from Congressional Directories 1953–1961.

to the general impression, much less than half the one-party districts are in the solid South. Although the South is constantly exhibited as the prime example of the sectional disease, actually it has only a slight aggravation of a condition found throughout the rest of the country.

Many Northern and Western cities and parts of rural New England, New York, the Midwest, and the Far West are just as thoroughly dominated by one party. This intense sectionalism is mitigated somewhat when both parties have a domain in one state. Party conflict, though excluded locally, is necessary in all state-wide elections in states like Illinois where rural and suburban Republicanism is balanced by Democratic hegemony in Chicago. The election of governors has the same effect locally as the election of the President does nationally. But even this duo-partisan influence is largely lacking in the eleven states once of the Confederacy, in Vermont, the Dakotas, Oklahoma and Oregon, and latterly, at least, in Maine, Rhode Island, Kansas, and Nebraska (twenty states in all), where the second party is so insignificant that, although it may occasionally frighten, it cannot really threaten the party in control.

Thus, although the two-party system is clear enough on the national scene, in most localities all really relevant political activity is inside just one party. Consequently a sort of multi-party system prevails because there are so many splinter factions. When most voters hold identical opinions on the important issues, when, for example, white Mississippians agree on white supremacy or upstate farmers in New York agree on the superior virtue of farm folk or the steelworkers of Gary agree in hating the steel companies, no great disputes can instigate faction. At most men can differ on local personalities, tax rates, patronage, or graft; and these have not sufficient force to mold either large or durable factions. The electoral forms by themselves cannot mold either, so politics consists of the temporary compromises of minute and ill-defined interests. Of course, great issues do occasionally agitate the dominant party and thus achieve the two-party result if not its form. In North Dakota, for example, Republican Regulars and Non-Partisan Leaguers are almost like two parties; so are the Long and anti-Long factions in Louisiana; and in Wisconsin from 1934 to 1945 Republican factionalism was actually formalized in the Progressive party. But the socialism of the Non-Partisan League, the demagoguery of Huey Long, the "progressivism" of the LaFollettes are rare issues. Furthermore, they do not last. The progressivism of the LaFollettes has now been fully transferred to the Democratic party, while in Louisiana, in the absence of an alternative party, the issues raised by the Longs have simply disappeared. Hence, most of the time one-party politics means that the rationalizing effect of majorities is lacking. The work that the two-party system usually does in making politics coherent simply is not done.

The supreme function of the two-party system is, as noted previously, to insure that a determinate majority always exists. There are other ways to insure it, of course: Parliamentary forms themselves (i.e. roll calls, divisions, and no-confidence votes) automatically produce temporary majorities on every issue. But, unless these procedural forms are supplemented with a two-party division, majorities are, for reasons already set forth, indistinct, temporary, weak, and hence not responsible to the people. In a distressingly large number of sections, the absence of the binary political form results in just this situation.

No better illustration of the irresponsibility of multi-factionalism can be found than the recent failure of two alert commentators to penetrate the maze of alliances, hatreds, local traditions, etc. in the politics of one-party states. No less skilled a reporter than John Gunther was baffled by it. In preparing his encyclopedic *Inside USA,* he asked in every state "Who runs it?" In most two-party or two-faction states he was able to elicit some sensible, though often oversimplified, answer. But in Kansas, for example, he was able to get no coherent answer at all. "The people run Kansas" was, he reported, the conventional reply.[34] The reason he could not report clearly on Kansas is evident: Few people had intimate enough knowledge to say "a combination of these and those factions runs Kansas," and the experienced politicians who did know probably could not verbalize their delicate and intuitive understandings. Similarly, in a far more thorough and scholarly study of the South, V. O. Key was equally disconcerted by state politics where the Democratic party had no stable factions. Of Arkansas, for example, he could at best explain that a host of local factions interplayed in no discernible pattern, around no issues except patronage and graft.[35]

Where dozens of factions thrive, where there is no majority to sharpen party conflict, politics is certainly not understandable. Where the voter cannot understand, he cannot control. Hence to the degree that multi-factionalism exists, local and state government responsible to the people is at best difficult and often impossible.

Fortunately, however, most of the great disputes of American politics

[34] John Gunther, *Inside USA* (New York, Harpers, 1947), p. 257. See also pp. 265–66, 268, 799–800.
[35] V. O. Key, *op. cit.,* pp .183–204. See also pp. 100–5 on Florida.

are not confined to local government. They have, in fact, been mostly transferred from the local to the national arena in a geometric progression which will be analyzed in detail in Chapter 8. Local politics is, therefore, much circumscribed by national politics and local government by national government. However, irresponsible parties may be in one-party sections, the two-party conflict nationally lends some responsibility to them and limits the amount of harm their irresponsibility can do to the democratic way. The two-party system, which is the best institution we have to make majorities, may not be everywhere complete; but we find it persistently enough on the national level and often enough on the local level to insure that majorities will exist whenever there is anything to dispute about.

That being true, the important question is not what causes the two-party system or where it exists, but rather how it works. How, briefly does the conflict of two parties make a majority? The surface mechanics are, of course, simple enough: It makes a majority because, when there are only two sides, some candidate must win with more than half the votes. To some degree this simplicity is deceptive. Majorities are in fact assured *only* when a two-choice system of voting exists. When there are three or more choices, it is impossible to create institutions which satisfy our tradition of fairness and yet guarantee that a majority exist.[36] In short, the two-party system creates a consensus, regardless of whether or not such consensus pre-exists. But behind the obvious hides the complex: No one believes himself to be a part of the Great Majority, yet in this Leviathan conglomerate of minorities a majority mysteriously shapes up.

Whoever thinks of himself primarily as a voter, that cipher among millions in election-made majorities? Few people, even few professional politicians, could be obsessed enough with partisanship to accept a character so drab and statistical. Rather men's stereotypes of themselves are in characters which set them off from the whole, which explain their social relations, and which particularize their interests in society and the world. In the family, people are husbands and wives or sons and daughters; at work, they are farmers and dairy farmers, mechanics and lathe operators, businessmen and brokers; when voting they are rich and poor, traditional and radical, Texans and Buckeyes, Republicans or Demo-

---

[36] See on this point: Kenneth J. Arrow, *op. cit.*, and William H. Riker, "Voting and the Summation of Preferences," *American Political Science Review*, LV (1961), pp. 900–11.

crats or Independents or (that curious compound of the opinion poll-sters) a "Don't know"; at play, they are golfers, hunters, bowlers, baseball players; to the world, they are Americans and Dutchmen; upon reflection, they are materialists, idealists, relativists, and adherents of a thousand brands of commonsense among which philosophical anarchism probably dominates; in anxiety, they are Christians or Buddhists, Cath-olics or Presbyterians, animists or free thinkers; in short, in every con-ceivable activity, men classify themselves in a category, adopting the values, beliefs, interests, and social position which they think goes with it. The curious thing about such categories is that they are almost always minorities—or at least only the minority ones are relevant to politics. When the category is a real majority, there is no question that its cup will be filled; hence, politcal disputes radiate only out of the cups which are not filled. Parodying Rousseau, the general will rules—but the question of politics is to decide which particular wills shall be called general.

Although minorities are probably more numerous than people because every person is conscious of attachments to many, they are yet amal-gamated artificially into a majority. Parties and politicians, in their restless quest for office, endeavour always to attach specific minorities to their cause. They distribute as widely as they can campaign promises, legislative rewards, patronage, graft, and public recognition. When politics is honest, the voter receives most of these quasi-bribes as a member of a minority rather than as an isolated person. The politician's basic technique, therefore, is to appeal to as many minorities as he can. Even in those decisive elections like 1800, 1860, 1896, 1964, when parties seemed to sharpen conflict between two large minorities, each party made appeals to the minorities thought to be attached to the other side and countless side issues were raised to weave undecided minori-ties into the majority pattern.

Parties make majorities, therefore, under the pressure of elections; but the majorities they make are lumpy, uneven mixtures indeed. What good is a majority made this way? What meaning can it have? What power to act can possibly come out of such heterogeneity?

Election-made majorities are, as has so often been pointed out, prac-tically indistinguishable from election-made minorities. This explains why both parties promise in their platforms almost the same things, often in the same words. Much worse for responsible government is, however, the fact that the majority disintegrates almost as soon as it is made. In our legislature, at least, party labels seem to be campaign adornments quietly discarded as soon as the election is over. Despite the popular belief that parties made laws, A. Lawrence Lowell pointed out as long ago as 1901 that legislative majorities are seldom party majorities, that the majority which makes a law is hardly the majority which wins elections. Lowell analyzed roll calls in Congress, several state legislatures, and the House of Commons to determine how many of them showed "party votes," that is, votes in which 90 percent or more of one party voted on the same side.[37] He found few Congresses in which party votes from either party were recorded on more than half the roll calls. In the state legislatures he examined one or both parties cast party votes in from 10 percent to 66 percent of the roll calls, the mode being about 25 percent. This is to be contrasted with the House of Commons where, even in the 1890's, over 90 percent of the divisions involved party votes by one or both parties. No equally detailed statistical studies have been made since Lowell's time; but a number of less elaborate analyses have shown that the situation is not greatly changed, except perhaps toward even less party cohesion.[38] As indicated by Table IV, on the most impor-

TABLE IV. Party Regularity in Congress

Percent of Congressmen in Eighty-seventh Congress (1961–62) Voting With Their Party on Roll Calls in which a Majority of Republicans Opposed a Majority of Democrats

| | Percent of | |
	Democrats	Republicans
First Session	67%	66%
Second Session	71%	72%

tant roll calls Congressmen vote with their party only about two-thirds of the time.[39]

All such analyses of Congress, of course, underestimate the significance of the electoral majorities because they leave out the President, who, more inescapably than Congress, embodies the electoral decision. Still, they do point out that the party majorities which win elections

[37] A. Lawrence Lowell, "The Influence of Party Upon Legislation," *Annual Report of the American Historical Association for the Year 1901*, Vol. I, pp. 321–542. See especially pp. 336–42 and pp. 532–41.

[38] Julius Turner, "Party and Constituency," *Johns Hopkins Studies in Historical and Political Science*, XLIX (1951), pp. 1–190.

[39] *Congressional Quarterly Almanac*, 1962, p. 762.

are so artificial that they disintegrate as soon as elections are over. Artificial majorities which bring together in campaigns men so diverse as, for example, Senators Case and Goldwater or Senators Eastland and Humphrey cannot long endure.[40]

Election-forced majorities disintegrate in this way precisely because they are election-forced. Majorities might be expected to stick together permanently if they were constructed around a systematic ideology or if the party leaders who constructed them were strong enough to discipline wayward legislators. But neither condition exists. Majorities are made around many campaign issues and party positions on them are often inconsistent. Although the necessity of winning the Presidency and other single-member district elections gives party leaders the power to organize their followers for the campaign, beyond the election they cannot often control because parties are diffuse federations of many minorities.

If we are to have government responsible to the people, the people must have something they can hold responsible. The agent of responsibility in our two-party system is the majority party. But if the majority disintegrates as soon as the voice of the people speaks, then the whole process of responsible government slows up—and in one case (the Civil War) it even broke down entirely.

The great question about our party institutions is, therefore: Can they make their majorities meaningful and effective? That they can make majorities is clear enough: the parliamentary forms are enough for that and the two-party system lends precision to the process. But if electoral majorities disintegrate, what power and meaning can they have? Is not irresponsibility fostered in the degree to which they fall apart? Of course the anwer is yes. And so our problem is to discover ways by which we can impart power and meaning to the majorities we already have.

Here, however, are two obstacles. First, the ineffectiveness of majorities certainly arises out of the very method by which they are made. Hence may it not be that so long as they are made this way—and there

---

[40] A theoretical proof that winning parties tend to ignore their extremists is presented in William H. Riker, *The Theory of Political Coalitions* (New Haven, Yale University Press, 1962), *passim* and chapter 4. A practical proof that it is impossible to use electoral alliances (i.e., parties) as a basis for predicting the behavior of Congressmen on roll calls is set forth in William H. Riker and Donad Niemi, "The Stability of Coalitions in the House of Representatives," *American Political Science Review*, LVI (1962), pp. 58-65.

is no better known—we cannot hope to give them more meaning and power? And second, the constitutional system within which parties operate and which in fact created them seems deliberately constructed to enervate majorities. Hence may it not be that, so long as it exists, government will necessarily continue to be in part irresponsible? These paradoxes are really two sides of one coin, so they will be considered together in the ensuing chapters. But lest the reader now feel doomed by a trick of logic, let him be reassured that neither paradox is unbreakable. With good will and luck, this government could be made a true democracy, fully responsible to the people.

4.

The Constitution and the Theory
of the Separation of Powers

A difficulty arises when we turn to consider what body of persons should be sovereign in the polis. [We can imagine five alternatives]; the people at large; the wealthy; the better sort of men; the one man who is best of all; the tyrant. But all these alternatives appear to involve unpleasant results. . . . It may perhaps be urged that there is still another alternative; . . . that it is better to vest [sovereignty] in law. [But this does not solve the difficulty.] The law itself may incline either towards oligarchy or towards democracy; and what difference will the sovereignty of law then make. . . .

. . . the first of the alternatives suggested—that the people at large should be sovereign rather than the few best—would appear to be defensible, and while it presents some difficulty it perhaps also contains some truth. There is this to be said for the Many. Each of them by himself may not be of a good quality; but when they all come together it is possible that they may surpass—collectively and as a body, although not individually—the quality of the few best. Feasts to which many contribute may excel those provided at one man's expense. In the same way, when there are many [who contribute to the process of deliberation], each can bring his share of goodness and moral prudence; and when all meet together the people may thus become something in the nature of a single person, who—as he has many feet, many hands, and many senses—may also have many qualities of character and intelligence. This is the reason why the Many are also better judges [than the few] of music and the writings of poets: some appreciate one part, some another, and all together appreciate all.

—ARISTOTLE, *Politics*, 1281a–1281b

". . . THE POOR SNAKE DIED WITH THIRST."

The Constitution under which our majorities are made and under which our Many work is characterized chiefly by the theory of separation of powers. To an analysis of that theory, therefore, this chapter will be devoted.

The separation of powers idea in its most abstract form is this theorem: Proposition: oppression most often occurs when one man or one group has full power to govern. Corollary: When the power to govern is divided up, therefore, oppression is usually impossible.

Half-truthful though this reasoning may seem today, it enjoyed tremendous popularity in the eighteenth century. Its popularity no doubt stemmed from the several rationalizers (especially Locke) of the Whig settlement of 1689—a Parliament to make laws and a monarch to execute them. But Locke, who fully realized that in the end Parliament was omnipotent, controlling even the Crown, never raised his description to the level of an abstract theory. Later and less empirical writers did that.

The chief of these was Montesquieu, who expressed the idea well for his whole century. "The political liberty of the subject," he wrote "is a tranquility of mind arising from the opinion each person has of his safety. In order to have this liberty, it is requisite the government be so constituted that one man need not be afraid of another." He contrasted the supposed liberty in England (where he mistakenly thought Locke's description still applied in 1748) with Turkey "where those powers [i.e. executive, legislative, judicial] are united in the Sultan's person" and "the subjects groan under the most dreadful oppression." [1]

Montesquieu's definition of liberty is to us curiously negative; it emphasizes peace of mind and freedom from fear rather than the power to act or the power of self-control. Negativity is, in fact, the definitive characteristic of the whole theory. The separation of powers is not a way to make use of freedom; it is only a limit on government, a "defense of liberty against tyrants." Naturally, therefore, all the eighteenth century parties which adopted it were fighting what they regarded as op-

[1] Baron de Montesquieu, *The Spirit of Laws*, Bk. XI, ch. 6.

pression. Those who scorned it feared impotence more than a resurgence of tyranny.

In this generalized and abstract form, the separation of powers has much in common with the method of democracy. Both are defenses against oppression. The one restricts government so that power, however evil, cannot work much harm; the other seeks to transform the nature of power, making it responsible to the people and hence incapable of harming them. In the limiting and restricting aspects they approach by different routes what is substantially the same goal. The difference between them is this: That democracy is in addition a positive way to use freedom for self-respect. Simply separating sovereignty into three or more parts does nothing to make power responsible. It retains the same propensity to oppression as if it were absolute. The separation only makes the oppression milder; it does not, like democracy, turn power to a popular use. Considered simply as defenses, however, democracy and the separation of powers are complementary techniques and seemed more so in the eighteenth century. "A dependence on the people is, no doubt, the primary control on the government"; said Madison in the fifty-first *Federalist,* "but experience has taught mankind the necessity of auxiliary precautions." These auxiliaries, he said, consisted of "giving to those who administer each department the constitutional means and personal motives to resist encroachments of the others. . . . Ambition must be made to counteract ambition."

Yet despite the similarity of purpose, the conviction has grown upon students of our public law that the separation of powers is a hindrance, even an outright obstacle, to the democratic technique. Even in the eighteenth century a few exceptional, far-sighted democrats, like Rousseau and DeMably in France and Priestley in England, doubted the almost universal faith in the separation of powers. The pragmatic Franklin could not be seduced by the ethereal logic of the theory and he compared a two-house legislature to a "Snake with two Heads and one Body." [2]

She was going to a Brook to drink, and in her Way was to pass thro' a Hedge, a Twig of which opposed her direct course; one Head chose to go on the right side of the Twig, the other on the left; so that time was spent

[2] William Cabell Bruce, *Benjamin Franklin Self-Revealed* (New York, Putnam, 1917, 2 vols.), II, p. 249.

in the Contest; and, before the Decision was completed, the poor Snake died with thirst.

Similarly Samuel Bryan, the author of the *Centinel* letters and much the most acute of the Anti-Federalist pamphleteers, observed that: [3]

The highest responsibility [i.e. to constituents] is to be attained in a simple structure of government. . . . If you complicate the plan . . . , the people will be perplexed . . . about the sources of . . . misconduct; some will impute it to the senate, others to the house of representatives, and so on, that the interposition of the people may be rendered imperfect or perhaps wholly abortive.

Once the Constitution was adopted, however, the separation of powers theory was no longer questioned. Criticism of our constitutional principles in the hands of men like Chancellor Kent and Justice Story was turned for almost a century into sedulous praise of all the framers' works. The Constitution became the chief symbol of our nationhood. Around it clustered a variety of other symbols—democracy, federalism, judicial review—and all these were woven into one great social myth. Like the English Crown or, as W. Y. Elliott observed, like Plato's "noble lie," faith in this national mythology is what united the United States.[4] Consequently, even scholarly criticism of the myth seemed lese-majesté or even indeed blasphemy. Charles Francis Adams remarked in 1851 that: [5]

Speculations upon government have gone out of vogue. . . . No leading political man, since his [i.e., John Adams'] day, has been known to express a serious doubt of the immaculate nature of the government established by the majority. The science [of politics] has become reduced in America to a eulogy of the Constitution . . . ; and we are compelled to look abroad, to Sismondi, De Tocqueville, Lord Brougham . . . for the only philosophical examinations that are free from . . . bias [sc. in favor of the Constitution].

It took the great national crisis of the Civil War to reawaken speculation about the separation of powers. Even in spite of the speculation,

---

[3] Samuel Bryan, *Centinel*, No. 1, from John Bach MacMaster and F. D. Stone, *Pennsylvania and the Federal Constitution* (Philadelphia, 1888), p. 569.

[4] William Y. Elliott, "The Constitution as the American Social Myth" in Conyers Read, ed., *The Constitution Reconsidered* (New York, Columbia University Press, 1938), p. 214.

[5] Charles Francis Adams, ed., *The Life and Works of John Adams* (Boston, Little, Brown, 1851, 8 vols.), IV, pp. 276–77.

most Americans still regard the separation of powers as the bulwark of liberty. Nevertheless, since the Civil War, a small but growing critical tradition has interpreted the constitutional checks and balances as a blight that prevents the fruition of American democracy. This stream of criticism has two tributaries which latterly have tended to converge. One views the separation of powers as the cause of ineffective government, hindering the majority in action even when action is desperately necessary. The other views it as forestalling majorities, vitiating democracy by preventing their very existence.

The former view appeared first as a result of the Civil War. "We are the first Americans," said Woodrow Wilson in 1885, "to hear our own countrymen ask whether the Constitution is still adapted to serve the purposes for which it was intended . . ."[6] Frontal attack on the separation of powers was begun by Sidney George Fisher, a conservative Philadelphia lawyer and Lincoln Republican, in a remarkably brilliant but now forgotten book, *The Trial of the Constitution* (1862):[7]

A government [he said] which cannot supply the wants, satisfy the intelligence, or accomplish the objects of a people so eager, so impulsive, so educated as ours, cannot be permanent. Whatever power is essential for these purposes, the Government must possess. . . .

And indeed a government in which ambition is made to counteract ambition is hardly strong enough to carry through a great national effort. This was the juristic lesson of the Civil War, nowhere set forth more succinctly than in Wilson's *Congressional Government:* [8]

. . . the federal government lacks strength because its powers are divided, lacks promptness because its authorities are multiplied, lacks wieldiness because its processes are roundabout, lacks efficiency because its responsibility is indistinct and its action without competent direction.

Or, again: [9]

[6] Woodrow Wilson, *Congressional Government* (Fifteenth edition, Boston, Houghton Mifflin, 1900), p. 5.
[7] Sidney George Fisher, *The Trial of the Constitution* (Philadelphia, Lippincott, 1862), p. 38. For a commentary on this trail-blazing book, see: William H. Riker, "Sidney George Fisher and the Separation of Powers During the Civil War," *Journal of the History of Ideas,* XV (1954), pp. 397–412.
[8] Wilson, *op. cit.,* p. 318.
[9] *Ibid.,* p. 93.

It seems evident . . . that . . . the more power is divided the more irresponsible it becomes. A mighty baron who can call half the country to arms is watched with greater jealousy, and, therefore, restrained with more vigilant care than is vouchsafed the feeble master of a single solitary castle. The one cannot stir abroad upon an innocent pleasure jaunt without attracting the suspicious attention of the whole country-side; the other may vex and harry his entire neighborhood without fear of let or hindrance. It is ever the little foxes that spoil the grapes.

Wilson's great prestige, both as scholar and as politician, lent authority to this interpretation; each national crisis since his time has produced a large number of similar critiques. In recent years the three most closely reasoned are W. Y. Elliott's *The Need for Constitutional Reform*, which was occasioned by the great depression, Thomas K. Finletter's *Can Representative Government Do the Job?*, occasioned by the second World War, and James M. Burns, *The Deadlock of Democracy*, occasioned by the lackadaisical tone of government in the 1950's.[10]

The other stream of criticism sprang forth in volume from the progressive movement of the early twentieth century. Its first able exponent was J. Allen Smith, who wrote *The Spirit of American Government* in 1907 "to call attention to the spirit of the Constitution, its inherent opposition to democracy, the obstacles which it has placed in the way of majority rule." The chief obstacle in his view was "the system of checks which . . . made the legislature largely an irresponsible body." [11] Inspired in no small part by Smith's critique, other scholars and publicists of the progressive era expanded his analysis. Some of the most notable of the books produced were Charles Beard's *An Economic Interpretation of the Constitution*, Vernon Parrington's *Main Currents in American Thought*, and Herbert Croly's *Progressive Democracy*.[12] By the time of the New Deal, this position had become so commonplace that much of the pro-New Deal literature simply

[10] William Y. Elliott, *The Need for Constitutional Reform*, especially part III; Thomas K. Finletter, *Can Representative Government Do the Job?*, with an introduction by Senator Robert F. Wagner (New York, Reynal & Hitchcock, 1945), *passim*; James M. Burns, *The Deadlock of Democracy* (Englewood Cliffs, Prentice-Hall, 1963), *passim*.

[11] J. Allen Smith, *The Spirit of American Government* (New York, Macmillan, 1907), pp. vii and 353.

[12] Charles Beard, *An Economic Interpretation of the Constitution of the United States*, especially ch. 7; Vernon L. Parrington, *Main Currents in American Thought* (New York, Harcourt, Brace, 1927, 3 vols.), I, pp. 267–320; Herbert Croly, *Progressive Democracy* (New York, Macmillan, 1914), especially chs. 15–17.

reiterated it. See, for example, Robert Jackson's *The Struggle for Judicial Supremacy* and Walton Hamilton and Douglass Adair, *The Power to Govern.*[13]

By the one hundred and fiftieth anniversary of the Constitution, disenchantment with the separation of powers idea was quite general among serious students of American history and public law. In the commemorative volume sponsored by the American Historical Association in 1938, not one of the essayists writing on the contents of the Constitution had a good word for the separation of powers. Some, like Charles McIlwain, argued:

The cause [of a "tidal wave of despotism sweeping over the world"] . . . is the feebleness of government. . . . If weakness is the cause, no true remedy can lie in increasing that weakness, it can only lie in making government effective, in removing such "balances" as prevent prompt and decisive action. . . .

Others, like Max Lerner, observed that "The Constitution was born in a century obsessed with the notion of limited powers. . . . Conservative thought clung to the rights of minorities against the tyranny of the majority," implying that the constitutional system is, therefore, a method to prevent majorities from existing. Still others combined both points of view. None, however, displayed the eighteenth and nineteenth century faith in the separation of powers.[14]

So much scholarly opinion developing over the last ninety years cannot be disregarded. We can no longer accept uncritically Madison's conception of the separation of powers as "auxiliary" to a "dependence on the people." We must dig beneath the surface similarity of the two methods. In light of our own version of a "dependence on the people," we must reassess the system of checks and balances. We must determine how and why so many scholars can, in the name of democracy, criticize our fundamental institutions. We must ask, in short, why can the separation of powers, which seemed so desirable in the eighteenth century, seem so undesirable today?

[13] Robert Jackson, *The Struggle for Judicial Supremacy* (New York, Knopf, 1940), *passim;* Walton H. Hamilton and Douglass Adair, *The Power to Govern* (New York, Norton, 1937), especially ch. 7.

[14] Conyers Read, ed., *op. cit.,* pp. 14, 195. See also the essays by Stanley Pargellis, R. M. MacIver, Roland Bainton, Walton Hamilton, Henry Steele Commager, and Carl Becker.

EIGHTEENTH CENTURY VERSIONS OF THE
SEPARATION OF POWERS

The answer is simple: Even in the eighteenth century the separation of powers idea carried different connotations in different circumstances. Certain forms of the theory then did indeed accord closely with democratic thought. Other forms did not. But the great prestige of the quasi-democratic forms carried over to the anti-democratic forms also. Thus it is that the antagonism of purpose between democracy and the kind of separation of powers embodied in our Constitution passed almost unnoticed in 1788 because other, earlier forms of the separation of powers theory had served democratic goals.

At the beginning of this chapter, the separation of powers theory was set forth in its most generalized form. But at least three different specific meanings were attached to that generalization in eighteenth century America, according to the source of the oppression which particular writers feared.

For Montesquieu and for most pre-revolutionary American Whigs, the oppressor feared was the executive. Montesquieu feared the king or the senate (to him, as to others of his time, Roman institutions seemed almost contemporary). He betrayed his preoccupation with executive tyranny when he defined political liberty in terms of "subjects" rather than "citizens." Indeed the practical danger to liberty in France and in the *ancien régime* was the sun-king, not the defunct estates or the circumscribed *parlements*. Montesquieu's prescription is, therefore, simply to separate the branches of government so that the king has not too much power for harm. A mechanical balance of offices is sufficient to allay the "apprehensions" which "may arise, lest the same monarch or senate should enact tyrannical laws, to execute them in a tyrannical manner." [15] In colonial America the oppressor feared was the same as Montesquieu's, that is, the Crown and its agents, the royal governors. W. S. Carpenter has discovered in the records of the Massachusetts General Court an expression of the theory which antedates *The Spirit of Laws* by six years but which might easily have come from that book itself. The colonial legislature refused to give the governor a permanent salary because it "would greatly tend to lessen the just weight of the

---

[15] Baron de Montesquieu, *op. cit.*, Bk. XI, ch. 6.

other two branches of the government, which ought to be maintained and preserved, *especially since the governor has so great authority and check upon them."* [16]

After the Revolution, the theory in America necessarily changed its real meaning. There was no monarch to fear. Nor was there a powerful, irresponsible governor. While most of the revolutionary state constitutions gave lip-service to the separation of powers, their authors had adjusted so slowly to freedom that they made their new governors elected figureheads in misapplied vengeance against the agents of the king.

Legislatures became the "vortex of power." Hence, the separation of powers theory was applied to limit them, either because, as Jefferson thought, they were too aristocratic or, as most of the founding fathers thought, they were too popular.

While he was yet governor of Virginia (1781) and no doubt influenced in part by his own official frustrations, Jefferson began the revision of the theory in the *Notes on Virginia:* [17]

"All the powers of government [i.e. in Virginia], legislative, executive, and judiciary, result to the legislative body. The concentrating these in the same hands is precisely the definition of despotic government. It will be no alleviation that these powers will be exercised by a plurality of hands, and not by a single one. 173 despots would surely be as oppressive as one. Let those who doubt it turn their eyes on the republic of Venice. As little will it avail us that they are chosen by ourselves. As *elective despotism* was not the government we fought for. . . ."

Jefferson's fear of an elective, legislative despotism was not a fear of the popular will—although ever since Madison misused this paragraph in the *Federalist* it has been quoted out of context to align Jefferson against responsible government. As the reference to Venetian aristocracy indicates, what Jefferson feared was an unrepresentative legislature, omnipotent, oligarchic, and irresponsible. The foregoing quotation is from the fourth item of a list of defects of the Virginia constitution, the first three of which specify the undemocratic features of the legislature. Not only, he said, were over half the militiamen and taxpayers unable to vote, but "among those who share the representation, the shares are very unequal." The Tidewater, dominated by the Virginia "aristocracy,"

---

[16] Quoted in W. S. Carpenter, "The Separation of Powers in the Eighteenth Century," *American Political Science Review,* XXII (1928), p. 37 (emphasis added).

[17] Thomas Jefferson, *Notes on Virginia,* Query XIII (emphasis in original).

was, he showed, mostly overrepresented in rotten boroughs, while the western country with the majority of the people was in turn under-represented. The bias thus injected into the legislature was made worse, he believed, because no part of it was set aside for ordinary people. When "wealth and wisdom have an equal chance for admission into both houses," it seemed to him certain that wealth would dominate entirely. Jefferson thus visualized the separation of powers primarily as a defense of democracy. It was the only way short of revolution to forestall the violation of basic popular rights by an oligarchical assembly.

The latter-day student, so conditioned to hearing the separation of powers preached as a defense of classes against masses, may think Jefferson's converse view most irrational. Yet it was frequently set forth during the Revolution and just afterwards. The developing democracy was still weak and good democrats were impressed with the need of protecting it. John Adams, for example, though he valued the rich and well-born far more than did Jefferson, praised the separation of powers on much the same grounds. The argument of his *Defense* rests on this thesis: [18]

The rich, the well-born, the able, acquire an influence among the people that will soon be too much for simple honesty and plain sense, in a house of representatives. The most illustrious of them must, therefore, be separated from the mass, and placed by themselves in a senate; this is, to all honest and useful intents, an ostracism.

What would happen, he asked, if Massachusetts had a one-house legislature: [19]

"There being no senate nor council, all the rich, the honorable, and meritorious will stand . . . for . . . the house of representatives, and nineteen in twenty of them will obtain elections. The house will be found to have all the inequalities in it that prevailed among the people at large."

This Jefferson-Adams form of the separation of powers, while it is directed against the legislature more than the executive, is still with Montesquieu a defense of freedom for the whole people. It goes beyond Montesquieu to the deeper perception (reminiscent of Aristotle and

[18] *A Defense of the Constitutions of Government of the United States of America* in Charles Francis Adams, *op. cit.*, IV, p. 290.
[19] *Ibid.*, IV, p. 399.

Polybius) that classes as well as office holders can oppress.[20] Naturally, therefore, its remedy involves a balance of classes in office as well as a balance of offices themselves. It is a hesitant kind of democratic faith, for it thus displays fear that the propensity of self-government is recessive. But in the infancy of our democracy, it was on the democratic side; it sought to develop the propensity, not to repress it.

CHECKS AND BALANCES IN THE CONSTITUTION: THEIR SOCIAL AND POLITICAL ORIGIN

Very soon it seemed unreasonable to fear that the rich and well-born might freeze the rest of the people out of government. The tendency in the 1780's was toward the other extreme, that the Many might boil up and overwhelm the Few. Although the *Notes on Virginia* was published in 1786 and Adams' *Defense* in 1787, Jefferson wrote in 1781–1782 and Adams, who had been abroad continuously since 1779, necessarily wrote from experience prior to then. Neither could thus take account of the aggressive advance toward democracy during the 1780's.

Popular control of government was immensely expanded during that decade. Not only were formal suffrage requirements lowered in most of the states, but more significantly many non-voting eligibles began to vote. Leaders of society had been accustomed to voting before the Revolution, ordinary folk less so. The democratic form took on democratic substance with the rise of political parties organizing small farmers: the Clinton group in New York, the Qo'hees in Virginia, the Constitutionalists in Pennsylvania, the Hancock and Sharp factions in Massachusetts, the Willie Jones party in North Carolina, etc. Although these perhaps never awakened the majority of the people to the democratic promise, they nevertheless did increase political interest and participation.

All this led in turn to a popular campaign against special privilege. A few states actually disestablished churches and in all other cases the establishment was weakened. Most states abolished entail of land and some got rid of primogeniture, thus toppling over the aristocratic pretensions which Revolutionary confiscations had undermined. Statute

---

[20] Gilbert Chinard, "Polybius and the American Constitution," *Journal of the History of Ideas,* I (1940), pp. 38–58.

law was quite generally substituted for common law, a development which not only adjusted the law of property to the more equalitarian condition of America but also reinforced some of the democratic liberties in state bills of rights. Penal law was reformed, especially in regard to capital punishment and mutilation for crimes against property. And in a few Northern states, Negro slaves were emancipated.

At the same time also aggressive, radical economic measures were enacted in the interest of the poor. The spread of paper money inflation, which helped the small farmer in debt, has been so much emphasized in the textbooks that other equally important aspects of this agrarian radicalism are often overlooked. Mortgages were stayed, export controls were instituted, tax burdens were shifted somewhat from land to personal property and mercantile pursuits. Confiscation of Tory property, begun during the Revolution under patriotic guise, now took on an almost socialist rationale, and proposals were even heard for the redivision of land.

In sum, most states witnessed the same kind of aggressive radicalism as occurred after the "revolution of 1800" and during the Presidency of Jackson. Naturally, therefore, this democratic upsurge occasioned a regrouping of conservative forces.

Historians now generally agree that the Constitutional Convention was their great retaliatory effort. Men of all parties were dissatisfied with the Confederation government for its weakness in foreign affairs. Nearly everybody thought that the Articles needed revision. But brilliant conservative leaders had the foresight also to use the necessary revision to impose restraints on popular rule.

The Constitutional Convention has been latterly much misinterpreted because we read back contemporary ideas into the setting of the 1780's. The founders, it is true, feared popular rule; but they feared oligarchy just as much. The theoretical position of the moderate Whigs was a fear of any arbitrary government, whether by the mob or by a small clique. Since in 1787 the propensity to arbitrary popular government seemed growing, the moderate Whigs like Wilson and Madison attempted to curb it. In this endeavor they were naturally joined by the really conservative Whigs like Hamilton and Pierce Butler.

The founding fathers were not democrats, which is not strange, for democracy was a rare faith then. Most of the influential delegates proclaimed, with varying degrees of intensity, anti-democratic opinions. Farrand's collection of the *Records* is well sprinkled with diatribes against popular rule: Hamilton's contemptuous remarks on Republican-ism,[21] for example, Gerry's reiterations "that in Massachusetts the worst men get into the Legislature," [22] and even the warnings of the milder, more scholarly Madison against majority tyranny.[23] Hardly a word during the entire summer was spoken in praise of democratic ideals. In the debate on suffrage restrictions, for example, exclusion of the poor was insisted on by a determined minority (including quasi-demo-cratic Whigs like Madison and George Mason as well as the quasi-oligarchic ones like Hamilton and John Dickinson). They failed because the more realistic majority wearily explained that, though exclu-sion would be desirable, no Constitution providing it could possibly be ratified. In these twenty pages of democracy by expediency, Frank-lin's commonsense idealism about the civic virtue of the plain people appears as refreshing as a desert oasis. He was about the only delegate there still impressed by the democratic enthusiasm of the Revolution.[24]

But, on the other hand, the founding fathers were not wholly un-democratic either. To James Wilson, as to most other moderate Whigs, it was an article of faith that "No government could long subsist without the confidence of the people." [25] Leaving opinions aside, how-ever, it is the document itself that counts, not what was said at Philadelphia. The Constitution embraced, in fact, a considerable portion of the best democratic thought of its day: election of Repre-sentatives by state-determined suffrage, which by 1790 had been quite widely extended; several guarantees of liberties, such as the *habeas corpus* provision; and a Bill of Rights added in 1790 as the price of ratification by Virginia, North Carolina and Massachusetts. It was not as democratic, for example, as the Pennsylvania constitution with its omnipotent unicameral legislature and the freest suffrage in America. On the other hand, it was not as anti-democratic as the New Jersey constitution with its elaborate devices to forestall popular control. It was, in fact, a rough average of the democratic features found in the thirteen states. Furthermore, it was general enough in form to allow democratic practices to creep into it as they developed: Observe how the electoral college, intended to exempt the President

[21] Max Farrand, *The Records of the Federal Convention of 1787* (New Haven, Yale University Press, 4 vols., 1911–1937), I, pp. 288, 308–9.
[22] *Ibid.*, I, p. 132.
[23] *Ibid.*, pp. 134–36.
[24] *Ibid.*, pp. 118–28, 200–12.
[25] *Ibid.*, I, p. 49.

from responsibility to the people, was by 1804 practically transformed into a democratic device. Only philosophers in a still half-feudal Europe could interpret the Constitution as a democratic advance, except in the sense that it united the people; but it was still not in 1790 a democratic retreat.

A fair and temperate judgment of the framers' work and purpose leads to this conclusion: that, as true Whigs, they thought that government must depend on the people but also that the people must be restrained. At the same time they laid the foundation of a national government, therefore, they took care to provide for both these apparently contradictory ends.

It is the restraint on the people with which we are here chiefly concerned, for that was inspired and justified by a new form of the separation of powers theory.

What needed restraint, in the framers' opinion, was the legislature. It was the most direct agent of the people and in the states it was generally omnipotent. Madison, in the forty-seventh *Federalist,* noted that of the eleven state constitutions adopted after the Revolution, seven declared adherence to the separation of powers principle and two more applied it in practice. And yet, as he argued in the next paper, in at least Virginia and Pennsylvania the legislature, the popular body, had usurped complete control. In the Convention he often remarked upon the same phenomenon, "a tendency in our governments to throw all power into the Legislative vortex." "The Executives of the States," he added "are in general little more than Cyphers; the legislatures omnipotent." [26] Despite lip-service to separation of powers, most of the state constitution framers intended exactly that. They had in most cases provided for the election of governors by the legislature for short terms. Appointments were to be made or closely supervised by legislatures. Few governors were given veto powers. And, in fact, what was said of the Governor of North Carolina was true of most: He had only the power "to sign a receipt for his own salary." In the case of Pennsylvania, Georgia, and Vermont, the unicameral legislature with an executive responsible to it by yearly election approached closely the centralized democracy of the present English government. The legislatures not only made law and controlled the executive, they also often controlled judicial activity. They, of course, appointed judges, usually for short terms; what is more they not uncommonly vacated

[26] *Ibid.,* II, p. 35. See also II, p. 74.

judicial proceedings and took cases before themselves. Frequent instances of the legislature acting as court in the medieval fashion were reported by the Pennsylvania Council of Censors in 1784; [27] E. S. Corwin has discovered many similar proceedings in New Hampshire between 1784 and 1792; [28] and the prohibition of bills of attainder in the federal constitution was no antiquarian reminiscence, as the controversy over it in the Virginia ratifying convention shows.[29] Finally, the legislatures considered themselves the only authority on interpretation of constitutions. Judicial review was unknown, as indicated by the elaborate provisions for Councils of Censors, Councils of Revision, periodic constitutional conventions and the like—all of which were floundering substitutes for judicial review. So in the absence of courts to interpret the constitutions, legislatures necessarily did so. Truly legislatures were omnipotent. And since they had become radical, no wonder the delegates at Philadelphia proposed to restrain at least the federal legislature.

The great problem of the Convention in this connection was to invent institutions which would subordinate the legislature. As Randolph remarked in his peroration on the Virginia plan, the plan which served as the basic model for the Convention's work: "Our chief danger arises from the democratic parts of our constitutions. It is a maxim which I hold incontrovertible, that the powers of government exercised by the people swallows up the other branches. None of the [state] constitutions have provided sufficient checks against democracy." [30] State experience showed further, said Madison, that "mere demarcation on parchment" was not enough.[31] So, in addition, a variety of "checks and balances" were adapted from state constitutions. Since the states with the most radical governments were those with unicameral legislatures, the delegates were agreed from the beginning on a strong Senate, not popularly elected. An independent executive was

[27] Federalist, No. 48.
[28] E. S. Corwin, "The Progress of Constitutional Theory Between the Declaration of Independence and the Meeting of the Philadelphia Convention," American Historical Review, XXX (1925), p. 514.
[29] Jonathan Elliott, Debates on the Ratification of the Federal Constitution (Washington, 1836, 5 vols.), III, pp. 66, 140. The issue involved the case of Josiah Philips, who was attainted during the Revolution as the leader of bandits, attainted, moreover, in three days and by unusual legislative procedure. When he was caught, however, he was tried, convicted and hanged by ordinary judicial processes. See W. P. Trent, "The Case of Josiah Philips," American Historical Review, I (1896), pp. 444–54.
[30] Farrand, op. cit., I, pp. 26–27.
[31] Federalist, No. 48.

also regarded as an essential restraint and this was partially secured by the President's power to veto laws, nominate officials, grant pardons, and command the army.

The most important check of all in the finished document was the method of electing the President that made him independent of Congress. Nothing displays better the determination of the framers to restrain the legislature than the development, during the summer, of the electoral college system. Early in the Convention, it seemed natural for the legislature to elect the executive: that was the procedure in eleven states. The Virginia and New Jersey plans both suggested it; and even so stalwart a conservative as Roger Sherman remarked that he: [32]

was for the appointment by the Legislature, and for making him absolutely dependent on that body, as it was the will of that which was to be executed. An independence of the Executive on [sic] the supreme Legislative, was in his opinion the very essence of tyranny. . . .

But Sherman was converted by the end of the summer,[33] largely by the persistence of Wilson and Madison who insisted that the executive and legislature be "as independent as possible of each other." [34] Wilson and Madison eventually won, but only after much wrangling. Twelve different methods were proposed and two others were actually adopted (one several times) before the electoral college was finally devised.[35] Truly, as Hamilton remarked in the sixty-seventh *Federalist,* "hardly any part of the system could have been attended with greater difficulty in the arrangement of it than this."

The difficulty arose thus: the method used in most states and in England for electing the executive made him dependent on the legis-

---

[32] Farrand, *op. cit.,* I, p. 68.

[33] *Ibid.,* II, p. 499.

[34] *Ibid.,* I, p. 68; II, p. 34.

[35] Suggestions: Election by the national legislature, *ibid.,* I, p. 21; by the people, I, p. 68; by electors chosen by the people, I, p. 80; by state governors, I, p. 175; by electors chosen by the people for life tenure, I, p. 292; by electors chosen by state legislatures, II, p. 32; by state legislatures directly, II, p. 101; by not more than fifteen Congressmen chosen by lot, II, p. 103; for the first term by the national legislature, for the second and successive terms by electors chosen by state legislatures, II, p. 108; by the national legislature from a list chosen by popular election in each state, II, pp. 114–15; by electors especially selected for the purpose in the manner prescribed in each state by the legislature thereof, II, pp. 497–98; by six Senators and seven Representatives chosen by joint ballot of both houses, II, p. 514.

Adoptions: Election by the national legislature, I, p. 77; II, pp. 32, 101; by electors chosen by state legislatures, II, 58; by the electoral college, II, p. 515.

lature, which was exactly the relation the followers of Montesquieu and the curbers of legislatures wished to avoid. It is often and mistakenly said that the framers did not understand the English trend toward executive responsibility to the Commons, the definitive incident of which was Pitt's victory in 1784. Those who fall into this error assume that the framers would have copied the fledgling cabinet government if they had understood it. Nothing could be further from the fact. Gouverneur Morris described these English developments succinctly in the Convention in terms of extreme disapproval: [36]

"In all public bodies there are two parties. The Executive will necessarily be more connected with one than with the other. There will be a personal interest therefore in one of the parties to oppose as well as in the other to support him. Much had been said of the intrigues that will be practiced by the Executive to get into office. Nothing had been said on the other side of the intrigues to get him out of office. Some leader of party will always covet his seat, will perplex his administration, will cabal with the Legislature, till he succeeds in supplanting him. This was the way in which the King of England was got out, he meant the real King, the Minister. This was the way in which Pitt (Ld. Chatham) forced himself into place. Fox was for pushing the matter still farther. If he had carried his India bill, which he was very near doing, he would have made the Minister, the King in form almost as well as in substance."

Despite the brevity of Madison's notes, Morris' position is quite clear. He feared above all a responsible majority party in control of the whole government. He speaks of "intrigues" and "cabals," of "coveting" and "perplexing"—which in neutral language is simply the political maneuvering that makes parliamentary majorities—and, like many others at the Convention, he was eager to find some device to circumvent it.[37]

The only feasible alternative to election by the legislature seemed at first to be election by the people. To many delegates this was a step from frying pan to fire. The people would be led, said Pinckney, "by a few active and designing men." That is why so many other proposals were put forward, even absurd ones like election by state legislatures or governors. The final decision, the electoral college composed of electors (who could not be Congressmen or office holders)

[36] *Ibid.*, II, p. 104. Hamilton shows a similar understanding in the *Federalist*, No. 71.
[37] C. C. Thach, *The Creation of the Presidency 1775–1789*, Johns Hopkins University Studies in Historical and Political Science, Series XL, #4 (Baltimore, Johns Hopkins University Press, 1922), *passim* and especially pp. 174–75.

chosen in each state in the manner prescribed by the state legislature, solved both difficulties. The President was not to be popularly elected nor was he to be very dependent on Congress. It is true that the framers expected the House of Representatives to choose among the five highest candidates in the electoral college, that is they expected that the required full majorities in the electoral college would be rare; but choosing among preselected candidates is very different from choosing in the first instance. The President was thus to be relatively independent of Congress and only indirectly responsible to public opinion.

CHECKS AND BALANCES: THEIR JUSTIFICATION BY A NEW VERSION OF THE SEPARATION OF POWERS THEORY

The rationalization of the independent executive and other restraints on the legislature is a third form of the separation of powers theory. Here the prospective oppressor is the poor or the many or, in short, the "mass of the people." In the secrecy of the Convention, Hamilton presented the argument as boldly as it could possibly be stated: [38]

"All communities divide themselves into the few and the many. The first are the rich and well-born, the other the mass of the people. The voice of the people has been said to be the voice of God; and however generally this maxim has been quoted and believed, it is not true in fact. The people are turbulent and changing; they seldom judge or determine right. Give therefore to the first class a distinct, permanent share in the government. They will check the unsteadiness of the second, and as they cannot receive any advantage by a change, they therefore will ever maintain good government."

Hamilton could not visualize the "mass of the people" losing their place. What seemed so reasonable to Jefferson and Adams less than a decade earlier, seemed impossible in 1787. To the framers it was "the rich and the well-born" who seemed in need of constitutional protection, in need of a "distinct, permanent share in the government." Of course, democratic practices were then far too generally distributed to permit ratification of a constitution providing a "distinct, permanent share." What was produced at Philadelphia was, therefore, what conservatives regarded as the next best thing. Offices were separated as thoroughly as possible in their "dependence on the people," while at the same

[38] Farrand, *op. cit.*, I, p. 299.

time each branch was given a constitutional basis for interfering with the others, in order, as Madison said, "to guard one part of society against the injustice of the other part." [39] Even in the *Federalist,* a campaign pamphlet written to attract support from all interests, Madison made it clear which part of society would thus be guarded. Speaking of the enlargement of the Union—the very act of which he regarded as a further application of the checks and balances theory—he said: [40]

A rage for paper money, for an abolition of debts, for an equal division of property, or for any other improper or wicked project, will be less apt to pervade the whole body of the Union than a particular member of it.

Madison, like Hamilton, often expressed the view that property is "the object deemed least secure in popular Governments"; [41] and so he also believed that means should be found to protect it. "One object of the Natl. Legislre.," he told the framers, "was to controul this propensity [of state legislatures to pernicious measures]. One object of the Natl. Executive . . . was to controul the Natl. Legislature, so far as it might be infected with a similar propensity." [42] For him, therefore, as for most of the framers, the separation of powers was at least in part a means to protect property.

It was thus radically different from the version of Montesquieu or Jefferson. This third form of the separation of powers arises not out of fear of an aristocratic class or a monarch, but out of fear of the "mass of the people," the great majority. The two earlier versions are directed to the defense of popular liberty, the constitutional version to the defense of class liberty. By verbal magic, the phrase thus came to mean its own antithesis, a common trick in the history of philosophy, though in its own day almost always unperceived. The transvaluation of meaning persuades men to accept new ideas under the guise of old and honored phrases. But no word play at all can hide the fact that the new theory had a spirit and effect entirely different from the older ones.

It is usually said that the constitutional version of separation of powers, regardless of its origin and original justification, protects everybody. And this is true in the sense that the separation of powers is

[39] *Federalist,* No. 51.
[40] *Federalist,* No. 10.
[41] Farrand, *op. cit.,* II, p. 204, note.
[42] *Ibid.,* II, p. 110. See also his argument in the tenth *Federalist* and his first statement of that argument, Farrand, *op. cit.,* I, pp. 134–36.

roughly equivalent to the negative side of democratic theory. Both are aimed at restraining rulers, the one by electoral sanctions, the other by limits on their power to do harm. In this sense the framers' Whiggism led to a general protection of liberty.

Nevertheless, it is also true that the separation of powers has a different significance in different circumstances, just as colonial nationalism differs from imperial nationalism. Separation of powers as a defense against royal governors and unrepresentative legislatures differs from separation of powers as a defense against democratic legislatures. The former kinds are directed against an established, powerful oppressor; the latter kind is directed against an anticipated oppressor. They limit a sovereign that has full power to govern; it limits a government that has no sovereign authority. They restrict abuses of power; it forestalls the accumulation of power to be abused. For Montesquieu there is no question that the monarch can govern, even if deprived of judicial and legislative power; but in the institutions of the third version, which presuppose no center of power at all, one doubts if any power to govern can really exist. In sum, the earlier versions limit and restrict a strong government; the third version enfeebles government from birth.

The process of infant emasculation is this: since all three branches of the government depend on the people in different ways (and some very indirectly) and since each branch possesses a series of qualified vetoes over the others, no clear and effective majority can ever exist. The President and Congress are elected by different majorities, each one of which has the power to limit the other. Hence, instead of one majority to govern, this third form of the separation of powers theory contemplates the several majorities hindering each other until, perhaps, no governing is possible at all.

The streams of criticism of the Constitution, which were recited earlier, are thus seen to have a foundation in fact. The one stream which views the constitutional theory of separation of powers as enfeebling and the other which views it as destructive to majorities are both clearly applicable. Both are indeed the same criticism in different perspectives. It is, of course, true that political parties and institutional changes have made the present-day Constitution very different from the Constitution of 1787. Yet neither men nor institutions can escape life-long direction by their ancestry and childhood. No matter how much use and wont revise constitutions, as they have revised ours, still the fundamental forms and theories remain.

The Separation of Powers and
Majority Tyranny: Is the Remedy
Appropriate to the Disease?

The constitutional forms of this version of separation of powers abort majorities lest they be tyrannical. The forms prevent tyranny by slowing down action, action which may just as easily be wise and good as impetuous and unjust. They fetter the democratic politician as much as the demagogue. They thus presuppose an obsessive fear of popular injustice, a fear so dominating that its victims are willing to forego popular wisdom in order to avoid popular mistakes.

So stated the theory seems to throw the baby out with the bath. Whether it really does or not depends upon two considerations: (a) Is the fear of majority tyranny a reasonable anticipation of an ever-present danger or is it a childish anxiety about "things that go Bump in the night"? (b) If the fear is reasonable, are the checks and balances appropriate institutions to allay it? A mature judgment on the separation of powers system requires, therefore, an analysis of these two questions.

Many contemporary democrats regard "majority tyranny" as a chimera maliciously conjured up by anti-democratic interests. It is an impossible delusion, they say, provoked by fear and diffused as a bogey for faint-hearted democrats. And indeed, if one accepts the quotation set at the head of Chapter 3, "majority tyranny" is wholly fantastic. Defining justice as the majority will inescapably means that the majority cannot be unjust (or incidentally, then, tyrannical). Tautologies do not settle the matter, however; they merely shift the question to the nature of justice: Is it, as Aristotle says democrats think, the will of the majority?

It is out of place in this discussion of institutions to launch an elaborate inquiry into the central question of political philosophy. But it is perhaps appropriate to point out here that, whether they like it or not, democrats must for logic's sake agree with Aristotle. Logic controls them thus: Every definition of justice, no matter how precise, requires interpretation in each new circumstance. What day-to-day justice is depends on who intreprets it; justice is, in fact, the will of the interpreter. The only interpreters who can be reconciled with the democratic ideal of self-respect by self-direction are democratic politicians. They are responsible first to the majority; and, because majorities fluctuate in content, they are ultimately responsible to the whole people.

Their interpretation of justice then necessarily roots in popular concep-
tions. Through them, therefore, all men can be self-directing and self-
respecting because men achieve their self-respect by setting their own
ethical standards for life (that is, by establishing justice). Any interpreters other than responsible politicians deprive people of the opportunity for self-direction.

Even when using definitions of justice as simple and clear as Plato's
or as the Ten Commandments, interpreters are necessary. If justice is
minding one's own business, someone must decide whose business is
whose; and if it is following the Law, someone must decide for example
when war is permissible or when a curse is blasphemy. Plato provided
philosopher-kings, wisest of men; and ancient Israelites utilized the
priests; both thus deprived most people of a chance to control their
future. More elaborate definitions of justice require more elaborate
interpretation. If, for example, justice is "natural law," then a whole
corps of jurists and philosophers usurp men's self-direction. That clear-
sighted cynic Hobbes succinctly described the usurpation by self-
proclaimed wise men; and what he said of them applies equally well
to priests, aristocrats, monarchs, demagogues, and philosophers.[43]

And when men that think themselves wiser than all others, clamor and
demand right Reason for judge; yet seek no more, but that things should be
determined, by no other mens reason but their own, it is as intolerable in
the society of men, as it is in play after t[r]ump is turned, to use for trump
on every occasion, that suite whereof they have most in their hand. For they
do nothing els, that will have every of their passions, as it comes to bear
sway in them, to be taken for right Reason, and that in their own controversies: bewraying their want of right Reason, by the claym they
lay to it.

Democrats must, therefore, willy-nilly accept the will of the majority
as justice if they would live up to their ideal of life. If they misgive
themselves shuddering over majority mistakes, they can find comfort
in the quotation set at the head of this chapter. And indeed, even in
the face of such dubious majority actions as the American Civil War
—if indeed that was a majority action—who is to say that the Many
are not wiser than the Few. Majorities are fallible; but all mere humans
are fallible. In the absence of demigods to lead us, the wisdom of many
seems the surest guide. It may be blasphemy to say *vox populi, vox dei;*

[43] Thomas Hobbes, *Leviathan,* Chapter V.

but is it not even more arrogant to imply, as, for example, in the quotation on page 138, *vox Hamiltonii, vox dei?*

Even though democrats must logically say that justice is the will of the majority, the institutions with which they practice contradict their theory. Nations that profess democracy have seldom trusted simple majorities to make fundamental law, thus displaying a Madisonian fear that majorities might oppress. In the United States, extraordinary majorities are required both to propose constitutional amendments and to ratify them; in Great Britain custom suggests that major constitutional changes be the subject of a general election; in the Fifth Republic in France, constitutional amendments require either an extraordinary legislative majority or a national referendum. Nor do these provisions for restraining simple majorities occasion much democratic complaint. In fact, most contemporary democrats seem to agree with Rousseau who, though he identified justice with the general will, still also urged that: [44]

> The more grave and important the questions discussed, the nearer should the opinion that is to prevail approach unanimity.

In short, the practice of democracies here belies democratic ideals, and democrats themselves seem afraid of majority tyranny. No one has set forth the problem more clearly than De Tocqueville who, though a reluctant democrat, was a just observer: [45]

> When an individual or a party is wronged in the United States, to whom can he apply for redress? If to public opinion, public opinion constitutes the majority; if to the legislative, it represents the majority and implicitly obeys it; if to the executive power, it is appointed by the majority and serves as a passive tool in its hands. The public force consists of the majority under arms; the jury is the majority invested with the right of hearing judicial cases; and in certain states even the judges are elected by the majority. However iniquitous or absurd the measure of which you complain, you must submit to it as well as you can.

And then he added in a footnote: [46]

[44] Rousseau, *The Social Contract*, Bk. IV, Chapter 2.
[45] Alexis De Tocqueville, *Democracy in America*, edited by Phillips Bradley (New York, Knopf, 2 vols., 1945), I, p. 260–61.
[46] *Ibid.*, p. 261 note. De Tocqueville here evidently refers to Alexander Contee Hanson, editor of the *Federal Republican*. It was not the editor who was killed, but rather a citizen of Federalist convictions, one General James Lingan, who had undertaken to defend the press. De Tocqueville should have modified his indictment by pointing out that the near martyrdom made Hanson a hero and helped to elect him to the United States Senate.

A striking instance of the excesses that may be occasioned by the despotism of the majority occurred at Baltimore during the War of 1812. At that time the war was very popular in Baltimore. A newspaper that had taken the other side excited . . . the indignation of the inhabitants. The mob assembled, broke the printing presses, and attacked the house of the editors. The militia was called out, but did not obey the call; and the only means of saving the wretches who were threatened by the frenzy of the mob was to throw them into prison as common malefactors. But even this precaution was ineffectual; the mob collected again during the night; the magistrates again made a vain attempt to call out the militia; the prison was forced, one of the newspaper editors was killed upon the spot, and the others were left for dead. The guilty parties, when they were brought to trial, were acquitted by the jury.

Toward the end of his discussion of majority tyranny, he remarked: [47]

If these lines are ever read in America, I am well assured of two things: in the first place, that all who peruse them will raise their voices to condemn me; and, in the second place, that many of them will acquit me at the bottom of their conscience.

If his comments seem remote in time, let us recall contemporary lynchings, our almost nationwide Jim Crow, the local statutes bedeviling Jehovah's Witnesseses which throng through Supreme Court reports of the last two decades. All of these are undoubtedly the works of majorities. Can we not still silently acquit De Tocqueville?

And so a paradox: The will of ᵗʰe majority is justice; yet the majority can and does oppress. We have reached the Thrasymachan absurdity that justice is injustice. Where is the fallacy?

The will of the majority is the best guide democrats have to the distinction between political right and wrong. In the end it is their only guide. But that does not mean majorities are infallible or that time will not prove them wrong. Consider the Eighteenth Amendment, which today usually seems a serious invasion of private judgment. Yet it was adopted even by an extraordinary majority. Certainly majority tyranny is more than a bad dream; it is, as the constitutional fathers thought, an ever-present danger which wise men must guard against.

The explanation of the paradox is, therefore, simple enough. The justice which the majority makes is not absolute or eternal. Like all things human, it is halting, half-truthful, relative. So all wise democrats, while recognizing that in the end the only justice to be found is

[47] *Ibid.*, p. 267.

in majorities, should yet also carefully hedge against mistakes majorities are bound to make. When majorities oppress, as it seems inevitable they will, they actually vitiate the democratic ideal because they deprive minorities of self-respect. Consequently, democrats have a positive obligation to guard democracy by guarding against majority tyranny.

This was one major purpose of the framers' work: to apply just such precautionary devices. And so we are led to the second question. Were the devices effective?

And for the answer, let us examine the most extreme case of majority tyranny in American experience, the Civil War. However democratic were the ideals of emanicipation and free soil, however important to democratic politics was the rooting out of the cotton aristocracy, it remains true that the Northern majority was oppressive. Vast amounts of Southern property were destroyed and confiscated; large numbers of citizens were deprived of civil rights. While Lincoln, Sherman, Sumner, and Stevens were no doubt milder than Cromwell, Robespierre or Lenin, the victors made the vanquished suffer even to the third generation. Still today the effects of lost capital and lost opportunity are apparent in the deep South.

All this occurred in spite of constitutional safeguards. Why did the separation of powers fail completely to restrain an arbitrary majority?

This question need not involve inquiry into the causes of the sectional conflict. We can accept without discussion the conclusion both of participants and of today's historians that sectional conflict was irrepressible, that a house divided could not stand. Incompatible economies and incompatible civilizations within one nation are sufficient and incontrovertible explanations of the sectional division.[48]

The question which is here important is why the conflict led to war and occasioned so much majority oppression? Why was peaceful adjustment impossible? Why was the Northern majority unable to continue the policy of containment started in the Compromise of 1850? Why was it unable to transform containment into gradual emancipation, perhaps with compensation? Why was war necessary to pass the Homestead Act of 1862? Why, in short, could not the majority establish its justice peacefully and without oppression?

The answer is simple and shocking: The separation of powers made

[48] Arthur C. Cole, *The Irrepressible Conflict* (New York, Macmillan, 1933) and bibliography there cited.

majority tyranny the only feasible solution to the conflict of the 1850's. Instead of restraining tyranny as it was supposed to do, the separation of powers was actually the immediate occasion of the worst majority tyranny in our history.

What made war and the ensuing oppression inevitable was the inability of either side to compromise.[49] And this uncompromising wilfulness was a direct consequence of politics within a system of separated powers. On the one hand, a divided up legislature and a remote judiciary strengthened Southern extremists in the belief that they might perpetually defy the majority will. On the other hand, the Senate and the Supreme Court frustrated the Northern majority for so long that it eventually turned to extreme leaders like Stevens and Sumner to whom victory meant the chance for tyrannical revenge.

Southern wilfulness stemmed from the separation of powers in this way: Throughout the abolitionist and free soil agitation of the thirties and forties, the South learned to think of slaveholding as an inalienable right confirmed by the structure of the national government. As late as 1850 Southern and Border states were a majority in the Senate. What need had the South to compromise, however small its citizen minority, when it controlled one branch of the legislature? What need had it to compromise when the independent Supreme Court seemed far more Southern than Northern in sympathy?

During the decade of the fifties the scene changed quickly, however, because the North expanded westward far more rapidly than the South. By 1860 the North controlled the Senate, despite the Kansas-Nebraska law and the grandiose schemes of cotton imperialists to annex Cuba, Nicaragua and Mexico. Since, further, the North showed little disposition to heed what they thought the Dred Scott decision ordered, both of the South's minority vetoes disappeared. Clearly this was the time for graceful compromise; but Southern extremists had gone too far to turn back. Secession was inevitable by 1860. It was inevitable because the separation of powers had so far obscured the democratic base of the government that the minority was lulled into the belief that it possessed a perpetual veto. However untenable in a democratic society, the belief persisted even when its institutional basis disappeared. If power had not been separated, if the South had not thought it had a perpetual veto, then, when in the 1820's cotton made slavery profitable and abolitionists were aroused in the North, compromise would have

---

[49] See Roy Nichols, *The Disruption of the American Democracy* (New York, Macmillan, 1948), *passim.*

been possible on both sides. But power was separated: Hence the inevitability of secession.

Northern wilfulness likewise stemmed from the separation of powers. Free soil agitators, confident during the 1850's that they spoke for an overwhelming majority of the voters, were constantly frustrated in their efforts to limit slavery, pass a homestead law, guarantee free soil, or build a western railroad. Thwarted so often by Senate and Court, Northern leadership was deeply permeated with resentment and intransigence, which are the foremost barriers to democratic compromise. Why should, in fact, the majoity in a democracy make overtures for compromise when the minority insists on a perpetual veto?

It is not strange, therefore, that during the course of the war, Northern radicals divided up Virginia without its consent—a clear violation of Article IV. Nor is it strange that, at the end of the war, they broke the power of Southern slaveholders, with three constitutional amendments, passed, it is true, with the show of constitutional forms, but actually imposed by the victor's physical force. If, as the proverb says, tyranny consists of taking away what men think they possess, then these actions were tyranny itself, however much we may today think they contributed to the ultimate improvement of American society.

And whence came the tyranny? Fundamentally, of course, from all those things which fostered two cultures inside one nation. But immediately and directly, from the separation of powers. By this constitutional structure the minority came to expect the right to refuse to compromise —certainly an illegitimate expectation in a democracy. And, at the same time, the very use of the constitutional structure to thwart the majority will, made the majority impatient of constitutional forms and justified in the majority's opinion its neglect and misuse of them—which is where tyranny begins.

The separation of powers has had similar significance in every political crisis of our history, though fortunately it has never had quite the same inflammatory effect. Most recently, for example, in the 1930's large business interests assumed that the Supreme Court would protect them no matter what Congress and the President did. And so for several years they adopted an intransigent attitude, even refusing to obey such laws as the Wagner Act. When the courts eventually capitulated to the will of the other two branches the necessary adjustments seemed all the more tyrannical simply because the minority had assumed that the structure of government would save it from the necessity of compromise.

The obstacles which the separation of powers system inserts in the democratic process were originally justified as protection for minorities when majorities were impatient. But after a century and a half of experience we can see clearly that the system simply makes majorities more impatient and hence more tyrannical. It protects not at all and it contributes far more majority tyranny than it discourages.

It makes for majority tyranny precisely because it is an obstacle to the democratic process. The real protection against majority tyranny is the next election. Regular elections mean shifting majorities. Shifting majorities mean that every minority has a chance to be on the winning side. This chance means that no ruler responsible to the ruled will for long use the force of government against voters in a really tyrannical way. Thus it is that the minorities that have been oppressed in our history are for the most part those, like Negroes in the South, who are excluded from the voting booth or those, like Southern whites at the conclusion of the Civil War, who had been trapped by the deceptiveness of the separation of powers.

And this ironical footnote: The authors of the *Federalist Papers* repeatedly castigated institutions such as the Polish *librum veto* and the requirement of unanimity in ancient and modern confederacies because the perpetual minority veto they involve disrupted government and instigated civil war. Yet they never realized that the kind of separation of powers which they so fervently advocated was a modified version of the same thing. It is a *librum veto* in disguise, and what Hamilton said of the Articles of Confederation applies almost as well to a Constitution of separated powers: [50]

In our case, the concurrence of thirteen distinct sovereign wills is requisite, under the Confederation, to the complete execution of every important measure that proceeds from the Union. It has happened as was to have been foreseen. The measures of the Union have not been executed; the delinquencies of the States have, step by step, matured themselves to an extreme, which has, at length, arrested all the wheels of the national government, and brought them to an awful stand.

THE SEPARATION OF POWERS AND THE OPERATION OF GOVERNMENT

The argument of this chapter leads to two important conclusions. First, the separation of powers was designed to impede majority action. It is, as it was intended to be, the primary obstacle to those effective, legitimate majorities which, as explained in Chapter 3, are an indis-

[50] *Federalist*, No. 15.

pensable necessity for realizing the democratic ideal. Second, although the separation of powers has been justified as a protection of minorities, it has in reality the opposite effect. Genuine protection for minority groups is the process of compromise inherent in democratic politics.

Thus is exposed the central paradox of American institutions. We are trying to operate with democratic methods inside a constitutional system which is designed to impede them. And so the great problem for American democrats is to refashion their institutions to compensate for the separation of powers.

This is no easy task. American democratic leaders have for a century and a half groped for methods and struggled for the power to tie together what the Constitution separates. How much they have accomplished and how much remains to be done will be set forth in the next four chapters. But at this point one brief note of warning: The facile and unrealistic proposal to import parliamentary institutions is no solution at all. For one thing, whole systems cannot be imported because particular parts often change their significance in a new environment. The surer, more pragmatic approach is to exploit the centralizing tendencies in the institutions we already have. But the more important reason to beware of large-scale importation is that the separation of powers cannot be suddenly removed without real danger to liberty. As was pointed out in the beginning of this chapter, the separation of powers is a real portection against tyranny in the absence of democracy. In the measure that we lack institutions that are completely democratic, we need the protection that the separation of powers provides. It would be folly, for example, to subordinate the judiciary to Congress while yet so many Southern Negroes cannot vote. The separated, independent courts are today their only protection, when they cannot be a party to democratic compromises.

Rather, the achievement of a full representative democracy and the abandonment of the separation of powers ought to go hand in hand. We must eliminate the inequities of the suffrage system at the same time that we add to the devices invented by five generations of American statesmen to overcome the separation of powers. We must, in short, complete the work of centralization for effective government which the founding fathers started. Paradoxically, we must do it by abandoning the separation of powers they held so dear and by strengthening the democracy of which they were so dubious. It is to the detailed working out of that gradualist formula that the next four chapters will be devoted.

5.

The Congress

> There are several examples of democracies collapsing from contempt—Thebes, where after the battle of Oenophyta democracy was ruined by misgovernment; Megara, where it perished as the result of a defeat which was caused by disorder and anarchy; Syracuse, where it began to collapse before Gelon became tyrant; and Rhodes, in the period before the rising of the notables. . . .
> —ARISTOTLE, *Politics*, 1302b

THE TRI-PARTITE LEGISLATURE

Chapter 3 emphasized how sorely democracy needs institutions to make majorities effective. Chapter 4 pointed out that despite the need, the constitutional plan of separated powers stands deliberately in the way. And so the problem: How can we compensate today for the constitutional theory we inherit? De Tocqueville, writing in the 1830's, observed that our forefathers knew how to compensate: [1]

I have never been more struck by the good sense and the practical judgment of the Americans than in the manner in which they elude the numberless difficulties resulting from their Federal constitution.

But can we elude them today? Can our majorities consciously bridge the gaps among the separated powers in order to direct themselves through the complexities of the modern world? Politicians and publicists alike have been perplexed by this question throughout United States history. Each generation of them has had to find an answer in terms of the available institutions in the legislative process.

Just what are the available institutions for majority-making is some-

---

[1] Alexis De Tocqueville, *Democracy in America*, edited by Phillips Bradley (New York, Knopf, 2 vols., 1945), I, p. 167.

what confused. The first sentence of Article I of the Constitution states flatly that "all legislative powers herein granted shall be vested in a Congress of the United States"; but Section 7 of the same article inconsistently provides that the President also participate in law-making. Although his signature is only conditionally required on laws, the extraordinary majority necessary to dispense with the condition transforms the Presidency into a third legislative body. Where the Constitution actually lodges legislative power, despite the verbal definition in the first sentence of Article I, is in the President-in-Congress which is comparable to the King-in-Parliament. The only operating examples of the division of the power to govern which the founding fathers had before them were the English government and colonial adaptations of it. Quite naturally, therefore, they divided up American government the same way. They gave the President less power than the Crown in theory possessed; but they did give him legislative power. Even in 1789 astute legislators were aware of it; William McClay noted in his *Journal* that Senators Izard and Ellsworth and Vice-President Adams wanted to recognize the President explicitly in the enacting clause of the first bill to pass the Senate, "Be it enacted by the President and Congress . . ." [2] That this and all later enacting clauses say instead "Be it enacted by the Senate and the House of Representatives in Congress assembled . . ." is not the least of the reasons that verbalisms obscure for us the constitutional reality.

The tri-partite legislature, there is the problem. How can this trinity act as one? Ambition must be made to counteract ambition, said Madison; but after 160 years of experience we say, ambition must be subordinated to the majority will. If it be not, then surely perpetual deadlock and the consequent impotence will bring our democracy into popular contempt. Aristotle thought that contempt for a government too feeble to govern destroyed democracy in Thebes, Megara, Syracuse, and Rhodes; and surely it destroyed a half-dozen practicing democracies in twentieth century Europe. How can we avoid contempt? How can we subordinate particular ambition to the general welfare?

Whether or not we can do either depends upon our chance of finding leadership which can create a majority in all three branches, even out of highly competitive ambitions. Let us therefore review the leaders

[2] William McClay, *Journal*, edited by Edgar S. McClay (New York, Albert and Charles Boni, 1927), pp. 16, 18–19.

available in our legislative process in order to discover if any can fill the requirement.

In our formally separated legislative branches, the power to govern and hence to lead is necessarily divided up into small parts. The legislative process takes place in a shallow pool, the surface of which is covered with many eddies, no one of which seems strong enough to impart a current to the whole. And yet it is obvious from the very fact that this government has existed and operated for a very long time that the eddies do have enough force to make the water move, however slowly. Competitive ambitions do not wholly dam the current. Some people can lead the legislature. But who are they?

The answer evades us today, as it has evaded skilled observers in the past. Woodrow Wilson, writing in 1885, observed of Congress: [3]

Like a vast picture thronged with figures of equal prominence and crowded with elaborate and obtrusive details, Congress is hard to see satisfactorily and appreciatively at a single view and from a single standpoint. Its complicated forms and diversified structure confuse the vision, and conceal the system which underlies its composition. It is too complex to be understood without an effort, without a careful and systematic process of analysis. Consequently, very few people do understand it, and its doors are practically shut against the comprehension of the public at large.

And the doors are still shut today; as Roland Young remarks in his study of Congress: [4]

The mosaic of Congressional power is confusing to anyone without a professional knowledge of how Congress operates. . . . [It] is in many respects similar to the game of button, button, who has the button? One knows that someone has the button, but it is at times difficult to tell precisely where it is. The responsibility for action lies in many hands and in many groups. As soon as you think you know where the responsibility lies, where the button is, it is slipped to someone else. The internal organization of Congress is so involved and so complicated that only very few men, and they specialists in the legislative process, know who are the individuals and the groups concerned with any specific piece of legislation, and there is hardly a man alive who can solve the mystery of Congress for every issue that comes along.

[3] Woodrow Wilson, *Congressional Government* (Fifteenth edition, Boston, Houghton Mifflin, 1960), p. 58.
[4] Roland Young, *This Is Congress* (New York, Knopf, 1946, 2nd edition), pp. 80–82.

Diffusion of Power: The Evidence of Idiom

Any one of the 537 men [5] constitutionally endowed with legislative power may at times become a leader of Congress. The chance to lead is diffused throughout it; and no more reliable proof of the diffusion exists than the idiom by which we name laws. Political scientists may differ in describing congressional leadership but the idiom embraces the collective, intuitive judgments of all its users—Congressmen, journalists, scholars, and citizens. It has thus more penetrating hindsight than any one man. The idiom knows at least who *had* the leadership, though it, like people, is never sure about who has it right now.

The significant point about this contemporary idiom is that, while we call most laws by their short titles or popular nicknames (e.g., the Fair Labor Standards Act, the GI Bill of Rights), we single out some for christening after the men who piloted them through Congress (e.g., the Wagner Act, the Taft-Hartley Act). The distinguishing characteristic of all laws known by persons' names is that some one or two Congressmen who are usually not permanent leaders have made heroic efforts on the laws' behalf. What the idiom thus implies is that there are two kinds of legislative leadership, the customary and permanent leaders who are expected to push through laws, and the temporary opinion leaders—any one of the 537 men—who may on occasion seize the chance to lead.

This usage, intuitive though it may be and, so far as is known hitherto unrationalized, is quite strict. Specific Congressmen are honored only if they have given peculiar, extraordinary, and effective leadership in managing the bill. Bills managed by permanent leaders are seldom known by personal names. The non-personal category includes all the recurrent legislative business (such as appropriations and general revenue bills) and all the bills of the President's legislative program, which are necessarily managed by the majority leaders (e.g., Medicare, Civil Rights, etc.). Even when the bills managed by the permanent leaders are known by personal names in the bill stage, the idiom will not tolerate them once the bill is law. For example, the Selective Service Act of 1940 was in Congress often called the Burke-Wadsworth bill, partially to distinguish it from other draft bills and partially to suggest

[5] The President, the Vice-President (as President of the Senate), 100 Senators, and 435 Representatives.

by a Republican name that it was bi-partisan. But the bill was managed by party leaders as part of Roosevelt's program; the idiom recognized that Senator Burke and Representative Wadsworth had done no more than lend their names and so it forgot them once their usefulness was over. Probably no slight was intended: it is only that the idiom requires more significant contributions than name-lending before it will acknowledge parenthood.

Sometimes the idiom may err in not properly crediting temporary leaders, leaving unrecognized the managers of minor bills. But considering the very large number of important laws that carry personal names, it is apparent just how much the chance to lead is spread through Congress.

The niceties of the idiom prove even more impressively than does its major distinction the diffusion of Congressional leadership. For example, from the middle of the nineteenth century—when the idiom became widespread—on to the end, it was customary to name laws after only one sponsor, the Senator (e.g., the Pendleton Act) or the Representative (e.g., the Morrill Act) who originated the bill, managed it through his house, and lobbied it through the other. The legislative complexities of the twentieth century, however, have led us to credit the sponsor in each house by means of a hyphenated name. (Witness the change of the idiom in the names of tariffs: The Walker, Morrill, and McKinley tariffs of the nineteenth century as against the Payne-Aldrich, Fordney-McCumber, and Smoot-Hawley of the twentieth.) But in spite of this development toward double recognition, we still name a law after only one man if in fact one man is peculiarly the force behind its passage (e.g., the Underwood tariff, the Volstead Act, the Wagner Act, the Hatch Acts). When we use the hyphenated name, it is customary to put the Senator's first, perhaps thus implying that it is harder to get bills through the Senate, perhaps simply accepting the Senate's judgment of its own worthiness. But if the Representative is the real leader, we do not hesitate to transpose the usual order (e.g., the Smith-Connally Act). The idiom may be discourteous, but it is accurate. Its accuracy is all the more impressive because it is willing, although indeed reluctantly, to recognize that genuine legislative leadership may lie outside Congress. A few laws have recently been named after lobbyists (e.g., the Frey rider, named after an officer of the American Federation of Labor). The idiom even sometimes recognizes administrative officers. Properly speaking, it should never do this because the chief administrator, that is the President, is a permanent leader of Congress charged by the Constitution with suggesting laws. But sometimes Cabinet members so dominate the legislative scene that their bills are known by their names. This is often the case with treaties, which are, however, only partially the work of Congress (e.g., the Jay Treaty, the Kellogg Pact). It is also rarely true of other measures, such as the Walker tariff (named after Polk's Secretary of the Treasury) or the Marshall Plan Act (named after Truman's Secretary of State). Altogether, in its selection of the number of personal names, the order of personal names and the kind of personal names, the idiom sufficiently indicates the extremely wide diffusion of the chances for legislative leadership. Really, any one of the 537, and more besides, may on occasion get control.

And its history, too, indicates the same thing. The idiom originated in the English Parliament and was in common use at the time our Congress began operation (e.g., Pitt's India Bill, Fox's Libel Act); but it has almost disappeared from English usage today. About the only contemporary example of a personal name for an English law is Herbert's Marriage Act (i.e. a divorce law) and it is just as commonly known as the Matrimonial Causes Act of 1937. Why should the idiom disappear in England while examples of it were multiplied profusely in the United States? The answer is clear: So completely did executive and party leadership by the Cabinet come to dominate Parliament that private members almost wholly lost their chance to lead. Government bills (i.e. Cabinet bills) so greatly overshadowed private member's bills that the distinction on which the idiom is based lost its significance. So archaic is the idiom now that Englishmen even hesitate to use Herbert's name for the law, although it was a private member's bill, lobbied and managed largely by Herbert, and hence rightly identified by his name. In the United States, on the other hand, personal names were increasingly attached to laws throughout the nineteenth century. Thus the idiom recorded the intuitive recognition that, as a Congress without centralized or Cabinet control grew larger and larger, the variety of potential leaders multiplied in geometric series.

Note well, however, that the linguistic variants are all devices to point out aberrations from a general rule. The personal names do show that many individual opinion leaders have chances to lead temporarily; but the impersonal titles, which are by far more numerous, show even more impressively that the permanent leaders lead most of the time.

And it is these permanent leaders who are therefore most interesting here. This chapter is devoted to a search for leaders who can unite the separated powers; and clearly they will be found among the usual leaders rather than among the chance, occasional ones. The question here, then, is: Who leads Congress when it passes bills that get impersonal names? Who are its permanent leaders?

PARTY LEADERS AND STRUCTURAL LEADERS

In every modern legislative body, the permanent leaders can be classified into two sorts: the formal leaders required by the constitutional structure of the house and the informal leaders of parties or blocs. The formal, structural leaders, that is, presiding officers, committee chairmen, and the like, are supposed to direct the whole body; presumably they are responsible to the whole body; and usually the forms of selecting them are based on the fiction that parties do not exist. On the other hand, the party leaders, that is, floor leaders, whips, and the like, are supposed to direct only the members of the party caucus; they are responsible only to the caucus which chooses them; and the forms of selecting them are based on the equally fictitious assumption that the majority party is a legislative majority.

Conscious self-direction in the democratic society is necessarily the self-direction of a coherent majority. And, as was pointed out in Chapter 3, a coherent majority is necessarily a party majority. Ideally, therefore, in the permanent management of a democratic legislature, party leaders ought to displace structural leaders entirely. Such displacement can conceivably occur in two ways: by reducing structural leaders to impotence (as in the case of the Vice-President) or by combining party and structural leadership in one person (as in the case of the Speaker of the House). But, regardless of the method used, party leadership must dominate if majorities are to be either coherent or effective. When party and structural leaders are different men, when leadership is atomized in the conflicts of ambition, then majorities are certain to be both volatile and meaningless.

The most noteworthy fact about our Congress is that the party and structural leaders are often not the same men. Of course, much of the structural leadership has indeed been replaced; but enough of it has independent existence to preclude majority action frequently. The proof of this proposition is to be got simply by a survey of the sources and limits of power of the several permanent leaders in each house. And so it is to such a survey that the rest of this chapter will be devoted.[6]

The Speaker: Presiding Officer and Caucus Spokesman

In the House of Representatives the greatest single portion of the power to lead is lodged in the Speaker; but the extent of his power is often misinterpreted. One widely used contemporary textbook suggests that the present-day Speakership is but a shadow of the office before 1910; another one says flatly that the Speaker is the second most powerful man in Washington. Neither extreme view is correct. The most accurate way to describe the Speaker's power is to say that he can, with the active support of the Rules Committee and party leaders and with the passive acquiescence of a majority of his caucus, force through some bills of which he approves and block some other bills of which he disapproves. In this way he has more chance to lead than any other Congressman, and this for two reasons: He is the most important structural leader and he is the chief leader of the majority party. And since each kind of leadership is involved in every specific action, the fused powers reinforce and expand each other.

The partisan element of the Speaker's power is easily defined, although its real extent is never certain. The election of the Speaker is one of the few roll calls on which all members of one party vote on one side and all members of the other party vote on the other side. So rarely do Representatives vote against their party's nominee that it is doubtful if one who did so could still be recognized as a member of the party caucus. Even the insurgent Republicans in 1910, who were in revolt against "Cannonism," refused to vote Speaker Cannon out of his job. And since the choice of the Speaker is now the one certain point of internal party agreement, nominating him has become the most important activity of the caucus. Thus, while the Speaker may represent a compromise between conflicting blocs in his own party, he can always be confident that such party cohesion as exists is personified in him—and this the more surely because the House is reorganized every two years.

[6] Since much of what follows presupposes some familiarity with the technical aspects of legislative practice, a chart of the procedure by which a bill becomes law is placed on page 158 and, for those who wish more detail, the appendix to this chapter contains a concise summary of legislative operation.

Introduced by a Representative; referred to a STANDING COMMITTEE by the Clerk of the House; → Studied by a STANDING COMMITTEE, reported to the House, with amendments proposed; → → Pigeonholed,

Placed on a Calendar to await consideration; → Selected for consideration by the RULES COMMITTEE (or sometimes by a special device); → Left on the Calendar until the end of the Congress,

Debated clause by clause in the Committee of the Whole House, the debate being led by its MANAGER: (amendments proposed); → Debated in the House under the chairmanship of the SPEAKER; amended; passed; sent to the Senate; → → Rejected or recommitted,

Referred to a STANDING COMMITTEE by the Senate; → Studied by a STANDING COMMITTEE; reported favorably or unfavorably with amendments; → → Pigeonholed,

Placed on the Calendar to await consideration; → Selected for consideration at some future time by the Senate, usually after agreement between its MANAGER and FLOOR LEADERS; → Left on the Calendar until the end of the Congress,

Called up for consideration; → Debated; amended; passed; returned to the House; → → Rejected or recommitted,

Its Senate amendments disagreed to by the House and a conference requested; → Conferred upon by CONFEREES for each house appointed by presiding officers;

Compromise amendments to it proposed by the CONFERENCE COMMITTEE; → Passed in each house in the form reported by the CONFERENCE COMMITTEE; → → Rejected,

Sent to the PRESIDENT; → Signed by the PRESIDENT; → → Returned to Congress by the President without his signature, ⌐

Considered immediately by the House; → Passed by 2/3 of the House; considered immediately by the Senate and passed by 2/3; → → Rejected by either house,

→ BECOMES A STATUTE   └→ FAILS.

If the Speaker's power rested simply on caucus support, however, he would be no more influential than the majority leader. But he is in fact much more so because he exercises a structural leadership as the presiding officer. When he uses his structural power in a partisan way with partisan backing, he can sometimes control the whole legislative process in the House of Representatives.

The Speakership developed into a powerful office largely through the accretion of several kinds of structural leadership. The Speaker always had, of course, the usual duties of a presiding officer: to moderate debate, to recognize members for the floor, to appoint committees, etc. As the office became the means by which the majority party controlled the House, the Speaker acquired also the right to rule irrelevant debate out of order, to appoint committees in such a way as to influence legislation, and to serve as chairman of the Rules Committee. During the 1880's when minority obstruction threatened to forestall legislative action entirely, the majority regained control largely by expanding the Speaker's powers. In the bitterness of Reconstruction, Democrats had invented and developed a wide variety of obstructionist devices, which, of course, Republicans also put to good use when they lost control of the House. The legislative impotence thus produced could not be endured forever. Speaker Reed spoke truly for the frustrated majority when he complained that "We undertake to run Niagara through a quill" and just as truly when he boasted jubilantly after the great rules change of 1889, "Thank God, the House is no longer a deliberative body." [7] It was no longer simply deliberative because the concentration of leadership in the Speaker gave it the power to act. Although speeches had been limited to one hour ever since the 1840's, filibustering was still in 1880 both feasible and common in the House by means of roll calls on dilatory motions, the "disappearing quorum," and a rigid calendar. After

[7] William A. Robinson, *Thomas B. Reed* (New York, Dodd, Mead, 1930), pp. 114, 255.

CHART III. CASE HISTORY OF A BILL

A schematic and greatly oversimplified history of the lengthy and complicated procedure by which an important bill becomes law in the United States (with the PERSONS who have most power over its fate indicated in CAPITAL LETTERS; and with many of the untimely deaths it escapes listed in the right hand column).

the parliamentary overhaul, however, filibusters were impossible unless the Speaker himself encouraged them.

Prior to the eighties the minority often forced interminable roll calls on minute and purely dilatory parliamentary issues. A first step, taken in 1881, to discourage such action was the Speaker's refusal to entertain one of the most fruitful of dilatory motions, an appeal to the floor on the Speaker's decision on recognition. In the great rules change of 1889, the Speaker was further empowered to refuse to entertain any dilatory motion, a power since used with crushing effect against any sort of filibuster. "The object of a parliamentary body," said Speaker Reed, "is action, not stoppage of action." Both these changes aimed at Reed's goal *by means of an increase in the Speaker's power of recognition.*

Similarly, the minority could completely disrupt the business of the House by the "disappearing quorum," that is by refusing to answer on roll calls even though they were physically present in the House. Since the Constitution fixes a quorum at one-half the membership and since some members are necessarily absent at any particular moment, the refusal of a large minority to answer often forced temporary adjournments. In a bold move which occasioned the rules change of 1889, Speaker Reed, thereafter popularly known as "Czar" Reed, counted the silent members as present. The House was in pandemonium for three days—one of the most exciting and dramatic events in congressional history. Order was completely banished by the tumult and namecalling; and, when Reed ordered the doors locked for a quorum call, one enraged Texan actually kicked them down. But then the Republican majority changed the rules to legalize Reed's action and thereby set a precedent for many other new and forceful uses of the Speaker's gavel.

Finally, the minority could under the old rules easily prevent the two-thirds majority required to consider bills out of their calendar order. Hence only unimportant bills were passed early in a Congress while the pressure at the end was so great that only appropriations bills could get through. "Special orders" were invented to vault this obstruction. Thomas B. Reed, not yet the Speaker, reported for the Rules Committee a temporary rule to be adopted by majority vote, a rule which arranged the procedure to pass the tariff bill of 1883. Under Speakers Reed, Crisp, and Cannon (1889–1910) special orders enabled the Speaker (then always chairman of the Rules Committee) to control House business entirely. Speaker Cannon in his old age recalled the

Committee meetings as a farcical false front for the Speaker's real control: [8]

> The Democratic members would come to the Speaker's room and jokingly inquire the purpose of the meeting. Reed, in his drawl, would respond, "Another outrage," and read it. The Special Order would be made, Reed, McKinley and I voted to report it, and the two Democrats voted adversely. That would be the end of the meeting.

Control as centralized as this could continue only if political parties were truly national and nationally led. But they are not. Inevitably, the House diluted the concentrated power of the Speakership. Republican insurgents, thwarted by Cannon and resentful because Cannon had used his power against Theodore Roosevelt and "progressive" measures, carried through the Revolution of 1910 which transferred committee appointment from the Speaker to the whole House and deprived the Speaker of his place on the Rules Committee. (This latter provision was dropped in 1946; but no attempt has yet been made to reassign the Speaker to the Committee.)

The insurgents of 1910 did not, and indeed could not, subdue the Speaker simply by slicing off these two prerogatives. They decentralized leadership somewhat, of course, but they did not affect the Speaker's partisan support nor did they take from him his powers acquired in 1889. So the Speaker still has important partisan powers. He is the main leader of his party in the House and can use this power to affect the structure of committees. Thus in 1961 Speaker Rayburn was able to force through an enlargement of the Rules Committee, an enlargement that sharply changed its ideological composition. And furthermore, the Speaker still has these important structural powers which he is expected to use in a partisan way to control the House.

First, he rules on all points of order, that is, on all questions involving an interpretation of House rules. It is his control of order which makes him still the master of the Rules Committee even though he is no longer a member of it. As explained by George Galloway, secretary of the committee that wrote the Legislative Reorganization Act of 1946, his control works this way: [9]

---

[8] L. White Busbey, *Uncle Joe Cannon.* Copyright 1927 by L. White Busbey, pp. 243–44.
[9] George B. Galloway, *Congress at the Crossroads* (New York, Thomas Y. Crowell, 1946), p. 117.

He cannot compel it [i.e. the Rules Committee] to act, but he can thwart it when it does act . . . he can prevent the adoption of any rule reported by that committee of which he disapproves by getting one of his trusted lieutenants to make a point of order against the rule on some technicality and by sustaining it. There is no effective appeal from decisions of the chair on points of order under the existing rules of the House.

Second, the Speaker and the Speaker alone has the power of recognition. Presumably he is bound by precedent to recognize certain types of Congressmen in specified situations, for example, the manager of a bill for all allowable motions to expedite it. But precedent is weak if the Speaker's partisan support is strong. Since no appeal to the floor is possible on questions of recognition the Speaker is really bound by nothing except his judgment of what his own party will tolerate. John G. Carlisle, a Democratic Speaker from 1883 to 1889, often boasted about an excise tax repealer that "no man with that damned bill in his hand can ever secure recognition"; and he added that, if anyone got the floor for another subject and then tried to introduce the bill, he would say, "The Speaker has been deceived in the purpose for which recognition was obtained, and the recognition is withdrawn." [10] In a more recent case, Rayburn, a Texas Democrat, ignoring the regular order for the call of committees under the twenty-one-day rule (see page 167), passed over Representative Lesinski, who wanted to bring up that anathema to Southerners, a Fair Employment Practices bill, and recognized instead Representative Peterson to bring up an Alaska Statehood bill.[11] The Speaker's arbitrary action occasioned considerable debate— all of which had the undertone of "but nobody can do anything about it." If it be objected that these are really special situations, the one old, the other arising from a rule not now in force, consider Speaker Rainey's control of the House in March, 1933. President Roosevelt and the Democratic leaders in Congress were trying to push an economy bill through quickly. But there was much opposition inside the Democratic party, especially from Congressmen who wanted a veterans' bonus. The party caucus had been almost disrupted over the issue, yet the party leaders put it through, largely by use of the Speaker's power of recognition. Pendleton Herring tells the story well: [12]

[10] James A. Barnes, *John G. Carlisle* (New York, Dodd, Mead, 1931), p. 153.
[11] *Congressional Record*, XCVI (Jan. 23, 1950), pp. 772, 773, 776, 778, 779, 781.
[12] Pendleton Herring, *Presidential Leadership*. Copyright 1941 by Pendleton Herring, p. 60.

The floor leader introduced a resolution providing that debate on the economy bill be limited to two hours and ruling out amendments. It was hoped that the amendment that had disrupted the caucus could thus be kept out of the House, but Representative Browning proved too experienced a parliamentarian to be thrust aside so easily. He saw that even under the resolution it would be in order for an opponent of the bill to offer a motion to recommit the bill to committee. An opening for amending the measure appeared in possible instructions to this committee. It was up to the Democratic leaders to forestall Representative Browning. How could the leader of the proveteran rebels be prevented from crippling the economy bill by his limiting amendment? A loophole was seen in a motion sponsored by Representative Connery of Massachusetts. This champion of the veterans wished to kill the economy bill entirely by returning it to committee without instructions. The leaders grasped this slender chance, for Connery's motion made possible a vote to recommit *without any modifying amendment.* The speaker used his right to recognize with decisive effect. Connery was called upon, Browning ignored. When the latter insisted that his amendment deserved recognition "after what occurred in the caucus this morning," the speaker coldly rejoined that the House had no knowledge of the caucus.

So the Connery motion was defeated, as the leaders had hoped; the bill itself was voted on immediately and passed without any amendments.

Third, the Speaker has a host of other powers in the ordering of debate. He may rule dilatory motions out of order. He decides whether or not proposed amendments are germane, and sometimes actually decides the meaning of propositions. He may rule irrelevant or discourteous remarks out of order, etc. All of these powers, none of great significance in themselves, can be used by a strong Speaker to control the substance as well as the process of House action. This possibility is nicely revealed in the House parliamentarian's annotation of Jefferson's *Manual of Parliamentary Practice.* Jefferson had observed: [13]

If an amendment be proposed inconsistent with one already agreed to, it is a fit ground for its rejection by the House, but not within the competence of the Speaker to suppress as if it were against order. For were he permitted to draw questions of consistence within the vortex or [sic—sc. of] order, he might usurp a negative on important modifications, and suppress, instead of subserving, the legislative will.

[13] *Constitution, Jefferson's Manual and Rules of the House of Representatives,* House Document, No. 459, 86th Congress, 2nd session (Washington, Government Printing Office, 1961), section 466.

The annotator agreed that the "practice of the House of Representatives follows and extends the principle set forth by Jefferson." But then he added this revealing comment: [14]

This principle has been the subject of conflicting decisions, from which may be deduced the rule that the Chair may rule out the proposition unless it presents substantially a different proposition.

All of which is to say that, since Jefferson was Vice-President, the American Speaker has enormously increased (Jefferson would say "usurped") the power to influence legislation.

THE RULES COMMITTEE: TOLL BRIDGE ATTENDANTS

The Speaker's power is, however, less than it once was, largely because one important part of it was transferred to the Rules Committee, now the second great concentration of the power to lead in the House.[15] The leadership once exercised by Reed and Cannon is now exercised by the Speaker and the fifteen members of the Rules Committee. The Committee's power differs from the Speaker's in one important respect, however, for it is more structural and less partisan in origin. Of course, selection of new members of the Committee is a highly partisan process in which the Speaker and the caucus are deeply involved. But once the selections are made, seniority determines advancement and to some degree separates the Committee from its partisan base. Its power to lead is therefore almost entirely derived from its grip on the mechanisms of the House.

What gives the Committee its extraordinary control is the great development of special orders, which are temporary rules prescribing the procedure to consider a particular bill. While they are of course adopted by majority vote in the House, they can be brought up for consideration only by the Rules Committee. It is its power to propose—or not to propose—special orders that gives the Rules Committee its authority. So crowded are the calendars of the House that few important bills could possibly come to the floor in the regular order of business. Hence,

[14] *Ibid.*
[15] See: James A. Robinson, *The House Rules Committee* (Indianapolis, Bobbs-Merrill, 1963).

if the House is to have time to consider important bills, some device is necessary to give them a special privilege. The rules provide the unanimous consent procedure for private bills and non-controversial public bills; and they permit committee chairmen to call up at any time certain important and recurrent public bills (e.g., appropriations and revenue bills). All other controversial public bills must wait their turn on the calendar (which is likely never to come) or be brought to the floor by some sort of privileged procedure, usually a special order. This means that the Rules Committee is first of all the traffic officer of the House, able to prevent or to expedite consideration of bills. The Committee's influence is far more pervasive, however, than the simple traffic officer metaphor implies. Indeed Chairman Smith is widely quoted as having said, "My people did not send me here to be a traffic cop." Hence, more accurately, it is a toll bridge attendant who argues and bargains with each prospective customer; who lets his friends go free, who will not let his enemies pass at any price; who may sell some customers the right of way, keeping all other vehicles off the bridge; and who may merely allow others an entry to a crowded and dangerous passage, permitting and even expecting all sorts of collisions and disasters for them *en route*.

It is the special order which gives these toll bridge attendants the power to coerce their customers. If the majority of the Rules Committee is unalterably opposed to a particular bill, it can refuse to report a special order for it and thus usually keep it from coming before the House. The greatest power of the Rules Committee, however, is not its power to obstruct so much as its power to bargain. In the words of Representative Eberharter: [16]

Many a chairman of a legislative committee which had considered legislation for months and months was ordered by the Committee on Rules to change the provisions of legislation before a rule would be granted.

And usually the chairmen obey, for half a loaf is better than none.

More than this, however, the Committee can by the form of special orders definitely control the result of roll calls. The simplest form of a special order usually sets a specific time for consideration of the bill, limits debate, divides the debating time between supporters and oppo-

[16] *Congressional Record*, XCVI (Jan. 3, 1951), p. 12.

nents, and prescribes the procedure by which the bill will be brought to a vote on final passage.[17] But special orders may do much more than this. They may, for example, prohibit all points of order, thus preventing the Speaker from ruling against certain expected amendments; or they may prescribe the succession in which amendments shall be put to a vote or even permit only certain specified amendments. They may even be used to kill a bill which has passed both houses by keeping it from going to a conference committee; the federal aid to education bill of 1960 was killed in this way. More rigidly still, they may effectively forestall amendments from the floor, the so-called closed rule. Thus the bill broadening social security in 1949 went through the House under a rule providing that "No amendments shall be in order to said bill except amendments offered by the direction of the Committee on Ways and Means . . . but said amendments shall not be subject to amendment." [18] Since the Committee had spent six months writing the bill and had no intention of offering amendments, this meant that no amendments would be possible. Without this rule, many enervating amendments would certainly have passed the House—a possibility which the supporters of social security greatly wished to avoid. By the kindness of the Rules Committee, they were able to pass their bill intact. Why, one asks, should the House adopt a special order like this when as Chairman Sabath of the Rules Committee admitted, well over half the House apparently wanted to amend the bill? The answer is clear: For the majority that wanted some kind of social security bill— and they were an overwhelming number—it was a choice of this special

[17] Here follows a typical, uncomplicated, special order (H. Res. 205, 71st Congress):

> *Resolved:* That upon the adoption of this resolution it shall be in order to move that the House resolve itself into the Committee of the Whole House on the state of the Union for the consideration of H. R. 10381, a bill to amend the World War veterans' act, 1924, as amended. That after general debate, which shall be confined to the bill and shall continue not to exceed 12 hours, to be equally divided and controlled by the chairman and ranking minority member of the Committee on World War Veterans' Legislation, the bill shall be read for amendment under the 5-minute rule. At the conclusion of the reading of the bill for amendment the committee shall rise and report the bill to the House with such amendments as may have been adopted, and the previous question shall be considered as ordered on the bill and the amendments thereto to final passage without intervening motion except one motion to recommit.

From Clarence Cannon, *Cannon's Precedents of the House of Representatives* (Washington, Government Printing Office, 1907–1935, 8 vols.), VII, section 798.

[18] *Congressional Record,* XCV (Oct. 4, 1949), p. 13,008.

order or none at all. The House usually cannot adopt a special order unless the Rules Committee reports one; so, if it wants the bill and if the Committee will report no rule but this, then the House must adopt it willy-nilly—clearly a Hobson's choice.

Such octopus-like control of the House agenda has, of course, occasioned much criticism, especially since the Rules Committee power— more structural than partisan in nature—does not emanate from the party caucus. Prior to the enlargement of the Committee in 1961, much of the criticism revolved around the fact that four of the eight Democratic members were conservative Southerners out of harmony with a majority of the Democratic caucus.

When the Speaker was separated from the Rules Committee in 1910, the House also fastened on a safety valve, a procedure by which in extreme cases the House might by-pass the Committee to consider special orders. As this rule now stands, a motion to discharge the Committee from consideration of a special order may be made after half the House (218 members) has signed the discharge motion. But a procedure which requires 218 signatures is manifestly difficult to use. Typically, twenty to thirty discharge petitions are started during a Congress but only two or three are actually signed by 218 Congressmen.

Discouraged by the difficulty of discharge motions, the Democratic majority in 1949 adopted the so-called twenty-one-day rule in hope of getting President Truman's civil rights program past the Rules Committee. If the Rules Committee refused to report a proposed special order for twenty-one days after receiving it, the chairman of the legislative committee that had reported the bill involved was permitted to move consideration of the special order. The twenty-one-day rule redistributed a considerable portion of the Rules Committee's power. The beneficiaries were, of course, the chairmen of other committees and the Speaker, who could choose which chairman to recognize on the two days per month set aside for this procedure. The twenty-one-day rule was successfully used eight times during the 81st Congress, which is perhaps why Southern Democrats and Republicans combined to repeal it in January, 1950. So now the Rules Committee has again its monopoly of the toll bridge. But in 1961 the Committee was enlarged from twelve to fifteen members in order to allow the Democratic party to add two persons sympathetic to the majority of that party. Thus, the criticism of the Committee was dampened not by destroying it but by changing its ideology. There is plenty of criticism still, but now it centers more on the very conservative chairman, Howard Smith of Virginia, than on the Committee.

THE LITTLE LEGISLATURES

After the two major concentrations of power, come nineteen smaller concentrations: the legislative committees and especially their chairmen. Like the Rules Committee, their power is more structural than partisan, for they too are only incidentally responsible to the caucus. Their strategic position is this: The Rules Committee has immediate control of the House agenda, the legislative committees exercise a more remote control. The Rules Committee decides which bills on the calendar will get to the floor; the legislative committees decide which introduced bills will get on the calendar. Both the Rules Committee and the legislative committees are winnowers of bills; but the power of the legislative committees is less because their winnowing is farther from the House floor.

The legislative committees are, as Woodrow Wilson said, little legislatures. All bills must be reported out by them before the House can act. Most bills they simply pigeon-hole; the politically important ones they study carefuly, often by public hearings at which interested citizens, bureaucrats, etc., are invited to testify. While hearings may greatly influence public opinion if they are well reported by the press, newsreels, and television, the legislatively significant committee work is that done in secret session. Here the committee decides what amendments, that is what compromises, can satisfy or can be forced on the House, what report, favorable or unfavorable, to make, what strategy to use on the bills, etc. The committee decisions are important because they carry great weight with the House as a whole. Representative Clarence Cannon probably much overestimates committee wisdom, but his advice is certainly what most senior Congressmen would give a freshman colleague: [19]

Generally speaking, and in the absence of convictions to the contrary, Members are justified in voting with the committee. Committees are not infallible but they have had long familiarity with the subject under discussion, and have made an intimate study of the particular bill before the House

[19] Clarence Cannon, *Procedure in the House of Representatives,* House Document #18 (Washington, Government Printing Office, 1963), p. 221, emphasis in original.

and after mature deliberation have made formal recommendations and, other considerations being equal, are entitled to support on the floor. *Members should be particularly wary of proponents of amendments disapproved by the committee who station Members or employees at the doors to accost Members arriving in response to the bells and who have not heard the debate.* It is a questionable practice and should serve to put Members on their guard until they have ascertained the committee's point of view.

So generally, do Congressmen rely on committees for their opinions, so generally do they believe that committee compromises reflect accurately the strength of factions in the House, that committees ordinarily influence the shape of legislation more than the House itself. Even when committees dare not obstruct bills, they can materially alter them. Consider the case of the Employment Act of 1946. While the Full Employment bill went through the Senate substantially as written, it was, from the sponsor's viewpoint, thoroughly mangled in the House. Nearly every section was watered down, a process symbolized by the change of title from "Full Employment" to simply "Employment." Why? Partially it was that the House was then more conservative in temper than the Senate, less likely to sympathize with a measure which embodied Keynesian economics and the spirit of the New Deal. But even more, at least in the opinion of two scholars who have studied the history of the bill in detail, it was that the managers of the bill accidentally allowed it to go to the wrong committee. Because they did not ask the Speaker (who would probably have granted it) for a favorable reference, and instead allowed the Clerk to use his own judgment, it was referred to the minor and highly conservative Committee on Expenditures in Executive Departments instead of either the Committee on Banking and Currency or the Committee on Labor, both of which could just as easily have claimed jurisdiction and both of which were liberal enough to accept the Senate version of the bill. In consequence, the sponsors "were never able fully to surmount the initial disadvantage of reference to the wrong committee." [20]

Of the several members of each little legislature, the chairman is

[20] Carl Brent Swisher, *The Theory and Practice of American National Government* (Boston, Houghton Mifflin, 1951), p. 243. Swisher's brief history of the bill is based on the very complete study by Stephen Kemp Bailey, *Congress Makes a Law: The Story behind the Employment Act of 1946* (New York, Columbia University Press, 1950), which analyzes the unfortunate referral at pp. 150–53 and 178. The best study of the work of committees is Richard F. Fenno, Jr., "The House Appropriations Committe as a Political System," *American Political Science Review*, LVI (1962), pp. 310–24.

by far the most important. He schedules meetings, appoints subcommittees and determines their charges, determines the agenda of the whole committee and presides over its discussion; and, while he is therein presumably subject to committee control, the control procedures are so cumbersome that they are seldom used. Nearly always also the chairman and the ranking minority member serve as the House conferees in conference committees between the House and Senate on their committee's bills. His greatest responsibility, however, is bill management. Once the committee reports, he—or someone chosen by him —plans the strategy of the bill and advocates it before the House. Taking all these duties together, it is clear that the chairman has considerably greater influence than other committee members.

Little legislatures with little presidents would be appropriate time-saving devices if they were small editions of the House as a whole. But they are not, chiefly because they are only half-way partisan. And they are only half-way partisan because seniority as well as caucus politics plays such a large part in their selection.

The caucus does slightly influence committee composition, however, for each committee's seats are divided between the two parties roughly on the basis of their strength in the House. If the House is split in the proportion 56 to 44, the majorty party will probably take 60 percent of each committee's seats, leaving the minority 40 percent. In 1964, the House was split in the ratio of 58 Democrats to 42 Republicans; so on the Agriculture Committee the Democrats took 61 percent of the 36 seats, on the Ways and Means Committee the Democrats took 58 percent of the 24 seats, etc. Considering the feebleness of party discipline, this narrow three-to-two margin is not enough to permit much caucus influence on committee action. Individual members can ignore party lines in committee decisions. While partisan leaders (e.g., Speaker, majority leader, minority leader) have much to say about committee assignments, seniority allows the personnel to slip out of partisan control.

Within the party, committee seats are assigned this way: In the Republican Conference, the Committee on Committees (composed of one Republican from each state having Republican members, each one chosen by the state Republican delegation) nominates Republicans for committee assignments. In the Democratic caucus, the Democratic members of the Ways and Means Committee serve as a committee on committees. In each case the nominations are perfunctorily ratified by the caucus and even more perfunctorily elected by the House. In making assignments the two committees on committees follow as much as possible the rule of seniority. This means that the chairman of each committee is always the member of the majority party with the longest continuous service on the committee. ("Continuous" here means just that, for, if a member's service is broken, he must start again like a freshman Congressman with no seniority at all.) Once a member is assigned to a committee, he keeps his place on the basis of accumulated seniority as long as he is re-elected. When fellow party members senior to him on the committee die, retire, move to other committees, or lose an election, he moves up one notch toward the chairmanship or ranking minority membership. When there is a change in party control of Congress, some of the junior members of the defeated party are pushed out of their committee places. But the seniority they have accumulated gives them first call when a minority seat on the committee next falls vacant. Naturally not all committee assignments are equally attractive. Rules, Appropriations, Ways and Means are regarded as the most desirable committees, and few Congressmen want such politically insignificant assignments as District of Columbia or Post Office and Civil Service. Even though members are limited to one committee place, there are still not enough desirable assignments to go around. Hence freshmen Congressmen with no seniority at all must be content with what places they can get. Thereafter, however, as important committees' seats fall vacant, seniority of service in Congress frequently determines which claimant will fill the vacancy. Thus, over a number of terms of service, Congressmen move from the Committee on Post Office and Civil Service to the Committee on Military Affairs to the Committee on Rules, in each case on the basis of seniority. So pervasive is the system of seniority that partisan judgment usually enters into committee assignment only when two members have exactly the same seniority claims, and that is usually when as beginners they have none at all and are certain to get unimportant assignments. And so far does seniority substitute for partisanship that, as Representative Plumley of Vermont has written: [21]

The new Member meets the rule of seniority when he applies for his first office room. . . . He meets with [it] at any official dinner he attends. The new Member sits near the foot of the table. . . . The new Members find the rule of seniority when they apply for committee assignment. The older

[21] *Congressional Record*, XCVI (May 5, 1950), pp. 6,554–55.

Members are given the favored places. . . . The new Member finds it in the committee room when he attends the first meeting of his committee. He finds his name on the place at the foot of the table. . . . The chairman of every committee is . . . the longest serving majority member of the committee. . . . Almost invariably the conferees appointed by both House and Senate are the oldest—in point of service—Republicans and the oldest Democratic Members serving on the committees reporting out the bills in each House. Conferees have had much to do with the final writing of . . . bills in which there is a difference between House and Senate. Members may orate and the two Houses may vote, but the conferees, the old boys, bring back the language agreed upon, and it will be adopted.

The seniority system tends greatly to separate party and structural leadership. Congressmen hold seats on important committees and eventually committee chairmanships only if they represent "safe" districts—districts, that is, like rural Alabama or rural New York where the Representative is not even likely to meet opposition in primaries. In 1964, in the middle of the 88th Congress, the average service of all Members was eleven years; but the average service of committee chairmen was twenty-six years, and of ranking minority members, over twenty. For the men with long service from safe districts, the electoral sanction means relatively little; hence they often represent extremist elements in their own party. Representatives from marginal districts are, of course, much closer to the partisan scene nationally. They must worry constantly about the next election in much the same terms as national party leaders like the President. In this sense the positions of a Democrat from Iowa or a Republican from Connecticut are much more relevant to party success than the positions of a Democrat from Texas or a Republican from South Dakota. In the majority party caucus—which is the majority because it has won a number of marginal districts—there are, perhaps, many more Congressmen who worry about the next election than there are those who do not. Yet the seniority system tends to promote the unworried to important structural leadership.

There is something to be said in favor of seniority rules, however. For one thing, they guarantee that committee leaders have learned something about the unique parliamentary procedure and the hundreds of informal channels of authority in the House. For another thing, they reduce the opportunity for factional fights inside the party. Every alternative to seniority would be almost certain to foster irrational personality conflicts. If the caucus, for example, were to elect committee chairmen, certainly some of the defeated candidates would find it hard to work with their rivals. Party harmony is precarious enough as it is, without the interjection of purely personal factionalism.

A favorite reform proposed by those who wish "to strengthen Congress" is therefore to eliminate seniority, at least in the choice of committee membership. What is not usually recognized in such proposals is that some other persons would be greatly strengthened—almost surely the Speaker and the majority leader. This would take us back to the situation of 1890 to 1910, to the era of Czar Reed and Uncle Joe Cannon. In short, it would make the Speaker better able to help or obstruct the President. Given these alternatives, most of the proponents of reform—who are typically exponents of Presidential leadership and who simply misunderstand where their proposals lead—would, I believe, prefer no change.

Yet when all this is said, it remains true that seniority's separation of party and structural leadership greatly dilutes the power to lead. Instead of laws made by party majorities working under the leaders of the party caucus we get laws made by highly temporary majorities working usually under the committee chairmen and the Rules Committee as well as the majority leader and the Speaker. It is this dilution of leadership which accounts for the phenomenon of bill managers and the inordinate emphasis placed on political strategy.

THE CAUCUS AND ITS LEADERS

Even if much of the power to lead is lodged in men who owe most of their influence to the structure of Congress, the power of the caucus is far from negligible. The caucus itself is, of course, too unwieldy to make many decisions; but the officers elected by the caucus are indeed influential men.

On the surface party organization in the House is absurdly weak. Early in the nineteenth century, when parties were smaller and more homogeneous, party policy was often actually thrashed out in caucus. But now, with parties divided internally into left and right, urban and rural, nationalist and isolationist, the caucus cannot possibly make policy. The Republican party acknowledges this fact openly. It calls the party group simply a "conference" and it regards its policy decisions as merely advisory, in no way binding on members. The Democratic caucus presents a façade of discipline, but it too can make only advisory decisions on policy. Furthermore, it seldom meets. Presumably, when a decision is reached by two-thirds of the Democratic members, the whole party is bound to abide by it in the House; but no member is bound if he did not attend the caucus, if the subject involves an interpretation of the Constitution, or if the caucus policy is inconsistent with a pledge made to constituents. When there are so many loopholes, caucus discipline is clearly unreal.

But even if the caucus itself is insignificant, the officers it elects are not. These are the Speaker, the majority and minority leaders, the whips, and the policy committee. Of these, the Speaker and the leaders should be regarded as the real centers of the party. The whips are simply the leaders' aides whose duty it is to explain the party position to recalcitrant members, to round up party members for roll calls, etc. The policy committee, consisting of members chosen to represent areas of the country and presided over by the party leader, serves chiefly to advise him. With him it plans the party policy and serves as a transmission belt of ideas back and forth between the leader and the party rank and file.

The really important agents of the caucus are the leaders and the Speaker. Since the Speaker spends much time as presiding officer, the majority leader necessarily makes most of the routine agreements and compromises on party policy. In the words of Representative Plumley: [22]

> The leader is all the title implies. He leads in party debate, brings forward party programs and policies. His advocacy of or opposition to proposed legislation indicates the party preference. The majority leader has much control over what comes up, and when, on the legislative program from week to week. When he makes a motion it is nearly always carried. He usually makes the motion to adjourn, and it always carries. If someone else, not authorized to do so, makes a motion to adjourn, it is nearly always defeated.

One must not infer from this, however, that the majority leader is an independent agent. He is rather the compromise-maker. The reason his motions always carry is not any sort of dictatorial power, but simply the fact that he and the whips have obtained party agreement on them beforehand. He collects opinions and weaves them together; and, while the weaver can determine the width of the weave, he has to work with whatever thread he has. He is, in short, a broker in a free market, not

[22] *Congressional Record*, XCVI (May 5, 1950), p. 6,554.

a monopolist in a closed one. The real extent of the majority leader's power is pretty well implied in this congressional interchange: [23]

Mr. McCORMACK. [Democratic majority leader] . . . I said to the gentleman [Mr. Farrington, Delegate from Hawaii] further back than 3 months ago . . . that I think both these bills should come up one after the other [i.e. an Alaska statehood and a Hawaii statehood bill]. I frankly told him I thought Alaska should come up first. That is the gentleman's agreement that I made with the distinguished Delegate from Hawaii, and if anyone had asked me the same question, I would have told them th. same thing.

Insofar as I am able to keep my agreement, I intend to do so. I hope the House will enable me to carry out an agreement that I think is fair, an agreement that I think is just, and an agreement that I think is honest. . . . I intend to keep my word. Of course, the House is supreme, and I am but the servant of the House. I will keep my word unless the House insists otherwise. If this rule [i.e. a special order for the Alaska bill] is adopted today, which I hope it will be, I also have a hope that the other rule might be adopted, but if not, it is my intention not to bring the consideration of the Alaska bill up until the Hawaii rule is adopted. That is my intention. Now, I am just an individual, but I have made an agreement, and my agreement means something to me. I think it is the fair thing to do, and I think that the proponents of both bills ought to recognize from a practical angle as to their mutual advantage to have the House know of both coming up one after the other, and to have a situation exist where this can be done.

* * *

Mr. HALLECK. [Republican, Indiana.] The gentleman from Massachusetts has said that he insisted on the Alaska bill coming up first. I wonder if he could tell us why he was so insistent about that.

Mr. McCORMACK. Certainly, I do not want Hawaii to go through and have Alaska defeated, or have Alaska encounter difficulty. We are all practical men. You cannot object to my doing that. I am keeping my word with the gentleman. I have said that both should come up with Alaska, in my opinion, coming up first. Alaska is good Democratic Territory and Hawaii is Republican. Let us be frank about that. Does the gentleman object to that?

Mr. HALLECK. Certainly not. . . .

The majority leader's job, as this colloquy indicated, is to plan party strategy and the House agenda (here to devise a strategy that will bring Democratic Alaska, whose claims to statehood were perhaps weaker, into

[23] *Ibid.* (Jan. 23, 1950), p. 777.

the Union at the same time as Republican Hawaii). But Mr. Mc-Cormack is very conscious that his plans may go wrong. Like every other majority leader, he is aware that party discipline is weak, that many Congressmen often vote against their party. If political parties were nationally centralized and if party attachment really determined each Congressman's position, then he might be as self-assured as party leaders in the House of Commons. But this is not the case. Mr. Mc-Cormack is called a leader; but he does not speak as one having authority.

SENATE LEADERSHIP

The power to lead is diffused even more through the Senate than the House. The Senate knows no great concentration of party and structural leadership like the Speaker; nor does any group like the Rules Committee have a grip on its mechanisms. Although the Vice-President has about the same formal power as the Speaker, he dare not use it arbitrarily, for the Senate, unlike the House, does not hesitate to reverse the Chair's decisions. Similarly, the Senate Rules Committee is an innocuous body. It cannot report special orders, which are really a kind of cloture, because the Senate carefully protects the freedom to filibuster. In the absence of a strong presiding officer or an effective traffic director, the chief centers of Senate leadership are, therefore, committee chairmen, floor leaders, and the informal leaders of little coteries, factions and blocs.

The committee chairmen and the majority and minority leaders have about the same power and position in the Senate as in the House. They are chosen in the same way and have the same duties. The Senate chairmen are probably a little stronger because Senators divide their time among several committees, thus giving less attention to each one and by default leaving more power in the hands of the chairmen. The floor leaders are perhaps a little weaker, for the sense of party —on which they subsist—seems weaker in the Senate than in the House. Furthermore, since 1947 there have been majority and minority policy committees, elected by the caucus, staffed with research assistants, and charged with planning party strategy. To some degree, as yet indeterminate, these committees probably dilute the leaders' powers simply because they have the same job as the leaders.

The power of the informal leaders of blocs is, however, unique in the Senate. It is impossible to imagine a group of fifteen or twenty Representatives who hold no important party or structural office, bending House to their will. Yet even one Senator can by the freedom of unlimited debate sometimes force the rest of the Senate to agree with him.

The popular image of the filibuster today is something of a mixture of Huey Long and "The Man" Bilbo: Flamboyant megalomaniacs, raucous and self-willed demagogues, sometimes droning irrelevant statistics, othertimes declaiming impassionedly on the glories of fried oysters, pot-likker, and Southern womanhood. But one lone, petulant Senator is merely an amusing symptom of a much more serious disease. When ten or twelve or twenty Senators determine to obstruct action, they can spell each other on the floor; they can invent all sorts of dilatory motions, roll calls and quorum calls; and they can thus avoid the necessity of heroic action by one man like "Fighting Bob" LaFollette's famous eighteen-hour spech in 1908. Twenty Senators can keep the Senate at a standstill for more than a month—as a group of Southerners did when they filibustered against the anti-lynching bill from January 6 to February 21, 1937.[24] In fact, any "little group of wilful men," as President Wilson angrily described the eleven Senators who filibustered against the Armed Ship bill in 1917, can render "the great government of the United States helpless and contemptible." So great is the power of little coteries to obstruct that the mere threat of a filibuster is often enough for a small minority to extort fundamental concessions from the majority. Roland Young cites this colloquy, which occurred during the discussion of the conference report on the Food, Drug and Cosmetic Act of 1938, as an excellent example of the effectiveness of the threat: [25]

Mr. OVERTON. May I inquire of the Senator from New York what was done with reference to the provisions of the House bill making whiskey "misbranded" if distilled from a source other than grain?

Mr. COPELAND. I told the House conferees that some of the most able filibusterers in the Senate were so opposed to that amendment that we could not accept it, and it was stricken from the bill.

Mr. OVERTON. Let me make the observation that the Senator from New York gave correct information to the House conferees.

[24] For good descriptions of this and other famous filibusters, see Franklin L. Burdette, *Filibustering in the Senate* (Princeton, Princeton University Press, 1940), pp. 191–99 and *passim*.
[25] Cited in Young, *op. cit.*, p. 144 from *Congressional Record*, LXXXIII (June 10, 1938), pp. 8,737–38.

Thus unlimited debate makes the threat of filibustering real and thereby sometimes permits minority control of the action of both houses.

Such continual travesty of democratic procedure is, of course, denounced, often and irately. Every few years some particularly flagrant minority triumph shocks us to the realization that this "democracy" can be very undemocratic. We ought not be shocked, however, for is not the very structure of the Senate, the geographic misrepresentation, hostile to majority rule? That basic fear of majority rule, which the Constitution embodied in both indirect election of Senators (abolished as recently as 1913) and equal representation of States, is the root of filibustering. This is why the attempts to reform the Senate, to impose cloture, have so regularly failed. After the famous Armed Ship bill filibuster in 1917, when the eleven Senators' names were inscribed on "rolls of dishonor" throughout the country and LaFollette was hanged in effigy on many college campuses, public and Presidential pressure impelled the Senate to adopt a cloture rule. But the rule required a two-thirds vote to end debate and was successfully invoked only four times. In 1948, Southern Democrats, afraid of Truman's civil rights program, managed with Republican help to change the requirement from two-thirds of those voting to two-thirds of the whole Senate (sixty-seven out of one hundred). Since a few Senators are always legitimately absent and since quite a few more are very likely to defend the Senate's freedom to filibuster (even though at the same time they may publicly deprecate each particular filibuster), this made cloture almost impossible.

In 1959 the old rule (two-thirds of those voting) was once again adopted under pressure from liberals who were hoping to put through a reasonably strong civil rights bill. Interestingly enough, this slightly easier cloture rule failed of use on the civil rights bill in 1960 but was used successfully for the first time in thirty-five years in 1962, not for the sake of civil rights, but to stop a liberal filibuster to prevent American Telephone and Telegraph Company from having excessive ownership of the Communications Satellite Corporation. Two years later, in 1964, cloture was successfully used for the first time on a civil rights bill. It took literally four months of debate to bring the Senate to the point of using it; but they did use it—which indicates that when a majority is very large and very determined it can overcome the advantage cloture gives to relatively small minorities. The civil rights majority of 1964 consisted of all Northern Democrats, most Northern Republicans, and some Border Democrats. This vast majority was created only by the construction of a bill which, while emanating originally from Northern Democrats, could have a tone and content acceptable to the Lincolnesque traditions of Northern Republicans and which could be construed as a project not of its originators but of its newest supporters. Such a bill is difficult to fashion. In this case it took four months and then was concluded only with the shadow of the forthcoming Presidential election cast over the whole proceedings. But I reiterate: It is possible to construct such a bill and it is possible to invoke cloture to pass it—but only under extraordinary circumstances, such as a four-month period of concentration on one bill by one hundred Senators. There is no prospect of closing debate by a simple majority; one should not expect it as long as the Senate continues to have its present structure.

STRATEGY IN CONGRESS

No one can deny that the power to lead in Congress is divided up among many people: permanent leaders, temporary and informal leaders, and even occasionally every member. Some scholars have attempted to find coherence in the system, however, in the existence of semipermanent blocs. David Truman, for example, has applied the Rice method of bloc analysis to roll calls in the Congress and discovered some theretofore barely visible blocs. Niemi and I, however, applied a less static and less summary statistic to roll calls in the 81st Congress (First Session) and discovered that the so-called blocs themselves shifted considerably in membership during the course of a single session. We calculated a "power index," based on members' appearance on the winning side of roll calls, and discovered that, in general, a member's high power index in the first half of the session did not indicate he would have a high power index in the second half.[26] I conclude, therefore, that since the chance to win is divided up in almost—but not quite—random ways, the power to lead is divided up almost randomly also.

It is this fact that makes parliamentary strategy so important. "Given the present Congressional set-up," says Roland Young, "where the lines

[26] David Truman, *The Congressional Party* (New York, John Wiley and Sons, 1959); and William H. Riker and Donald Niemi, "The Stability of Coalitions on Roll Calls in the House of Representatives," *American Political Science Review*, LVI (1962), pp. 58–65.

of political power are never clear, legislation cannot be enacted without an extensive use of political maneuvering." [27] Good strategy, that is the sum of all the plans and tricks to influence events, is the key to success in every social activity, war, business, poker, and politics; but no place is a sense of strategy more important than in the United States Congress.

Strategy enters into every stage of the legislative process. It is involved in those grand political combinations by which great leaders construct a party majority which lasts for a generation. Presidents like Jefferson and Franklin Roosevelt and political manipulators like Mark Hanna are counted as great politicians simply because they had enough sense of strategy to make a majority combination in congressional elections, a combination which facilitated the passage of their legislative program.

Similarly, strategy is involved in every stage of the passage of a bill. Bills are passed because some people know how to manipulate parliamentary procedure. Witness the examples already cited of Speaker Rainey's use of recognition for the economy bill of 1933 or Majority Leader McCormack's control of the agenda for the Alaska Statehood bill in 1949. Even such simple procedures as the choice of a title may involve strategic consideration. For example, the Employment Act of 1946 was named by its sponsors the "Full Employment Bill" because they believed that no one could oppose "full employment." Here, however, the strategy backfired. The opposition was able to point out that the title implied a promise of far more than the bill could reasonably be expected to deliver.[28]

Even though debate on the floor seldom influences votes and is on the whole an unimportant part of legislative procedure, a skilled strategist can sometimes debate a bill through. In his memoirs Speaker Cannon recites one case in which strategy in debate provided the margin of success for a bill. The White House was being enlarged and President Theodore Roosevelt had, with an authorization of $50,000, made plans for repairs costing $650,000. When Cannon reported a deficiency appropriation of the large amount, he "started a sensational debate": [29]

[27] Young, op. cit., p. 133.
[28] Stephen Kemp Bailey, op. cit., p. 46. This fascinating case history of a bill points out many other examples of strategic considerations involved in apparently routine and minor procedures.
[29] L. White Busbey, op. cit., pp. 228–29.

I explained the bill as fairly and clearly as I could, knowing there would be much opposition. I sat down waiting an opportunity to ask for a vote. As the debate increased in personal abuse, John Wesley Gaines, of Tennessee, sprung a new line of attack by calling attention to the sale, at auction, of the sideboard presented to Mrs. Hayes by the W.C.T.U. as a testimonial of her prohibition of liquor at the White House table. Mr. Gaines gave the history of the sideboard, and then, in a dramatic manner, such as Gaines was master of, he demanded that I explain why the sideboard of the W.C.T.U. now rested in an Avenue saloon for the service of whiskey. The House was in an uproar and some of the Republicans who did not like Roosevelt, and were afraid of the temperance vote, were getting restive. The situation seemed to call for a diversion, and I, rising to reply to Gaines, tried to assume the same dramatic attitude as my interrogator and said very solemnly: "Mr. Chairman: We are told that good Abigail Adams was wont to hang the White House wash in the East Room to dry. Great God! What has become of that clothes line?"

The House broke into a roar of laughter and as it began to subside, I demanded a vote. The item was passed without division. That one minute bit of buffoonery—you could not dignify it with the name of speech—created the diversion to get away from debate that had no place in considering an appropriation bill. It saved time and embarrassment to many Members who would have felt compelled to vote against the item if the debate had continued along the line of Mr. Gaines' criticism. A laugh turned the tide and passed the bill. It was not wit or humor. It was only a diversion. . . .

Here is suggested in brief and clear form some of the essential problems of parliamentary strategy. Cannon's buffoonery worked because he knew the temper of the House and all the intricacies of the political issues and side-issues involved in the question, because he knew how to use parliamentary procedure in exactly the right way at exactly the right time, because he knew what kind of debate would be appropriate at just that moment, and above all because he had the wit and skill to use his knowledge as he did.

Strategy includes more than more quick wittedness in debate or an exploitation of parliamentary rules. Fundamentally, strategy involves negotiation over the content of bills to create a majority. In this sense, the essence of strategy is the manipulation of ideology. Every important bill that passes is the end product of a process that can be described abstractly thus: In original form, a bill satisfies the ideological goals of its sponsors and supporters who are presumably less than a majority. (If they were a majority, as is the case on unimportant bills which go through the consent procedure, strategy in modifications would not be necessary.) To attract additional supporters, the ideological content of the bill must be modified. Hence, the problem of its original supporters is to select those modifications (1) that they find least objectionable and (2) that are sufficient to attract a majority to the support of the bill. The modifications are then admitted at appropriate moments and thus a majority is formed. On the other hand, the problem of the opponents of the bill is to find some ideological combination that will render the bill distasteful—even perhaps to its original supporters. The day-to-day operation of a legislature is largely concerned with these two kinds of strategic problems, for each of which I now offer an example.[30]

In the struggle over civil rights bills in the last decade, the main problem for the supporters has been the fact that strong civil rights bills could easily get a simple majority in the House (and in the Senate, for that matter), but they could not get the two-thirds majority required for cloture in the Senate. Of course all Southern Democrats would oppose cloture on civil right bills, and usually as many Republicans who presumably oppose cloture on principle have joined them. Twelve times since 1938 the advocates of civil rights tried to impose cloture on a House-passed civil rights bill. Only in 1964 did they succeed. This fact presented the sponsors with this dilemma: that the civil rights bills coming out of the House were either (1) very strong and thus so distasteful to the crucial one-sixth in the Senate (i.e. those who might join a simple majority to vote for cloture) that cloture could not be obtained or (2) very weak and thus able to pass the Senate with or without cloture. The Civil Rights Acts of 1956 and 1960 fell in the latter category.[31] The sponsors of the Civil Rights Act of 1964 by clever strategic maneuvers were able to break through this dilemma by writing a strong bill in the House (many of the provisions of which they were willing to abandon in bargaining for cloture votes in the Senate) and allowing the Senate Minority Leader (Senator Dirksen) to pick the portions to be abandoned. Thus they allowed their bill to become Senator Dirksen's bill and at the same time obtained the strongest civil rights bill since Reconstruction. Senator Dirksen did not in fact greatly weaken the bill (he modified the power of the United States to prosecute for

[30] For a general discussion of the theoretical features of legislative strategy see: William H. Riker, *The Theory of Political Coalitions* (New Haven, Yale University Press, 1963), chapter V.

[31] See Daniel M. Berman, *A Bill Becomes a Law* (New York, The Macmillian Company, 1962).

violations until a "clear pattern" of local violations occurred, and he modified the procedures for convictions on criminal contempt to provide for jury trials); but he did get credit for passing it, which he certainly believed important in an election year.

The strategy by which the Civil Rights Act was passed embodies the essential elements of successful affirmative strategy. The strategy by which the aid to school construction bill of 1956 was defeated embodies, on the other hand, the essential elements of successful negative strategy. In the case of that bill, there probably was a clear majority prepared to vote for it in the House. But this majority was split between those who would and those who would not like to amend it to provide that no federal money be spent in states which had segregated public schools. This is the situation that the opponents of the bill exploited. By voting to attach the amendment they could make the amended bill so unpalatable to some of its original supporters that these offended persons would vote against the bill on final passage. This is precisely what happened. Nearly one hundred Northern and Southern Republicans who were opposed to federal aid voted with Northern Democrats and Republicans who favored federal aid to attach the so-called Powell amendment prohibiting aid to segregated schools. Then those Northern Republicans who had helped attach the amendment voted with the Southern Democrats (many of whom had originally favored federal aid but who were of course deeply offended by the amendment) to defeat the bill.[32]

This chapter ends with an emphasis on the crucial significance of parliamentary strategy for this simple reason: No important bill goes through Congress smoothly. Stephen K. Bailey, at the conclusion of his careful case history of a bill, remarks that: [33]

Put in its baldest form, the story of S. 380 adds up to the fact that majority sentiment expressed in popular elections for a particular economic policy can be, and frequently is, almost hopelessly splintered by the power struggles of competing political, administrative, and private interests, and is finally pieced together, if at all, only by the most laborious, complicated, and frequently covert coalition strategies.

[32] This is an instance of the so-called paradox of voting, the main weapon in the arsenal of defenders of the *status quo*. On the paradox see: William H. Riker, "Voting and the Summation of Preferences," *American Political Science Review*, LV (1962), pp. 900–11.

[33] Stephen K. Bailey, *op. cit.*, p. 237.

The liberty head dime is stamped with the Roman *fasces* to symbolize the united power of the American people. But the symbolism distorts the reality. In America the bundle of rods is often untied and the axe is often without force to act for the popular will. How can it be otherwise when the power to lead is divided up into such small bits of conflicting ambition?

6.

The President

> Goodness by itself is not enough: There must also be a capacity
> for being active in doing good.
>
> —ARISTOTLE, *Politics,* 1325b

". . . THE GREAT PRESIDENTS WERE ALSO STRONG PRESIDENTS . . ."

Many readers probably sensed an atmosphere of unreality throughout the preceding chapter because, in a description of the legislative process, the President, the greatest legislator, was only incidentally mentioned. Indulgent ones will of course recognize that analysis requires abstraction; but the real justification for the omission is that the President is important enough to deserve separate study. His office unconsciously denies the separation of powers theory; it combines the executive power with the main legislative responsibility. Here then ends the search begun in Chapter 5 for an agent of the majority who can cure the constitutional palsies.

To bring the separated powers together for majority action, one branch must lead, even dominate the other two. And this only the executive can conceivably do. Despite the misleading division of sovereignty in the Constitution, government is actually a continuous, indivisible process of which legislation is the beginning, judgment is the end, and execution is all that lies between. Congress and the Court cannot lead the other branches, because the Constitution formally vests each of them with power over only a small part of the process. Of course such formal division of authority is unrealistic. Power over a part is enough to cast a shadow over the whole. But, while shadowy influence may check and balance, it cannot give coherent leadership. The President can. His formal authority extends not only over execution but over legislation and judgment as well. And of course, therefore, his informal influence extends much further.

The Constitutional and actual arrangements of power can perhaps be schematically portrayed: Divide a line into three parts corresponding to the Constitutional separation; draw beneath it three other parallels representing the three branches, solid parallels where authority is formally vested by the Constitution, dotted parallels where influence is indirect. The parallel representing the President should be solid for almost its whole length, while each of the others should be dotted in many places:

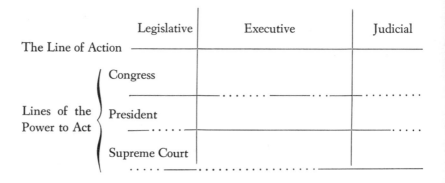

If this schematization even roughly represents reality, then certainly neither Congress nor the Court have much chance to lead. Such, in fact, is the lesson of history. The Court, relegated to the very end of the process, has seldom tried to dominate the whole. And when it has tried, the Thirteenth Amendment and the threat of Roosevelt's court reform bill have sufficiently denied its pretensions. Congress has a surer foothold on the whole line, however, so that its attempts to control have sometimes succeeded. From the assassination of Lincoln to the Spanish War we almost had what Woodrow Wilson called "congressional government." Writing in 1885 when for twenty years the White House had been occupied by a bewildered general and several dark horses who allowed Congress to usurp their prerogative with such devices as the Tenure of Office Acts, he observed that "the balances of the Constitution are for the most part only ideal. Congress is predominant over its so-called coordinate branches." [1] But "congressional government" was

---

[1] Woodrow Wilson, *Congressional Government* (Fifteenth edition, Boston, Houghton Mifflin, 1960), p. 52.

already in decay when Wilson wrote; and in the second edition in 1900 he predicted that Presidential resurgence might "put this whole volume hopelessly out of date." [2] "Congressional government" failed then, never to be revived again. It failed because Congress was (and is) too disorganized internally. But more, it failed because the President's prerogative stretched farther over the line than Congress's. Even at the height of "congressional government" an independent President like Hayes could thwart Congress by exploiting its internal divisions. Though he was unable to lead it to positive action, Hayes still could dethrone Conkling and Blaine and carry out his major administrative policies.

The Presidency stands athwart most of the governing process. Surely this was not what the founding fathers intended if we take seriously their elaborate separations. Still, the Constitution is a paradox. The Presidency may have been originally designed to be no more than the name implies, a presiding officer, simply a focus of national loyalty, a pseudo-monarch from whose person might radiate a new myth of American nationality and self-governing liberty, a role for Washington and Washington alone. But beyond Washington's republican dignity is the office that overshadows all else, a one-man depository of prerogative and a third, one-man house of the legislature.

The explanation of this paradox is, as set forth in Chapter 4, that the founding fathers wanted to counterbalance legislative power. They wanted to avoid what seemed to them the chief defect of state constitutions, the plenary power to govern in popular state legislatures. As men of action, they knew how impotent was government by assembly; as conservative Whigs they feared too much popular rule. And so they tilted the scales the other way toward executive vigor, making the President potentially the greatest officer of all, with enough power to dominate the other branches of government.

Interpreted this way, the Constitution is seen to embody a greater compromise than any of those the glosses usually mention. Between the closet philosophy of Montesquieu and Madison and the administrative commonsense of Wilson and Hamilton stands the final draft of the Constitution—a compromise the greater for being only half-conscious and misunderstood.

This reconciliation of a strong executive with separated powers dominates both our constitutional theorizing and our constitutional history.

[2] *Ibid.*, p. xiii.

It is visible microscopically in the internal inconsistency of that primary rationalization of the Constitution, *The Federalist Papers*. Usually they are interpreted as the classic American formulation of the separation of powers dogma. But they are more. At the same time their authors quoted Montesquieuian aphorisms to allay the scepticism of the common man, they also pointed out to the elite who understood: [3]

A feeble Executive implies a feeble execution of the government. A feeble execution is but another phrase for a bad execution; and a government ill executed, whatever it may be in theory, must be, in practice, a bad government.

"Energy in the Executive" was what Hamilton wanted. And, in spite of his cryptomonarchist principles, he was relatively satisfied with the framers' work. "The executive department," he observed, ". . . combines, as far as republican principles will admit, all the requisites to energy." [4]

Similarly, this great compromise between sovereignty and impotence is visible macroscopically in the whole course of our constitutional history, in the variegated tempo of governing in America, those curious decade-long shifts from energetic action under a strong President to almost psychopathic lassitude when three haggling ambitions allow great crises to develop. The great constitutional compromise explains this curious periodicity. The Presidential office is a fluctuating star, never at any certain position in our national constellation. When Presidents are great heroes elected by a vast and vigorous majority, or when they are forced by catastrophe and crisis to unexpected greatness, then the Presidency is as powerful as the sun, obscuring all other stars with its own light. But when neither heroic personality nor calamitous circumstance expands its influence, then it is only one star among many, almost unnoticeable in a Milky Way. Yet through all this fluctuation one can discern a long-run trend of increasing brightness: [5]

The great Presidents [says Arthur Schlesinger] were also strong Presidents, magnifying the executive branch at the expense of the other branches of the government. . . . From Washington's time onward, each conceived of the office in heroic proportions, and each left it more powerful and influential than he found it.

[3] *The Federalist*, No. 70.
[4] *The Federalist*, No. 77.
[5] Arthur M. Schlesinger, *Paths to the Present* (New York, Macmillan, 1949), p. 105.

The successors of each hero President have institutionalized and bureaucratized a part of the hero's legacy. But however much the next hero stands on the shoulders of the great men before him, Presidential leadership is still, as Edward S. Corwin observed, "the function of two highly variable factors—Crisis and Personality" and it is for that reason still also "a highly discontinuous feature of our constitutional system." [6]

Here then is the crux of our problem: The President can unite the separated powers to express the majority will; yet a great enough President is not always available when majorities need him. Only occasionally do we get the proper combination of crisis, personality, and prerogative for democratic self-control. The lesson of our political history is that we can overcome the separation, *if the crisis is great enough.* But almost never have we been able to avert the crises everyone expects. Hence our solutions have always been temporary expedients, devised in crisis.

And so this great question of our day: Can the American democracy learn to govern effectively *before* crises as well as *in* them? We have met the challenge of many crises successfully, so our record should give us confidence; but it should also make us pause. For observe: each crisis, each time a hero President has proved his heroism is evidence that in ordinary times our government lacks the power to govern well. Were the twentieth century exactly like the nineteenth, perhaps we could continue to assume that our proven reserves of power would be forthcoming in the future. But we are not our grandfathers. Our society is vastly more complex than any in the world before; and yet it lacks the delicate integration by custom that characterizes simpler societies. It is always liable, therefore, to devastating breakdown, unless we can learn conscious social control. We must learn to plan, in the brief interludes of quiet, for the time of troubles always ahead. But can we plan through a government based on irrational conflicts of ambition? Can we work the plans with a government based on deadlock? Of course not— and so our problem: How can we transform the President from an intermittent miracle-maker to an ever-effective agent of the majority? "Goodness by itself is not enough: there must also be a capacity for being active in doing good."

The rest of this chapter will be devoted to a detailed examination of the current status of the Presidency, always with a view (in Aris-

[6] Edward S. Corwin, *The President: Office and Powers* (2nd edition, New York, New York University Press, 1941), p. 306.

totle's phrase) toward making goodness active, toward strengthening Presidential leadership. For the sake of comprehensible analysis the Presidential character will be arbitrarily divided up into three parts:

(1) Chief Executive: his power here actually corresponds to the middle category of the tripartite division.

(2) Chief of State: this includes the power to act when not directed by law, mostly in war and foreign affairs, what Locke called the federative power.

(3) Chief Legislator: his power here rests on his party leadership and certain constitutional prerogatives.

But in so separating these functions for analysis we must not forget that to the incumbent they are inseparable. For him the problem invariably is, as Neustadt expresses it, to "make those powers work for him." [7]

THE EXECUTIVE POWER:
MORE THAN MERE DOING

The executive power is the prime element of Presidential authority. It rests on the absolute declaration, "The executive Power shall be vested in a President, . . ." and on the admonition "he shall take care that the Laws be faithfully executed." [8] Thereby the President is given authority over and made responsible for the vast administrative machinery of the national government, to the tune of 2,500,000 civilian employees in 1963. But the executive power comprehends more than mere doing, more than mere execution of law. It includes as well making plans and policy, providing the men to execute, and even interpreting law—powers that will be described in detail in the following paragraphs.

Over and above the tremendous amount of routine doing, the President also makes national policy. To the degree that policy is expressed in law, he shares his power with Congress; but, though shared, his power is probably the greater because, usually, he initiates new policy. That the executive should initiate seems inconsistent with the democratic tradition in which it is often assumed that Congressmen are the authentic voice of the people. Yet the President, also elected, is just as

[7] Richard Neustadt, *Presidential Power* (New York, John Wiley and Sons, 1960), p. vii.
[8] Article II, sec. 1, clause 1; Article II, sec. 3, clause 1.

authentic a voice as all of Congress; and more, by reason of his executive responsibility, he is in the best position to know what to do. Engaged in day to day routine, he is learned in the actual problems of doing. And so, in the conflict between two expressions of the popular will, fortune favors him because he knows how to give the will effect. Thus it is that the initiation of policy is inseparably linked with the actual execution of it. Almost all the great new departures of the last fifty years have been sponsored originally by the President. What is true of the grand form of public policy is equally true of year-to-year planning. Although the Constitution specifically provides "All bills raising revenue shall originate in the House of Representatives," the financial complexity of contemporary government has lately overwhelmed it. Through the budget procedure Congress asks the President to tell it how much money ought to be raised and how it ought to be spent. Final decisions, both on grand policy and yearly planning, of course remain with Congress. But in a variety of ways it has asked the President, who knows because he executes, to tell it what to do.

Besides doing and planning, the executive power also includes choosing the men to do and to plan. The Constitution provides that the President "shall nominate, and by and with the Advice and Consent of the Senate, shall appoint" public officials, and then notes the exception that "Congress may by Law vest the Appointment of . . . inferior officers . . . in the President alone, in the Courts of Law, or in the Heads of Departments." But political development has modified these commands in several ways. Most "inferior offices" are now filled by thoroughly routinized civil service procedures (85 to 90 percent of federal employees), which makes appointment irrelevant in the assessment of power. While the President nominates for all the important offices and some "inferior" ones, so jealously has the Senate preserved its power to advise that today Congressmen or state chairmen of the President's party not only advise but actually control nominations for most patronage jobs physically located outside Washington (that is, district attorneys and judges, tax collectors, postmasters, etc.). So strong is the pull of localism that Congressmen customarily control the appointment even of heads of agencies when the central office of the agency is in their district (e.g., directors of Federal Reserve Banks and Land Banks). Thus the President's prerogative to nominate has in many cases actually shifted to Congress, though of course for the appearance of legality the President proposes to the Senate the names that Congressmen tell him to. The sanction for this reversal of roles is "senatorial courtesy," the custom by which the Senate refuses to consent to nominations if the Senators from the state in which the offices are located object. Occasionally Presidents have tried to assert their constitutional prerogative only to find the sanction applied, as Eisenhower found during much of his second term, when Democratic Senators held back consent on many nominations, hoping for a Democratic President in 1960 who would submit Democratic names. I suspect that senatorial courtesy has influenced many Presidents to advocate civil service reform, since they have preferred to neutralize patronage that they could not control.

But the President does control the appointment to the highest offices. They are located in Washington and "senatorial courtesy" does not apply. Since the Civil War the Senate has only thrice actually refused to consent to nominations for the Cabinet. In 1877 the jealous Blaine and the corrupt Conkling actually proposed to reject all of Hayes' Cabinet nominations. Had they carried the Senate with them, possibly they would have altered the whole nature of the Presidency. But they did not. The general rule then as now seems to be that mere political opposition is not enough for rejection; there must also be a reason, however specious, like corruption or statutory disqualification. In 1869 A. T. Stewart, the inventor of department stores, was not confirmed as Secretary of the Treasury on the ground that an old statute disqualified merchants. In 1925 Charles B. Warren was not confirmed as Attorney-General because he would have been responsible for enforcing anti-trust laws which as head of a beet-sugar company he had been accused of violating. And in 1959 Lewis Strauss was not confirmed as Secretary of Commerce after prior service as chairman of the Atomic Energy Commission, apparently because in that post he had personally incurred the wrath of the Democratic majority. But that is all. Much as many Senators disliked Henry Wallace, for example, they still confirmed him as Secretary of Commerce in 1945, satisfying their resentment by rejecting him for the RFC directorship to which he had been nominated at the same time.

The Presidential record in lesser appointments is not so impressive, though relatively few ambassadors, commissioners, agency chiefs, etc. fail to pass the Senate. Of course Presidents must consider what the Senate will accept, especially if the opposition party controls the Senate. But though he must sometimes trim sail, the President most of the time has the hiring power he needs if his executive power is to be real.

The power to fire is the complement of the power to hire. Without it the President may discover his subordinates are more loyal to his opponents than to him. So President Johnson, for example, discovered during the post Civil War experiment in "congressional government" when the Tenure of Office Acts were passed to require Senatorial consent to the removal of Cabinet (and lesser) officers. Secretary of War Stanton directed the army in the South, not as Johnson wished, but in agreement with the Republican Radicals in Congress. Only since the Myers case in 1926—after Cleveland, McKinley, Roosevelt, and Wilson had definitely reestablished "Presidential government"—have Presidents indisputably possessed the power to discharge subordinates.[9] In 1920 President Wilson fired one Myers, even though his term as a postmaster had yet over a year to run, without the required concurrence of the Senate. Myers sued for his lost salary, and Chief Justice (ex-President) Taft held for the Court not only that the particular statute was void but also that Congress could not possibly limit the President's removal power. In 1934 the Supreme Court had a chance to backtrack somewhat from the broad dicta of the Myers case in *Humphreys' Executor (Rathbun)* v. *United States*. In August, 1933, President Roosevelt asked William Humphreys, a Republican member of the Federal Trade Commission to resign because, as Roosevelt put it, "I do not feel that your mind and my mind go along together on either the policies or the administering of the Federal Trade Commission." [10] Humphreys refused, was fired, sued for his back salary, and won in the Supreme Court. The Court distinguished his case from the Myers case on the ground that the Federal Trade Commissioners were legislative subordinates of Congress rather than administrative subordinates of the President. For the President to remove them would, Mr. Justice Sutherland argued, prevent "maintaining each of the three general departments of government entirely free from the control or coercive influence . . . of either of the others" [11]—a curious legalism, of course, this use of the separation of powers principle to deny the President a part of executive power which in the separation of powers theory he ought to possess completely. But the total effect of the Humphreys case is less than might be imagined. The six commissions which it exempts from Presidential control are only a small part of the administration. In all other parts

[9] *Myers* v. *United States*, 272 U.S. 52 (1926).
[10] 295 U.S. 602, 619.
[11] 295 U.S. 602, 629.

the Myers decision still holds; [12] and it guarantees the President's control of his subordinates.

Besides doing, planning, and staffing, the executive power also includes interpreting law or, to speak bluntly, legislation. The vast amount of executive ordinance-making is possibly the most startling of our departures from traditional separation of powers. One fundamental proposition of Whig constitutionalism was, in Locke's words, "the legislature neither must nor can transfer the power of making laws to anybody else." [13] But inevitably the man who executes law must interpret before he acts, and the power to interpret carries with it the power to legislate. If Chief Justice Hughes' quip "the Constitution is what the judges say it is" has any meaning at all, it is equally true that law is what the law-enforcer makes it. The contemporary breadth of the President's power to interpret derives from two trends in our political development. One is the vast arena of contemporary legislation which necessitates that even the most energetic executive pick and choose among statutes to enforce. The other is the baffling complexity of contemporary social problems which necessitates the delegation of ordinance-making power to the President. Let us briefly examine the effect of each of these.

No executive today, or at least no human one, can enforce all the laws, or all laws with the same energy: The corpus of law is too vast; the propensity to transgress is too ingrained; the modern opportunities to gratify the propensity are too varied; and above all too many laws today are almost unenforceable because, opposed by large and recalcitrant minorities, the rate of violation is astronomic (recall prohibition and price control). So, the appropriations for enforcement being limited, the executive must choose which laws to enforce vigorously. And in the choice lies interpretation: [14]

So the President's duty to "take care that the laws be faithfully executed" has come to embrace a broad power of selection among the laws for this purpose; and that this power is today without statable limits the history of the Sherman Act alone is sufficient proof. In a word, the President's very *obligation to* the law becomes at times an authorization to *dispense with* the law.

[12] In *Morgan v. Tennessee Valley Authority,* 115 F. (2nd) 990 (1940), a circuit court held—and the Supreme Court refused to review, 312 U.S. 701 (1941)—that the tenure of a member of the TVA board was controlled by the Myers case rather than the Humphreys.
[13] John Locke, *Of Civil Government,* sec. 142.
[14] Edward S. Corwin, *op. cit.,* pp. 114–15 (emphasis in original).

Striking as was the example of the Sherman Act when Corwin wrote, it has become even more striking today. The Act was passed in 1890; but under Harrison, Cleveland, and McKinley there was almost no enforcement, partly because the Supreme Court was hostile, but partly also because the Presidents were too. Theodore Roosevelt, Taft, and Wilson enforced as well as they could, while Harding, Coolidge, Hoover, and Franklin Roosevelt—for diverse ideological reasons—substantially abandoned enforcement. Truman, Eisenhower, Kennedy, and Johnson in the last two decades, however, finally enforced it as its authors probably intended. The recent Presidents have been vigorous prosecutors partly because the Supreme Court has welcomed it, but partly also because enforcement has fitted their ideologies. So the ups and downs of enforcement at least in part reflect variations in Presidential styles of law-making.

Much the most important kind of executive ordinance-making today, however, is derived from the incompetence of legislatures. In the slower-moving eighteenth century world it was perhaps reasonable to insist that legislatures make the laws. But in the twentieth century insistence would only mean the abdication of government from the control of society. So complex are our economic problems that legislatures cannot conceive of all their facets, let alone make workable regulations for all contingencies. The President, however, with a larger staff and less formal methods, can at least comprehend more facets than Congress.

Consider, for example, the case of wage and hour regulation, a relatively simple legislative policy, but interesting because it occasioned a definitive judicial statement on the delegation of legislative power. The authors of the Fair Labor Standards Act of 1938, which Roosevelt conceived of as a substitute for the NRA,[15] faced a difficult drafting problem. The National Recovery Act, which authorized the President to adopt (on the advice of "industry committees") and to enforce as law "codes of fair competition," had been declared unconstitutional, partly because the legislature did not even "undertake to prescribe rules of conduct" but simply authorized "the making of codes to prescribe them."[16] Even Mr. Justice Cardozo, sympathetic as he was to the problems of the New Deal, was horrified by the "unconfined and

---

[15] Frances Perkins, *The Roosevelt I Knew* (New York, Viking Press, 1946), pp. 249–53.
[16] *Schecter* v. *United States*, 295 U.S. 495 (1935), 541.

vagrant" delegation of legislative power, which gave the President, without any standards at all to guide him, "in effect . . . a roving commission to inquire into evils and upon discovery correct them." [17] After this decision the Presidential assistants who wrote the wage and hour bill were faced with two alternatives: If they established a flat minimum, it would, if too high, be unworkable in low income industries or regions or, if too low, be meaningless. On the other hand, if they provided that an administrative board fix minimum wages, industry by industry, there was real danger the Court might call this unconstitutional delegation of legislative power. In colonial America this dilemma could not have arisen, for legislatures simply wrote specific wage rates for each occupation into statute.[18] But in 1938 neither drafters nor Congressmen nor anyone else know enough about actual economic conditions to attempt such a gigantic job. Even if they had known enough, they had no crystal ball to tell them what would be needed a year or ten years hence. And so they did the only reasonable thing: They authorized an Administrator to promulgate specific minimum wages for specific industries somewhere between 25 and 40 cents per hour. Both the Administrator and the "industry committees" which were set up to advise him were required to consider how proposed minimums would affect price levels, consumer demand, collective bargaining contracts, and regional differences in production cost in each industry. Thus, while the law left specific rates to the Administrator's discretion, it did set standards of how he should think and, within broad limits, what conclusion he should come to.

This delegation was tested in the Opp Cotton Mills case and a unanimous court sustained the law. Mr. Justice Stone admitted that the Administrator was permitted considerable "exercise of judgment" in fixing minimum wages but he immediately added that "the Constitution, viewed as a continuously operative charter of government, is not to be interpreted as demanding the impossible or the impracticable." [19] Expressed more bluntly, this means that, if effective execution requires the executive to make law, why then, let the executive make it.

Law-making by interpretation is usually regarded as a judicial func-

[17] 295 U.S. 495, 551.
[18] Richard B. Morris, *Government and Labor in Colonial America* (New York, Columbia University Press, 1946), pp. 55–135.
[19] *Opp Cotton Mills v. Administrator*, 312 U.S. 126 (1941), 145.

tion. And so it is. But judging and executing are not so far apart as they often seem. Indeed, as the great contemporary jurist, Hans Kelsen, has pointed out: [20]

. . . there does not exist any clear-cut separation of the judicial and executive powers. . . . One identical function is distributed among different bureaucratic machines, the existence and different denominations of which can be explained only on historical grounds.

And from an entirely unrelated source we get the same incisive perception. Chester I. Barnard, who philosophizes about business administration, suggests that "Were it not for the separation of powers in American government, we should better recognize that the judicial process is a highly specialized executive process." [21] And what is shown by verbal analysis is shown as well by fact. Observe how courts and administrators cooperate to change the meaning of law. No one would have thought in 1938 that the new minimum wage law, for example, applying only to interstate commerce, affected elevator operators in a building in which rooms were rented to clothing manufacturers. But by 1942 the Supreme Court, needled by aggressive lawyers of the Wage and Hour Division, had so broadened the meaning of "interstate commerce" that those local elevator operators were covered by the Act.[22] Is it not clear that legislation by interpretation, presumably the heart of the judicial function, is necessarily executive too? [23]

[20] Hans Kelsen, *General Theory of Law and State* (Cambridge, Mass., Harvard University Press, 1945), p. 275.

[21] Chester I. Barnard, *Functions of the Executive* (Cambridge, Mass., Harvard University Press, 1938), p. 280.

[22] *Kirshbaum* v. *Walling*, 316 U.S. 517 (1942); for a similar expansion of perhaps greater constitutional significance, see the comment on Lincoln and the Prize Cases on page 220.

[23] The ordinance-making described in the text is all based on legislation. But according to the Supreme Court in the famous and leading case, *In re Neagle*, 135 U.S. 1 (1890), an order of the Attorney-General based only on the Constitutional admonition that the President "take care that the Laws be faithfully executed" was also law. At least it issued a writ of *habeas corpus* to free Neagle for the murder of one Terry committed while guarding Mr. Justice Field on order of the Attorney-General, justifying the writ on the ground that Neagle was "in custody for an act done in pursuance of a *law* of the United States" (emphasis added). In his criticism of *In re Neagle*, however, James Hart suggests that this kind of executive ordinance-making power extends only to rules for administration, not to rules regulating the society. (*Ordinance-Making Power of the President of the United States*, Baltimore, Johns Hopkins University Press, 1925, pp. 226–27.) It is hard to see, however, in what way the Attorney-General's order regulated only Neagle: Neagle acted upon the order so that it had some effect on Terry as well.

CONGRESSIONAL LIMITATIONS ON THE
EXECUTIVE POWER: DO THEY LIMIT?

The foregoing paragraphs should have amply demonstrated that the executive power is more than mere doing. It is also planning what to do, selecting the men to do it, and at least partially making rules about how it is to be done. That the executive power is so tremendous implies two observations of great constitutional significance: First the Presidency is so great that other branches can never really dominate it. Hence, Congress and Court are forever foreclosed from uniting the separated powers. Second, the Presidency is so great that, filled by a vigorous man, it can sometimes dominate the other two. But tremendous as the executive power is, it is genuinely limited. It is shared with Congress, specifically and in the general congressional control of money and statute. And at the same time it is physically limited too, for no President has yet organized the executive branch to exploit fully the constitutional grant of power. Whether or not the Presidency can be made a regularized source of leadership depends upon whether or not these limitations are enough to enfeeble it. In the following paragraphs, therefore, the limitations will be carefully analyzed in order to estimate their significance.

As the light of the Presidency has brightened, the light of Congress has necessarily faded. Consequently, as Roland Young suggests: [24]

> Most Congressmen are frustrated, and I mean this in the political sense only. They are frustrated because, to paraphrase Browning, their reach for power exceeds their grasp, for the great positions of power are held by the President and the heads of the departments and agencies. . . . The important everyday policy of the government is decided by those at the top of the administrative hierarchy, and these positions are not filled by Congressmen. . . . Any ambitious Member of Congress is consequently thwarted, because however wise or politically strong he may be, he cannot as a Congressman become the authoritative, responsible spokesman for any governmental policy.

Every frustration, psychologists tell us, provokes aggression; and so in the few decades past Congress has attempted, sometimes frantically, sometimes petulantly, to seize back the power it has lost. It has at its

[24] Roland Young, *This Is Congress* (New York, Knopf, 1946, 2nd edition), pp. 28–29.

disposal three major weapons. It can change law, supervising administrators by revising the basic norms of their action. It can investigate administrators, and in recent years this power has become administrators' most terrifying nightmare. Above all, it can alter appropriations—and no administration whatever goes on without salaries. Let us examine how each one of these weapons works.

The power to change law is probably the weakest weapon, even though it is the fundamental congressional activity. It is weakest because it usually involves Congress in an almost inextricable dilemma. Consider the typical case, that is, when Congress approves of a law in principle but not in application. To change it in any essential particular—the one horn of the dilemma—means to revoke a public policy it favors. Of course, over time Congress does exactly that, but in the short run—and this is what counts in supervising—Congress cannot abolish the Bureau of Labor Statistics, for example, simply because it is annoyed by some of the uses to which the Bureau's statistics are put. To allow a law to stand unaltered—the other horn—is to permit administators to subvert what Congress regards as its intent. Faced with these perplexing alternatives, Congress can at best amend statutes in minor details, sometimes with telling effect, sometimes not.

Much of the supervision Congressmen want to give, however, cannot be written into law because it is directed at such tenuous things as the personality and political orientation of administrators. No amount of statutory change could affect what many Congressmen regarded as the provincial self-righteousness of Sherman Adams, the didactic conservatism of Lewis Strauss, the mystic fuzziness of Henry Wallace, or the suave assurance of Dean Acheson, to name but a few who have been pilloried in the last twenty-five years. What can get at these indefinables, however, is committee investigation, an ancient device in law-making, latterly redesigned for supervision.

The significance of committee investigation is that it can install the fear of Congress into administrators' hearts. Hence the system of investigation, even when it seems carried to excess, is an essential and effective sanction for democratic responsibility. To most people outside Washington it seems perhaps inexplicable that a Cabinet officer, for example, should tremble at the prospect of a morning of interrogation by a half-dozen Congressmen. Reading the journalistic diatribes against supposedly irresponsible bureacrats, one imagines them regularly thumbing their noses at Congress. Many frustrated Congressmen imagine just that. Yet the picture is unreal, especially when one has seen the entire disruption of a large office for nearly a whole day simply because the head of the department had to be briefed for an unexpected summons before a Congressional committee. If a Cabinet officer is thus disturbed, consider how much arteriosclerosis hostile committees on Capitol Hill occasion among lesser bureaucrats. Ironical note: Congressmen are frustrated because they cannot control administration; but administrators fear Congressmen more than anything else. The fear is justified. Protracted needling by a Congressional committee is a painful experience, especially when the humiliation is magnified and broadcast by a thousand newspapers. It is enough, on the one hand, to drive men out of the government service. Recall that Sherman Adams was driven out of the office of President Eisenhower—who to the very end said "I need him"—because of the revelations of Adams' probably innocent (though certainly unwise) associations with a corrupt businessman. It is enough, on the other hand, to convince the President that even a good administrator so publicly vilified is a political liability. Recall that after Lewis Strauss was rejected after a vilifying investigation of his fitness for the Secretaryship of Commerce, Eisenhower could find no place for a man whom he had previously thought to be a devoted public servant.

Perhaps the fairest estimate of Congress's investigatory power can be derived from the history of the National Labor Relations Board, which has been investigated probably more than any other agency. After the opponents of the Wagner Act failed to get it declared unconstitutional, they began an attack in Congress. From 1937 until the war directed attention elsewhere, the Board and the Act were investigated in every session of Congress, culminating in the two-year hearings by the Special Committee to Investigate the National Labor Relations Board (1939–1941). Regardless of whether one interprets the criticism as justified or not, its cumulative effect was quite clear. The Board modified one of its most important administrative policies [25] and abandoned some of its senior employees.[26] Finally, the reputations of the original members had been so besmirched that, when their terms

[25] The Board early claimed the right to determine election districts; but two weeks after an investigation was proposed, it reversed itself in *Matter of Globe Machine and Stamping Co.*, 3 NLRB (1937) 294.

[26] D. O. Bowman, *Public Control of Labor Relations* (New York, Macmillan, 1942), p. 355.

expired, Roosevelt replaced them, despite their experience, with others who would be less of a political liability to the Board.[27] Lest these events seem overly significant, however, it should be recalled that the opponents of the Wagner Act were not really satisfied until the Taft-Hartley amendments of 1947 substantially revised public policy. And so the moral: Investigations may kill off a few men or induce a few conciliatory moves, but the President always has other men and other measures available.

The prime supervisory power of Congress, however, is control of the purse, that which, centuries ago, made legislative supremacy possible in England. The Commons bargained with the Crown, withholding supply until the Crown accepted its advice on administration. Ever since both the Commons and its children overseas have followed the behavior pattern established in the infancy of popular rule. In the heyday of "congressional government" Congress had many and varied sanctions over the President; but today, when the subsidiary sanctions have played out, the power of the purse remains.

The appropriations procedure is about the same as that for any other bill in Congress except that the first draft of the several appropriations bills is always taken directly from the President's Budget and that all of them are studied in subcommittees of the two Appropriations Committees. Unlike the procedure with some other bills, however, the crucial stage of an appropriations bill is nearly always in the subcommittee, where five or six Congressmen study a small section of the Budget with extraordinary care. In an important subcommittee the hearings ordinarily run to several thousand pages. This is where genuine supervision is possible. True, it is not really Congressional supervision, for the few Congressmen on, for example, the two subcommittees on appropriations for agriculture may be quite unrepresentative of Congress as a whole. But at least administrators do sit at a Congressional table, some even in the Seat Perilous for which they are utterly destroyed, as, for example, was the chief of the Bureau of Agricultural Economics in 1946, when the House Committee reported a cut in the BAE appropriation of $485,000 (about one-fourth the total estimate). As it was explained in the House, the subcommittee on agriculture, which was then dominated by cotton Congressmen, intended to rebuke those employees of the BAE who had publicly proposed to let the price of cotton fall to world

[27] *New Republic*, CI (Dec. 27, 1939), p. 285.

levels instead of supporting it at parity.[28] Even though the Senate repaired most of the damage, the Bureau had been taught, for a while at least, to walk humbly before its Congress. Ordinarily, however, the appropriations committees need not use such sensational tactics. Sharp questioning is usually enough to warn administrators to stay closer to the subcommittee's version of Congressional intent.[29]

Congress's limitation of the Executive is not as great today, however, as the foregoing catalogue may suggest. Rather, Congressmen are frustrated simply because they cannot supervise as much as they want. Why they cannot is obvious: Modern government is so complex that only a full-time executive can attempt to manage it, if indeed it can be managed at all. Congress with dozens of centers of power, internally antagonistic, is certainly not organized to supervise, even if it had the time to. All over the democratic world it is the same. In England, for example, where in juristic theory sovereignty resides in the legislature alone, the Commons has been forced by the complexity of modern government to relinquish its control of administration to the Cabinet. And for good reason: Management of the vast administrative machine is no part-time job; it cannot be sandwiched in among legislative sessions, errands for constituents, and trips to the home-town.

Perhaps the clearest sign of Congressional failure is its transfer to the President of much of its control of the purse, that uniquely legislative function. As late as 1911, A. E. Zimmern found it natural to explain to sceptical Europeans how Greek city-states of antiquity could work without a budget by observing that the great government of the United States worked without one too.[30] Indeed both governments were legislatively oriented; and legislative government cannot endure a budget. Its finances must be totted up by party leaders in the legislature itself. In a complex fiscal system, however, haphazard legislative judgments cannot bring probable revenue into even rough alignment with necessary supply. So budgeting is introduced—which transfers financial control to the budget maker. It is no accident of idiom that we speak of the *executive* budget. It means that the real initiative in appropria-

---

[28] *Congressional Record*, XCII (March 7, 1946), p. 2,007.

[29] See, for example, Richard F. Fenno, Jr., "The House Appropriations Committee as a Political System," *American Political Science Review*, LVI (1962), pp. 310–24.

[30] A. E. Zimmern, *The Greek Commonwealth: Politics and Economics in Fifth Century Athens* (Oxford, Oxford University Press, 1911), pp. 212–13 note.

tions is in the President, a proposition which deserves detailed examination.

The Budget, a quarto volume of over a thousand pages, is compiled by two hundred examiners in the Budget Bureau, all high-level civil servants, working all year under the fairly close direction of the President; by budget officers of every agency working all year too (in the Department of Agriculture, for example, twenty-five men); and finally by the agency chiefs who necessarily spend much time on their budget problems. Produced thus by the concentrated, dovetailed effort of so many people, the Budget is a coherent and rational division of funds. When Congress attempts revision, it is always therefore somewhat baffled. It finds that every departure, however minute, from the Budget as a whole is very difficult. Increases mean more taxes or more debt— and what Congressman likes that? Decreases mean abandoning projects which Congress in another mood approved. Reallocations mean constructing a new plan for the next year when the Budget is already about the best available. Thus, having lost the budget initiative, Congress has lost the appropriations initiative also. No wonder Congressmen often dislike and distrust the Budget Bureau.

Each year Congress does a war dance with the Budget and then goes home without fighting. Table V shows Congress's failure to control the size of the Budget as a whole; Table VI its failure to control specific items.

TABLE V.* Congressional Action on the President's Budget,
1956–61

Year	Budget Estimate (in billions	Actual Appropriations of dollars)	Actual as Percentage of Estimate
1956	62.4	66.5	106.0%
1957	65.9	69.4	105.0%
1958	71.8	71.9	100.1%
1959	73.9	80.7	109.0%
1960	77.0	76.5	99.3%
1961	79.8	81.5	102.0%

* Source: Compiled from the Budget of the United States for the years 1956–63.

In Table V the actual appropriations exceed the estimate in all years but one and in 1960 the cut was only seven-tenths of one percent—

all this in the face of a Congressional tradition that control of the budget means cutting it. In five of six recent years, Congress has raised rather than cut the President's estimates, although typically most of the increase has come in supplemental appropriations. So, in general, Congress has appropriated what the President has asked. To consider the Congress which in recent years has displayed the most antagonism toward the incumbent President, even the Republican Eightieth Congress, while it pared Truman's Budget ten percent for 1948, actually appropriated more than he asked for 1949. Table VI shows why grants and requests are so close together. Congress goes through the motions of careful examination—only nine minor items in this group were voted as asked in 1951. But what Congress really appropriated was the 1950 amount plus about half the requested increase. On item after item this mechanical, split-the-difference technique appears: The Farm-

TABLE VI.* Congressional Action on the
Department of Agriculture Budget for 1951

Number of items on which the actual appropriation was

more than the amount requested	25
exactly the amount requested	9
less than the amount requested	45

Total number of annual and permanent appropriations
(exclusive of trust accounts)   79

. . . .

1951 budget estimate	$925,789,656
1950 appropriation (original and supplemental)	883,024,554
Increase of 1951 estimate over 1950 appropriation	$ 42,765,102
1951 appropriation (original and supplemental)	$906,264,514
1950 appropriation (original and supplemental)	883,024,554
Increase of 1951 appropriation over 1950 appropriation	$ 23,239,960

* Source: Based on The Budget of the United States, 1950, 1951, 1952.

ers' Home Administration, for example, asked for $35,000,000 when it had had $23,649,000. It got $29,150,000, or an increase of almost exactly half the increase it had requested. Surely Congress has lost both real and rational control when it resorts to a meaningless rule of thumb.

Naturally Congressmen resent their failure and have several times encouraged national competitions for the invention of a device to re-establish their control. The latest gadget, patented by the Hoover Commission, is the "performance budget." The present arrangement of items in the Budget is neither readable nor rational. As the Commission pointed out, a naval hospital at Bethesda, Maryland, is supported by twelve different items of naval appropriations, only six of which relate to medicine, and the Bureau of Indian Affairs had 100 items on the Interior appropriations for about $50,000,000, the largest of which was more than $11,000,000 and the smallest $114.53.[31] That is why, the Commission implied, Congressional control was so superficial, tending to concentrate on minor expenses like the purchase of automobiles. It therefore suggested a "performance budget"—arranging items by the activity paid for—to redirect Congressional attention to the real question: the desirability of a specific program.[32] But would a simple mechanical innovation really do that? It would, of course, make the Budget easier to read. But is Congressional impotence a matter of illiteracy? If the real reason is the new Presidential initiative, then no amount of redesigning of accounts can affect that constitutional fact. In all likelihood the performance budget would not even permit Congress to use its rule of thumb control, an intuitive fear of which is perhaps why Congress has been reluctant to adopt the recommendation.

PHYSICAL LIMITATIONS ON THE EXECUTIVE POWER

The foregoing review suggests that Congress can limit the President much less in real practice than in constitutional theory. The President's executive power is sufficiently limited and shared that he cannot use it to master Congress; but subject to occasional, intermittent limitation, it is enough to do what he wishes to do, *if he is able.* And there is the rub. The main limit to his power is physical, an inability to perform what in theory is performable.

[31] The Commission on Organization of the Executive Branch of the Government, *Budgeting and Accounting: A Report to Congress* (Washington, Government Printing Office, 1949), pp. 7, 9.
[32] *Ibid.,* p. 12.

Our great administrative machine was not created in one day and for one purpose. Rather it is a conglomerate of many agencies created over the last 160 years to meet an amazing variety of public problems. No one of the agencies is the lengthened shadow of one man. Instead inconsistent systems of value struggle with each other in each agency as well as in the machine as a whole. "Coordination" is the prime word in administrative gobbledygook because it expresses what we have not got. The lack of it is why the theoretically performable is so often unperformed.

The grossest case of the failure to harmonize is seen in the independent regulatory commissions. They place the President in a curious position: [33]

The Constitution commands the President to "take Care that the Laws be faithfully executed" . . . but obviously he cannot see that the Interstate Commerce Act or the Federal Trade Commission Act is faithfully executed, because the job has been given to someone else.

The acts establishing the commissions provide that the President can remove commissioners only for incompetence, etc. and not for political reasons.[34] These restrictions the Supreme Court affirmed in the Humphreys case.[35] Thus the commissioners are free of any formal responsibility to him. He does control their budget somewhat; and most commissioners realize that they must, in order to operate, keep some friendly relations with the rest of the executive branch. But the only formal sanction the President has is reappointment; and since the terms range from five to fourteen years, this cannot count for much.

The irresponsibility of commissions is usually justified on the ground that regulation of business ought to be non-political. Thus the commission device is one of thousands of reflections of the nineteenth century *laissez-faire* principle. But now that we recognize how inac-

[33] Robert E. Cushman, *The Problem of the Independent Regulatory Commissions*, vol. III of *Studies for the President's Committee on Administrative Management* (Washington, Government Printing Office, 1937), p. 15.

[34] The Federal Power Act, the Securities and Exchange Act, and the Federal Communications Act—all passed between the Myers decision in 1926 and the Humphreys decision in 1935—do not limit the President's power of removal. But as the Hoover Commission pointed out, "these three commissions were and are nevertheless treated as independent."—Committee on Independent Regulatory Commissions, *Task Force Report on Regulatory Commissions Prepared for the Commission on the Organization of the Executive Branch of the Government* (Washington, Government Printing Office, 1949), p. 14.

[35] See page 193 above.

curate is the sharp separation of economics and politics, the justification is clearly inaccurate too. More in the spirit of our constitutional system, the irresponsibility is also justified on the ground that the commissions are quasi-judicial and ought therefore to be set apart like federal judges. But this argument too is semantically loaded, for it is used to justify their irresponsibility not only in their judicial duties but also in their administrative and quasi-legislative duties as well.

Inadequate as both justifications are, however, they both greatly influence our national political life. The President's Committee on Administrative Management described the Commissions as a: [36]

. . . headless "fourth branch" of the Government, a haphazard deposit of irresponsible agencies and uncoordinated powers. . . . The Congress has found no effective way of supervising them, they cannot be controlled by the President, and they are answerable to the courts only in respect to the legality of their activities. . . . Power without responsibility has no place in a government based on the theory of democratic control, for responsibility is the people's only weapon, their only insurance against the abuse of power.

Even the Hoover Commission, concerned about economy more than democracy, and composed of men deceived perhaps by the semantic confusions used to justify irresponsibility, reluctantly admitted that coordination of the commissions "requires careful attention." While its final reports defended irresponsibility because of a supposed paucity of examples of direct conflict between commissions and the President, their conclusion was not based on their facts. The most serious criticisms they made of the commissions involved a failure to harmonize with the rest of the government.[37]

[36] President's Committee on Administrative Management, *Administrative Management in the Government of the United States* (Washington, Government Printing Office, 1937), p. 36.

[37] Committee on Independent Regulatory Commissions, *A Report with Recommendations Prepared for the Commission on the Organization of the Executive Branch of the Government* (Washington, Government Printing Office, 1949). There it is said that, for example, the Maritime Commission has been in conflict with the State Department ever since the war (p. 62); and the Interstate Commerce Commission is said to be justifiably criticized because "it ignores too completely general economic conditions and basic Government policy in other fields (p. 84). For similar comments, see: on the Federal Power Commission pp. 105–6; on the Federal Reserve Board p. 110; on the Federal Trade Commission pp. 132–33; on the Securities and Exchange Commission pp. 149–50; on the Civil Aeronautics Board see: The Commission on the Organization of the Executive Branch of the Government, *The Independent Regulatory Commissions* (Washington, Government Printing Office, 1949), pp. 14–15; 19–22.

President Eisenhower for the most part allowed commissions to go their way, fully tolerating their conflicting regulations, which in at least one instance in the 1950's became a national scandal: The independent Interstate Commerce Commission ordered railroad actions which the Presidentially controlled Anti-Trust Division of the Department of Justice then prosecuted as violations of the Sherman Act. President Kennedy, however, placed high on his list of reforms the reordering of the relationship between the commissions and the President. He instituted several investigations of this relationship and undertook to make his appointments to them in such a way as to solidify his personal control of their activities. Unfortunately, his three years in office were not enough to affect the basic relationship. President Johnson apparently abandoned this effort; it therefore seems unlikely that any basic change will occur in the foreseeable future.

Enfeebling as the direct conflicts between commissions and the President are, the simple isolation of the commissions is worse. Central bank manipulations, transportation and power rates, anti-trust enforcement, etc.—all are potential avenues through which to meet the challenges of war and the business cycle. Can the President travel them? In the long run he can. The commissioners are not powerful enough to withstand his pressure. But in the short run—and this is what counts in the affairs of twentieth century man—it is never certain whether he can or not, for independence grows into irresponsible pig-headedness.

The independence of the commissions is, however, simply a morbid aggravation of the normal centrifugal tendencies in our administrative system. The normal condition of the bureaucracy is bad enough with its jousting among empire-builders and its stalemates among self-willed zealots. And, in sum, perhaps, the normal bickering of administrators impedes action more than the pathological tissues of commissions, for it slows down every single part of the organism. If the President were truly the sole directing center, the impediments would count for naught. But he is not and never has been and probably never can be. So, though we carelessly speak of "the" administration, we should always remember that it is not one but many, only roughly coupled by the President.

The most obvious symptoms of administrative centrifugality are the cases of constant, disruptive bickering among officials in high places, such as the feud between Secretary of Labor Durkin and Secretary of Commerce Weeks in the Eisenhower Cabinet, which finally drove

Durkin out of the Cabinet and aliented one important kind of support for the Republican party. But personal feuds even as vicious as this one are not in sum nearly as disrupting as the wars of attrition between agencies. Men and their personal passions come and go, but bureaus and their conflicting value systems rooted in statute go on forever. Whenever the duties of two agencies overlap, disputes are sure as death and taxes, surface disputes about how specific jobs ought to be done, disputes on the lowest level of consciousness about who will do them.

Consider how much bickering there is over even so routine administration as that of the civil service system. Between the Civil Service Commission and the rest of the executive departments is a feud on the grand scale, now nearly seventy years old. The subject of the dispute is clear enough, although the discussions of it are confusing because it has been in the interests of all participants to obscure with irrelevancies. Beneath the charges of red tape and the counter-charges of spoils is the unashamed struggle for power: Are departments to hire their own employees or are they to take what the Civil Service Commission sends? Floyd Reeves describes very well the nature of the feud: [39]

One personnel director of a federal agency likened the system imposed by the Civil Service Commission to the situation under the Volstead Act. Because many of the rules seem unreasonable, personnel directors spend much time and use great ingenuity in discovering ways to evade them. More often than not, ways can be found. But the service suffers because of the time lost and, often, because of the nature of the means used to evade the rules.

And what goes on in day-to-day evasion and recrimination is mirrored on a theoretical level. The Civil Service Commission was established originally because of long agitation against the spoils system and on the occasion of public horror over the assassination of President Garfield by a disappointed office-seeker. The spoils system, perhaps justifiable at first as a method of democratic responsibility, had degenerated in the latter half of the nineteenth century to cynical wholesale job-selling. The Commission, derived from an atmosphere of self-righteous condemnation of spoils, has ever since been dominated by a single ideal: To substitute merit for partisanship, to guarantee every civil servant procedural equality in appointment, promotion, and dismissal. It has of course never admitted that partisanship is often a merit, nor has it ever

[39] Floyd Reeves, "Civil Service as Usual," *Public Administration Review*, IV (1944), pp. 327, 335.

recognized that enthusiasm for the public service is sometimes a better recommendation than a high grade on an examination. It is the negative ideal of procedural equality, excluding, so most agency personnel officers think, any interest in the good of the service as a whole, which has occasioned so much hostile criticism.

Up to 1937 academicians had usually praised the Commission's ideal; but then even they began to besiege it too. The President's Committee on Administrative Management blew the first blast of the trumpet: [40]

After more than 50 years experience with civil service in Federal, State, and local governments, there is overwhelming evidence to show that the original theory of merely protecting appointments from political influence through a legalistic system of civil service administration is inadequate to serve democratic government under modern conditions.

It went on to propose more positive methods of recruitment than examinations and, more significantly, the decentralizaion of the Commission's work. In 1939 the President's Committee on Civil Service Improvement, even questioning the career service shibboleth, spoke up more definitely still on the departments' side of the feud. Arguing that lawyers should be hired for their imaginativeness, not for their skill in passing a test, it wrote: [41]

Whatever name is given to this quality, whether it is called imagination or is thought to come from some even less definable combination of natural gifts and intellectual training, it is rare and . . . can [not] be precipitated from the mass by any standardized catalyst. . . . In this all-important field of recruiting . . . the Committee believes that no "system" can take the place of good judgment founded upon personal experience.

And again the Hoover Commission made most of the same criticisms that the two earlier Committees had made.[42] Clearly, in this struggle between Civil Service Commission and the operating agencies over the power to hire and fire, the agencies have persuaded the theorists

[40] President's Committee on Administrative Management, *op. cit.*, p. 7.

[41] The President's Committee on Civil Service Improvement, *Documents and Reports to Accompany the Report on Civil Service Improvement* (Washington, Government Printing Office, 1942), *Report of the Advisory Committee on Lawyers,* p. 1.

[42] Commission on the Organization of the Executive Branch of the Government, *Personnel Management* (Washington, Government Printing Office, 1949), see especially p. 39.

that they are right. But that does not end the quarrel. In the 1950's and 1960's the disagreements have been less charged with emotion than formerly, partly because the Civil Service Commission has accommodated to the agencies and partly because, in an era of high-level employment, the agencies have had to take the people they can get rather than pick and choose among alternative candidates. Nevertheless, all the grounds for the disagreement are still present. Indeed, one suspects that bickering on this subject, with all its consequent demoralization and disorganization, will last as long as this government itself.

Bickering between the line agencies and a staff agency are annoying; but, since the staff agency is likely in the long run to get its way, they are not nearly so debilitating as bickering between two line agencies. As an example of the latter consider the relationship between the Army and Navy in the Department of Defense. The original intention of combining the two forces under one department was not, of course, to submerge their individual identities but to coordinate those basic policies—e.g., on personnel, on procurement, and the like—which might reasonably be coordinated for the sake of efficiency and effectiveness. But even in these elementary things, coordination has proved difficult. The office of Secretary of Defense was established in 1946, but even by 1963 the services were totally unused to cooperation on procurement, as illustrated by the great conflict over the TFX fighter plane. Early in the Kennedy administration, Secretary of Defense McNamara, the first Secretary to attempt coordination on a large scale, ordered the Air Force and Navy to plan a joint fighter plane, which with a maximum number of interchangeable parts, etc., could be more effectively maintained. For nearly two years the departments bickered, each insisting that the design satisfy primarily its own requirements, the Navy wanting a plane with a long range (to protect carriers) and able to land on the deck of a carrier, the Air Force wanting a plane designed with a shorter range for tactical superiority in a local fighting area. Eventually, the two forces realized the Secretary was indeed serious in requesting agreement, so they produced the TFX specification which was then sent to various contractors for design. In the design competition, the choice was narrowed to two contractors. A military board chose one of them, but the Secretary overruled the board and chose the other, presumably because the former's plane was essentially two planes with some common parts while the latter's was essentially one plane with adaption to two uses. Once this choice was made, a great public dispute arose in Congress, with the agencies fighting the Secretary *sub rosa*. The Secretary was vilified and accused of improper motives, but by now he seems to have settled the matter in his favor, really the first achievement of a common procurement program that was planned in 1945–46 but delayed by the bickering of agencies until 1963–64.

THE PRESIDENTIAL STAFF AND THE PHYSICAL LIMITATIONS

The disharmony of subordinates is clearly the greatest restriction of the executive power. Constitutionally, the President has tremendous power to act; one might therefore assume that his executive power is enough for all democratic self-control. But a formal grant is not the same as the real ability to exercise it. All recent Presidents have been frustrated by the physical limitation and all have tried hard to overcome it.

Richard Neustadt opens his discussion of *Presidential Power* with the observation that in the summer of 1952 President Truman often remarked that if Eisenhower were to win, "He'll sit there and he'll say 'Do this! Do that!' *And nothing will happen.* Poor Ike—it won't be a bit like the Army. He'll find it very frustrating." And he did. Neustadt also reports that an Eisenhower aide said in 1958, "The President still feels that when he's decided something, that *ought* to be the end of it . . . and when it bounces back undone or done wrong, he tends to react with shocked surprise." [43]

Here is the great administrative question of our times: How can an executive dovetail the work of many, many people toward a common purpose? Military men have grappled with it ever since the development of the mass army, and now it is the constant preoccupation of civil officials as well. Even businessmen, executives of the corporation and the cartel, have discovered that it is their question too. In the answering of it both politicians and manufacturers have adopted a military technique, one which soldiers discovered and applied long before the others had to face the question. The technique is the staff, the executive's extra eyes and ears, a group which has no direct operating responsibility, but which makes plans for him and then checks up to see if

---

[43] Neustadt, *op. cit.*, p. 9, emphasis in original.

operating (or line) officers have carried them out. Militarily, the distinction is between the persons of the joint chiefs of staff concerned with strategy and the field commanders concerned mostly with tactics. The former plan and control, the latter fight.

It is with applications of the staff idea that Presidents have tried to harmonize their administrations. While there is no civil staff like the military one, the half-dozen agencies in the Office of the President are what makes this government as effective as it is: (1) the President's secretaries, et al., (2) planning agencies, (3) the Budget Bureau, and, from time to time, (4) "assistant presidents." Are these enough to subdue the agency feuds that disrupt executive operations? Let us examine them.

But first a note: Most listings of the President's assistants begin with the Cabinet; but it is simply a council of operating officers, not a staff. While it could conceivably act collectively as such, no President has ever so used it, or given it a separate secretariat. Most Presidents treat Cabinet meetings simply as briefing conferences, reserving the really delicate political questions for private discussion.

Every President from Washington's time onward has had personal secretaries whom he has used as extra eyes and ears as well as amanuenses. Lincoln had four at once, including John Hay, later Secretary of State, and this was the largest personal entourage in the nineteenth century. McKinley's secretary, George B. Cortelyou, raised the office to a significance it has had ever since, though today the number of aides is much larger.[44] Franklin Roosevelt equipped himself with three secretaries (Louis Howe, Stephen Early, and William Hasset); military and naval aides (especially General Watson); a number of imaginative and vigorous men, the so-called brain trust, borrowed from the departments, installed in the White House, and made into a "kitchen cabinet" (at various times Rexford Tugwell, Raymond Moley, Benjamin Cohen, Thomas Corcoran, Harry Hopkins, and Judge Rosenman); and besides these a clerical staff sometimes of two hundred. And outside it all, but very important, Mrs. Roosevelt served as an amazingly peripatetic information service. The President's Committee on Administrative Management (composed of Louis Brownlow, Charles Merriam, and Luther Gulick, all outstanding pioneers in the study of public

---

[44] On this development see Pendleton Herring, *Presidential Leadership*, pp. 101–9.

administration) was so impressed with Roosevelt's improvised staff that the committee proposed to institutionalize it: [45]

The President needs help. . . . He should be given a small number of executive assistants . . . probably not exceeding six . . . to assist him in obtaining quickly . . . all pertinent information . . . so as to guide him in making his responsible decisions; and then when decisions have been made, to assist him in seeing to it that every administrative department and agency . . . is promptly informed. . . . They should be possessed of high competence, great physical vigor, and a passion for anonymity.

Their suggestion was adopted but it has not worked out quite as the Committee hoped. The institutionalization will probably remind new Presidents, as it reminded Truman, that loyal personal aides are necessary.

Subsequent Presidents have enormously expanded the White House office. President Eisenhower brought to the office his experience both as a staff officer and as a commander with a large staff. Consequently, he expanded the functions of the White House office. Not only did he continue the usual set of liaison men with Congress and the agencies, press secretaries, etc., but he also apparently used the staff in a more thoroughgoing way to brief him on prospective decisions. President Kennedy continued the expansion of the White House staff, as has President Johnson, so that today the office is much larger and more useful than the Committee on Administrative Management envisioned. But it seems clear that no President has used it in quite the same manner. Thus, President Kennedy relied on his brother, the Attorney-General, more than on the administrative assistants, though of course he had an elaborate staff organization, often referred to by the press as the Irish mafia. Apparently the relationship between the President and his personal staff is too delicate to standardize. According to Wendell Willkie, Roosevelt explained his need of Harry Hopkins thus: [46]

But—someday you may well be sitting here where I am now. . . . And when you are, you'll be looking at that door over there and knowing that practically everybody who walks through it wants something out of you. You'll learn what a lonely job this is, and you'll discover the need for somebody like Harry Hopkins who asks for nothing except to serve you.

[45] President's Committee on Administrative Management, *op. cit.*, p. 5.
[46] Robert Sherwood, *Roosevelt and Hopkins: An Intimate History* (New York, Harper & Brothers, 1948), p. 3.

The mark of a good executive is his ability to attract aides like Hopkins. But they cannot be created by drawing an organization chart: They are made with the heart.

Even a good personal staff is far from enough to compensate for all the disputes and passive resistance inherent in a large bureaucracy. Personal aides are trouble shooters; that is all they have time to be. What the President needs besides is a regularized staff with authority to help plan and inspect the whole executive branch. It should be large enough to keep tab on the whole in order to forestall trouble in any part. While he already has some such assistance, it is not yet complete enough to coordinate the whole government.

Consider the planning function, for example: There are a host of devices available, but none of them seem to be suited for comprehensive national planning. For one thing the President can use the vast number of interdepartmental committees, a device first popularized here and in England during 1914 to 1918, to smooth out particular problems. Even such an elaborate committee as the National Security Council, on which sit Cabinet officers and which has over 400 employees, is too limited in scope. Though such committees carry considerable prestige and attract the best type of civil servant, they are also, like personal aides, simply trouble shooters, designed to iron out particular problems, not to exert systematic control. The same can be said of committees of lay specialists. Many important new departures have been initiated by them, e.g. President Taft's Committee on Economy and Efficiency (Budget and Accounting Act of 1921), Franklin Roosevelt's Committee on Economic Security (Social Security Act of 1935), or the Attorney-General's Committee on Administrative Procedure (Administrative Procedure Act of 1946). Like the English Royal Commissions of Inquiry from which they are copied, they avoid the indecisiveness of Congress, clarify public discussion, and reassure the public about innovations. But, of course, they are only appropriate for those specialized problems on which specialists' advice is valuable.

Perhaps encouraged by the success of interdepartmental and lay specialist committees, Franklin Roosevelt set up the supposedly permanent National Resources Planning Board. It was unfortunate. In a short life (1939–43) it aroused distrust in Congress without accomplishing much else. It was cremated in 1943, but its soul transmigrated to the Council of Economic Advisors, established in 1946. The Council has a narrower field, fiscal policy; but since fiscal policy is basic to everything else the government does, it perhaps approaches being an all-inclusive planning agency. Since Truman, Eisenhower, and Kennedy all appointed economists whose views on policy coincided with the President's preferences, the Council has been truly in the President's confidence, which is essential if the Council is to plan effectively.

There is more to executive supervision, however, than planning; there must also be a check to see that plans are carried out. Yet control and inspection is the weakest part of the President's staff. Within the narrow field of financial control he does have the Bureau of the Budget, once not a staff agency at all, merely "an economy-minded, restrictive agency, skilled only in saying 'no,' " [47] but since 1939 "one of the primary instruments . . . for effective overall management of the executive establishment." [48] But the budget sanction is too indirect to be always effective; and yet the President has nothing else.

Such managerial assistance as the Bureau can give depends on the fact that every administrative act costs money. The President must decide with each Budget which activities ought to be expanded, which curtailed, which reorganized, etc. These are the delicate political questions of low taxes versus more social services or simply perhaps of guns versus butter. Whatever the decisions, it is the function of the Bureau of the Budget to plan appropriations for the coming year in a way that enforces the President's choice. If, for example, the decision is guns, then the two hundred or so budget examiners must see that the Army gets all it needs, while cutting down on, say, the Office of Education. Of course, the Bureau's decisions are not final; but usually only his favorites—and they rarely—can persuade the President to overrule it.[49]

The Bureau, making yearly budgets, cannot, however, enforce the President's policy daily; and, further, the budget sanction is by itself often insufficient to enforce anything. Consider this case: In 1943 the Office of War Information believed that the Army and Navy were

---

[47] Harold D. Smith, *The Management of Your Government* (New York, Whittlesey House, 1945), p. 61.

[48] This is what the President's Committee on Administrative Management hoped it would be when it recommended its transfer from the treasury to the Office of the President, *op. cit.*, p. 15.

[49] The best brief descriptions of the managerial aspects of budgeting are in Charles Hyneman, *Bureaucracy in a Democracy* (New York, Harpers, 1950), p. 335 note; and Fritz Morstein Marx, "The Bureau of the Budget: Its Evolution and Present Role," *American Political Science Review*, XXXIX (1945), pp. 653–84, 869–98.

withholding news of defeats, and that domestic war administration consequently suffered because the public did not appreciate the need for rationing, job freezing, and other disagreeable things. The armed forces, on the other hand, apparently feared that really bad communiques would be even worse for morale. Assuming for a moment what is untrue, that the Budget Bureau is close enough to the President to deal with a dispute in which each side has a reasonable argument, still how could it reconcile ghoulish journalists and vain generals? Reduce budgets? How silly! Fortunately the President then had the Office of War Mobilization under James Byrnes to minimize just such conflicts. In this minor case, "he urged immediate action by the services to end the basis of OWM complaints." [50] Much more important, his office coordinated all the domestic war agencies with the military ones and near the end of the war made a plan, the most inclusive and effective this government ever used, for contract termination, surplus property disposal, and factory reconversion.

The great success of the OWM as a real staff to the President suggests that he needs something like it permanently. Its historian, quoted just now, proposed that an assistant to the President with an Office of Program Coordination (actually a domestic chief of staff) integrate major policies among all agencies.[51] President Eisenhower, with all his experience with military organization, apparently saw the need for such a thing when he made Sherman Adams his assistant. President Kennedy and Johnson did not, however, seem to feel the same need, although clearly some device like this is necessary if the President is to do what he is elected to do—if, in fact, democratic self-control is to exist.

The Federative Power:
". . . Must Be Left to the Prudence and Wisdom of Those Whose Hands It Is in . . ."

In the treatise *Of Civil Government*, that first great textbook on popular rule, Locke suggested that the Chief of State has two kinds of authority, the one executive, the other including "the power of war

---

[50] Herman Somers, *Presidential Agency: OWMR, the Office of War Mobilization and Reconversion* (Cambridge, Mass., Harvard University Press, 1951), p. 61.

[51] *Ibid.*, pp. 219–23.

and peace, leagues and alliances, and all the transactions with all persons and communities without the commonwealth." This latter, he said, "may be called federative, if any one pleases." [52] He distinguished it from the executive power thus: [53]

These two powers, executive and federative . . . [are] really distinct in themselves . . . one comprehending the execution of the municipal laws of the society within itself upon all that are parts of it, the other the management of the security and interest of the public without. . . . [The federative power] is much less capable to be directed by antecedent, standing, positive laws than the executive, and so must necessarily be left to the prudence and wisdom of those whose hands it is in, to be managed for the public good. For the laws that concern subjects one amongst another, being to direct their actions, may well enough precede them. But what is to be done in reference to foreigners depending much upon their actions, and the variation of designs and interests, must be left in great part to the prudence of those who have this power committed to them, to be managed by the best of their skill of the advantage of the commonwealth.

This discussion of the President follows Locke's distinction because, it seems to me, the founding fathers did too. In Article II they enumerated the powers of the President in such a way that the executive seems to be one among several. Along with the direction to "take Care that the Laws be faithfully executed," he is granted most of Locke's federative power as well as others (i.e., to pardon, to appoint judges to convene special sessions of Congress, etc.) neither executive nor federative but customarily included in the royal prerogative. While the Courts have always called all the President's power executive, they have always also recognized that in war and diplomacy his acts are different from ordinary executive actions. Under the federative power he has more leeway to bypass Congress and to act for the "advantage of the commonwealth."

Because it permits more leeway, the federative power deserves separate study. Were federative actions legally the same as executive, there would be no point to the separation. But, although they may be less time-consuming and less frequently involved in elections, they do have fewer constitutional or Congressional limitations. The great Presidents have consistently exploited the federative power to dominate the whole national government.

[52] John Locke, *Of Civil Government*, section 146.
[53] *Ibid.*, section 147.

Just as the founding fathers gave Congress some executive power, so also they divided up the federative—but with difficulty, for, as Locke pointed out, it must be in the hands of the Executive: [54]

Though . . . the executive and federative power . . . be really distinct in themselves, yet they are hardly to be separated and placed at the same time in the hands of distinct persons. For both of them requiring the force of the society for their exercise, it is almost impracticable to place the force of the commonwealth in distinct and not subordinate hands, or that the executive and federative power should be placed in persons that might act separately, whereby the force of the public would be under different commands, which would be apt some time or other to cause disorder and ruin.

Still the founding fathers did formally divide the power. "The President shall be Commander-in-Chief of the Army and Navy . . ." says Article II; but from Article I Congress has the powers:

to declare War, grant Letters of Marque and Reprisal, and make Rules concerning Captures on Land and Water; To raise and support armies; . . . To provide and maintain a Navy; To make Rules for the Government and Regulation of the land and naval Forces; To provide for calling forth the Militia to execute the Laws of the Union, suppress Insurrections and repel Invasions; To provide for organizing, arming, and disciplining the Militia. . . .

In diplomacy the President is instructed to "appoint Ambassadors, other public Ministers and Consuls," to "receive Ambassadors and other public Ministers" of other countries and to "make Treaties." But half the Senate must confirm his appointments and two-thirds of it must concur in treaties.

In spite of this check and balance, the President is not much restricted *because he has the initiative.* Executive initiative is intermittent, for often the President must administer laws he has not helped enact. But the federative power is "much less capable to be directed by antecedent . . . laws" and must be left to the "prudence and wisdom" of the chief of state. Executive acts are spawned of a marriage of President and Congress. But federative acts occur asexually. Jupiter's child springs forth from his head; and Congress must perforce accept it, not as mother but as nursemaid.

Presidential initiative and Congressional docility are impressively

[54] *Ibid.*, section 148.

demonstrated at every military crisis of our history. The Commander-in-Chief tells the army what to do, what is done cannot be undone, and Congress must appropriate money. Consider Lincoln's action early in April, 1861. Largely disregarding the Cabinet's advice, he decided to defend Fort Sumter.[55] Between the evacuation of it on April 14 and July 4 when Congress convened there was truly a "presidential war," [56] during which Lincoln molded the "rebellion" theory as the pattern for the next four years. Had Congress been able, it would probably have done the same. But, significant fact: Congress was not in session; Lincoln summoned it only after the pattern was set. In the crucial ten weeks, Lincoln not only called out the militia, as authorized by the Constitution, but also seized telegraph lines and offices without warrant and suspended the writ of *habeas corpus,* both acts of dubious legality. Much more important, he proclaimed a blockade of Southern ports, thereby, so the Supreme Court subsequently held, exercising the Congressional power to declare war.[57] He paid out of the Treasury to private persons $2,000,000 for war materials in direct violation of the prohibition that "no money shall be drawn from the Treasury but in consequence of appropriations made by law." And the crowning audacity, he enlisted 80,000 new soldiers by his proclamation, although only Congress has the power to raise armies. As a legal precaution Congress later (August 6, 1861) declared all these measures to be as valid as if they had been "done under the previous express authority and direction of the Congress." [58] But in the *Prize Cases* the Supreme Court upheld the President's blocade proclamations as within the power of the President alone "without admitting that such an act [i.e. Act of August 6, 1861] was necessary under the circumstances," [59]—which is to say the military prerogative is almost unlimited.

If the Presidential vigor in the spring of 1861 stood alone, it would be merely a curious interlude in our constitutional history. But it does not. It is a logical development of the way Polk prepared for the Mexican War.[60] It foreshadows the Emancipation Proclamation in

---

[55] Carl Sandburg, *Abraham Lincoln: The War Years* (New York, Harcourt, Brace, 1939, 4 vols.), I, pp. 189, 193.
[56] James G. Randall, *Constitutional Problems under Lincoln* (New York, D. Appleton, 1926), p. 51.
[57] *The Protector,* 12 Wall. 700 (1871).
[58] 12 U.S. Stat. 326, Act of August 6, 1861.
[59] *Prize Cases,* 2 Black 635 (1863).
[60] Milo Milton Quaife, ed., *The Diary of James K. Polk* (Chicago, McClurg, 1910, 4 vols.), *passim* and especially Vol. II.

which Lincoln freed the slaves "by virtue of the power in me vested as Commander-in-Chief of the Army and Navy." And, although no later President has ignored Congress as much as Lincoln did, his precedents remain valid law, valid enough to justify the military initiative of Woodrow Wilson and Franklin Roosevelt.[61]

Presidential initiative in war is paralleled by Presidential initiative in diplomacy, "war by other means." In the diplomatic half of the federative power, the President conducts all foreign relations up to Senate confirmation of treaties. Hence he is almost always able to present Congress with irreversible situations. No better illustration of his initiative exists than the failure of the several Neutrality Acts of the 1930's, ill-considered, floundering attempts to control foreign policy by "antecedent law." That they failed and that Roosevelt had to make policy contrary to their spirit while they were yet in force clearly demonstrates that foreign affairs must be left to what Locke called the "prudence and wisdom" of the Chief of State.

From 1935 through 1939, as European war seemed imminent, Congressmen generally were convinced, ostrich-like, that neutrality acts were enough to isolate us from the rest of "one world." And so they passed the Neutrality Acts of 1935, 1937, and 1939, on the theory that we might avoid war simply by avoiding any contact with belligerents. They forbade the sale of arms to nations at war; after 1937, they permitted the sale of other war materials but only on a "cash and carry" basis; they forbade also the arming of American merchantmen, travel by Americans on ships of belligerents, etc. Their folly lay in this: They gave Europe the impression that we would condone aggression, no matter how hideous or detrimental to our interests. Perhaps, as some sarcastically said when the Acts were passed, they would have kept us out of the first World War very well. But in the 1930's the United States was, willy-nilly, a great power and so the whole world watched fascinated as we tied our arms behind us. As Roosevelt pointed out when he proposed the repeal of the arms embargo provision in 1939: [62]

At the very least, we can and should avoid any action, or any lack of action, which will encourage, assist or build up an aggressor. We have learned that when we deliberately try to legislate neutrality, our neutrality laws may oper-

[61] Edward S. Corwin, *The President: Office and Powers* (2nd edition, New York, New York University Press, 1941), p. 184.

[62] *The Public Papers and Addresses of Franklin D. Roosevelt, 1939*, pp. 3–4.

ate unevenly and unfairly—may actually give aid to an aggressor and deny it to the victim. The instinct of self-preservation should warn us that we ought not to let that happen any more.

Had the Act been applied to the invasion of Manchuria in 1937, for example, it would almost certainly have aided the aggressor. Japan, with a lucrative foreign trade, had the exchange to buy on a cash and carry basis, while China did not. Fortunately Roosevelt refused to apply the Act—on the legalism that war had never been declared —and thus helped China a little. Merely by its existence, however, the Act encouraged European wars, for it gave Hitler some assurance that we would not fight and took hope away from England and France. Thus part of the blame for the shameful capitulation at Munich actually rests on our shoulders.

Clearly the attempt to legislate a foreign policy was disastrous. But to some degree the President was able to reverse the policy legislated, thus displaying that the initiative was still really his. He arranged to lend China $25,000,000 and organized a "moral embargo" on the sale of airplanes to Japan. In the "Quarantine the Aggressors" speech he made clear that, regardless of the Act, our influence was on the side of Britain and France. He refused to recognize Japanese conquest in China or the partition of Czechoslovakia. He led in organizing an inter-American defense system based on collective security, not skulking isolation. And through it all he instructed an innocent Congress in the realities of international politics patiently enough to get the Act modified in 1937 and the arms embargo repealed in 1939. Congressional usurpation did unquestionably hamper him; but in making foreign policy, though the President may "lose . . . particular battles; he retains, and is understood to retain the power of the offensive in the campaign. . . ." [63] So indispensable is his leadership in federative affairs that, even when Congress attempts diplomacy by law, the initiative still is his.

CONGRESSIONAL LIMITATIONS ON THE FEDERATIVE POWER

Hence also, Congressional limitations are far less significant on his federative than his executive acts. The great case of the Versailles

[63] Harold Laski, *The American Presidency* (New York, Harper, 1940), p. 181.

treaty to the contrary, Congress can seldom revoke federative acts because these usually set in motion a train of events in which, once started, it must perforce acquiesce. Those who remember Senator Lodge's hatchet work on the Versailles treaty may, however, be inclined to discount Presidential initiative. What good is initiative if one-third of the Senate can negate all the President has done? Yet the significance of Wilson's failure in 1919 can be overestimated. It is true that a minority of Senators defeated the Versailles treaty. (The final vote was 49 yea to 35 nay, seven short of the necessary two-thirds.) It is also true that this treaty was one of the most important ever to come before the Senate. (Might the League of Nations have kept the peace if the United States had been in it?) Still, the Versailles treaty was but one event, and not all its results were bad. True, having tasted blood the Senate isolationists twice later defeated American membership in the Permanent Court of International Justice; but in the long run Versailles left only the taste of shame. It gave rise to many proposals to amend the Constitution in order to eliminate the Senate's minority veto.[64] It encouraged more use of executive agreements which can be approved by a simple majority of both houses or, when previously authorized by statute, do not need Congressional approval (e.g., reciprocal trade agreements).[65] Finally, it greatly influenced the passage of the Charter of the United Nations. Thirty-five Senators voted against the League Covenant; only two against the Charter. The point is clear: When a Senate minority defeats a major treaty, popular reaction will probably forestall repetition for a long time in the future.

Aside from the treaty veto, Congress can limit federative acts much less than executive ones. Ambassadorial appointments, for example, are scrutinized less carefully than domestic ones. Similarly, the delegation of legislative power, broad enough today in domestic affairs, is in federative affairs greater still. The judicial tradition is that, when the delegation involves war and diplomacy, it should be sympathetically reviewed. Thus, even in 1936, when the Court had just nullified the NRA mainly because of excessive delegation of legislative power, it still upheld almost as much delegation in a Neutrality Resolution because it involved foreign affairs.[66] Even the control of the purse is

[64] Kenneth Colegrove, *The American Senate and World Peace* (New York, Vanguard Press, 1944), pp. 94–112 and 168–76 for a discussion of these.
[65] *Ibid.*, pp. 99–100.
[66] *United States* v. *Curtiss Wright Export Corporation*, 299 U.S. 304 (1936).

weaker. Army appropriations are, indeed, often reviewed with great care in peace time, perhaps because of our traditional distrust of the military. But in war time what money the army wants the army gets, usually with no serious questions asked. The most remarkable example of Congressional abdication is the financing of the atomic bomb. From 1941 to 1945 Congress appropriated about two billion dollars for the "Manhattan project," knowing only that it was for a secret weapon and with only the word of a few generals that the weapon was feasible.

Less limited in the federative power, the President can use it to control all of government—and this is the great significance of his having it. Neither in actual fact nor in constitutional interpretation is there a sharp distinction—here drawn for the sake of informative analysis—between the federative and executive powers; hence the prestige the President acquires from one spills over into the other, thereby strengthening Presidential leadership as a whole.

The Presidency of Theodore Roosevelt precisely illustrates this expansionist effect. He earned much hero-worship by ordinary executive action, his vigorous enforcement of anti-trust laws, for example. But it was his daring use of the federative power that brought him almost religious adoration. He later reminisced: [67]

I did not usurp power, but I did greatly broaden the use of executive power. . . . I acted for the public welfare . . . whenever and in whatever manner was necessary, unless prevented by direct constitutional or legislative prohibition.

Since he was least limited as Commander-in-Chief and Chief of State, it was as these that he did the broadening.

Very soon after he took office came the great anthracite strike of 1902. Public sympathy was clearly with the United Mine Workers; even Mark Hanna, the rich and hard-boiled boss of the Republican party, "viewed some of the great Pennsylvania owners with a distinguished and rather visible contempt." [68] It was the spokesman for the owners, George Baer, who uttered that classic blasphemy: [69]

The rights and interests of the laboring man will be protected and cared for, not by the labor agitators, but by the Christian men to whom God, in

[67] Theodore Roosevelt, *Autobiography* (Second ed., New York, Charles Scribner's Sons, 1920), p. 357.
[68] Thomas Beer, *Hanna* (New York, Knopf, 1929), p. 216.
[69] John R. Commons, ed., *History of Labor in the United States*, vol. IV by Selig Perlman and Philip Taft (New York, Macmillan, 1935), p. 43.

His infinite wisdom, has given control of the property interests of the country. . . .

The operators, mule-like, refused to talk to union leaders; but Roosevelt acted the muleteer, threatening to break with troops what had become a lock-out, and frightening the Wall Street community so much that in turn it forced the owners to compromise.

Most domestic problems cannot, however, be settled by military *fiat;* hence on them Roosevelt had to cooperate more often with Congressmen less easily hypnotized than the citizen-voters. But not in diplomacy. "I took Panama," he exulted in 1913, "without consulting the Cabinet." [70] And here his often overdramatic memory did not deceive. When "believers in a do-nothing policy" called the taking unconstitutional, he replied the accusation held "only if Jefferson's action in acquiring Louisiana be also." [71] Jefferson did not, however, encourage a revolution in New Orleans, simply because he was piqued by Napoleon's cupidity. But Roosevelt? When "those contemptible little creatures in Bogotá" [72] refused to ratify the Hay-Herran treaty, he helped along the revolution which agents of the French company that was selling us its Panamanian rights were trying to foment. He sent warships to Colon, which turned back the Colombian army from the new Republic of Panama on November 4, 1903. On November 6, one hour after he learned that the revolutionaries held Panama City, he recognized their government, and, of course, soon thereafter negotiated a canal treaty with it. How different the liver of the strenuous life from the Sage of Monticello! But Roosevelt was right: he did act within the Constitution. Certainly the President has full power under it to transfer destroyers and exchange ambassadors.

Panama began Roosevelt's vigorous new diplomacy. In the next years he projected the United States, almost entirely without Congressional control, into the power politics of the whole world. Isolationist Republicans today are wont to blame the Democrats, Woodrow Wilson and Franklin Roosevelt, for the European wars that ended our traditional distrust of "foreign entanglements." They should remember, however, that the first and crucial steps toward a global foreign policy were taken by the Assistant Secretary of the Navy who sent Dewey

[70] Theodore Roosevelt, *op. cit.,* p. 548.
[71] Theodore Roosevelt, *op. cit.,* p. 512.
[72] Quoted in Henry Pringle, *Theodore Roosevelt* (New York, Harcourt, Brace, 1931), p. 311.

to Manila, by the Colonel who charged through fire and smoke up San Juan Hill. How did T.R. do it? For one thing, it was the Peace of Portsmouth. Very conscious of our new Melanesian empire and disturbed by the Russian osmosis into China, he repeatedly offered to mediate in the Russo-Japanese War and was able finally to bring both sides together at Portsmouth, New Hampshire. Neither side really liked the compromises he engineered, but Roosevelt himself was delighted, for he had taught his countrymen to recognize their Oriental interests. Interference in Japan led to interference in Morocco because Japanese and Russian alliances were world wide. And although European diplomats may have been alternately amused and disturbed by his ferocious idealism, they had to deal him into their game, which was what he wanted. He himself got a Nobel prize for the "Peace of Righteousness" and made our entry into *realpolitik* the more palatable by playing the peacemaker's role.

His champion exploit with the federative power was the famous cruise around the world. After Portsmouth, Japan rather than Russia seemed too heavy in the Pacific balance of power. So he counterbalanced with a show of force, cruising the whole fleet into the Pacific and hoping thereby to impress everybody, not least his own countrymen. But it did not impress Congress. Senator Hale of the Committee on Naval Affairs, announced that Congress would not pay for it; and since Roosevelt's term was nearly over, his influence waning, the Senator's threat was ominous. "However," Roosevelt recalled,[73]

I announced in response that I had enough money to take the fleet around to the Pacific anyhow, that the fleet would certainly go, and that if Congress did not choose to appropriate enough money to get the fleet back, why, it could stay in the Pacific. There was no further difficulty about the money.

The coal strike, Panama, Portsmouth, the world cruise, perhaps just his phrase "speak softly and carry a big stick," are what heroized him. And heroes, once made, do not have to show their credentials often— which is the real contribution of the federative power to the strength of the Presidential office.

The reason that the federative power can make this contribution to the office is that the President, in using it, is less restricted by the usual impediments to direct and forceful action—the immobility of

[73] Theodore Roosevelt, *op. cit.*, p. 553.

the bureaucracy and the recalcitrance of Congress. As an example of the significance of action in areas without these impediments, consider the relatively brief Presidency of John Kennedy. Though he achieved a reputation as a strong leader in less than three years, in the management of legislative and bureaucratic affairs he actually accomplished relatively little. In his first Congress his main new program was medical care for the aged, which not only failed to pass but also failed so completely that, even when it was revived by President Johnson as an election issue in the election year of 1964, it again failed rather ignominiously. In his second Congress, his two main programs were a small cut in the income tax and a civil rights bill, both of which passed under the skillful legislative management of President Johnson. It is not clear that they would have passed had Kennedy lived, for it was Johnson's promise to cut the budget that put through the former and Johnson's presence as a bargainer and a moderate that put through the latter. Much the same record appears in the management of the bureaucracy. Kennedy was ambitious in this area, more so than any President since Franklin Roosevelt. Kennedy especially wanted to make the regulatory commissions less responsive to the appeals of the regulated and more responsive to the appeals of the "public." By imaginative appointments to the commissions, Kennedy did begin to affect the tenor of their decisions and investigations. But three years is too short a time to bring about the desired transformation, and Johnson has not had the same ideas. So it seems unlikely that Kennedy's goals will be achieved in more than an occasional and haphazard way.

The only significant new program distinctively associated with Kennedy's leadership is the Peace Corps, which, significantly, is in the field of federative affairs. It went through Congress easily, partly because it was interpreted as an inexpensive substitute for expensive foreign aid, and partly just because it was a federative affair.

But in the management of business not impeded by the difficulty of forming a majority coalition in Congress or by the difficulty of coordinating a massive bureaucracy, Kennedy's achievements were considerable. After the fiasco of the Bay of Pigs incident, which much of the press attributed to the semi-independence of the Central Intelligence Agency and to the disorganization of the new President's office, Kennedy apparently reorganized his staff to deal more effectively with crises. And so effectively did he prepare that in just three subsequent crises, two domestic and the other federative, he acquired on his handling of these three matters alone the reputation of being a strong leader.

The first crisis was domestic, an increase in the price of steel.[74] Throughout the period since the second World War, steel labor and management have developed an accommodation with each other which took this form: Management conceded substantial wage increases with the expectation and understanding of meeting the increased costs by raising the price of steel and by eliminating (by automation) some jobs. Many believed that this policy in a basic industry contributed heavily to the persistent inflation of the 1950's. By the end of the 1950's, however, this bargain could no longer be struck because the price of steel had risen to the point that the market could not absorb further increases. Hence followed a protracted bitter strike in 1959, which was settled, so steel management believed, to their disadvantage by the intrusion of Vice-President Nixon, who presumably acted for political advantage. In the steel wage negotiations of 1961–62, President Kennedy, motivated by a desire to minimize inflation, sought to persuade steel labor to accept what was called a non-inflationary settlement. The union did so and then, after all negotiations were completed, management announced a price increase. Kennedy interpreted this as breaking the unspoken agreement he had made with all parties, so he denounced the perfidy of the steel management and called upon them to rescind the price increases. After a few days of feverish discussion, recrimination, and counter-recrimination, some of the smaller companies rescinded the increases, whether because of the President's pleas and the unpleasant position he had put them in or because of a genuine belief that the market could not support a price rise, we shall never know. Quite probably it was a combination of these motives that led all companies then to rescind the increase and thereby to give the President a great public victory.

The second crisis was federative, the Soviet missile build-up in Cuba. In the autumn of 1962, when the United States was presumably occupied with a political campaign and during a period in which weather conditions prohibited aerial photography, the Soviet Union began swift installation of medium-range missiles. United States in-

---

[74] For an interpretation of this event see: Grant McConnell, *Steel and the Presidency, 1962* (New York, Norton, 1963).

telligence reported the unusual activity but not its exact nature; it was not until some of the launching mechanisms were nearly constructed that the nature of the installations was known. As soon as the information was verified, President Kennedy threatened to blockade until the missile-launching bases were dismantled and to carry the conflict to the Soviet Union if military action occurred. After brief vacillation, the Soviet government backed down. The bases were dismantled and medium-range missiles were returned to the Soviet Union. By acting with calmness and determination in a great crisis, Kennedy achieved the reputation of a strong negotiator.

The third crisis was a domestic police action, requiring the coordination of civilian police and military forces at the University of Mississippi. In this controversy the refusal of the Governor of Mississippi to allow university authorities to register a Negro student, James Meredith, as ordered by United States courts, precipitated a crisis in which Kennedy was faced with a clear choice between literal enforcement of the court order and some kind of compromising delay which, of course, would negate the entire order. Kennedy chose to enforce the order; and when the Governor announced his intention to resist physically, Kennedy sent a large enough force of marshals, backed up with military forces, to ensure compliance. After the initial riot, Meredith was able to attend classes and, ultimately, to graduate. From this series of incidents Kennedy emerged with a reputation as a decisive administrator, able to enforce the law without fear of political consequences.

The point of this summation of the Kennedy Presidency is simply that, in those areas of action which require the joint action of President and Congress or which require the joint action of several branches of the bureaucracy, Kennedy's three years were not enough to make a great impact on the system; but in those areas of action in which the President can act on his own, Kennedy did make a significant impact on the system, giving it a sense of direction and the people a sense of triumphant self-confidence.

Since most of the time the opportunities for such direct action arise in federative affairs, it follows that it is especially in federative affairs that a President can prove he is a hero, thus earning the right to lead in all aspects of political life. Again, this is the real contribution of the federative power to the strength of the Presidential office.

THE PRESIDENT'S LEADERSHIP OF HIS PARTY

Yet great as the executive and federative powers are, not by these alone does the President stretch octopus-like over the whole of government. At best these are enough only to overawe Congress, to allow him legislative initiative, but they cannot actually project him into the Congressional scene. What does do that is his leadership of a national political party.

The President is Chief of Party just as much as he is Chief of State. The founding fathers did not plan it that way, of course. They expected the President to stand aloof from the muck of faction in order to moderate Congressional cabals. But instead of the many parties they foresaw, only two emerged and the Presidency quickly became identified with one of them for very understandable reasons. The Presidential candidate is, as pointed out in Chapter 3, the one issue upon which all the factions of a party must agree every four years, the one thing definitely differentiating the two parties. Elected in a constituency of the whole nation, he personifies his party and speaks its dogma in the loudest, most authentic voice. Attitudes toward the President affect attitudes toward other candidates of his party; and to some degree people vote on Senators and mayors because of their judgment on the President, a habit revealed in election statistics. In every Presidential election but one since the Civil War the President's party has won more seats in Congress than they have at the midterm following, presumably because the President pulls votes for other candidates of his party. The only exception in this statistical series was 1934 when Democrats won more seats than at Roosevelt's election in 1932; but surely this is no exception to the rule. Democrats won more seats because of the President who had led us out of the wilderness.

As party leader the President has a double role: he helps his party win and then becomes its spokesman on dogma. And as spokesman he leads his party in Congress. This too, the founding fathers did not plan, although they did vest him with legislative powers. They required his conditional assent to laws (the so-called veto); they asked him to give Congress information and to recommend measures; they authorized him to convene Congress in special session and permitted him to adjourn it when the two houses could not agree on a time—all of which, combined with party leadership, is enough to make him Chief Legislator too.

"Chief Legislator," however, is merely an abstract formula. What the President is in fact is often very different. His legislative leadership varies between two historical extremes, one in 1867, the other in 1933. In 1867, Johnson had so lost influence in Congress that the Senate failed to convict him on impeachment by only one vote short of the necessary two-thirds. But Johnson was not convicted, which implies an irreducible minimum of Presidential leadership. At the other extreme, Franklin Roosevelt's leadership was so magnetic that Republican Floor Leader Snell supported the emergency banking bill, saying,[75]

The house is burning down, and the President of the United States says this is the way to put out the fire. . . . I do not know that I am in favor of all the details carried in this bill, but whether I am or not, I am going to give the President . . . his way. He is the man responsible, and we must at this time follow his lead.

Seldom, however, are these extremes approached in practice. Consider two more typical examples, Roosevelt's leadership in 1937–38 and Truman's in 1947–48. In the first, the President had just been elected by the largest popular majority ever recorded, certainly as much of a "mandate from the people" as one could ask. Yet only by the most difficult maneuvering did he get any part of his program through Congress. The Court reform plan, his first great proposal, was debated throughout the spring and summer of 1937, was reported adversely from committee, and finally failed in the Senate. Perhaps if Senate majority leader Robinson had not died before the vote, perhaps if the plan itself had been better prepared, perhaps if the sit-down strikes had not frightened marginal Senators, perhaps if Roosevelt had been less imperious in his dealings with Congress—but then, the plain fact was that the plan lost. And although the minor procedural reforms subsequently passed and the Supreme Court itself compromised with Roosevelt, so definite a rebuff at the beginning weakened his leadership during the rest of his second term. Roosevelt proposed a wage and hour bill in May of 1937. It got nowhere then and failed again in a special session convened in November to reconsider it.

[75] *Congressional Record*, LXXVII (March 9, 1933), p. 76.

Finally it passed in June, 1938, but only after frequent revision under pressure and almost constant White House attention. The reorganization bills, the proposals of his Committee on Administrative Management, were cut to pieces but finally passed in very modified form in 1938 and 1939. The Neutrality Act of 1937 Roosevelt signed "with reluctance" and then only because he had persuaded Congress to include the "cash and carry" provisions. In 1938 a number of riders to WPA appropriations materially restricted his administration of it. In other less important issues he was somewhat more successful, for example, the Trust Indentures Act of 1938. A very mixed record, however, for a President elected by so large a majority in 1936.

Truman's case was somewhat different: Elevated by Roosevelt's death, he lacked the self-confidence that comes from popular approval. Faced with a Republican Congress, aggressively hostile with their first majority in sixteen years, he had to cope with the widest possible separation of powers. But in spite of his initial handicaps, he did not fail entirely in domestic affairs: Congress of course ignored most of his "Fair Deal" proposals, but it did repass such no longer controversial New Deal policies as reciprocal trade agreements. He vetoed often, and several times Congress repassed bills over his veto, especially the Taft-Hartley bill, which was the most important domestic issue of the 80th Congress. But Truman shone more brightly in foreign policy. By taking advantage of and encouraging certain renegade Republicans, he was able to force through bills for Truman Doctrine aid to Greece and Turkey, Marshall Plan aid to Europe, the Voice of America, aid to China, etc. Almost the only federative issue on which he even had to compromise was the immigration of displaced persons. Considering his initial disadvantages, the record indicates not only his strategical skill but also the basic strength of the Presidency.[76]

In neither case did the President achieve all that he proposed. Yet each achieved enough to prove that Presidential leadership exists. Both Presidents guided Congress most in budget and federative affairs, which suggests this rule: The greater the need for decisive direction, the greater the President's domination. Roosevelt accomplished a little more in controversial domestic affairs, probably because his party

[76] Floyd M. Riddick, "The First Session of the 80th Congress," *American Political Science Review*, XLII (1948), pp. 677–93 and "The Second Session of the 80th Congress," *American Political Science Review*, XLIII (1949), pp. 483–92.

following was larger and more loyal than Truman's. And this suggests another rule: that the Presidential leadership deriving from party loyalty is, except for the greatest crises such as in 1933, generally weaker than that deriving from his constitutional prerogative. Thus, while most new departures in domestic policy in this century have originated with the President, they have come slowly and late because his party leadership is so tentative.

THE PREVENTIVE OF CAESARISM

Strong in prerogative, weak in party: It is this dual nature of his legislative leadership that makes it so curiously intermittent. The prerogative is always present, even for the weakest Presidents, although, of course, they do not always have courage to use it. But party is a "function of . . . Crisis and Personality." Party leadership rests on party loyalty—which is realized only when some great crisis or some great personality creates it. The executive and federative prerogative have been continually expanded because in a thousand crises Americans have understood that only the President is able to use all of government to overcome them. Each new addition of prerogative remains to magnify the office. But party leadership, also born of crisis, disintegrates once the crisis is passed, as Franklin Roosevelt's did during his second term. Party leadership has to be won anew by each incoming President, and often the occasion to win it is lacking. For considerable periods, therefore, Presidents have let the power to govern slip from their grasp. Unable to lead their party, they fear as well to use their prerogative. Then ambition really counteracts ambition and our impotent government drifts into new distress. Then we hope, but with no assurance, that a hero will materialize to save us.

This is the problem with which the chapter started, that heroes are not always available, that the power to govern appears only in crisis, not before. By this chapter we have got this much further in the analysis: We know the conditions for this curious periodicity. The President's formal powers guarantee that he is always important, but they are not enough for him always to lead the whole. Intermittent government depends, therefore, on the President's intermittent leadership of his party. Democrats have often feared the heroes they heroize, but they have not always understood that we rely on heroes because our institutions cannot be operated by ordinary men. Thus our next problem is to understand why his party leadership is intermittent in order to find a remedy for it. The great danger to our constitutional system and democratic procedures generally is that in some future crisis a President may destroy Congress rather than lead it. Hence we need to regularize the President's party leadership in order to prevent Caesarism.

7.

The Supreme Court

> Another attribute of democracy is to dispense with all life offices
> —or at least to curtail the powers of any such offices, if they have
> been left surviving from some earlier epoch of change. . . .
> —ARISTOTLE, *Politics,* 1317b–1318a

THE SUPREME COURT AND THE
SEPARATION OF POWERS

Although a discussion of the Supreme Court may seem on the surface only a parenthetical interlude in this analysis of the power to govern, it relates closely to the argument, because the President cannot unite the separated powers if one branch has the strength to withstand him. If the Court neither needs nor wishes to cooperate, if —as has actually happened several times in our history—the Court is unaware of belonging to the government, the separation of powers is then irremediable. A latent obstructiveness lies deep in the Court's nature. Although most of the time it is rationally repressed, now and again it breaks loose and springs upward to direct judicial action. The perpetual danger that the obstructiveness be uncaged is what occasions this chapter.

But first a note to indicate just which conflict about the Supreme Court this chapter considers, for there are two quite different controversies. One is between the Court and elected officers of the national government; the other is between the Court and elected officers of states. Throughout most of our history these conflicts have occurred, sometimes simultaneously, so that many writers have tended to confuse them. But from the point of view of political analysis, they are different conflicts, and I distinguish them sharply here. When the Court conflicts with state officials, it acts as a branch of the central government supervising subordinate governments. One may disagree with particular acts of supervision, but one may not disagree with the general need for such supervision if the American political system is to be maintained. On the other hand, when the Court conflicts with national officials, it acts as part of the central government in conflict with another part of the central government. In such an instance, it expresses all the worst features of the separation of powers. So long as the Court has life tenure and some share of the power to govern, it is able to obstruct the elected branches. We say that sovereignty resides in elected officials, yet we regularly permit the Court, whose responsibility to the people is very indistinct, to exercise a sizeable share of it. It is this inconsistency, its source and effects, that will be analyzed in this chapter.

JUDICIAL SOVEREIGNTY AND JUDICIAL REVIEW

The Supreme Court's share of sovereignty, one of its two resources for obstruction, is its power to make law, and especially law concerning the most delicate political questions of our society. It has: [1]

. . . ceased to be a common law court. The stuff of its business is what on the continent is formally known as public law and not the ordinary legal questions involved in the multitudinous law suits of Doe v. Roe of other courts. The construction of important federal legislation and of the constitution is now the staple business of the Supreme Court.

To say that it constructs law and the Constitution is to say that it makes our fundamental law.

Obvious as this comment is, however, it directly disputes one of the most persistent (and deceptive) traditions of Western political thought from antiquity onward, the popular fallacy that judges merely announce law that already exists. This Blackstonian misconception is one aspect of natural law theory, the idea that law is infallible and complete, laid up in Heaven for eternity. If law exists always perfect, then judges cannot possibly add to it. They can merely deduce the law of particular cases by a series of syllogisms from general principles. Were judges really limited to "finding" law in this logical way, they

[1] Felix Frankfurter, "Supreme Court," *Encyclopaedia of the Social Sciences*, XIV, p. 479.

could neither legislate nor obstruct the elected legislature. Their irresponsibility would not then trouble democrats.

Yet this is not the case. All judges make law, even in lowly traffic courts. Every driver knows that he can usually get away with minor violations of traffic ordinances. If one is picked up for driving 33 miles per hour in a 30 mile zone, very likely the magistrate will rebuke the policeman for making frivolous arrests. But let the same magistrate be needled by a newspaper campaign against speeding or even let him have an argument with his wife at breakfast, then some luckless fellow will pay $25 for the same speed in the same place in the same amount of traffic. The ordinance remains the same, but its meaning changes. Who changes it but the magistrate? Indeed every analysis of law and judging must, with Justice Cardozo, "take judge-made laws as one of the existing realities of life." [2]

Nevertheless, it dies hard, this thing Morris Cohen called the: [3]

. . . phonographic theory of the judicial function—according to which the judge merely repeats the words that the law has spoken into him.

It clings especially to the Supreme Court, possibly because its judges have so much law-making to hide. As recently as 1936, when the Court refused to enforce the first AAA, Justice Roberts set forth an up-to-date version of the phonographic theory, although in his form it ought perhaps to be called the "t-square" theory: [4]

It is sometimes said that the court assumes a power to overrule or control the action of the people's representatives. This is a misconception. The Constitution is the supreme law of the land ordained and established by the people. All legislation must conform to the principles it lays down. When an act of Congress is appropriately challenged in the courts as not conforming to the constitutional mandate the judicial branch of the government has only one duty,—to lay the article of the Constitution which is invoked beside the statute which is challenged and to decide whether the latter squares with the former. All the court does, or can do, is to announce its considered judgment upon the question . . . and, having done that, its duty ends.

[2] Benjamin N. Cardozo, *The Nature of the Judicial Process* (New Haven, Yale University Press, 1921), p. 10.

[3] Morris Cohen, *Law and the Social Order* (New York, Harcourt, Brace, 1933), p. 113.

[4] *United States* v. *Butler*, 297 U.S. 1 (1936), pp. 62–63.

In this view of the judicial function, law is assumed to be a wholly logical, unemotional science, one in which the judges' philosophies, their prejudices, if you like, do not enter. Yet to assume so is to deny what modern logicians and psychologists alike affirm: that the crucial s*ep in logic is the selection of premises. Analyzing the split decisions of the 1960 term of the Court, Schubert found that almost all the judges' votes are explainable (using two quite different statistical techniques) as affirmations of their political preferences.[5] Truly, every judge, being human, adopts his premises from his experience in the same way that other people do. Hence between two judges there are always two personal histories and therefore two different sets of premises to control their logic. And judging emotionally as well as logically, they not only decide whether the Constitution "squares" with statute, but also whether one *ought* to square with the other. Indeed the Supreme Court does make law; and the popular phrase, "overrule . . . the people's representatives," to which Justice Roberts so much objected, is really accurate idiom. What else did Roberts and his colleagues do when they found that the authors of the Tenth Amendment of 1791 foresaw and forbade the Agricultural Adjustment Act of 1934?

It is often said, however, that constitutional law is simply a body of precedents which judges use according to the common law rule of *stare decisis* (literally: to stand by decisions). Constant repetition of this incantation is enough to convince the naive that the law is a wholly logical system, revealing itself in each application of the principles derived from precedents which stretch back in series to unrecorded history. It is indeed true that our legal forms make much of standing by precedents. The very structure of the lawyer's brief—with each proposition supported to tedious length by citations of earlier cases —is enough to indicate that. And it is true also that *stare decisis* is intended to and does introduce a modicum of certainty into law, that most inexact of sciences. But it is true as well that precedents are never so decisive as the lawyer arguing his case asserts. Even the layman quickly understands that there would be neither lawsuit nor appeal if the precedents were clear-cut. Controversies exist, in fact, just because law is uncertain, because there are no precedents or, more likely, too many and conflicting ones. Indeed judges do follow the rule of *stare decisis*; but on the Supreme Court at least they themselves can choose

[5] Glendon Schubert, "The 1960 Term: A Psychological Analysis," *American Political Science Review*, LVI (1962), pp. 90–107.

the decisions by which to stand. And that is sufficient power of legislation.

Of course, like all other courts, the Supreme Court makes law only when it decides particular cases. But particular cases come to the Court for decision only if they present occasions to make important additions to law, a fact well indicated by the Court's rules of jurisdiction. The Court is required to hear appeals only when there is a serious question of constitutionality, such as (a) when a state or federal court has held a federal law unconstitutional, (b) when a federal court has held a state law unconstitutional, or (c) when a state court has held against a litigant's claim that a state law is unconstitutional. Other cases it accepts at its pleasure, when, as the rules say, there are "special and important reasons therefor." These special and important reasons usually turn out to be that the case involves "an important question of federal law which has not been, but should be, settled by this court." Hence the Court actually sits, as Chief Justice Vinson has said, only on those "cases which present questions whose resolution will have immediate importance far beyond the particular facts and parties involved." [6] And hence also, the Court really is, as Mr. Justice Frankfurter once said: [7]

. . . the ultimate organ—short of direct popular action—for adjusting the relationship of the individual to the separate states, of the individual to the United States, of the forty-eight states to one another, of the states to the union and of the three departments of government to one another.

As the "ultimate organ" for adjusting, the Court is, at least in paper calculations of sovereignty, superior to Congress and the President. Judicial supremacy is to some degree characteristic of all governments because judges make law in particular cases always after the legislature enacts general rules. But judicial supremacy is more pronounced in the United States than anywhere else in the world: Our courts have the power of judicial review, that is the power to pass upon the "constitutionality" of acts of Congress. In other countries, courts make law roughly within the general norms established by statute. Our courts, however, can choose also whether or not to enforce the statutory norms themselves. The power to interpret is broad enough; but the power of judicial review is greater still—and that is what makes our judicial supremacy unique.

[6] 69 S. Ct. v at vii (1949).
[7] Felix Frankfurter, "Supreme Court," *Encyclopaedia of the Social Sciences,* XIV, p. 474.

Here then is the real problem of this chapter: The Supreme Court makes ultimate law, subject only to the usually ineffectual procedure for constitutional amendment. Yet this last legislature is isolated by constitutional plan from the President and Congress. Democratically responsible leaders obviously cannot lead if the Court makes ultimate laws that forbid their leadership, as it did, for example, in 1857 and again in 1934 to 1936. In this search for leadership to unite the separated powers for majority action, it is therefore necessary to determine how great an obstacle the Court is or can be. The Court and a judicial bureaucracy are, of course, indispensable; but is the Court's share of sovereignty a real barrier to majority action? Or is it, on the other hand, possible to integrate the Court's sovereignty with that used by the responsible leaders of the majority? And if it is possible, what conditions make it so? To answer these questions it is necessary to analyze carefully judicial review, which is judicial supremacy in its most extreme form.

But first a note: The phrase "judicial review" is here used in a narrow sense to refer only to the Court's consideration of the constitutionality of acts of Congress. Many writers use it to refer also to the Court's consideration of the constitutionality of acts of state legislatures. In this latter activity, however, the Court is presumably acting as agent of the national government in supervising the states. Here the narrow sense is preferred because only in it is the question raised of the relation of the Court to the rest of the government.

THE HISTORY OF JUDICIAL REVIEW: DID THE FRAMERS INTEND IT?

The only way to appreciate the exact significance of this unique judicial authority is by an understanding of the history of its development. Judicial review was largely unanticipated. Its rationale reflects, therefore, experience, even historical accident, more than philosophy and constitutional plans. Who made the judicial review? When and how was it made? These are the questions we must answer if we are to understand what it is today.

The easiest of these questions is "when," for we can answer it with objective statistics. Ever since 1792 the Court has heard objections to the constitutionality of the acts of Congress, but only three times before the Civil War did it actually refuse to enforce one for that reason. The first case, *United States* v. *Todd* (1794) went unnoticed and unreported until 1851; the second, *Marbury* v. *Madison* (1804) was atypical, more a legal trick than a serious precedent (see pages 247 to 249); and the third, the Dred Scott case (1857), was so confused that historians ever since have debated whether or not it actually held the Missouri Compromise unconstitutional.[8] After the Civil War, however, clashes between the Court and Congress occurred regularly; and even now that the Court has learned self-restraint, the pertinacity with which lawyers challenge statutes suggests that judicial review is still very much alive: [9]

Number of Cases in Which the Court
Held Acts of Congress Unconstitutional, 1860–1949

1860–69......4	1890–99...... 5	1930–39......16
1870–79......9	1900–09...... 8	1940–49...... 2
1880–89......4	1910–19...... 7	1950–59...... 1
	1920–29......18	

To say that judicial review became especially characteristic in the decade or so after 1865 is not to say, however, that it began then. Early evolutionary forms of the species have been unearthed in strata ante-dating the Constitution. One interesting, but unprofitable, intellectual exercise, therefore, is the question of whether or not the framers intended that the Court have it. The Constitution itself is quite vague, saying only: [10]

The judicial Power shall extend to all Cases, in Law and Equity, arising under this Constitution, the Laws of the United States, and Treaties made, or which shall be made, under their Authority;

Since this says nothing directly about the power of the Court to refuse to enforce statutes, scholars pursuing the question have had to gather evidence of the framers' intent from other sources. And some of the

---

[8] Reported at 13 How. 52 (1851); 1 Cranch 137 (1804); and 19 How. 393 (1857) respectively.

[9] Based upon Library of Congress (W. C. Gilbert), *Provisions of Federal Law Held Unconstitutional by the Supreme Court of the United States* (Washington, Government Printing Office, 1936) and *The Constitution of the United States: Analysis and Interpretation*, Senate Document #170, 82nd Congress, 2nd session.

[10] Article III, section 2.

evidence has unfortunately been misinterpreted out of zeal to provide judicial review with a respectable genealogy. It is true that Dr. Bonham's case (1610), in which Sir Edward Coke set forth something a little like a judicial review, was often on the lips of colonial lawyers; but it is far from clear that Coke's words meant what later generations thought they did.[11] It is also true that colonial litigants appealed to the Judicial Committee of the Privy Council. But it invalidated only three statutes between 1630 and 1776. Nor were these actions, properly speaking, judicial review: They were supervision by a superior government of an inferior one, analogous to the Supreme Court's control of state legislation.[12] And while it is true that state courts did, several times between 1780 and 1787, hold state laws unconstitutional, the cases were probably far less widely known then than they are today.[13] Finally, it is true, as Charles Beard conclusively showed, that most of the active members of the Philadelphia Convention knew about judicial review, at least hazily; but they did not think enough about it to mention it in the Constitution.[14] And so the question of whether or not the framers intended judicial review is really unanswerable; indeed it is irrelevant: how could they intend an institution of which they had no knowledge, an institution which matured seventy-five years later?

The History of Judicial Review:
Does the Constitution Imply It?

While most of the framers had only a hazy idea of judicial review —too hazy and unrationalized to write it into the Constitution—still there is a persistent tradition among constitutional lawyers that the Constitution clearly implies judicial review. In the seventy-eighth *Federalist*, written of course soon after the Constitution, Alexander Hamilton first asserted that it did so imply. So effective was his argument, so widely influential was it in our constitutional development

---

[11] S. E. Thorne, "The Constitution and the Courts: A Reexamination of the Famous Case of Dr. Bonham," in Conyers Read, ed., *The Constitution Reconsidered* (New York, Columbia University Press, 1938), pp. 15–25.

[12] Arthur M. Schlesinger, "Colonial Appeals to the Privy Council," *Political Science Quarterly*, XXVIII (1913), pp. 279, 433.

[13] See Andrew C. McLaughlin, *A Constitutional History of the United States* (New York, D. Appleton-Century, 1936), pp. 312–13 note, for a listing of the cases and a convenient bibliography.

[14] Charles A. Beard, *The Supreme Court and the Constitution* (New York, Macmillan, 1912), *passim*.

that many scholars since have thought that judicial review was indeed set forth in the Constitution itself. But that the tradition exists today does not mean that the Constitution does really imply judicial review; and that Hamilton stated his proposition in 1788 does not mean that he inferred it from the document of 1787.

Indeed, just as it is impossible to say that the framers intended judicial review, so it is impossible to say that the document they wrote implies it. To deduce judicial review from the Constitution is, however, so traditional and so persuasive an argument that it deserves summary here. It appeared first in the seventy-eighth *Federalist* where, to justify judicial review, Hamilton had to prove, first, that the Constitution established a hierarchy of law, itself superior to statute; and, second, that the Court was the appropriate body to decide when inferior law conflicted with superior. Since in the Anglo-American tradition the reconciliation of conflicting laws is a duty for the judiciary, neither he nor his followers had much difficulty with the second proposition.

His really difficult job, therefore, was to establish the existence of a hierarchy of law. Concerning it he suggested two proofs, one historical and the other logical. The historical argument was simply that the Constitution is to be regarded as an act of the people, statutes as mere acts of representatives. Hence he argued: [15]

No legislative act . . . contrary to the Constitution, can be valid. To deny this, would be to affirm, that the deputy is greater than his principal; that the servant is above his master; that the representatives of the people are superior to the people themselves.

Unfortunately, Hamilton did not explain just how the Constitution was more significantly popular in origin than statutes. Yet some explanation seems necessary. Was not the Constitution proposed by convention delegates who had been chosen by state legislatures? And was it not ratified even more indirectly by state conventions elected by perhaps one-fourth the adult white males?

Hamilton could not raise the Constitution above statute by historical fact, nor can those who have quoted his argument a million times since. He was on sounder ground, however, when he asserted that the Constitution ought to be regarded as fundamental law, not so much in fact as in theory. He derived his argument from the familiar problem of

[15] This and other quotations from Hamilton in the next few paragraphs are from the seventy-eighth *Federalist* except when otherwise credited.

the conflict of laws, when two laws, "clashing in whole or in part," cannot be reconciled, the courts must as "a matter of necessity . . . give effect to one, in exclusion of the other." But which one? The customary rule for choosing had, as he observed, always been "that the last in order of time shall be preferred to the first." Against this he set a new rule: that the Constitution is superior to statute, and that the superior law ought to be preferred to the inferior.

The crux of this argument is the assertion that the Constitution is more fundamental law than statute. This assertion can be supported in one of two ways: by inference from specific words of the Constitution or by inference from the whole document. Hamilton did not try the first; he knew it was impossible. But his caution was not inherited by later theorists: it has been customary now for over a hundred years for judges to say that the Constitution makes itself supreme. But constant repetition of a misquotation does not alter the original document, even though it may becloud legal minds. The Constitution is not, as for example Justice Roberts asserted in the Butler case, "the supreme law of the land." What is supreme is:

this Constitution, and the Laws of the United States which shall be made in Pursuance thereof; and all Treaties made, or which shall be made under the Authority of the United States.

The supremacy clause makes the Constitution, federal statutes, and treaties superior to state law; but it does not make any one of the three kinds of federal law superior to the others. It can do so only by reading the words "in Pursuance thereof" as equivalent exactly to "in accordance with its principles"; yet the history of the phrase, as it develops in Farrand's *Records* suggests that it is equivalent rather to "subsequent to the adoption of the Constitution." [16] And if "pursuance" does mean "subsequent," there is no direct verbal basis in the Constitution for the hierarchy of law.

Unable to support his assertion by inference from specific words, Hamilton inferred it from the tenor of the whole document. It is, as he pointed out,

a limited Constitution . . . one which contains certain specified exceptions to the legislative authority; such, for instance, as that it shall pass no bills of attainder, no *ex-post-facto* laws, and the like. Limitations of this kind

[16] Farrand, *The Records of the Federal Convention of 1787* (New Haven, Yale University Press, 4 vols., 1911–1937), I, 245; II, p. 417.

can be preserved in practice no other way than through the medium of courts of justice, whose duty it must be to declare all acts contrary to the manifest tenor of the Constitution void.

It is this argument that Chief Justice Marshall amplified in *Marbury v. Madison*: [17]

To what purpose are powers limited, and to what purpose is that limitation committed to writing, if these limits may at any time, be passed by those intended to be restrained?

Thus he suggests that the Constitution must, by its very delegation of powers, limit Congress by a real sanction (judicial review) and that it must place itself above statute so that the sanction can work.

While Marshall's suggestion is persuasive, it does not follow that the sanction for the limitation *must* be judicial review. The framers themselves were very conscious of democratic responsibility and the separation of powers as limitations on government. It may well be that these, taken singly or together, are—instead of judicial review— the limitations implied in the Constitution. So far as the Constitution itself suggests, each branch of the government is as well qualified as any other to restrain itself by interpreting the Constitution. Hence the tradition that deduces judicial review from the Constitution is at best dubious. Hamilton himself acknowledged as much in the eighty-first *Federalist*:

. . . this doctrine [i.e. that in the case of "evident opposition, the laws ought to give place to the Constitution . . ."] is *not* deductible from any circumstance peculiar to the plan of the convention . . . [emphasis added].

But dubious as the inference is, the seventy-eighth *Federalist* and *Marbury* v. *Madison* planted it firmly in our constitutional system. In all honesty, however, we can at this distance of time say only that the Constitution perhaps does and perhaps does not imply judicial review.

Toward Judicial Sovereignty: What Encouraged Judicial Review

Since it is impossible to say either that the framers deliberately sanctioned or even accidentally implied judicial review, we must look outside the Constitution itself for its exact genealogy. The seventy-

---

[17] 1 Cranch 137, 176 (1803).

eighth *Federalist* and *Marbury* v. *Madison* were the first well-rationalized statements of it that were widely enough distributed to earn for their authors the credit for parenthood. But to say that these were the natal statements tells us nothing about how or why they and their doctrine were so generally accepted. To understand the acceptance itself, one must look at several peculiarities of our political history, at the supremacy clause and the special judicial function it implied, at life tenure for judges and the judicial isolation to which it contributed, and at the gloss applied over the Constitution in 400 volumes of opinions.

The earliest influence chronologically to prepare the way for judicial review was the Court's supervision of state law under the supremacy clause. Although the clause apparently requires only state judges to enforce the supremacy of national law, the Supreme Court in its very first sessions undertook enforcement itself. Hence it was immediately involved in an activity easily confused with judicial review. Nullifying state law because it conflicts with the Constitution is not, however, judicial review; it is simply supervision of acts of an inferior government, very different from review of acts of equal national authorities. But both activities involve overruling legislatures; and inexperienced citizens could easily confuse the two.

This confusion would possibly never have been important had not John Marshall been Chief Justice from 1801 to 1835. Marshall, who was both a great judge and a determined Federalist, apparently believed his calling was to save America from its democratic self, especially from its democratic self in state legislatures. In a series of famous decisions, *Fletcher* v. *Peck* (1810), *McCulloch* v. *Maryland* (1819), *Dartmouth College* v. *Woodward* (1819), *Cohens* v. *Virginia* (1821),[18] he boldly interpreted both fact and law to void state regulations of property as conflicting with the Constitution.[19] Thereby he habituated American lawyers and voters to judicial annulment of statutes, to the settlement of great political controversies by judicial order. The hierarchy of laws was so engrained in legal thoughtways that only in this century have we understood that supervision of state law is normal and necessary

[18] 6 Cranch 87 (1810); 4 Wheat. 316 (1819); 4 Wheat. 518 (1819); 6 Wheat. 264 (1821).

[19] See for example, the discussion of Marshall's argument in the Dartmouth College case in Charles Grove Haines, *The Role of the Supreme Court in American Government and Politics, 1789–1835* (Berkeley, California, University of California Press, 1944), p. 409.

while judicial review of acts of Congress claims ultimate sovereignty for judges. Justice Holmes set forth the distinction nicely: [20]

I do not think the United States would come to an end if we [i.e. the Supreme Court] lost our power to declare an Act of Congress void. I do think the Union would be imperilled if we could not make that declaration as to the laws of the several States . . .

But a distinction apparent to the foremost American judge who had lived all of his judicial life in an atmosphere of judicial review was not so obvious in the early nineteenth century. It was easy, therefore, for the frequent, aggressive, and much debated judicial supervision of state legislation to pave the way for judicial review of national law.

Life tenure for judges, or rather tenure during good behavior, contributed even more than the supremacy clause to judicial review. It guaranteed that the Court—and indeed the entire federal judiciary —would sometimes be out of sympathy with the rest of the national government. Were judges responsible either to the electorate directly or to Congress and the President, probably they would only rarely wish to nullify acts of Congress. But the judges are irresponsible, or at least their responsibility is very indistinct. Although they are politically appointed, no sanction can realign them with the popular will when, as sometimes happens, they are partisans of ideals long since abandoned by the electorate. With life tenure they can perpetuate their principles in law even after they have been defeated in elections. Hence this observation: Each time the Court is ideologically isolated, it adds a little bit to the theory and practice of judicial review.

The first isolation occurred after the election of 1800, when Jeffersonian Republicans controlled the popular branches while embittered Federalists sat on the Court. It was then that the Court first fully rationalized judicial review. Earlier Federalist judges had considered the validity of statutes; [21] but Marshall's Court nullified part of the Judiciary Act of 1789 and enshrined the elaborate justification of their act in the case books for as long as this government lasts. *Marbury* v. *Madison* was a minor case, which even conservatively

[20] Oliver Wendell Holmes, *Collected Legal Papers* (New York, Harcourt, Brace, 1921), pp. 295–96.
[21] *United States* v. *Todd* (1794), reported at 13 How. 52 (1851); *Hylton* v. *United States*, 3 Dall. 171 (1796).

slanted histories acknowledge needed no decision on constitutionality.[22] But it came at a time when Jeffersonians were attacking the judiciary, when they were planning to impeach the most intemperate of Federalist judges, and when they had just reduced the number of federal judgeships in order to get rid of some other Federalists in lower federal courts. And so, as Albert Beveridge observed in his great biography of the Chief Justice: [23]

Marshall resolved to make use of this unimportant litigation to assert, at a critical hour when such a pronouncement was essential, the power of the Supreme Court to declare invalid acts of Congress that violate the Constitution.

The details of the case are simple: Marbury, one of Adams' midnight appointments in 1801 as justice of the peace for the District of Columbia, sued in the Supreme Court for an order (writ of mandamus) to compel Madison, Jefferson's Secretary of State, to deliver Marbury's commission which had been overlooked in Adams' last hectic days. The political controversy was over the Court's power so to order an executive department. It was well known that Madison planned to ignore the writ if the Court issued it. And so Marshall's dilemma: If the order were issued and ignored, the Court's prestige would fall even lower. If the order were not issued, it would seem capitulation to Jefferson. In a bold and ingenious maneuver, he contrived to avoid issuing the order, to assert that the order ought really to be issued, and to establish the principle of judicial review. As permitted by the Judiciary Act of 1789, the suit had been started in the Supreme Court, although the Constitution says that the Supreme Court shall have original jurisdiction only in cases involving states and ministers of foreign countries. Marbury was neither of these and hence Marshall could hold void that section of the act which applied to his suit. He could just as easily, however, have reconciled the act with the Constitution, saying that the authority to issue writs of mandamus, given by the act to the Court, should be understood as limited by the clauses of the Constitution that define its jurisdiction. But this was high politics, not lifeless logic. So Marshall held the act unconstitutional and

[22] Charles Warren, *The Supreme Court in United States History* (rev. ed., Boston, Little, Brown & Co., 1928, 2 vols.), I, p. 242.

[23] Albert J. Beveridge, *Life of John Marshall* (Boston, Houghton Mifflin, 1919, 4 vols.), III, p. 111.

set forth the theory of judicial review in an opinion that is now the cornerstone of judicial supremacy.

Yet the importance of *Marbury* v. *Madison* can be overestimated. It decided only a narrow point of the Court's jurisdiction; the Court was regulating itself, not extending its authority over elected officers. Hence the case could not occasion a great controversy between the Court and Congress. Not until 1857 did the jurisdictional self-denial of the Marbury case become a precedent for judicial regulation of the whole government.

When, in the Dred Scott case, the Court again refused to enforce an act of Congress, it was again soon to be ideologically isolated: [24] Its majority fanatically supported a policy which soon the Congressional majority would scorn. After the long Federalist domination of the Court from 1789 to the mid-1820's, it was roughly aligned with national politics by Jackson's appointments. But life tenure means that the current of judicial ideas is sluggish. Pro-slavery judges, holdovers from the less inspiring elements of Jacksonian Democracy, approached the free-soil controversy convinced of the justice of their position and blinded to the politics of their day. They reasserted the claim of *Marbury* v. *Madison*; but the cases were not analogous. Marshall's Court decided a minor question of jurisdiction and did not deprive Congress of important powers. Taney's Court, however, meddled with the most insoluble problem of its generation and, moreover, denied Congress the power to govern.

Dred Scott, a slave, had been taken by his master in 1834 from Missouri to Illinois, where slavery was forbidden by state law, and thence in 1836 to Fort Snelling (near Minneapolis) in the Louisiana Territory north of 36° 30', where slavery was forbidden by the Missouri Compromise, and finally in 1838 back to Missouri. Arguing that he was freed by residence in free territory, he sued for freedom in Missouri courts and lost. Then he was sold to Sandford, a New Yorker—the sale made the diversity of citizenship necessary for a suit in federal courts—and he sued in them for freedom on the same grounds.

Six majority and three dissenting opinions were written and none of the judges on either side entirely agreed with the others. But five judges apparently agreed with Chief Justice Taney that the Missouri

[24] *Scott* v. *Sandford*, 19 How. 393 (1857).

Compromise was unconstitutional. Scott, he said, was not a citizen of the United States and hence could not sue. Negroes were not citizens of any state, nor therefore of the United States, when the Constitution was adopted, so Taney mistakenly asserted; [25] and no state (here Illinois) could by its own action enlarge United States citizenship. Nor could Congress, he said, abolish slavery in the territories, thus indirectly granting Negroes citizenship. To do so, Taney held, would deprive slave-owners of property without due process of law in violation of the Fifth Amendment. Hence the Missouri Compromise of 1820 was void, Scott was still a non-citizen slave, and as such could not sue in federal courts.

Temporarily, this decision brought the Court into popular contempt in the North. But by the strangest paradox of our constitutional history, the Court absorbed power out of infamy. After Lincoln appointed five Republicans or Unionists, Republican Congressmen did not object to judicial review by Republican judges. That the bitter taste of the Dred Scott decision was forgotten so soon is the crucial event in the history of judicial review. Had Republicans prohibited slavery by statute, wholly ignoring the case, judicial review would probably have died a-borning. But instead they prohibited it by the Thirteenth Amendment, thus indirectly acknowledging the Court's right to void acts of Congress. Throughout the debates on the Thirteenth Amendment, even the Radicals conceded the need for an amendment; and this agreement meant general acceptance of judicial review.

Judicial review was moderately exercised so long as all three branches were controlled by men whose partisan principles were derived from the Civil War. But in the next generation the Court was again ideologically isolated. From, roughly, 1890 to 1936 the Court itself and most Americans believed that the Court was the censor of Congress and should regularly exercise a judicial veto. During most of that time the Court was always far more conservative than public opinion. Appointments did liberalize it somewhat toward the end of Theodore Roosevelt's Presidency and again toward the end of Wilson's; during the 1920's public opinion seemed almost as conservative as the Court. But appointments did not turn out quite as expected and when the electorate voted conservatively the Court voted even more so. Life tenure ensured that the Court should lag behind the public opinion expressed in the

---

[25] See Gordon E. Sherman, "Emancipation and Citizenship," *Yale Law Journal,* XV (1906), pp. 263–82.

more responsible branches. Hence the Court had frequent occasion to thwart elected officials with judicial review.

In the post-Civil War period judicial review was much encouraged by the two tendencies heretofore discussed: first, habituation to judicial annulment of state law by the Court's use of the supremacy clause; and second, conflicts between the Court and other branches, conflicts inevitable because judges were (and are) out of touch with the electorate. But these tendencies were not alone enough to make judicial review. Both existed almost from the beginning, yet judicial review became especially characteristic only after the Civil War. Judicial supremacy needed something else, and that was a doctrinal gloss over the words of the Constitution, a gloss to give judges leeway for reading their own social philosophies into it.

The framers omitted petty detail from the Constitution, thus enabling us to adapt it to the twentieth century world. In the absence of detail, statutes can seldom conflict directly and verbally with it. In all but five of the seventy-seven cases in which acts of Congress have been held unconstitutional, they have conflicted more with judicial embroidery than with the exact words of the Constitution itself. (The five cases of direct verbal conflict all involved the procedural guarantees of the Bill of Rights, which are the most specific parts of the Constitution.[26]) Given such generalized wording, judicial limitation of Congress was difficult until the words were narrowed down. But by 1900 or so, seven judicial generations, each including some very ingenious sophists, each bombarded by the sophistries of ingenious counsel, had accumulated a remarkable set of extra-constitutional doctrines sufficient for the purpose.

What the Court needed was a set of doctrines that specifically limited the broad powers of the national government. For this the Tenth Amendment served well:

The powers not delegated to the United States by the Constitution, nor prohibited by it to the States, are reserved to the States respectively, or to the people.

This may seem to the layman indisputably plain English; but interpreted within different constitutional traditions, it can have entirely

[26] *The Justices* v. *Murray*, 9 Wall. 274 (1870); *Boyd* v. *United States*, 116 U.S. 616 (1886); *Callan* v. *Wilson*, 127 U.S. 540 (1888); *Wong Wing* v. *United States*, 163 U.S. 228 (1896); *Rasmussen* v. *United States*, 197 U.S. 516 (1905).

different meanings. The broad constructionist, who believes that the Constitution must always be interpreted as delegating whatever power the national government needs, neglects and ignores this amendment. When a broad constructionist like Marshall or the Roosevelt-appointed judges must decide whether or not a national law infringes upon powers reserved to the states, he asks: Is there any basis at all in the delegated powers for the exercise of it in the statute? And since the grants of Article I are very broad, the answer is almost always "yes." In his hands, therefore, the amendment can seldom limit the other branches. On the other hand, the narrow constructionist, who believes that the Constitution must always be interpreted to limit, even at the risk of a national debacle, the national government in favor of the states, emphasizes this amendment all out of proportion to the rest of the Constitution. When a narrow constructionist, like Taney or the justices of the early 1930's, must decide a question of the infringement of reserved powers, he asks: Can I deduce from the delegated power on which this statute rests a self-contained limitation that makes this statute infringe on the reserved powers of the states? Since 1870 an often narrow constructionist Court has twenty-nine times discovered limitations in the unlimited grants of power to Congress. The broad constructionists undoubtedly have the better argument. The amendment simply says that it reserves to the states those powers not delegated to the national government; it does not say, as the narrow constructionists insist, that it also reserves to the states part of the national government's delegated powers. But a poor argument has not deterred the narrow constructionists. Thus the Constitution gives Congress without restriction the power "to lay and collect taxes," but the Court has held that Congress cannot lay taxes if they concern a subject which the Court believes is reserved to the states.[27] Similarly, Congress has the unrestricted power "to regulate commerce with foreign nations and among the several states"; but the Court has held that many clearly interstate transactions (e.g. the refining of sugar imported from abroad and sold all over the United States) are not interstate,[28] and that special aspects of interstate business (e.g. railroad employment contracts) are not commerce.[29] Altogether, the Court has held that

[27] *United States* v. *Dewitt*, 9 Wall. 41 (1870); *Hill* v. *Wallace*, 259 U.S. 44 (1922); *Bailey* v. *Drexel*, 259 U.S. 20 (1922); *Trusler* v. *Crooks*, 269 U.S. 475 (1926); *United States* v. *Butler*, 297 U.S. 1 (1936).
[28] *United States* v. *E. C. Knight Co.*, 156 U.S. 1 (1895).
[29] *Adair* v. *United States*, 208 U.S. 161 (1908).

many of the power-delegating clauses of Article I (taxing, borrowing, government of territories, commerce, bankruptcy, and patents) as well as the Fourteenth and Fifteenth Amendments do not really mean what they say, but impliedly reserve to states some of the power that they apparently grant to Congress.

An interesting example of the effect of narrow construction is the story of Congress and child labor. Knowing that the Court had long regarded manufacturing as local commerce rather than interstate—and hence beyond the reach of direct Congressional regulation—Congress prohibited the interstate shipment of goods produced by child labor. In the famous case of *Hammer* v. *Dagenhart* the Court held that this really regulated local business and hence invaded powers reserved to the states.[30] The decision necessarily ignored what Congress actually did, for while Congress indirectly regulated local business, the commerce it directly regulated was clearly interstate—and that the Constitution gives it full power to control. Persevering in humanitarianism, Congress next passed a special profits tax on businesses employing children; but in *Bailey* v. *Drexel* the Court again held that the tax regulated local business, unconstitutionally invading the powers reserved to the states.[31] Again an unlimited power of Congress was whittled down by an interpretation of the vague words of the Tenth Amendment. Congress recognized its defeat and proposed a constitutional amendment for national regulation of child labor. It has never been ratified; but since the Court overruled *Hammer* v. *Dagenhart* in 1941, it is not really necessary.[32]

The narrow constructionist finds the due process clause of the Fifth Amendment almost as useful as this peculiar version of the Tenth for judicial review. Up to the middle of the nineteenth century the phrase no person "shall be deprived of life, liberty, or property without due process of law"—a free translation from the Magna Charta—was regarded simply as a guarantee of traditional procedure in trials. But then the phrase took on new meaning; it became a guarantee that statutes as well as trials be just. All the prejudices of *laissez-faire* economics were absorbed into the phrase: a minimum wage law for women in the District of Columbia, for example, was said to restrict the freedom of contract and thus to deprive employees of property in

---

[30] 247 U.S. 251 (1918).
[31] 259 U.S. 20 (1922).
[32] *United States* v. *Darby*, 312 U.S. 100 (1941).

their labor without due process of law.[33] So broad had the phrase become by the 1920's and 1930's that it could be used to prohibit almost any regulation of business that the Court did not like.

What these extra-constitutional doctrines accomplished was, in Edward S. Corwin's words, "the Court's emancipation from the constitutional document." [34] Instead of interpreting the Constitution, the Court's job became interpreting its own precedents—which explains the wisecrack of the lecturers on law that students shouldn't read the Constitution lest they become confused. Interpretation of precedents allows the Court much greater freedom of choice in holding statutes unconstitutional than does mere interpretation of the Constitutional document. And this increased freedom of choice is one very important reason for the increase in judicial review in the period since the Civil War.

Toward Judicial Subordination:
What Deters Judicial Review

Judicial review is a great power, but it is neither so absolute nor so irresponsible as it seemed in its heyday. According to the foregoing analysis, it was produced by the accumulated force of three circumstances: habituation to judicial supervision of state law; the influence of life tenure which, in occasional periods of ideological isolation, encouraged new applications of judicial review; and the development of an extra-constitutional gloss which was used to limit the powers of the other branches. But to each of these circumstances, there is a counter-circumstance limiting the scope of judicial review. The urgency of judicial self-restraint makes judges very conscious of the enormity of judicial review. Presidential appointment sometimes minimizes judicial isolation. And the doctrinal gloss is judge-made law, easily promulgated and even more easily repealed. During the heyday of judicial supremacy, these limitations seemed insignificant, as indeed they were so long as the Court did not too often act as if its theoretical supremacy were real. But they acquired a new force after the great orgy from 1934 to 1936, when in three years the Court nullified

---

[33] *Adkins* v. *Children's Hospital*, 261 U.S. 525 (1923).
[34] Edward S. Corwin, *Constitutional Revolution, Ltd.* (Claremont, California, Claremont Colleges, 1941), p. 31.

thirteen acts of Congress, ten of them the highest trumps of the New Deal. The misuse of power contains its own retribution: In reaction to the abuses of 1934 to 1936 judicial review declined so much that some students believe it has now become wholly atrophied. Let us therefore examine its limitations in some detail in order to estimate its present significance.

The great defect of judicial review is judicial pride. This is why Theodore Roosevelt so often talked of putting the "fear of God" into judges—for pride is the primary Christian sin. Judicial review depends upon judges' belief that their version of public policy is better and wiser than the version of Congressmen and Presidents. No judge can void an act of Congress signed by the President without self-confidence, even arrogance; and in return, each judicial nullification fortifies the intellectual pride of the nullifiers. Only arrogance could impel Justice McReynolds—who wrote ten opinions holding acts of Congress void, more than any other judge ever on the Court—to compare Congress with the Emperor Nero and to declaim from the bench of the Court itself about an act of Congress: "The Constitution is gone." [35]

To this kind of intellectual pride the theory of judicial self-restraint is an appropriate antidote. It proposes to instill humility in judges as they approach the acts of legislatures, to remind them that the laws they make are merely later than the laws that Congress makes, not superior to them. Its basic premise is, in Justice Holmes' words, "that legislatures are ultimate guardians of the liberties and welfare of the people in quite as great degree as the courts." [36] And its rule of constitutional interpretation is that judges should prevent their views on public policy from influencing their judgment on constitutionality. This is best set forth, again in the words of Mr. Justice Holmes in his dissent in *Lochner* v. *New York*, a dissent which began contemporary jurisprudence, a dissent in which Holmes protested holding a statute prohibiting more than a ten hour day for bakery workers an unconstitutional deprivation of the liberty of contract: [37]

[35] *New York Times*, Feb. 19, 1935, p. 1.
[36] *Missouri, Kansas, and Tennessee Railroad* v. *May*, 194 U.S. 267, 270 (1904).
[37] *Lochner* v. *New York*, 198 U.S. 45, 75–76 (1905), Holmes, J., dissenting. This case of course did not involve judicial review in the sense here used, but rather judicial supervision of an inferior government. Nonetheless, these remarks are appropriate to the problem of judicial review, and Holmes applied the sense of them to it several times later.

This case is decided upon an economic theory which a large part of the country does not entertain. If it were a question whether I agreed with that theory, I should desire to study it further and long before making up my mind. But I do not conceive that to be my duty, because I strongly believe that my agreement or disagreement has nothing to do with the right of a majority to embody their opinions in law. It is settled by various decisions of this Court that State constitutions and State laws may regulate life in many ways which we as legislators might think as injudicious or, if you like, as tyrannical as this, and which equally with this interfere with the liberty to contract. Sunday laws and usury laws are ancient examples. A more modern one is the prohibition of lotteries. The liberty of the citizen to do as he likes so long as he does not interfere with the liberty of others to do the same, which has been a shibboleth for some well-known writers, is interfered with by school laws, by the Post Office, by every State or municipal institution which takes his money for purposes thought desirable, whether he likes it or not. The Fourteenth Amendment does not enact Mr. Herbert Spencer's *Social Statics.* The other day we sustained the Massachusetts vaccination law. . . . The decision sustaining an eight hour law for miners is still recent. . . . Some of these laws embody convictions or prejudices which judges are likely to share. Some may not. But a constitution is not intended to embody a particular economic theory. . . . It is made for people of fundamentally differing views, and the accident of our finding certain opinions natural and familiar or novel and even shocking ought not to conclude our judgment upon the question whether statutes embodying them conflict with the Constitution of the United States.

As soon as judicial review began to be characteristic of our government some judges, notably Justice Miller (1862–90), protested the tendency to substitute "an undefined code of ethics for the Constitution . . . a court of justice for the National Legislature." [38] Justice Holmes' great contribution during his thirty years on the Court (1902–32) was his frequent reiteration of the argument of *Lochner* v. *New York.* Although his teaching went unheeded during his lifetime, the next generation of judges made it the dominant attitude on the Court. The judicial intemperance during the early years of the New Deal inspired Justice Stone to suggest "two guiding principles of decision which ought never to be absent from judicial consciousness": [39]

that courts are concerned only with the power to enact statutes, not with
their wisdom . . .
that . . . the only check upon our own exercise of power is our own sense
of self-restraint . . .

[38] *Hepburn* v. *Griswold,* 8 Wall. 603, 638 (1870), Miller, J., dissenting.
[39] *United States* v. *Butler,* 287 U.S. 1, 78–79 (1936), Stone, J., dissenting.

Remembering these principles, the Roosevelt-appointed justices, with some regularity, read themselves homilies on self-restraint. Listen to Mr. Justice Jackson, in what seems to be an invitation to Congress to re-enact a tax on stock dividends held unconstitutional in 1920: [40]

There is no reason to doubt that this Court may fall into error as may other branches of the Government. Nothing in the history or attitude of this Court should give rise to legislative embarrassment if in the performance of its duty a legislative body feels impelled to enact laws which may require the Court to reexamine its previous judgments or doctrine.

Considering the oracular pose the Court has often adopted, "nothing in the history . . ." is no doubt judicial humor; otherwise, this is an entirely serious statement of the Court's present dogma. And the Court really acts upon it: Only three times since 1936 has it held an act of Congress unconstitutional; two of these cases were minor and only one involved high politics; and in that case the Court substituted its judgment for the judgment of only one-third of the legislature. The rider that they nullified was attached to the appropriations bill in the House; it was twice rejected by the Senate; and the whole bill was signed by the President only after he declared his belief that the rider was "not only unwise and discriminatory, but unconstitutional." [41]

The kind of humility that the theory of judicial self-restraint instills in judges is of course far from democratic humility instilled by the sanction of the ballot box. And yet they have this in common: While no sanction enforces judicial humility, judges who strive for it at least recognize that the ballot box is greater than they are. Essentially, therefore, the theory of judicial self-restraint is an attempt to incorporate some democratic responsibility into an institution which is deliberately irresponsible.

It is not wholly accurate, however, to say that the Court is irresponsible. Judges are appointed by Presidents and approved by Senators, both of whom are in turn responsible to the people in elections. This is perhaps only a minute ingredient of the democratic method: There can be no electoral sanction over judges appointed during good behavior. Nor can more than a few Presidents (actually Washington, Jackson, Lincoln, Taft, and Franklin Roosevelt) appoint a majority of

[40] *Helvering* v. *Griffiths*, 318 U.S. 371, 400–401 (1943). The earlier case referred to is *Eisner* v. *Macomber*, 252 U.S. 189 (1920).
[41] *United States* v. *Lovett*, 328 U.S. 303, 313 (1946).

the Court; and these few cannot avoid imposing their choice upon their successors. Still, Presidents do appoint judges. The Court is hence occasionally revitalized (although not necessarily improved) by new men with new ideologies formed in a new set of political circumstances. Were the popular belief true that Presidents appoint men to the Court only because they are wise and learned lawyers, then even Presidential appointments would not induce political responsibility. But few Presidents have themselves been duped by the mythology. Rather they have given the judicial plums mostly to prominent politicians, rarely to men with much previous judicial experience, usually to men whose chief recommendations are attachment to the President's political principles. Of course, Presidents perpetuate the myth, speaking of their appointees as learned and just men and perhaps really believing that political sympathy with themselves is what constitutes learning and justice. Occasionally, however, one finds documented frankness about the politics of appointments. While investigating Oliver Wendell Holmes for appointment, Theodore Roosevelt wrote of his doubts to Senator Lodge: [42]

In the ordinary and low sense which we attach to the words "partisan" and "politician," a judge of the Supreme Court should be neither. But in the higher sense . . . he is not in my judgment fitted for the position unless he is a party man, a constructive statesman. . . . The Supreme Court of the sixties was good exactly insofar as its members fitly represented the spirit of Lincoln. . . .

. . . Now I should like to know that Judge Holmes was in entire sympathy with our views, that is with your views and mine . . . before I would feel justified in appointing him. . . . I should hold myself as guilty of an irreparable wrong to the nation if I should put in his place any man who was not absolutely sane and sound on the great national policies for which we stand in public life.

Lodge assured Roosevelt that Holmes was sane and sound enough, so he got the job. Most judges have apparently been appointed after the same sort of inquiries. To the degree that they have, judicial appointments have been democratically made and judicial irresponsibility has been minimized.

[42] Quoted in Elting E. Morison, ed., *The Letters of Theodore Roosevelt* (Cambridge, Harvard University Press, 1950 ff.), vol. III, p. 298. From Henry Cabot Lodge, *Selections from the Correspondence of Theodore Roosevelt and Henry Cabot Lodge, 1884–1918.* Copyright 1925 by Charles Scribner's Sons, I, pp. 517–19.

The satirical comment that the Supreme Court follows the election returns is occasionally true. Unfortunately for American democracy, however, it does not follow them often enough. But, whenever it does, we can explain it by the dual influence of Presidential appointment and judicial self-restraint. Consider the Court's action during the first two terms of the New Deal. At first enough judges were as stunned as the rest of the people by the immensity of the depression that they sanctioned some startling experiments in regulation of business: price fixing of milk by states and the abrogation of the gold clauses in private bonds by Congress.[43] But from 1934 to 1936 the Court set to work to negate election returns and destroy the New Deal. The National Recovery Act, regulating prices and production generally; the Guffey Coal Act, regulating wages, prices and production in coal mining; the Agricultural Adjustment Act of 1934, regulating prices and production of farm commodities; the Railroad Retirement Act, a precursor of social security; the Frazier-Lemke Act and the Municipal Bankruptcy Act, the one relieving bankrupt farmers, the other relieving bankrupt local governments—all these were in one way or another held unconstitutional.[44] After such passionate assertion of judicial supremacy, the WPA, the Wagner Act, social security, the TVA, and stock exchange control were about the only parts of the New Deal left. And in the summer of 1936 it seemed certain that a Court which followed the election returns in 1908 and 1920 instead of the returns of 1934 and 1936 would strike them down too. So certain did it seem that the Wagner Act, for example, would be struck down that the Liberty League, financed by extreme right-wing elements, actually published a statement signed by fifty-eight outstanding constitutional lawyers, assuring employers that they might ignore the act because it would soon be held unconstitutional.[45]

Then came the election of 1936 and the Court reform bill. With a tremendous popular majority, the election vindicated that legislative spirit which the Court had so thoroughly condemned; and three months

[43] *Nebbia v. New York*, 291 U.S. 502 (1934); *Norman v. Baltimore and Ohio R. Co.*, 294 U.S. 240 (1935).

[44] *Schecter v. United States*, 295 U.S. 495 (1935); *Carter v. Carter Coal Co.*, 298 U.S. 238 (1936); *United States v. Butler*, 297 U.S. 1 (1936); *Railroad Retirement Board v. Alton*, 295 U.S. 330 (1935); *Louisville Joint Stock Land Bank v. Radford*, 295 U.S. 555 (1935); *Ashton v. Cameron County Water Improvement District*, 298 U.S. 513 (1936), respectively.

[45] D. O. Bowman, *Public Control of Labor Relations: A Study of the National Labor Relations Board* (New York, Macmillan, 1942), pp. 412–14.

later Roosevelt proposed to reconstruct the Court. His plan was to appoint up to six new judges, one for each judge over seventy years old who did not retire at full pay after ten years' service. Assuming the older judges would wish to keep their jobs, this would have enlarged the Court to fourteen or fifteen members. The plan failed. But, coupled with the election, it had two notable effects: Justice Roberts, the fifth man of the conservative, narrow constructionist majority, was induced to change his mind. From at least February, 1937—and some argue from just after the election in November, 1936 [46] he was the fifth man of a new, liberal, broad constructionist majority which sustained the Wagner Act and the Social Security Act.[47] The second result was that Justice Van Devanter, also a narrow constructionist, retired in June, 1937. Within the next few years a new majority of judges appointed by Roosevelt rubbed away most of the extra-constitutional gloss with which the old Court had tried to void the New Deal.

And this suggests the third limitation on judicial review. The judges who tried to reign in 1934 to 1936 used as a weapon that vast gloss of precedents which, *laissez-faire* inspired, forbade, for example, that the national government set minimum wages, reserving that function to the states,[48] and which at the same time forbade as well that the states set them,[49] thereby not permitting any jurisdiction in the United States to tackle what was in the 1930's one of the most pressing of national problems.

But what if this gloss were chipped and sanded off? Then would be revealed the simplicity and strength of the Constitutional grant to Congress. And more important still, the Court could no longer use the decoration to withhold the power to govern. This is exactly what the Court of Roosevelt appointees accomplished. True, the process started with the old Court after Justice Roberts changed his mind. The Wagner Act, the Social Security Act, and the Securities and Exchange Act were all upheld in the spring of 1937. But it was the later Court that systematically removed the gloss. Consider two cases dealing with agricultural regulation, first *United States* v. *Butler,* the culmination in fact and logic of the struggle for judicial supremacy, and second, *Wickard* v.

[46] Charles P. Curtis, *Lions Under the Throne* (Boston, Houghton Mifflin, 1947), pp. 156–57.
[47] *National Labor Relations Board* v. *Jones and Laughlin Steel Corp.,* 301 U.S. 1 (1937); *Steward Machine Co.* v. *Davis,* 301 U.S. 548 (1937).
[48] *Carter* v. *Carter Coal Co.,* 298 U.S. 238 (1936).
[49] *Wolff Packing Co.* v. *Court of Industrial Relations,* 262 U.S. 522 (1923).

Filburn, one of the cases in which the Court subsequently recognized the power of the elected branches to govern. In both the primary question was whether or not agriculture was a local concern outside the regulatory power of Congress. In the Butler case a cotton mill denied the validity of a tax on the processing of cotton, the proceeds of which were used to pay farmers to limit production. In the opinion of the Court, Justice Roberts—this was in his narrow constructionist phase —asserted first that the federal government has only such powers "as are expressly conferred upon it and such as are reasonably to be implied from those granted." [50] Thus he hypothesized a system in which states are more essential than the national government. Where the Constitution lists what powers the federal government has, Roberts asked what it has not. Once he had established the primacy of states, what follows is perhaps logical enough: [51]

Congress has no power to enforce its commands on the farmer to the ends sought by the Agricultural Adjustment Act. . . . *It does not help to declare that local conditions throughout the nation have created a situation of national concern;* for this is but to say that whenever there is a widespread similarity of local conditions, Congress may ignore constitutional limitations upon its own powers and usurp those reserved to states.

No matter how horrifying the catastrophe, he says in effect, Congress may not transcend the limits which judges have in seventy years read into the Constitution. Agriculture cannot be a national problem even when it is a national problem.

Compare this with *Wickard v. Filburn,* in which Filburn, a small dairy farmer, sought to escape a penalty imposed under the Agricultural Adjustment Act of 1938 for raising 23 acres of wheat when his allotment was only 11.1 acres. Filburn argued that, since he intended to keep the excess wheat for use on his farm, his production was a purely local concern which Congress could neither regulate nor punish. How could this application of the AAA be a regulation of interstate commerce when his grain was not and never would be in the commercial market? A unanimous Court, including even Justice Roberts, refused to allow Filburn's complaints. Here Mr. Justice Jackson's argument is summarized in a quotation: [52]

[50] *United States* v. *Butler,* 297 U.S. 1, 63 (1936).
[51] *Ibid.,* pp. 74–75 (emphasis added).
[52] *Wickard* v. *Filburn,* 317 U.S. 111, 125–29 (1942).

. . . even if appellee's [Filburn's] activity be local and though it may not be regarded as commerce, it may still, whatever its nature, be reached by Congress if it exerts a substantial economic effect on interstate commerce. . . . The effect of the consumption of home-grown wheat on interstate commerce is due to the fact that it constitutes the most variable factor in the disappearance of the wheat crop. Consumption on the farm where grown appears to vary in an amount greater than 20 per cent of average production. . . . That the appellee's own contribution . . . may be trivial . . . is not enough to remove him from the scope of federal regulation where, as here, his contribution taken together with that of many others similarly situated is far from trivial. . . . This record leaves us in no doubt that Congress may properly have considered that wheat consumed on the farm where grown, if wholly outside the scheme of regulation, would have a substantial effect in defeating and obstructing its purpose to stimulate trade therein at increased prices. . . .

United States v. *Butler* has never been specifically overruled; but who can doubt that it is completely obsolete today after a series of decisions like *Wickard* v. *Filburn?* The Roosevelt-appointed judges have used the same pumice on many other glosses so laboriously laid on by their predecessors. So now, as Edward S. Corwin prophesied in 1934, this is the "twilight of the Supreme Court." It can no longer claim to be superior to Congress, for it has itself destroyed the tools with which it worked its claim.

The Present Status of Judicial Review

As the previous discussion indicates, judges hostile to the temper of their times can make judicial review into a most effective obstruction to majority leadership. While one thinks immediately of the two most striking examples of obstruction, the Dred Scott case and the thirteen cases during 1934 to 1936, still the steady operation of judicial review in its heyday (from, roughly, 1890 to 1936) thwarted Congress and the President just as significantly. Systematically, but seldom spectacularly, the Court discouraged national efforts to meet national problems, thereby undoubtedly contributing to their seriousness when they had to be solved during the New Deal. Not only did the Court nullify numerous minor regulations of business, but also by that very fact successfully warned Congressmen not to attempt any major renovations of the economy. Without too many notable examples of conflict between the Court and Congress, the Court stood perpetually in the way of the rest of the government, obstructing majority leadership and making impossible majority reconciliation of the separated powers.

Happily this obstructiveness is now at a minimum because of the decline of judicial review since 1936. To many writers just prior to that time this was a "government by judiciary." D. W. Brogan, who in 1933 published another one of those perspicacious European studies of American government in the De Tocqueville tradition, started out with two chapters on the Supreme Court and judicial review, apparently because he believed them to be the really significant characteristic of our government.[53] Neither he nor any other scholar would today choose to repeat the emphasis. Nor, indeed, *will* any, so long as the judges are appalled by their predecessors' work from 1934 to 1936, so long as they remember the Court-packing bill and cling to the theory of judicial self-restraint. Furthermore, judicial review is now greatly limited, not only by the judges' own inhibitions, but also by the destruction of doctrines by which they could formerly refuse to enforce acts of Congress. Those constitutional limitations we call civil liberties are probably the only bases now left by which to make declarations of unconstitutionality. And this is properly so, for constitutional limitations in favor of civil liberties are about the only specific limitations in the Constitution. And so judicial review is now in eclipse, except perhaps in this one area.

To say that judicial review is in eclipse is not to say that the Court is an unimportant or non-controversial organ of the central government. The activism that previously attempted to control the central government is now directed largely at controlling the state governments, which have, of course, resented the control bitterly.

It is important to note that supervision of the states carries with it the tacit approval of the elected branches of the central government. The Court's most extensive supervision has occurred in the area of school desegregation and civil rights for Negroes. And in the case of the latter subject, the Congress and the President have finally (in the Civil Rights Act of 1964) gone further than the Court in protecting Negroes' rights, especially in the area of public accommodations. There is no doubt that the Court initiated this kind of supervision, especially in the famous school desegregation case, *Brown* v. *Board of Education*.[54] But the Presidents have supported court decisions with the United States marshals

[53] D. W. Brogan, *Government of the People* (New York, Harpers, 1933).
[54] 347 U.S. 483 (1954).

and even United States troops and the Congress and the President have provided specific enforcement procedures for the maintenance of Negroes' civil rights.

In some other areas of supervision, however, the Court has not had the clear tacit approval of the elected branches, for example, in the prohibition of school prayers and the redistricting of state legislatures. Congress and the President have done nothing to approve the Court's actions in these areas and it is conceivable (though not probable) that the Congress may initiate a constitutional amendment to reverse the Court's action. It is, therefore, not clear what the eventual outcome of supervision in these areas will be.

The difference between the consequences of judicial supervision in these two kinds of subjects indicates that even here the Court is dependent on the elected branches. Judicial review is in eclipse and judicial activism in supervision is dependent on the approval of President and Congress.

But what of the future? Is the eclipse permanent or temporary? Some scholars believe that judicial obstruction is for all the future impossible. But this seems wishful thinking in some, dread in others. It was pointed out at the beginning of this chapter that the Supreme Court has two resources for obstruction: One is judicial review. The other is life tenure. And while these reinforce each other, they are also distinct institutions. Judicial review may be temporarily eclipsed, but life tenure remains, perhaps to relight judicial review.

"ANOTHER ATTRIBUTE OF DEMOCRACY IS TO DISPENSE WITH ALL LIFE OFFICES"

Life tenure, or more properly the holding of offices "during good behavior," can be understood in the United States only as a denial of responsibility to the people. It has no other purpose or justification than the one Hamilton phrased as directly as possible in the 78th *Federalist*:

The standard of good behavior for the continuance in office of the judicial magistry, is certainly one of the most valuable of the modern improvements in the practice of government. In a monarchy it is an excellent barrier to the despotism of the prince; in a republic it is a no less excellent barrier to the encroachments and oppressions of the representative body.

Probably only the most inept propagandist today would identify irresponsible princes and responsible legislatures, but the purpose and justification remain essentially the same. Charles Warren, for example, concluded his two-volume history of the Court with these words: [55]

. . . in spite of the few instances in which it has run counter to the deliberate and better judgment of the community, the American people will unquestionably conclude that final judgment as to their constitutional rights is safer in the hands of the Judiciary than in those of the Legislature, and that if either body is to possess uncontrolled omnipotence, it should be reposed in the Court rather than in Congress, and in independent Judges rather than in Judges dependent on election by the people in passionate party campaigns and on partisan political issues.

Similarly Senator McCarran, adversely reporting Roosevelt's Court bill, opposed it because the Court must then: [56]

. . . ultimately become subservient to the public opinion of the hour, which might at the moment embrace mob passion abhorrent to a more calm, lasting consideration.

There is not much else one can say. Many people may prefer an only vaguely responsible Court to elected representatives; but they cannot possibly reconcile their preference with the democratic method. What is democracy, but government by public opinion determined in partisan elections? and what public opinion can there ever be but the public opinion of the most recent election or "hour"? If one does not wish to speak as bluntly as Hamilton of legislative oppression or popular incapacity, one can then like Warren or McCarran cast slurs on the democratic process itself, suggesting by the words "passionate party campaigns" or "mob passion" that Congressional legislation is first cousin to lynch law. The slander is insidious. It does not argue the case; it merely hints of some vague dire peril. Mob passion there may be in the United States, but judicial review has never been used against it. Rather the statutes the Court has nullified have been enacted after mature and lengthy deliberation. Consider the AAA, for example. During the late twenties and early thirties, bills dealing with farm surpluses were, as Solicitor General Reed pointed out in his argument in the Butler

[55] Charles Warren, op. cit., II, pp. 754–55.
[56] Committee on Judiciary, Report #711, United States Senate 75th Congress, 1st Session, p. 15.

case, reported out eight times by the House Committee on Agriculture, ten times by the Senate Committee.[57] Of these the Senate passed five, the House four, and Presidents signed two. The slow and tortuous path of a bill through Congress, as described in Chapter 5, can hardly be called mob passion. And the proposal that finally matured as the AAA had been before Congress since 1923, so that it can hardly be called the product of a passionate party campaign. The mob passion, from which the proponents of judicial review say the Court saves us, was in this case a popular emotion stable and thoughtful enough to endure through five campaigns and a decade of argument.

A more sophisticated form of this defense of the Court is to say that it protects civil liberties which the more responsible branches are likely to deny. Yet here too the record does not support the assertion. Twelve times the Court has refused to enforce an act of Congress because it seemed to conflict with one of the constitutional limitations for civil liberty. The first of these, the Dred Scott case, protected the property of slave-owners—which seems today a curious sort of civil liberty. Three cases of the 1860's nullified minor sections of the Reconstruction laws.[58] Against these should be set the Court's failure to oppose the really great infringements of liberty during Reconstruction and its systematic toning down of the Fourteenth and Fifteenth Amendments so that they did not really give Negroes full civil equality. In six cases between 1886 and 1922 the Court did, it is true, nullify several provisions of federal criminal codes that partly denied grand jury indictment, trial by jury, etc.[59] And more recently the Court nullified a section of the military code in *Toth* v. *Quarles*.[60] None of these cases involved a severe conflict between Court and Congress, however, so that it is difficult to see why complete judicial independence was necessary for the decisions to be handed down. Finally, in *United States* v. *Lovett* (1946) the Court decided that a rider to an appropriations bill forbidding salary payments to certain named persons was an unconstitutional bill of attainder.[61] Only in this case and in *Ex parte Garland*, a Reconstruction

[57] 297 U.S. 1, 5.
[58] *Ex parte Garland*, 4 Wall. 333 (1867); *United States* v. *Dewitt*, 9 Wall. 41 (1870); the *Justice* v. *Murray*, 9 Wall. 274 (1870).
[59] *Boyd* v. *United States*, 116 U.S. 616 (1886); *Callan* v. *Wilson*, 127 U.S. 540 (1888); *Wong Wing* v. *United States*, 163 U.S. 228 (1896); *Kirby* v. *United States*, 174 U.S. 47 (1899); *Rasmussen* v. *United States*, 197 U.S. 516 (1905); *United States* v. *Moreland*, 258 U.S. 433 (1922).
[60] 350 U.S. 11 (1955).
[61] 328 U.S. 303 (1946).

case, did the Court protect civil liberties against an aroused Congress; and in the Lovett case it was clear that the President and Senate were on the Court's side. The Court has, it is true, often protected civil liberties against mob passion in local government, but in so doing it is exercising not judicial review against Congress but judicial supervision of inferior government. Since the supervision involves no conflict with the persons who appoint judges, the Court could control this kind of mob passion just as easily if judges had short terms. So the record stands: Twice, or rather once and a half, in 160 years the Court has protected civil liberties when they were in real danger from the national government; which indicates that the Court, for all its life tenure, is no place for minorities to look for defense. From the time of the Alien and Sedition Acts to the recent Japanese Exclusion Order, oppressed minorities have mistakenly appealed to the Court only to discover that their only real protection was political, in elections, not litigation.

American democrats should not be misled by insinuations about mob passion or by the suggestion that life tenure works better in democracy than the electoral sanction can. They should understand the justification of life tenure for what it is: a distrust of democratic government and a preference for irresponsibility. But life tenure for the judiciary is, however, firmly established with us. The Jeffersonians attempted and failed to impeach Justice Chase in 1804; Franklin Roosevelt failed to force retirement in 1937. The failure of these two concerted efforts to reform the judiciary is a precedent which only the greatest civil turmoil could overthrow.

The Future of the Court

Why have American democrats tolerated judicial independence, especially when the Court has so often thwarted majority plans and perhaps will again? At least once a generation the Court has been extraordinarily disaligned with elected officers: after the election of Jefferson, during most of Jackson's presidency, just before the Civil War, from the middle nineties through 1910 or so, and during the first part of the New Deal. At each time it has unhesitatingly elevated its will over popular will and has thereby always occasioned a great constitutional controversy. And yet "for a century every contest with the Supreme Court has ended in evading the basic inconsistency between popular government and judicial supremacy," and it has been left "to the Justices themselves to correct the errors of the Court." [62]

One explanation, frequently advanced, is that the American people are innately conservative. But it is reasoning in a circle to say that we keep the Court because we are conservative and then to prove it by showing that we are conservative because we have kept the Court. Conservative opinion has indeed, since Hamilton's day, regarded the Court as its peculiar property. But conservative values have not always dominated our political life; one cannot say that popular conservatism preserved the Court in 1861 or 1937. Yet radical attack has strenghened rather than weakened the Court, except perhaps during the New Deal. So the question recurs: Why? One reason may be that conservative judges have had a more profound appreciation of our politics than conservative publicists. Perhaps they have known that the ferocious manners of Hamilton's great beast, the people, cover up a soft heart and a tractable mind. Immediate victory in politics is often enough to distract it from the constitutional issue underneath. Thus, when judges have strategically retreated in the face of popular indignation or when court vacancies have allowed the radical party to fill it with sympathetic men, democrats have been content to leave the constitutional problem untouched.

But to say that radical parties have not appreciated constitutional issues is only half an explanation because radicals have stubbornly persisted on other constitutional questions (suffrage, for example, or Negro citizenship). We need, therefore, a complementary, more reasonable motive for radical hesitation. This, perhaps, is to be found in a popular misconception of the Court's function. The Court is not an ordinary law court, even though it works through the ordinary judicial forms. Its cases, as observed in the beginning of this chapter, are heard in order to proclaim general law, not to dispense particular justice. Hence there is a discrepancy between form and function; the form of the law suit, the function of judicial law-making. Hence also there is popular confusion. Democratic politicians want unbiased judgments on private rights; but they also want the electorate to supervise law-making. They attack the Court because it is an almost irresponsible legislature; but they hesitate to carry the attack to its logical conclusion because the Court seems to be simply the last appeal on private rights. Consequently

---

[62] These are the words of Mr. Justice Jackson, who, as Roosevelt's Solicitor General, had good reason to ponder this paradox. Robert Jackson, *The Struggle for Judicial Supremacy* (New York, Knopf, 1940), p. vii.

American democrats have seldom known what to do about the Court. They have packed it a number of times to settle particular controversies. But the basic irresponsibility they have not touched, partly because they have been confused by this discrepancy between form and function.

The Court is indispensable to the constitutional system. Without a highest court of appeal, differences in decision between equal courts would produce intolerable confusion. Even the basic outlines of law would be different in different jurisdictions. And without a supreme federal court, state courts could not be relied upon to enforce federal law. Hence democrats cannot simply abolish the Court. They might perhaps return to the medieval tradition, still partially continued in England, in which the legislature is the high court of appeal. So Senator LaFollette suggested during his campaign for President in 1924: appeal to Congress when the Court has refused to enforce one of its acts. Theodore Roosevelt had earlier (during this 1912 campaign) suggested popular referendums on Court-nullified law. Both these proposals really meant an easier method of amending the Constitution. Mr. Justice Frankfurter, when yet a professor of law, suggested another approach: repeal of the due process clauses by which the Court then expressed its most extreme arrogance. But one hears little of these propositions today: The need is less; but also they were intrinsically unsound, being remedies for the symptoms, not remedies for the disease.

The disease, as Theodore Roosevelt rightly saw, is judicial pride. And although in the democratic method the electoral sanction is the only way to substitute humility for pride, still many democrats today hope that after the great lesson taught by the controversy of the 1930's, humility will be self-imposed without a formal sanction. Judges must, said Mr. Justice Jackson in 1941, just before he was appointed to the Court: [63]

. . . return to the spirit with which our early judges viewed the function of judicial review of legislation—the conviction that it is an awesome thing to strike down an act of the legislature approved by the Chief Executive, and that power so uncontrolled is not to be used save where the occasion is clear beyond fair debate.

But to expect that judges can always restrain themselves requires a greater faith in fallen human nature than democrats dare have. The propensity to pride pervades the black-robed judges no less than other

[63] *Ibid.*, p. 323.

men; and as democrats are well aware, neither humility nor responsibility endures unless enforced by formal sanctions. So long as the arrogance of 1934 to 1936 lives in judicial memory, we may perhaps rely on judicial self-restraint. But should these moral sanctions fail to operate, should the Court again be about to thwart majority leadership, again about to harass us with the most unworkable of separated powers, we then ought to remember the advice of Jefferson: [64]

Before the canker is become inveterate, before its venom has reached so much of the body politic as to get beyond control, remedy should be applied. Let the future appointments of judges be for four or six years, and renewable by the President and Senate. This will bring their conduct, at regular periods, under revision and probation. . . . We have erred in this point, by copying England, where . . . it is a good thing to have the judges independent of the King. But we have omitted to copy their caution also, which makes a judge removable on the address of both legislative Houses. That there should be public functionaries independent of the nation, whatever may be their demerit, is a solecism in a republic, of the first order of absurdity and inconsistency.

[64] *The Writings of Thomas Jefferson,* H. A. Washington, ed. (Washington, Taylor and Maury, 1854, 9 vols.), VII, p. 256.

8.

Federalism

> A great change of the whole system of institutions may come
> about unperceived if small changes are overlooked.
> —ARISTOTLE, *Politics*, 1303a

FEDERALISM IN ACTION:
THE CASE OF THE "PURGE" OF 1938

Once it happened that a Democratic President tried to defeat Democratic Congressmen in primary elections. The time was the spring and summer of 1938; the President, Franklin Roosevelt; the Congressmen, some of those who had most strenuously opposed his program in the preceding session. The episode is unique in American politics: No President before or since has tried anything like it; and for that very reason it is both fascinating in itself as well as instructive in our present inquiry. We have made some progress in our search for an agency of the majority to unite the separated powers: Chapter 5 demonstrated that Congress is far too disorganized internally to provide our national leadership. Chapter 7 demonstrated that the Supreme Court now has neither the inclination nor the power to continue the struggle for judicial supremacy. Chapter 6, on the other hand, demonstrated that the President can, when crisis presents an occasion, unite a government for the United States. But Chapter 6 also demonstrated that Presidential leadership is sporadic, largely because the President only sporadically leads his own party associates. For the investigation, to which we now turn, of his sporadic party leadership, there is no more illuminating introduction than the so-called purge of 1938.

As the primary campaign started that year it did not seem to differ signficantly from earlier primaries. President Roosevelt did, it is true, try to smooth out intra-party disagreements. For example, he persuaded

Representative Disney of Oklahoma not to run in the primary against Senator Thomas.[1] He repeatedly and unsuccessfully urged John L. Lewis and the party regulars in Pennsylvania to support the same candidates in the primary;[2] but he was unable to prevent a vicious, mud-slinging campaign fight between the two factions, a fight disastrous to the Democratic ticket in the fall. He took much trouble to help the two Southern New Dealers, Senators Pepper of Florida and Hill of Alabama, in the spring primaries—for Pepper, the President's eldest son formally announced "we are interested" in seeing him returned.[3] Early in March, Roosevelt took a part behind the scenes of the Kentucky primary, persuading erstwhile supporters of Governor Chandler, who coveted Senator Barkley's place, to desert Chandler for Barkley.[4] All this activity was quiet maneuvering, however, not extensively reported in the newspapers; all the public statements were made by other people, not directly using the President's name; and his so-called interference was either in support of sitting Senators or in the interest of party harmony. What Roosevelt did, therefore, was no more than what many of his predecessors had done. It would have been very strange indeed had he not helped his loyal floor leader, Barkley; and it would have been stranger still if he had ignored Pepper, who was one of the few Southern Democrats in favor of the very controversial and—in the President's view—extraordinarily important wage and hour bill, and whose renomination would certainly swing some wavering Southerners to its support.[5]

The first intimation that Roosevelt intended a real break with political precedent came during a vacation at Warm Springs, Georgia, at the end of March. Reporters were quick to notice that he praised Governor Rivers and Representative Weichel without mentioning Senator George who was up for renomination.[6] Another hint was dropped a month later when Jim Farley, still then Postmaster-General and Chairman of the Democratic National Committee, was quoted as saying that Maryland Democrats should defeat Senator Tydings in the primary. Several Maryland politicians, eager to be the President's candidate, promptly scurried

---

[1] *New York Times*, Feb. 13, 1938, p. 32.
[2] *Ibid.*, Feb. 25, 1938, pp. 1, 12.
[3] *Ibid.*, Feb. 7, 1938, p. 1.
[4] *Ibid.*, March 1, 1938, p. 15.
[5] Frances Perkins, *The Roosevelt I Knew* (New York, Viking Press, 1946), p. 263.
[6] *New York Times*, March 25, 1938, p. 3.

to the White House to beg for approval.[7] By the end of May the President's new role in the primaries was clear to journalists, if not to the public generally, and the word "purge" had begun to appear in the headlines. When the Governor of Oregon, a very conservative Democrat, implied that the President favored his renomination, Roosevelt's press secretary issued a sharp denial and a few days later Secretary of the Interior Ickes advised Oregon Democrats to vote for the other, more liberal Democrat in the primary.[8] At the same time Governor Johnson of South Carolina, a New Dealer, emerged from an interview with the President to announce that he would try to get the Democratic senatorial nomination over the incredibly reactionary Senator "Cotton Ed" Smith; and Governor Rivers of Georgia, also after seeing the President, intimated to reporters that he had been urged to run in the primary against Senator George.[9] These were clear enough indications that Roosevelt was trying to defeat those Democratic Senators who were lukewarm about the New Deal.

Then came the first clear evidence of a plan to purge. Harry Hopkins, then the Administrator of the WPA, told a reporter that, if he were voting in the Iowa primary, he would support, not Senator Gillette who was seeking renomination, but Representative Otha Wearin who was seeking promotion.[10] Senator Gillette, and other Democratic Senators who fearfully visualized a similar pronouncement about themselves, were outraged and excited by what they thought was a threat to use WPA money against Democrats. They spent the whole day debating it in the Senate.[11] Faithful Administration Senators, like Barkley and Mrs. Caraway, defended Hopkins, saying that he had been badgered by reporters into an indiscretion; even they did not then conceive of arguing that the Administration ought to campaign publicly against sitting Democratic Senators in the Democratic primaries.[12]

After the excitement aroused by Hopkins' remark, Roosevelt evidently wavered. The next day, coming out of a conference with the President, Representative Eicher of Iowa, announced his support of Wearin; [13] but a few days later at a press conference Roosevelt refused to discuss

[7] *Ibid.*, April 26, 1938, p. 4.
[8] *Ibid.*, May 15, 1938, p. 8; May 17, 1938, p. 18.
[9] *Ibid.*, May 17, 1938, p. 18.
[10] *Ibid.*, May 26, 1938, p. 1.
[11] *Congressional Record*, LXXXIII (May 25, 1938), pp. 7,460 ff.
[12] *Ibid.*, pp. 7,479 ff.
[13] *New York Times*, May 27, 1938, p. 1.

the Iowa primary and said that Hopkins' comment had been off-the-record and ought not to have been published.[14] Roosevelt's wavering reflected the division among his official intimates. While Hopkins, Corcoran, and Ickes were evidently urging aggressive action, Jim Farley seemed to support Gillette; and Henry Wallace, the only Iowan high in the Administration, kept discreetly, even noticeably, silent.[15] Roosevelt, uncertain and unwontedly indecisive, did nothing. Gillette won, and a few days later the two sat down to a hatchet-burying luncheon, in shirtsleeves, so reporters said.[16]

If Roosevelt intended to appeal to the people for support, the Iowa primary was an inauspicious start—ill-prepared, ill-timed, ill-managed, and necessitating at the end an embarrassing reconciliation. Perhaps Roosevelt was piqued by the failure; perhaps he had gone too far to stop —he had, for example, already selected Governor Johnson of South Carolina to oppose Senator "Cotton Ed" Smith; he had already given his blessing to one Lawrence Camp in the Georgia primary against Senator George; [17] and Senator Guffey of Pennsylvania—always loyal, but always too blunt—had already been forced off the Democratic Senatorial Campaign Committee for proposing a purge of all those Democratic Senators who had voted against the Court reform bill.[18] In any event, whether piqued by a messy failure or trapped by events which in his hesitancy he allowed to slip from his control, he told the people in a fireside chat that he intended to intervene in Democratic primaries: [19]

As the head of the Democratic Party . . . charged with the responsibility of carrying out the definitely liberal declaration of principles set forth in the 1936 Democratic platform, I feel that I have every right to speak in those few instances where there may be a clear issue between candidates for a Democratic nomination involving these principles. . . .

Do not misunderstand me. I certainly would not indicate a preference in a State primary merely because a candidate, otherwise liberal in outlook, had conscientiously differed with me on any single issue. . . . [but]. . . . We all know that progress may be blocked by outspoken reactionaries and also by those who say "yes" to a progressive objective, but who always find

---

[14] *Ibid.*, June 1, 1938, p. 4.
[15] *Ibid.*, June 3, 1938, p. 2; June 8, 1938, pp. 1, 14.
[16] *Ibid.*, June 13, 1938, p. 8.
[17] *Ibid.*, June 2, 1938, p. 1.
[18] *Ibid.*, June 2, 1938, p. 5.
[19] *The Public Papers and Addresses of Franklin D. Roosevelt, 1938.* Copyright 1941, by Franklin Delano Roosevelt, p. 79.

some reason to oppose any specific proposal to gain that objective. I call that type of candidate a "yes, but" fellow.

Soon thereafter he started out on a trip through the South to California, presumably to campaign in the Democratic primaries for New Dealers and against the " 'yes, but' fellows," the ones who had opposed not only the Court bill, but also the wage and hour bill, the administrative reorganization bill, and the public utility holding company death sentence clause. He made four speeches for Senator Barkley in Kentucky; but after that the "purge" was, as an editor of *Nation* complained, allowed "almost to peter out." Instead of campaigning forthrightly for his supporters, he ceased to mention primaries, substituting: [20]

an elaborate code of graduated approval—with candidates designated as "friend," "old friend," and "dear old friend" according to the degree of White House enthusiasm for their respective nominations.

In Covington, Kentucky, he had asked Democrats to renominate the Senate floor leader because: [21]

We in this county operate principally through what we call the party system. We so operate because we believe that party responsibility eliminates a large part of the confusion which would result from a complete lack of party leadership.

But by the time he spoke for Senator Thomas in Oklahoma, he had cheapened the argument from an appeal for effective democratic government to an appeal to sordid self-interest: [22]

Senator Thomas has been of enormous help to me and to the Administration in keeping me advised as to the needs of your State, and as to how we, in Washington, could help meet them.

In Colorado and Nevada, where Senators Adams and McCarran, two who really qualified for the "yes, but" category, were up for renomination, he ignored their opponents and referred to McCarran as a "friend," albeit the lowest degree of approval.

Back again in the Old South, and encouraged perhaps by the news of Barkley's victory, he was more forthright. At Barnsville, Georgia, he made a full-dress speech for Lawrence Camp, the Federal District At-

[20] *Nation*, CXLVII (July 23, 1938), p. 79.
[21] *The Public Papers and Addresses of Franklin D. Roosevelt, 1938*, p. 438.
[22] *Ibid.*, p. 444.

torney whom he had encouraged to run against Senator George. In South Carolina he obliquely supported Governor Johnson who was running against Senator "Cotton Ed" Smith. In Maryland, he made the most powerful and partisan speech of the campaign endorsing Representative Davey Lewis, who was trying to unseat Senator Tydings. Finally in a New York City Congressional district, he strongly supported one James Fay, a deputy collector of internal revenue, against Representative O'Connor, a Tammany Democrat, chairman of the House Rules Committee, and the man who more than anyone else delayed consideration of the wage and hour bill.

And the result of his campaigning? Senator Barkley won in Kentucky, Senator Caraway, whom he had mildly supported, won in Arkansas, Senator Thomas won in Oklahoma. Three victories. But Senator George won in Georgia, Senator Smith won in South Carolina, Senator Tydings won in Maryland. Three defeats. James Fay won in the New York 16th District. A victory. As many journalists and scholars have pointed out, every sitting Congressman, with the exception of O'Connor, won—which suggests that Roosevelt's campaigning had no significant effect, except perhaps in New York City.[23] Of course, 1938 was a bad year for the New Deal in the fall elections and it may be that he did at least save Barkley and Thomas from defeat. Otherwise, however, he did not accomplish very much, certainly not enough to compensate for the bad feeling he engendered among conservative Democrats.

Why the meagre result?

Perhaps in part Roosevelt failed because of simple lack of preparation. While some of his advisors may have conceived the plan in 1937, Roosevelt himself probably did not decide just what to do until late in the campaign year. How else can one explain his wavering over the Iowa primary? How else can one explain the elaborate trip West, starting out just after the promise made in the fireside chat to "indicate preferences," a trip taking him through eleven states during their primary campaigns, and yet a trip on which he indicated a preference plainly in only three states and hinted at a preference in only two more? Reconstructing the events now, it seems likely that, with his advisors divided, he planned at first merely to have certain recognized intimates speak out, as his son James did in Florida, or as Harry

---

[23] This is the conclusion reached after a careful examination of several campaigns by J. B. Shannon in "Presidential Politics in the South—1938," *Journal of Politics*, I (1939), pp. 146–70, 278–300.

Hopkins did in Iowa, but that he changed his mind after the Iowa fiasco. No doubt it is futile now to pry into long-forgotten thoughts, but one fact is certain: He did not select his candidates in Georgia or Maryland until sometime in May, unfortunately after the junior Senator in each state—both good New Dealers—had agreed to campaign for the men he was trying to purge.[24] Yet one rule upon which most experienced politicians would agree is that, in a primary campaign to unseat a fairly popular office holder, the aspirant ought to work full time at his campaign for at least six or nine months before the election. By this standard the purge was ill-planned; the hesitancy on his trip West indicates that the affair was ill-managed. In his own campaigns, Roosevelt was extraordinarily astute; but here he blundered.

The blunder is understandable. He was attempting something theretofore never tried on a grand scale in American politics.[25] Furthermore, he was running counter to the tradition of localism and state sovereignty in American politics. So it is not strange that he blundered in an explored land. Consider the blank amazement and unbelief displayed by Hiram Johnson when Hopkins' remark about the Iowa primary was reported to the Senate: [26]

Mr. JOHNSON. . . . I take it Mr. Hopkins is a resident of Iowa.
Mr. WHEELER. I do not know.
Mr. JOHNSON. He must be, or he would not think of doing such a thing.
Mr. WHEELER. No, he is not, I am told.
Mr. JOHNSON. The Senator must be in error. Mr. Hopkins must be a resident of Iowa, or he would not think of doing such a thing.
Mr. WHEELER. Mr. Hopkins, I am informed, votes in New York. . . . [H]e is being talked of as a candidate for Governor of the State of New York.

And having considered Johnson's incredulity, consider then how difficult to plan and execute was Roosevelt's self-imposed assignment.

It is a superficial explanation, however, to say that the meagre result of Roosevelt's campaign was due only to blundering. Behind the blundering lies the fact of federalism. What this whole episode demon-

[24] *Ibid.*, pp. 283, 290–91.
[25] Presidents have of course frequently tried to influence nominations in their own parties. And every President since Wilson has at least once publicly endorsed a candidate in a primary of his own party. See William L. Bast, "Presidential Participation in Congressional Primary Elections of His Own Party" (Appleton, Wis., Lawrence College Library, typewritten, 1958). What makes Roosevelt's action unique is its grand scale and great national publicity.
[26] *Congressional Record*, LXXXIII (May 25, 1938), pp. 7,460–61.

strates more than anything else is the resistance of local politicians to national leadership. With their own well-oiled local machines, all the sitting Senators won, whether Roosevelt favored or opposed them. The only place where Roosevelt unseated a Congressman was in his own state of New York; and there he was perforce a local politician himself, the leader of a local faction; so his victory must be attributed as much to his residence as to his national leadership.

POLITICAL LOCALISM: NATIONAL COMMITTEES

The localism of our politics which this episode concretely displays is equally apparent in abstract analysis of the structure of our political parties. Their ideal form, as diagrammed in the textbooks of the last generation, is two vast pyramids, each resting on approximately half the voters. Each rises from precinct captains just above the voter base through city and county committees, through state committees, to a national committee at the top. Human associations are so intangible that pictures always distort them; and this picture is worse than most. It has hardly any relation at all to what actually exists. One can too easily draw from it the absurd inference that party officials are clearly responsible to party voters. Yet we all know how muddled are primary elections and how rarely are even precinct captains responsible to the voters they serve. We all know as well that the pyramid picture is false at the top, for it leaves out the popularly recognized leaders of the party, that is, the party candidates in elections, the President, Congressmen, Governors, et al. But the worst distortion in this picture theory is the suggestion it makes that parties are compact enough, organizationally, operationally, ideologically, to be described as a pyramid at all. This is just exactly what they are not. Instead they are loose federations of local political groups, groups in such confusing array of relationships with one another that no chart or diagram could ever generalize their contacts accurately.

Since parties are loose federations, the national committee is only a figurehead, concealing the real centers of power underneath. Formerly the national committees always hibernated three years out of four, waking up only in Presidential campaigns. Although in the past thirty-five years each national committee, awakened to action by a series of bad defeats, has established a permanent publicity bureau, they have not thereby acquired any voice in the real management of the party. When its party is in power nationally, each committee does, it is true, share vicariously in party management through the person of its chairman. He is the President's campaign manager and patronage dispenser. From Cleveland to Truman, the chairman of the national committee of the President's party was also the Postmaster-General, the officer with the most federal patronage. Since the post office patronage has now been curtailed to relatively little, Presidents have sometimes appointed chairmen who are simply Congressmen or not even office holders. By this change, the chairmen have become even more obviously the personal agents of Presidents, while the chairmen of the opposition party have clearly been minor figures waiting to be replaced by the appointees of a Presidential candidate. In campaign years, of course, the committee (i.e. the chairman) collects the $3,000,000 which the committee is permitted by law to have. Most of it is spent for the Presidential campaign, but some is also passed on to other candidates. Here some real party control is possible because the committee (i.e. the chairman) can select the beneficiaries, favoring the party regulars, ignoring the undisciplined mavericks. In all this, however, the chairman works quite independently of the committee. He dispenses patronage not through his committee associates but rather through Congressmen and local party leaders whom he knows to be important. And in the management of the campaign he is really responsible to the Presidential candidate rather than the committee. Hence in both their staff work and their campaigning, national committee are only nominally the apex of a party pyramid. On the few occasions when they have presumed to be more, they have been promptly and effectively rebuked. In the 1940 Democratic convention Jim Farley, still national chairman and ambitious for promotion, used his position to run against Roosevelt for the nomination. He lost and he resigned. Or again, Carroll Reece, a Congressman from Tennessee and in 1946–1947 Republican national chairman, was once so bold as to criticize Republican Senators who did not follow the lead of the Republican Policy Committee in the Senate. Senator Morse at once announced: [27]

. . . I deny that the group of Republicans for whom Carroll Reece serves as a chore boy represents the rank and file of registered Republican voters.

[27] *New York Times,* March 4, 1947, p. 19.

One cannot regard as important a committee of which the chairman is so easily described as a "chore boy."

The insignificance of the national committee is further illustrated in its personnel, a man and a woman from each state. While the state organizations do occasionally send their real leader to the national committee, more frequently they use the job as an inexpensive honor for deserving party types: "fat cats" (i.e. rich men whose large campaign contributions are their only party service), retired politicians (sometimes also discarded ones, in which case the job serves as a consolation prize), second-rate party leaders for whom the job is the summit of their political careers, or prominent laymen whose names are decorative on letterheads and newspaper advertisements. In prestige the national committeeman ranks only a little above a Presidential elector, for example; and, since little work is expected of the committee, the job can appropriately serve as a reward.

The things the committees do *not* do are even more illustrative of their insignificance than the character of their membership. They are carefully isolated from the really important party affairs like the choice of a candidate for President and the making of the national platform. These are the functions of the national conventions, in connection with which the national committee has only these minor duties: the selection of the convention city, the dispatch to state committees of a call for delegates, and the choice of a temporary chairman. Precedent demands that even in this routine the national committee be strictly neutral among the important contenders for the nomination, avoiding the selection of a city or a keynoter that might conceivably benefit one candidate more than another. Once the national conventions have assembled, the national committee have no more influence than their individual members may have by reason of their position in state party machines.

Political Localism: National Conventions

Nor is the national convention the apex of the so-called party pyramid, for it is national in naught but name and function. It is a gathering of local leaders, a gathering so organized that they can make all decisions uninfluenced by the titular heads of the party. Were the individual delegates free to act individually, it is likely that national leaders like the President, national chairman, and former Presidential candidates might influence them directly, bypassing the state leaders and local bosses. But this is definitely not the case. For one thing the very unwieldiness of the convention (1,000–1,500 delegates) necessitates some intermediate level of leadership. Then also the delegates are chosen by state leaders in state conventions or in state primaries (which usually amounts to the same thing) and are therefore entirely responsible to the party leaders of their locality. Similarly, each state delegation chooses a representative for the convention committees and these committees (on permanent organization of the convention, on credentials of delegates, on rules, and on resolutions or the platform) usually control all the work of the convention except the actual nomination itself. Voting on roll calls is by states and the Democratic convention rules even permit the state delegations to vote as a unit (i.e. permit the majority of the delegation to control the minority). In short, the entire procedure is aimed at maintaining the state leaders' control of state delegations.

So it is that the choosing of a Presidential candidate—except when a President in office is renominated—is entirely a matter of alliances, bargains, and compromises among the local leaders. To the television viewer it perhaps seems unbelievable that anyone can control the bedlam he sees and hears. But the wild carnival, with its mob parades and cacophonic song, its frantic cheering and hypnotic name-chanting—all this violent enthusiasm is deceptive facade, too carefully controlled by cheer leaders to be as spontaneous as it sounds. Of course, the facade is desirable: It is a part of our tradition of circuses, and anyway the delegates are on vacation. Most campaign managers believe the myth that candidates must inspire frezny at the convention to prove that they can inspire frenzy in the voters in the fall—though of course they would not admit the corollary that only national frenzy could elect the duds they manage. Probably also the campaigners who engineer the giant demonstrations hope secretly that a display of enthusiasm, however spurious, will impel delegates to their candidates in one great St. Vitus dance, as it is said in the mythology that the ovation impelled the Democrats of 1896 to Bryan after he inflamed them with "you shall not press down upon the brow of labor this crown of thorns, you shall not crucify mankind upon a cross of gold." But they know or ought to know that, even in this remarkable case, Bryan had been traveling through the West and South for two years before the convention, making himself known and quietly lining up delegates. This is the usual procedure. The main contenders for the nomination start several years before the convention seeking pledges from local politicians. Farley reports that he started looking for Roosevelt delegates at the 1932 convention as early as November, 1930; [28] and Dewey had hardly lost the election in 1944 when he started to line up delegates for 1948. No sooner had Kennedy lost the Vice-Presidential nomination in 1956 than he began to act like a Presidential candidate and his victory in the convention in 1960 was undoubtedly owing in part to the fact that he had been working for the nomination for four years, while his opponents (Humphrey, Johnson, and others) had been working at it for only one or two years. Similarly Nixon, who as Vice-President had little else to do, had clearly been working for eight years on being Eisenhower's successor. In 1964 many liberal Republicans were dismayed by the ease with which Senator Goldwater won the nomination. They ought not to have been surprised, however, because they knew that he had been systematically working for delegates since at least 1956 by helping his followers to obtain crucial positions in the state party hierarchies, positions from which they could influence the selection of delegates. Nearly all the delegates from the South and the far Middle West and some of the delegates from the Midwest were assured for him in this way—and these alone were nearly enough to win the nomination.

So effective are the preconvention agreements among local leaders that they can seldom be upset by any amount of orgiastic enthusiasm on the convention floor. Theodore Roosevelt found this out in 1912 when he tried to carry away the delegates already pledged to Taft by an outburst of emotional oratory—"we stand at Armageddon; and we battle for the Lord." But He with whom the alliance was claimed did not see fit to change the minds of those Southern delegates who, cheering for Roosevelt, voted as they had been instructed by the local Taft managers who paid their traveling expenses. Governor Scranton found the same thing in 1964, when his 300,000 letters from citizens remained unopened and unsorted while the Goldwater delegates systematically voted down all attempts to liberalize their conservative platform and then went on to nominate their candidate.

What really happens at most conventions other than those in which Presidents in office are renominated is this: Several major contenders come to the convention with perhaps several hundred delegates pledged to them by preconvention agreements or Presidential primaries (these

[28] James A. Farley, *Behind the Ballots* (New York, Harcourt, Brace, 1938), pp. 62, 70.

are, in most states, simply a way for party voters to express a preference that will bind the delegates in the first few ballots). The suspense is maintained by the unpledged delegations and those pledged to "favorite sons" (that is, locally prominent politicians who usually have no chance for the big prize but to whom their state delegation is pledged either as an honor or the better to bargain with the major contenders for promises on jobs or policies). With many contenders, it has until recently been rare for any but a President in office to win on the first ballot. (Usually it takes at least five or six, but Garfield did not win in 1880 until the 36th and Davis in 1924 not until the 103rd.) Thus the balloting usually takes about two days and has taken as much as two weeks, in either case enough time for extensive horse trading. All sorts of considerations enter into this bargaining. When the local leaders are sure their party will win the election, the convention tends to be dominated by sordid deals of jobs later for delegates now, for example, the conventions that nominated Harding in 1920, Roosevelt in 1940, and Dewey in 1948. On the other hand, when the local leaders are really worried about the election results, they tend to look about for a genuinely appealing candidate as, for example, they did in the conventions that nominated Hoover and Smith in 1928, Roosevelt in 1932, Willkie in 1940, Eisenhower and Stevenson in 1952 and Kennedy and Nixon in 1960. Regardless of the specific considerations—and here are suggested only two extremes of the spectrum—the important points are that such deals are made by local leaders and that often the leading contenders prior to the convention are thrust aside by local bosses in favor of a "dark horse" who fits the kinds of deals they are making. Consider the Republican convention of 1920, which was pervaded with an expectation of certain victory and hence also with a hunger for spoils. Consequently the local leaders thrust aside Hiram Johnson and Herbert Hoover, both genuinely appealing candidates, for the pliable Harding. Consider in contrast the Republican convention of 1952, which was pervaded by a spirit of doubt. Taft, a reliable party regular, though not a sure vote-getter, was thrust aside for the clearly popular Eisenhower, not a party regular but the only man who seemed able to carry the party back into power after twenty years of opposition.

This analysis may suggest that it is never possible to nominate candidates who are not very similar to the candidate of the opposing party. Such is not, however, true, as the nominations of Bryan in 1896 and Goldwater in 1964 indicate. What happens in conventions like these two is that, by exploiting an ideological split in the party, the candidate persuades the delegates that he can win with a national coalition somewhat different from the one the party has been accustomed to winning with. Thus Bryan persuaded the Democratic party to abandon its traditional alliance of rural South and urban North for a much more heavily rural alliance of South and rural Middle West. Again Goldwater persuaded the Republican party to abandon its traditional alliance of Eastern and Middle Western mercantile interests for an alliance based on mercantile interests of the Midwest and racial interests of the South. Both changes involved radical reorganization of their parties' traditional electoral stance. So in addition to the usual bargaining kind of convention, there is a special class of party reorienting conventions.

Whatever kind of convention occurs, however the whole process of nomination bears the imprint of localism, of deals between candidates' managers and local bosses. National leaders of the party—the President who has been tested in elections and those Congressional leaders who have been elevated by their party colleagues—influence the nomination only insofar as they are local leaders too. Even though with their national reputations they are vastly more responsible to the voters of any specific locality than the local leaders are, it is the local leaders who control. Thus, although ten Presidents since the Civil War have conceivably been able to promote a lieutenant, only one has done so. (Theodore Roosevelt secured the nomination of Taft in 1908.) Even Franklin Roosevelt, whose hold on his party was greater than most, was unable both in 1940 and in 1944 to do more than veto certain aspirants for the nomination for Vice-President. Is there any better illustration of the fact that national conventions are in the hands of local bosses?

In recent years the evidence has been even more pronounced. Nixon and Kennedy in 1960 and Goldwater in 1964 used the new facilities of travel to influence local conventions in their favor by making local contact with local leaders prior to the conventions themselves. Thereby they both recognized and exploited the localism of "national" conventions.

And so the conclusion: if political parties are to be pictured as pyramids at all, there must be not two but hundreds of peaks, one or two rising over each local area. These smaller peaks have relatively little formal connection with each other, except that their top men meet every four years to agree upon a Presidential candidate. This is the decentralized localism of American parties, so different from the national parties of European democracies. In France and England especially, the party leaders at each geographic level in the hierarchy control the selection of party nominees for offices of that level. Thus national leaders control party nominations for the national legislature, local leaders the nominees for local councils and administrative offices. Not so here. In the United States national leaders control no nominations while local leaders control them not only for local offices but also for the national offices of Congressmen and President.

POLITICAL LOCALISM: PARTY PRINCIPLES

The discussion with which this chapter started showed by a concrete example how thoroughly local party leaders control nominations to the national legislature. The analysis just completed showed as well that local leaders control the nomination for the national executive. One important consequence of this localism is the great diversity of political belief in each of our two parties. Lord Bryce (and after him a host of more cynical and hostile students of our institutions) compared our parties to two bottles, saying "each bore a label denoting the kind of liquor it contained, but each was empty." [29] And unfortunately, Bryce and the cynics later are in large measure correct, for our parties are strikingly similar. Each of them covers most of the ideological spectrum. In both parties we find the kind of demogogic reactionaries who developed fascism in Europe. In both we find the traditionalist conservatism, which distrusts most innovation since 1900, a sentiment best represented by the Republican Goldwater of Arizona and the Democrat Byrd from Virginia. In both we find that modernized conservatism just right of center, eager to beat radicalism on its own ground, Scott of Pennsylvania in one, Maybank of South Carolina in the other. In both we find that mild radicalism—really old-fashioned liberalism and now the center—of which Republican Smith of Maine and the Democratic Gore of Tennessee are typical. In both we find that democratic radicalism, best shown in the spirit of the New Deal and in Roosevelt's description of himself as a "little left of center," in such Democrats as Humphrey of Minnesota and Douglas of Illinois and such Republicans as Javits of New York. Neither party has any prominent leader at the far left, but twenty-five years ago the Republican Marcantonio

[29] James Bryce, *The American Commonwealth* (revised edition, New York, Macmillan, 1923, 2 vols.), II, p. 29.

of New York City and the Democratic O'Connell of Montana stood in that position.

Until very recently the Republican party seemed far more homogenous than the Democratic. Republican variations from the party norm did cover the spectrum, but the variations were few in number. This seeming homogeneity was not, in fact, a harbinger of greater party centralization. Rather, it was a deceptive unity, often characteristic of each party whenever it has been out of office. The party in power attracts to it a large number of promoters who label their own opinions with the party's name for the sake of prestige and a few votes. So the bandwagon effect diversifies the ins. The outs, on the other hand, by the very fact of being outs, are usually stimulated to reconcile their ideological differences the better to fight for office. Sometimes, however, as in the Democratic party in 1896 and the Republican party in 1964, the outs (apparently in despair of ever regaining national office) split deeply in order to try out a new ideological appeal. If the appeal is successful, as was the Republican in 1860, then the party acquires a new ideological stance. If it is unsuccessful, however, the differences are composed (if not reconciled) in order to wage subsequent election campaigning. But underneath the public composure is the ideological divergence. Those who are surprised at the ideological divergence revealed in 1964 in the Republican party (after many years of apparent homogeneity) should recall the era of the 1920's when Republicans had been the dominant party for two generations and thus did not shrink from revealing their ideological split. In the 1920's Republicans won every election by considerable majorities and yet were so internally divided that they could accomplish almost nothing. Besides the mercantile conservatism from Wall Street to Main Street which today seems so dominant in the party, it then had two radical wings. One was the Northwestern and Midwestern rural radicalism which, having displaced Bryan-like Democrats, adopted Bryanesque attitudes: LaFollette of Wisconsin, Norris of Nebraska, Brookhart of Iowa—these were the extremes, the "sons of the wild jackass"—but many others like Borah of Idaho, Johnson of California, McNary of Oregon voted as often with the radicals as they did with the regulars. The other Republican radicalism of the 1920's was urban, centering in New York City and best expressed by Fiorello LaGuardia, who in his later career was a political intimate of Franklin Roosevelt. So we can say that the recent homogeneity of the Republicans is, as revealed by the split of 1964 and the splits of the 1920's, only a superficial phenomenon. Hence the proposition stand that each party is ideologically diverse within itself and has some representatives of nearly all political positions. The only real difference between parties is the label, for the bottles themselves are empty—or perhaps more accurately, filled with the same blend of whiskies and diluted, of course, with neutral spirits and water.

The background for this ideological confusion is again that localism of structure which blurs their platforms just as much as it disjoints their organization. Each party has all kinds of opinions represented in it simply because there is no national leadership that can bring all the elements of the party together. In alliances of local leaders simply for the purpose of nominating Presidential candidates, each local party takes on local characteristics so that as a result each party has just about as many ideological divisions as there are sectional differences of opinion in the country.

SECTIONALISM IN AMERICAN POLITICS

Localism dominates our political parties, in organization, in operation, in ideology. And this is not strange, for localism in this is simply a particular reflection of the sectionalism that dominates American culture generally.

Sectionalism today is somewhat on the decline. We are a mobile people and our system for the exchange of ideas (television, radio, movies, magazines, newspaper associations, etc.) is based on our national life and customs, not on provincial ones. But that the decline of sectionalism is so pronounced that it is no longer a constant fact in the mind of every citizen ought not to blind us to its influence on our history. From the very beginning the partially united states were always plagued with sectional secessionist movements culminating in the Civil War. Since then, sectionalism has no longer implied secession; but sectionalism itself remains. We cannot avoid recognizing that Kansas, for example, is today dominated by rural, Protestant grain farmers who have different ideals, different economic interests, different patterns of life and thought from the urban, Catholic factory workers who dominate Rhode Island. That these two states should have different political problems, different issues, different alignments is wholly to be expected. And so sectionalism continues to show itself in party alignment: The Republican party has not since the end of Reconstruction ever presumed to be more than a sectional party, for it has been almost entirely excluded from the eleven states of the old Confederacy except in the Presidential elections of 1928, 1952, 1956 and 1964, and most minor parties which have developed since the Civil War have been sectionally based (e.g., Populists in the South and Midwest, LaFollette Progressives along the Canadian border west of the Great Lakes).

Much the most significant influence of sectionalism in our history, however, is the federal structure of our government. Secessionist movements, sectional parties, and the like are simply particular manifestations of this always existent constitutional fact. It is federalism that, by encouraging quasi-autonomous local governments, made secession possible. It is federalism that, by so sharply separating local and national government, makes possible the localized structure and diverse ideology of our political parties. It is federalism, therefore, that stands behind the weakness of Presidential leadership, behind our failure to create stable majorities, behind our difficulties in rational voting, behind our only intermittent operation of the electoral sanction. As such, it deserves as careful analysis as can be made in the rest of this chapter.

The Origin of Federalism

Today, when federalism so often seems an obsolete form, impeding effective action and forestalling effective majorities, it is difficult to realize what a centralizing, unifying, nationalizing innovation it was in 1787. We worry now about how to make the national government effective; but the framers of the Constitution were worried about a much more basic question, how to make a national government at all. National government in the 1780's was little more than anarchy, one unforeseen consequence of the Revolution. For all their diversity in culture, in religion, nationality background, class origins, etc., the thirteen colonies were, when they were colonies, harmonized by the Crown. Southern colonies may have been indifferent to the French menace in the North, but the home government with its broader imperial vision taxed all colonies alike to fight the French and Indian wars. In Revolution, however, the colonists, rebellious against an imperial mercantilism which benefited Londoners more than themselves, inadvertently got rid also of the unifying influence of the London government. True, the initial steps in separation were taken by a "continental" Congress; but, when the revolutionaries devised new political forms to substitute for

the ones they abandoned, they forgot about the one unifying government. They mistook the local organizations of parliamentary control,
the several colonial governments, for government itself. Although there
was some excuse for the mistake because they had little contact with real
English government, at any rate they transformed colonies into states
as the ultimate political organization. Thereby, they forfeited the chance
of anything but anarchy once the joint interest in Revolution no longer
compelled cooperation, even though they did try to regularize the war-
time expedient of a Continental Congress by the Articles of Confederation, finally adopted in 1781.

The Congress of the Confederation had some characteristics of a
national government, more indeed than its critics then and since have
been willing to recognize. It could and did govern the western lands not
yet formed into states. Unlike most confederacies of times before, the
army it levied from the states was directed by the Congress—even
though the officers below field command were commissioned by state
governments. Most significant of all, the Articles contained several
provisions which, growing out of a sense of national solidarity, were
incorporated with little change into the Constitution (e.g., that citizens
of any state be entitled to the "privileges and immunities of citizens" in
other states, that each state give "full faith and credit" to the official acts
of every other state, etc.).

Nevertheless, it was a flabby government. Every important act by
Congress required the approval of nine state delegations (and amendments to the Articles required unanimity of the state legislatures). The
Congress could not directly govern the citizens of states unless they
were in the army, in the territories, or on the high seas. Since the taxes
Congress levied on the states were paid only at the pleasure of state
legislatures, each state had in effect a veto on every tax. Hence also most
states were constantly in arrears in their payments to Congress. Tax
collectors are the veins of the commonwealth, said Hobbes, treasurers
are its arteries, and what passes through them is its blood—and on this
analogy, the government of the Articles was a biological monstrosity,
still-born because the embryo lacked its most essential system.

Even worse, the democratic parties in the states developed an interest
in perpetuating this stage-scenery Leviathan. They controlled some state
legislatures easily enough, but they feared they could not control a fully
developed Artificial Man, the more so since conservative politicians
were the chief advocates of a stronger central government. That agrarian

democrats should act like anarchists is regrettable, but easily under-standable. Like the populists and progressives at the turn of this cen-tury, whose goals of anti-monopoly *laissez-faire* in domestic politics and isolation in foreign politics so closely parallel the radical goals of the 1780's, they superficially identified democracy with the least and least effective government. They were unaware of the deeper meaning im-plicit in the ideal, and they had not yet been granted the vision of a government good enough and effective enough to create the conditions of self-respect for everybody. And so they opposed every concrete attempt to strengthen the national government. In that incipient anarchy, when even the author of the *Centinel* letters, the most cogent of the Anti-federalist writers, could admit "that the present confederation is inade-quate to the objects of the union, seems to be universally allowed" [30] —in that incipient anarchy, the federalism invented at the Philadelphia convention restored national government. For that service we should be grateful.

After 160 years of habituation and of copying by foreign constitution-makers, the device of federalism seems so normal and simple that it is hard to understand how original it was in 1787. The idea was indeed original, however, that two governments, both sovereign in the portions of governing assigned to them, could operate on the same people simul-taneously. It was so new that the authors of the *Federalist Papers* had no word for it. In the thirty-ninth *Federalist* Madison explained that this new Constitution was partly "federal," by which he meant it was like loose leagues of still independent governments such as the Greek federations of antiquity or perhaps the United Nations of today, and partly "national," by which he meant it was like the centralized British or French governments of his time. The federal or league-like aspects were, he said, the facts that the Constitution was to be adopted by states, that states were to be represented in the Senate, and that the powers of the central government were to be limited to those enumerated in the Constitution. The national or centralized aspects were the representation of citizens directly in the House of Representatives and the operation of laws and courts and tax collectors directly on the citizens rather than on the states. In short, this new thing was neither flesh nor fowl, but a composition of both. What was unique about it was this: Although the central government was an association of states, a true league, still this

---

[30] Samuel Bryan, *Centinel*, No. 3, from John Bach MacMaster and F. D. Stone, *Pennsylvania and the Federal Constitution* (Philadelphia, 1888), p. 601.

central government governed not only states but their individual citizens also. This is what for Hamilton made it so superior to the government of the Articles, of which he said: [31]

The great and radical vice in the construction of the existing Confederation is in the principle of LEGISLATION for STATES or GOVERNMENTS, in their CORPORATE or COLLECTIVE CAPACITIES, and as contradistinguished from the INDIVIDUALS of which they consist.

This new federalism involved, however, legislation for both states and individuals and it was made possible only by the division of governmental functions between the state and national governments. The national government was delegated certain powers—mostly those enumerated in Article I, section 8; Article II, sections 2–3; and Article III, section 2—while all other conceivable powers were assumed to remain with states. Thus the national government was given the power to control foreign affairs and maintain an army, but state governments retained the power to raise a militia for internal police. The national government was given the power to levy taxes directly upon citizens— even the exclusive power to levy import taxes or tariffs—while the states retained also the power to tax everything except imports and exports. This division into two spheres thus made possible the creation of an effective national government without too greatly diminishing the powers of the states.

This was the secret of its success in the political situation of the 1780's. It did not destroy state governments which the radical parties so loved. It did not even greatly hamper their operation. Recall that still today the highest state offices carry as much prestige as, for example, Representatives in Congress. All that federalism did was to create an additional government. Hence it was an excellent propaganda device, an exactly appropriate arrangement to reconcile the vested interests in state government with the vested interests in a national one. It put the opponents of a stronger central government in a difficult position: Since they admitted the inadequacy of the Confederation, they could not object very much to the strengthening of the central government in itself. They could criticize only the particular form of the proposal. And here they were at a disadvantage because the state governments were quite clearly not to be destroyed. Hence about all the

[31] *The Federalist*, No. 15.

Anti-federalists could do was to question the purity of motive of the framers and to criticize the document for its paucity of democratic features. As it was, this criticism almost succeeded: The Constitution was adopted only by a minority and then only after a considerable amount of political maneuvering. Had federalism not characterized the whole structure, it is certain that the Constitution would not then have been adopted.

THE VALUE OF FEDERALISM

Thus we inherit federalism today because it was necessary in 1787 if the framers were to be able to bequeath us a national government at all. Simply because we inherit it, along with all the rest of our culture, does not, however, make it good. We do not revere poll taxes simply because we can trace them back to the forty-shilling freehold; nor do we respect the abracadabra of astrologers simply because we inherit their charlatanry from the Chaldees. Nor ought we in mistaken patriotism to venerate federalism simply because it was invented by our ancestors. They invented the electoral college too, an institution which we modified almost immediately (1804), and which is still so troublesome that we sporadically plan to revise it further. Rather, we ought to examine federalism, like all christening gifts, with a critical eye, asking whether it is really as useful or as pretty as it seemed the day it was received.

And so this question: What, precisely, is the effect of federalism today? And for answer there is no better concrete evidence than the story of Roosevelt's campaign in 1938. Federalism, by its maintenance of semi-autonomous state governments and hence of independent local political parties, makes it extraordinarily difficult to create a national party. This, in turn, contributes to the sporadic nature of Presidential leadership; and at the same time it makes rational, coherent voting difficult and rare. Observe how this was true in the 1938 campaign. That the local parties, based on local patronage, based on local elections wholly unconnected with national elections, were thoroughly independent of the national party is clear enough in Roosevelt's failure. Voters in every one of the primaries were asked to choose between local and national leadership. Quite generally they chose the local, which was in only about half the cases aligned with the national. Yet all these voters were Democrats, presumably followers of the national party and of its national leaders as indicated in the Presidential elections of 1936 and 1940. The federal structure no doubt hoodwinked them into believing that the election of the national legislature was a local affair. Only by the blindest chauvinism could such voting be called rational. Yet elections like this are far more common in our national life than those rare, once-a-generation contests like 1800, or 1828, or 1860, or 1896, or 1964 in which clear-cut decisions were made by popular vote.

It is a serious indictment, that federalism permits Congressmen to represent their local party interests almost always, the national interest and the national party almost never. So damning is the change that it makes us ask whether there is any advantage still left for us in federalism as a whole, a question which ought to be inquired into with some care. Three assertions are usually made in defense of federalism: first, that it strengthens local government, which is good because it is more democratic than national government; second, that the local government it strengthens is the most efficient governing unit; and third, that the diversity it permits in public policy is a positive value. Let us go behind the assertions to the real facts of experience to determine their degree of validity.

Throughout the eighteenth and nineteenth centuries, American democrats believed that local government from state to township was more democratic than the national government because it was geographically closer to the people. This postulate was fundamental in the American credo, even after the Civil War quashed the claims of state sovereignty. Even so nationalistic a President as Franklin Roosevelt, than whom no man did more to aggrandize the central government, really was: [32]

against the development of a strong central government . . . [he wanted] most governmental functions to be decentralized—carried on by the states and municipalities. . . . And when a permanent social security system came to be worked out, he settled an internal argument in his official family by coming down on the side of state rather than Federal administration. This was a momentous and revealing choice; it showed what side he would like to be on if he could.

But Roosevelt could not really be on the side of local administration. Even as he acted, the postulate was increasingly recognized as a kind of wishful thinking.

To the reasonably impartial observer, it ought to be fairly clear that

---

[32] R. G. Tugwell, "The Experimental Roosevelt," *The Political Quarterly,* XXI (1950), pp. 239, 241.

in a large number of cases local government, though physically close to the people, is not nearly so democratically responsible as the central government, and this for two reasons: First, at most times and in most places voters are both less informed and less concerned about local government and hence less prepared for and less interested in holding local officials responsible. And second, many local government institutions are such that the democratic sanction for responsibility is only partially effective.

That most of us know less about local government than national government is hardly a disputable proposition. Even well-educated and well-informed voters often do not know the name of a single school board member, city councilman, or state legislator. Yet almost all of us know the names of some Congressmen, sometimes even of our own. What is true of politicians' names is even more true of the things they do. Most of us have some knowledge of a few at least of the more important bills enacted in a Congress, especially tax bills, but few of us know even when the state legislature is in session, let alone what it does. Partly our ignorance of local government arises from faulty mechanics of communication. Almost all of our media of communications are produced for a mass audience, which means that purely local issues are ignored or standardized out of existence. National television and radio networks concentrate their news programs and public forums on national issues; national magazines can find a least-common-denominator in their audience only on the level of national issues; about the only medium that carries any news at all about local issues is the press, yet often the newspapers too are almost filled up with stories from the national news associations or boilerplate from propagandists. But ignorance arises out of more than these mechanical difficulties. We don't know much about local government largely because we don't care as much about it; and we don't care as much about it because it doesn't do much that affects us closely. How can it do much that affects us closely when the really great political problems of our lives are by definition national problems: war and peace, prosperity and depression. (Of course, part of the reason local government does not do much that affects us closely is that during the last half-century we have transferred many functions traditionally performed by it to the national government. Serious inadequacies in those functions it still has—schools, garbage disposal, and the like—do provoke a genuine, though usually temporary, interest in local politics until they are improved. Hence some people believe that the present unconcern about local government is a product of the transfer of its functions to the national government and could be remedied by a transfer back. But why were the functions transferred in the first place? As will be shown later in this chapter, the reason was usually that in these transferred functions local government proved inadequate to perform them, often because of this very unconcern.)

All these comments about local government are truisms which every citizen has already noted for himself. What is not so often noted, however, is that they cast some doubt on the premise that local government is more democratic than the national government. We cannot hold elected officials responsible in elections if we do not know and do not care who they are or what they do. It is a well-known fact that most of the time fewer people vote in elections of local and state officials than vote in national elections. It is almost as well known that the vote in local elections is less rational, that people are less informed about the character of the candidates. Hence it follows that the whole process of democracy, self-government for self-respect by means of officials held responsible in elections, tends to break down in local government by the very ignorance and indifference of the citizenry.

What responsibility might grow up in spite of ignorance and indifference is often blighted, moreover, by the very institutions of local government. The traditional American curse in local government is bossism. But bossism is itself simply a symptom of a deeper evil, the one-party system as it exists in most local governments. We have generally the republican forms in our state governments, and in most northern states, at least, we have the actual clarifying hand of the two-party or two-faction system. But on the local level this organization of parties is often almost entirely lacking. Party organization is expensive and difficult to operate; and hence, in most localities, one party is well run and active while the other exists only in name. Very often in fact the single major party is so dominant that the other party is operated as a bribed and corrupt adjunct to it—and this is what makes possible the most notorious of local bosses. In every city or township where the same coterie of politicians is returned to office year after year, where the second party is only a name and a committee of cranks, there we can be sure that the electoral forms are not really enough to work the electoral sanction. How can they be if the voters are in fact seldom presented with a choice, or worse still, if the voters are too uninterested to take notice or advantage of the choices that are presented?

The progressives of the early twentieth century, infuriated by bossdom in local government, devised a whole series of reforms that were supposed to eliminate the tyranny of bosses. Direct primaries were supposed to transfer the choice of candidates from bosses to rank and file party members. Direct legislation (i.e. the referendum) was supposed to circumvent the boss-dominated legislature. Judicial recall was supposed to hold boss-selected judges responsible to the people. Nonpartisan elections in local government were supposed to eliminate bosses by eliminating the party loyalty on which they lived. These things all together have slightly weakened the old-fashioned boss—who probably was already *passé* at the time they were enacted—but they have not succeeded in making local governments more responsible to the people. In fact, some of them have worked in exactly the opposite direction insofar as they have undermined political parties. The open primary, i.e. a party primary in which voters can participate regardless of party affiliation, permits voters of one party to help their opponents select the weakest candidate. The non-partisan election destroys the very basis of political responsibility by taking away from the voters the one instrument by which they can organize to enforce responsible government. The city-manager system, which purports to run city government on non-political principles, very often obscures the democratic sanction by obscuring the political character of governmental and administrative decisions. The referendum has become a device by which technical public issues are settled under the influence of high-pressure advertising rather than by responsible officials. While voters can always defeat legislators who pass a bad law, they have no sanction at all over the press agents who maneuver a bad referendum. The democratic millennium which these devices were supposed to herald is still as far away as ever. No doubt the direct primary contributed to more popular control of the nominating process, and this was a democratic gain. But otherwise, these devices were unwittingly a democratic loss, for they weakened political parties. Hence the local political scene, often irresponsible through lack of a well-developed two-party system, has been made all the more irresponsible by these well-intentioned but ill-advised progressive reforms.

And so this situation: even if voters are well informed about and interested in local government, they often cannot wield the electoral sanction because the two-party system by which they must necessarily wield it is absent. In the infancy of our democracy when most communities were small, when most voters had face-to-face contacts with their local office holders, it may well have been that the citizenry was both well enough informed and sufficiently interested to apply effective sanctions to local officials. But we are now 200,000,000 people and our political contacts are largely indirect and depersonalized. We must rely on press, television, and radio for our knowledge of men and issues and on political parties for the control of office holders. Since the knowledge of issues and the institutions of the sanction are for the most part a little more adequate on the national level than on the local, it follows that the democratic method is somewhat more effective there also.

This is not to say, however, that local government cannot be democratically effective. Of course it can be and often it is. Here it is simply urged that, taking the country as a whole and over a long period of time, the popular concern and political methods that democracy needs flourish more on the national level than the local. The election of the President excites more interest and educates the citizenry more thoroughly than the election of governors and mayors.

If, therefore, the democratic method is less effective in local government than in national government, it also follows that local government is the less efficient of the two. In the democratic system of thought, the efficiency of a government is a function of its responsibility to the people. Unfortunately, democrats have not always appreciated this point. Looking at the world scene, they have instead complained that dictatorships like Hitler's are more efficient than their own government and, looking at their own communities, they have substituted city managers for mayors, apparently believing that the less the responsibility the more efficient the government. But in so doing they underrate their own ideals and their own practice. The democratic system with its periodic check on governors instills in most politicians the question: "How will this or that action affect me in the next election?" And this has two important effects on the process of government. Negatively, it is the best sanction yet devised to control official corruption. We have, of course, our scandals, from Credit Mobilier to Teapot Dome to Sherman Adams to Bobby Baker; but however bad they seem to us, they are minor enough compared with the fortunes Goering and a host of lesser Nazis made or with the millionaire Communists of the Soviet Union today. For every case of a fortune built on graft it is possible for us to point to a private fortune dissipated while its possessor attended too much to public business. Those of our Presidents who have built a modest fortune in a lifetime of public service have done so like Taft by wise investing or like Coolidge by personal frugality. Here, where we have always had some democratic forms, corruption has never been really widespread, except when we were absorbing large numbers of immigrants untrained in democracy. But consider the history of public morality in England for an excellent example of the influence of democracy on corruption. Today in England bribery and graft are perhaps rarer than anywhere in the world; yet this is a recent development, almost entirely contemporaneous with the development of English democracy. In Pepys' *Diary* (circa 1665) one discovers from the complacent records of his own transactions that graft was the normal way of making a fortune; in the trial of Warren Hastings (circa 1787) one finds that graft is only just then becoming morally wrong (Hastings was impeached for corruption in India, but not convicted); in Trollope's Parliamentary novels (circa 1870, *Phineas Finn, Phineas Redux, The Prime Minister*) the conflict is beautifully portrayed between the older aristocratic ethic in which bribing voters and M.P.'s is thought customary and proper and the newer democratic ethic in which it is one of the primary sins. Clearly, the moral code changed in the same degree and at the same time as officials became responsible to the people. Who can doubt that the coincidence is more than temporally related?

However important the elimination of gross corruption, it is only a negative contribution to efficiency. Positively, the democratic system does much more because it provides a constant spur to official action. The tenure of officials in a democracy depends not on tradition, not on the fear they inspire, not on the deceitfulness of their tricks with monopolistic propaganda, but eventually on their productiveness as governors. Hence, their basic problem is how to do a job well, not how to force or trick the people into believing they do it well by means of ministries of propaganda, Gestapos, and MVD's. Admittedly the electoral sanction does not always work that way, especially when the party system is disorganized enough to render voting incoherent. But the long-run tendency is clearly in that direction, a tendency indicated well enough by the spurt of enormous productivity in this country during the last war. This is not to say, on the other hand, that despotisms are never efficient. Indeed they are, as we had occasion to realize in 1940 to 1945 and may shortly have occasion to realize again: but when so, the despots usually seem to have grasped the essential needs of the people and are themselves working to realize them. But as Aristotle said, "no constitutions are so short as oligarchy and tyranny"; [33] and when they change, the quasi-responsible despots are succeeded by wholly irresponsible ones. And with that transformation, efficiency vanishes.

Now if efficiency is in the long run a function of responsibility, it follows that the most efficient governing unit is in the long run the most democratic one. Since it has already been shown that most of the time the institutions of democracy work somewhat better on the national level than on the local, it follows also that the national government is somewhat more efficient too, at least in every affair that in any way transcends local boundaries. From this it follows also that some doubt is cast on the traditional justification of federalism as the protector of a supposedly more democratic and a supposedly more efficient local government. No one would deny, perhaps, that local government is appropriate for most of its present duties; but on the basis of the foregoing argument one might very reasonably deny that for its sake the national government should be weakened, that the national interest in strong parties should be sacrificed to the local interest in federated ones.

The third customary defense of federalism is that it allows for great diversity of administration and great diversity of public policy. This is indeed true for, as has already been emphasized, federalism encourages and perpetuates sectionalism; and diversity of administration and sectionalism are really two sides of one coin. Certainly this encouragement was a necessity in national life in the beginning of the Republic. Even so ardent a nationalist as Justice Holmes, speaking as lately as 1921, interpreted this as one of the great merits of the federal structure: [34]

. . . the making of social experiments that an important part of the community desires, in the insulated chambers afforded by the several States, even though the experiments may seem futile and even noxious to me. . . .

He spoke these words, however, apropos of a state law prohibiting injunctions against peaceful picketing, one minor aspect of the problem of labor relations which we have learned today is too great to be handled by state governments at all. It casts some doubt upon the value of diversity if the problems to be solved in the "insulated chambers" are so large that they cannot be contained. What good are the

[33] Aristotle, *Politics*, 1315b.
[34] *Truax* v. *Corigan*, 257 U.S. 312, 344, Holmes, J., dissenting.

experiments if the solutions must necessarily lie in Wagner Acts, Taft-Hartley Acts, Fair Labor Standards Acts, and other products of the national government? When the economy was much simpler, when each community was in some sense an isolated market, then one could reasonably expect successful experiment in "insulated chambers." But even in the beginning this was not wholly the case. Was not one of the main incentives for calling the Constitutional Convention just the fact that the experiments with money and markets in the "insulated chambers" of the states had thoroughly upset the national economy? As more and more problems have come to be regarded as national in scope, problems once so local in character as, for example, poor relief and the theft of vehicles, diversity in the government of them seems less valuable. Indeed sometimes diversity seems an evil: Attempts to meet national problems by forty-eight varying legal solutions simply incite to evasion. This is what numerous Northern states found when, after they regulated labor conditions in cotton mills, the mills moved to Southern states where regulations were either non-existent or unenforced. Wages and working conditions in the cotton mills were in fact, therefore, not adequately regulated in either the North or the South until the passage of the Fair Labor Standards Act of 1938.

It is this kind of situation that has led some people to conclude that federalism is now useless. This conclusion is, however, facile and oversimplified. Diversity still serves some purpose, as is suggested by the case of prohibition: the attempt to impose it upon all sections regardless of cultural differences was not only an administrative failure but also an inducement to the organization of syndicates of criminals, syndicates which have plagued us ever since in prostitution, gambling, dope-peddling, and the like. Local option, on the other hand, does satisfy the moral demands of both pietist and convivial neighborhoods. Diversity does indeed still serve an important purpose, allowing sections with different moral standards to live at peace with one another. Surely it was by this means that the South was reconciled after the Civil War. Yet as we approach true nationhood, with a standardization of morality, with a real general will, the need for diversity is less than it was.

And so this conclusion: Federalism does not today have all the advantages usually attributed to it. Valuable, yes; but not so valuable as formerly. And it has at the same time the great disadvantage of subordinating national interest and national politics to local interests and local politics as epitomized by the story of the campaign of 1938. And so this question arises: What chance have we today of revising federalism so that we can still use its remaining advantages and yet avoid the difficulties it brings on? And in answer, this hopeful point: Federalism is changing of its own accord and has been changing slowly now for a long time. And this is why:

THE DECLINE OF FEDERALISM

The federalism of 1787 was a political expedient to foster unity in people who thought they wanted anarchic diversity. Because it was a compromise of the moment, the relation is established between state governments and the superimposed central government was highly unstable, the more so since the Constitutional fathers, perhaps deliberately, left many aspects of the relation vague. Indeed, the word "federal" is itself unstable. It once meant "confederative"; now it is used to mean "national"—which is almost a complete reversal. But even when it means "national," it carries a "confederative" sense, so that it implies a theory both of states' rights and of nationalism. Much of our subsequent constitutional history can be written in terms of this unstable relation, in terms of the struggle between the two levels of government for the allegiance and control of the citizens to whom they are both responsible and over whom they both operate. Each generation faced with new problems has had to work out its own version of federalism. And each new version has occasioned violent dispute. (Do not misunderstand: Men have not fought over an abstract definition; rather one party has controlled the central government, the other has controlled some state governments, and each has used its base to attack or resist the other. The abstract relation has thus been a pawn in struggles over particular public policies. What makes the relation so interesting is that it has been so used in nearly all the important controversies of our history.) States' rights have been at one time or another the rallying standard of nearly every kind of party: Jeffersonians in their most radical phase adopted the Virginia and Kentucky Resolutions, while the most aggressively reactionary elements of the Federalist party called the Hartford convention of 1814; the Populists and Progressives were both strong states' rights parties, while most recently the opposition to the New Deal and the New Frontier has constantly raised the states' rights cry. In general one can say that the party out of power nationally tends to dignify its opposition with a political theory of federalism that emphasizes states' rights, greatly to its embarrassment when, on gaining control of President and Congress, it finds states' rights a galling hindrance. Thus embarrassed were the Jeffersonians after 1800 and the Democrats after 1932. When twitted for their inconsistency, for their abandonment of those principles which in opposition they had called immutable, they both could only answer petulantly that Federalists, so nationalist in the 1790's, and Republicans, so nationalist from 1860 to 1933, were strange ones to adopt the states' rights dogma the minute they lost control of Congress.

Since the party in power nationally tends always to be nationalist, the long-run effect has been a constant shift of power from state governments to central government until now it is hard to say whether or not we are still a federal republic. That such should be our development is not strange. Given the fact that states' righters out of power become nationalists in power; that Jeffersonians, the narrow constructionists, nevertheless purchased Louisiana; that Jacksonians, the apostles of regionalism, passed a Force Bill to meet South Carolina's nullification —given all this, increases in centralization have been inevitable. The only way to stop the transformation of the federal government into the national government was, as the architects of the *Confederate* States of America so clearly realized, to destroy the Union. That the Union has lasted is simply another way of saying that the central government has continually aggrandized itself at the expense of the states.

This shift of weight toward the national side is observable in three major changes in the federal relation: 1) national powers have been broadly rather than narrowly interpreted; 2) national action has become more and more independent of state action; and 3) national responsibilities have come to cover more and more of the whole field of governing. Each one of these changes, in roughly this chronological order, has been produced by a great party controversy in which the party in control of the national government has triumphed, incidentally thereby aggrandizing the national government.

The first important party controversy of the new republic concerned federalism in no small degree. The heart of the Federalist party program, Hamilton's financial proposals for funding the war debts, for setting a protective tariff, and especially for establishing a national bank, raised a clear question of the national government's power in relation to the states. In the bank controversy Hamilton, the broad constructionist, urged that the national government's power to establish a bank was implied in the Constitution, that, in addition to the enumerated powers, it possessed certain others reasonably implied by them. He rested his case chiefly on the "necessary and proper" clause in Article I, which, coming after the list of enumerated powers, says that Congress shall have the power to "make all laws which shall be necessary and proper for carrying into execution the foregoing powers. . . ." The word "necessary," he argued, meant "needful, requisite, incidental, useful, or conducive to" and the intent of the Convention was, he said, "to give liberal latitude to the exercise of the specified powers." [35] On the other hand, narrow constructionists and states' righters objected at just this point. Jefferson, then Secretary of State and the leader of the states' rights party, asserted that "necessary" and "convenient" were not synonyms, that the necessary laws of which Article I speaks are those "without which the grant of power would be nugatory." [36] Since Congress could easily lay taxes, pay debts, borrow money, and regulate commerce without a bank, not Congress but only the states had power to charter banks.

Hamilton's view prevailed in 1791, a national bank was established, and Hamiltonians on the Supreme Court defended the bank against all state interference. It was in a case involving the bank that John Marshall wrote that classic statement of the broad constructionist doctrine which later judges have so often quoted as they condoned reading still more and more implied powers into the Constitution: [37]

We admit, as all must admit, that the powers of the government are limited, and that its limits are not to be transcended. But we think the sound construction of the constitution must allow to the national legislature that discretion, with respect to the means by which the powers it confers are to be carried into execution, which will enable that body to perform the high duties assigned to it, in the manner most beneficial to the people. Let the end be legitimate, let it be within the scope of the constitution, and all means which are appropriate, which are plainly adapted to that end, which are not prohibited, but consist with the letter and spirit of the constitution, are constitutional.

Although Jackson destroyed the bank, which had become the symbol of national oppression of the states and mercantile oppression of

[35] *The Works of Alexander Hamilton*, edited by Henry Cabot Lodge (New York, 1904, G. P. Putnam's Sons, 12 vols.), III, p. 453.
[36] *The Writings of Thomas Jefferson*, edited by Paul Leicester Ford (New York, G. P. Putnam's Sons, 1895, 9 vols.), V, p. 287.
[37] *McCulloch* v. *Maryland*, 4 Wheat. 316, 421 (1819).

farmers, the principle of broad construction remained. While several times since, notably the late 1850's and the mid-1930's, the Supreme Court has tried to renege on the precedent of broad construction, the rest of the national government has not let it do so. And indeed so deep is broad constructionism in our constitutional theory that narrow constructionists of our own day unconsciously operate on broad constructionist principles. For example, Mr. Justice Roberts, in the *Butler* case, while denying Congress the power to regulate agriculture in the particular way in which it had tried to do so, still admitted that the power to tax was in practical effect unlimited.[38] In consequence of the principle of broad construction, our chief inheritance from the Federalist party in its days of domination in the 1790's, some constitutional basis has always eventually been judicially invented for whatever expansion of national power Congress has chosen to make.

The only effective opposition to this kind of gradual expansion of national power is formal resistance by the states. But this opposition is no longer possible, for if the Civil War settled nothing else, it did decide that states could not nullify national actions. The Virginia and Kentucky Resolutions of 1798 were the first state claims of the right to supervise the national government. Jeffersonian Republicans, aroused by the Federalists' use of the Alien and Sedition Acts to silence their political opponents, developed the theory that the Constitution was a compact between sovereign states. In the Kentucky Resolutions, Jefferson argued "that to this compact each state acceded as a State, and is an integral party, its co-states forming, as to itself, the other party." On that basis, then, the legislatures of the two states proposed that the other twelve state legislatures join with them in nullifying the Alien and Sedition Acts. Fortunately for the nation, none did; and the energies of the Republicans were diverted to the far more sensible project of electing the author of the Kentucky Resolutions to the Presidency. But the compact theory which Jefferson originated matured to plague the nation during the next two generations. It reappeared again in a more radical form among those New England Federalists as disaffected by "Mr. Madison's War" as Mr. Madison had been by the Sedition Act. The extremists of the Essex Junto planned that the Hartford convention of 1814 would threaten secession and a separate peace with England. Actually it did nothing of the sort, for Madison was making

---

[38] *United States* v. *Butler*, 297 U.S. 1, 65 (1936). Edward S. Corwin, "The Passing of Dual Federalism," *Virginia Law Review*, XXVIII (1950), p. 1.

peace as the Convention met. But it did something which was perhaps worse: It gave a new boost to the compact theory and twisted it to justify not simply united action by all states against the central government but instead secessionist action by several states. The Convention failed and the Federalist party never recovered from the reputation for treason that the Convention brought on it; but the compact theory lived on to reappear in an even more virulent form in South Carolina in 1828. There, after the tariff of 1828, the state legislature claimed the right to nullify all by itself the laws passed by Congress. And in 1832 it actually passed a bill forbidding national customs collections in South Carolina ports, threatening to enforce its nullification by secession. Andrew Jackson, the indomitable, who made the famous toast at a banquet of nullifiers "Our Federal Union—it must be preserved," forced South Carolina to compromise by mobilizing the army. By that time, however, the compact theory was so clearly worked out that the later secession was entirely possible.

In the next thirty years John C. Calhoun, Abel Upshur, and other Southerners transformed the compact theory into a theory of secession. It contained these propositions: [39]

that the people of the several States, while in a Colonial condition, were not "one people"; . . . That they did not become so by the Declaration of Independence, but that each State became a complete and perfect sovereignty within its limits; . . . [and that the Constitution was adopted by] no other agency than that of the States as such, and of Congress, which was strictly representative of the States.

From this it was but a short step to the theory that states could remove themselves from the compact whenever it was no longer to their advantage, as some of them did in fact in 1861. On the other hand, the nationalist theory which eventually prevailed was also worked out in the same thirty years by John Marshall, Joseph Story, and perhaps most impressively of all by John Quincy Adams, who put this poignant question to all the assertions of state sovereignty: [40]

Where did each state get the sovereignty which it *retains*? In the Declaration of Independence, the delegates of the Colonies in Congress assembled,

[39] Abel P. Upshur, *A Brief Inquiry into the True Nature and Character of our Federal Government*, By a Virginian (Petersburg, Va., E. and J. C. Ruffin, 1840), sections 54–55.

[40] John Quincy Adams, *The Jubilee of the Constitution* (New York, S. Colman, 1839), pp. 18–19.

in the name and by the authority of the good people of the Colonies, declare, not each Colony, but the United Colonies, in fact, and of right, not sovereign, but free and independent states.

The United States is one people, he said, one people in the Declaration, one people in the Constitution. This is the background of Lincoln's famous phrase in the Gettysburg address "one nation, indivisible." And this is what the Civil War determined, that part of one people cannot secede. Once secession became both legally and physically impossible, states could never claim to nullify national laws. This sanction was gone. Immediately after the Civil War the new theory of subordination of the states appeared in our constitutional law. Southern antiquarians, still true to the tradition of Calhoun, yet today speak with adamant precision of "the war between the states." But the phrase is meaningless, for in theory as well as fact it was a civil war, the verdict of which was recorded by Chief Justice Chase in the famous case of *Texas* v. *White* (1869): "When Texas became one of the United States, she entered into an indissoluble relation." [41] No longer would it be possible to view the Constitution as a compact or the states as sovereign and indeed we have ever since been sloughing off such vestigial remains of the league theory of the Constitution as election of Senators by state legislatures. We still have much to slough off—representation of the states in the Senate, for example—but who can doubt that states have lost most of the practice as well as the theory of sovereignty?

Once broad construction became both a settled congressional practice and an irremovable judicial precedent, once state sovereignty, the compact theory, nullification, and secession were forcibly destroyed, no barrier remained to prevent the national government's expansion into areas of administration long regarded as reserved to the states. Perhaps as good a date as any for the beginning of this tendency in recent times is 1887, the year the Interstate Commerce Act was passed. The year before the Supreme Court in the Wabash Railroad Case had held that states might not regulate interstate railroad rates.[42] This was a clear invitation to Congress to take over the regulation itself—and it did. Almost all the previous regulation of commerce had been merely encouragement of the shipping industry. But observe what happened

41 *Texas* v. *White*, 7 Wall. 700, 722 (1869).
42 *Wabash, St. Louis, and Pacific Ry. Co.* v. *Illinois*, 118 U.S. 557 (1886).

after this one great forward step. From regulating railroad rates to regulating railroad technology to regulating railroad employment to regulating railroad retirement plans. From regulating railroads to regulating businesses that ship on them to regulating the employees of businesses that ship on them to regulating the wages of employees of businesses that serve businesses that ship on railroads. During the administration of Grover Cleveland, the national government moved into the area of railroad regulation; during the administration of Benjamin Harrison it moved into the area of trust regulation; during the second administration of Grover Cleveland, into military control of labor relations; during the administration of William McKinley, into soil control; during the administration of Theodore Roosevelt, into food and drug regulation; during the administration of William Howard Taft, into forest management and natural resources conservation; during the administration of Woodrow Wilson, into central banking, further trust regulation, vocational education, and public utilities regulation; during the administration of Warren Harding, into regulation of advertising; during the administration of Calvin Coolidge, into regulation of radio industry; during the administration of Herbert Hoover, into general banking activity; during the administration of Franklin Roosevelt into house financing and apartment house building, farm financing, wage and price regulation, poor relief, old-age and unemployment insurance, stock market regulation, regulation of labor unions, of agricultural production, and of a host of other things; during the administration of Harry Truman into urban renewal; during the administration of Dwight Eisenhower into a vast program of interstate highways; and during the administration of John Kennedy into area redevelopment. Perhaps the most interesting of these new activities was poor relief, for which, in the Anglo-American tradition, the smallest unit of local government has always been responsible. So it was in eighteenth and nineteenth century America. But in the days of the Great Depression, few local governments and indeed few state governments had either the resources or the ability to deal with such prostrating poverty. As Mr. Justice Byrnes remarked in the case of *Edwards* v. *California*, ". . . the theory of the Elizabethan poor laws no longer fits the case." [43] Relief was therefore administered by the national government and from that it was but a short step to nationally administered old-age pensions, na-

[43] *Edwards* v. *California*, 314 U.S. 160, 174 (1941).

tionally supervised unemployment insurance, and nationally financed and controlled aid to indigent mothers and children. As a matter of necessity, perhaps, but also as a matter of party politics and national aggrandizement, the alms-giving functions of the monastic brotherhoods and Lady Bountifuls, of parish vestries and township trustees became a function of the national government.

Truly federalism is an unstable relation.[44] Paraphrasing the quotation set at the head of this chapter, a great change in the whole system of institutions has come about, unperceived, by a long series of small changes. The enumerated powers have been supplemented by the implied powers, the compact theory and state pretensions to sovereignty collapsed in the Civil War, and now the only real limits on the functions of the national government are the demands of the people and its own sense of self-restraint. Madison would be horrified and so even Hamilton. But it is they who are really responsible, for they were the authors of this unique but unstable compound of governments. Because it was unstable, small changes could easily occur in it; and, because it was unique, they could easily be overlooked.

It is this instability, this unrecognized instability, that permits us some optimism. Were the federal relation as absolute and unchanging as the founding fathers probably thought it would be, then we would be forever foreclosed from strengthening Presidential leadership and bridging the gap among the separated powers. But what has changed so much and so imperceptibly can be changed also by conscious rearrangement. What can we consciously do about changing it? That is the question for the next and last chapter.

[44] For a more detailed consideration of this instability, see William H. Riker, *Federalism: Origin, Operation, Significance* (Boston, Little, Brown, 1964).

9.
The Struggle for Democracy in the United States

> The sort of constitutional system which ought to be proposed is one which men can be easily induced, and will be readily able, to graft onto the system they already have. It is as difficult a matter to reform an old constitution as it is to construct a new one; as hard to unlearn a lesson as it was to learn it initially.
> —ARISTOTLE, *Politics,* 1289a

THE PROBLEM OF AMERICAN DEMOCRACY

These are the propositions of the democratic dogma: that pride and servility it exacts from others are the depths of human evil; that self-respect for everybody is the summit of human good and the final purpose of democratic government; that self-respect grows out of self-control, that in fact it is the adult, manly confidence in one's ability to live life as it seems good; that the fullest self-control is possible only when government, the greatest human institution, is so responsible to the people that they can control themselves with it as if it were an extension of their own faculties; that responsible government is effective only when it can control all the controllable elements in the environment; and that effective government requires the use of the best human intelligence to surmount the worst human difficulties. The democrat of course does not ask that his government imitate the pretensions of the witch doctor to eliminate death by magic or redesign the biological constitution of the species. But he does ask that the best knowledge of the age be set to work on the most pressing of its problems. Today he asks that it actually avert those natural catastrophes that are in theory avertible, flood, for example. And of those unavoidable catastrophes, like hurricanes and drought, he expects that government at least prepare for them and plan to alleviate their effects. Of our own man-made domestic environment, he asks more: that government really control, prevent, and eliminate depressions, inflation, epidemic disease, urban filth, the arrogance of place and possessions, or, in short, all those defects and breakdowns of our intricate Leviathan which bring on early death, poverty, and servility for so many people. Above all, given this world of surging imperialisms, he asks that it hide us as long as it can from those four terrifying horsemen, until the great day of His wrath is come and no one shall be able to stand.

This is the hope. What is the accomplishment? How far does our democracy, partial though it is, subdue the pride of high station or control the practicably controllable? How far, we ask, does it mitigate for us the violence of the planet and the nastiness of men? And the answer: Like all things human, it combines the good and the bad, hope fulfilled and hope deferred. The record of flood control suggests the complexity: We have both the skill and the resources to eliminate floods. And some rivers, like the Tennessee and the Columbia, we have systematically dammed up while taking measures also for the permanent control of soil erosion in their watersheds. But despite the demonstration of success on the Tennessee, we still do very little about the Missouri, the Ohio, the great Mississippi itself, and a dozen other rivers that periodically rise up to destroy the lives, property, and family happiness of those who live upon their banks.

The record in this relatively simple technical problem is mixed, much done and much left undone. So it is in more difficult things. Finally in the 1930's we acquired some of the means of controlling depressions. Now the great question of the future is whether or not we will be able to use the knowledge we have acquired. We know from recent advances of economic theory that the secret of a high and stable level of employment is a neat balance between money saved and money invested. We know also many ways by which government can steady that balance. If more money is saved than there are opportunities to invest it, the government can absorb excess savings by high taxes or heavy borrowing, by subsidies of consumers' goods, and the like. Or it can increase investment opportunities by bringing about lower interest rates (in which case less attractive investments become profitable), by subsidizing or easing taxation on new investment, or by directly investing money itself. On the other hand, if investment needs are greater than money saved, the government can of course enforce saving by borrowing or taxation, using the proceeds for public investment or subsidies of private investment.

Note well, however: Knowledge by itself of all these techniques is not power; it becomes power only when it is actually used. Do we have appropriate institutions to use our knowledge? Of course we have a government, one which can and does make and apply a fiscal policy. But we have also the separated powers and the stalemates of ambition. Can we really use tax policy to control the business cycle when there are approximately 155,000 units of government, most of which levy taxes, most of the time independently of one another? When the national government raises taxes as a matter of fiscal policy, local governments may, as they did during the last war, partially negate the national policy by lowering theirs. Or again, when the national government is itself investing heavily, state and local governments may, as they did in the 1930's, lessen their investment, thus also partially negating the national policy. So long as the system of federalism permits independent judgments on fiscal policy, the national government will be hamstrung, no matter how rational its intentions may be.

Even if the national government did not have to contend with state fiscal policies, we would still be justified in doubting if it could make a coherent one itself. Its own internal organization is not really adapted to that purpose. Interest rates, always an important tool in any fiscal policy, are controlled both by the Federal Reserve Board through its manipulation of discount rates to private banks and by the Treasury Department through its manipulation of offerings on government bonds, rules on credit buying, and the like. Were these two agencies integrated by the President, then we would have little cause to worry. But they are not. The Federal Reserve Board, supposedly responsible to Congress, but not really responsible to anybody, is able to, and, as was noted in Chapter 6, actually does, occasionally thwart both the Treasury and the President, attempting, for example, to raise interest rates when they are attempting to lower them. Or again, concerning investment policy, consider how many administrative agencies make decisions affecting the size, the location, and the kind of both private and public investment. Some of these, like the Treasury, the Interior Department, the Department of Defense, etc., are directly under the President and fairly well harmonized by him. But others, like the Interstate Commerce Commission, the Securities and Exchange Commission, the Federal

Power Commission, the Federal Reserve Board, the Federal Trade Commission, etc., are quite genuinely independent, able to go their own way, even when it is in a direction opposite to the rest of the government.

Even if the whole national administration were thoroughly harmonized by the President, however, it would still be doubtful if we could make a coherent fiscal policy. To do so, Congress and the President must work together; yet, in the absence of adequate party discipline to bridge these separated powers, they are more likely to work apart. Consider the control of inflation, the one great question of fiscal policy with which we grappled during the 1940's and 1950's. Angered daily by new price rises, avoiding ulcers and permanent irascibility only by making bitter jokes on ourselves about them, we need no treatise to tell us that the problem was not solved. It simply wore out after two decades of investment. Why did we fail to solve it? Surveying its history, it clearly appears that what we lacked for the solving was leadership capable of insisting on a coherent fiscal policy. And why did we lack the leadership? Because the President, who can use the Council of Economic Advisors or the Treasury or the Budget Bureau to devise a coherent policy, lacks the party leadership to persuade Congress to enact what he has devised. At the beginning of the second World War, when only systematic price control could prevent a sudden and dramatic price spiral, Congress passed the Emergency Price Control Act of 1942, though the sheer number of subsequent price control acts belied the first word of the title. As originally introduced, drafted by OPA Administrator Leon Henderson under the close direction of the President, the 1941 bill would probably have been adequate for the purpose. But its integrity was quickly compromised in Congress. Special interests, unchanneled by any party discipline, wanted to construct a bill which would exempt their prices from control. That is what too many of them got. Farm Congressmen of both parties combined to insert a general provision that would allow the prices of all farm products to rise considerably more than they had risen already. Then Congressmen representing special commodity interests devised still other special provisions to allow still higher prices for the constituents' products. One scholar remarks: [1]

[1] James M. Burns, *Congress on Trial* (New York, Harpers, 1949), p. 88.

Perhaps not since the Smoot-Hawley tariff of 1930 had Congress been the scene of such bold and naked log-rolling as in the consideration of price control, when blocs and individual Senators reduced action on price control to the lowest terms of sectional and local advantage. Indeed, the tariff affair was the less serious, for that was a case of a congressional majority dividing up the spoils, while here a minority was peddling its votes for a vitally needed war program and exacting a heavy price.

So it was that the first bill against inflation actually encouraged inflation of farm prices and thereby set the pattern for all subsequent bills. Manufacturers and wage-earners, naturally resentful and envious of the farmers' privilege, tried to imitate. And soon they had a good argument for imitation: The special privilege for farmers so upset the customary price relationships that further special adjustments seemed necessary. So manufacturers and wage-earners got the special privilege extended to themselves, gradually by particular appeals in 1943 and 1944, suddenly by a general revision in 1945. Thus the policy of price control was actually reversed—not by positive enactment, but by log-rolling compromises. Special privilege for one justified special privilege for another until so many special privileges were granted that we had a general price rise. The policy that we verbally supported we in reality negated by so many exceptions that, when landlords were at last given *their* special privilege in 1947, price control was no longer feasible. Although we did control prices fairly well for the first two years, thereafter the policy was naught but pretense, the ghost of hopes we once had.

Compare our experience with Great Britain's. There price control was initiated somewhat earlier and maintained throughout the decade. Except for a few adjustments necessitated by foreign trade, it actually prevented inflation. By 1951, prices in England had risen about 53 percent over 1939, while in this country they had risen to about 85 percent over the same base year. Why the difference? On the surface there is no reason. England has the same kind of pressure groups as the United States and, at least during the war, had a similar economic situation. In England, however, pressure groups cannot exert the same kind of pressure. Members of Parliament, unlike Members of Congress, are so well disciplined by their national party that they do not so readily give in to the importunities of lobbyists. Of course, public policy in England is a bundle of compromises, as it is in every democratic country; but the compromises are rationally formulated among the great national interests, not accidentally thrown together at the behest of interests great and small. Members of Parliament, under party discipline, can serve national interests just as much as local ones. Hence England's price control was a national policy, while ours was a series of local policies masquerading as an act of Congress.

This is the real evil of our separated powers and our lack of national leadership. Local interests and pressure groups representing small minorities are able to make hash of nearly any national policy. Even in so vital a necessity as the decentralization of war industries to avoid destruction by atomic bombing, it turns out that a Congress—superficially controlled by the President's party—snipes at the President's policy and, in the short-sighted interest of the old industrial areas, tries to keep industry in the places where it can most easily be destroyed.

Sometimes in great crises, our government does the things we want it to do and does them very well. More often, however, it drifts along, sometimes smothering good policies with exceptions for the benefit of local interests and effective lobbies, other times missing opportunities for real foresight and self-control. In the time of the English civil wars, James Harrington, so reported John Aubrey: [2]

. . . was wont to find fault with the constitution of our Government, that 'twas *by jumps,* and told a story of a Cavaliero he sawe at the Carnival in Italie, who rode on an excellent managed horse that with a touch of his toe would jumpe quite round. One side of his habit was Spanish, the other French; which sudden alteration of the same person pleasantly surprized the spectators. Just so, said he, 'tis with us. When no Parliament, then absolute Monarchie; when a Parliament, then it runnes to a Commonwealth.

Our jumps are not so obvious as were England's then; they are hidden and therefore, perhaps, the worse. The horseman jumps so quickly that the alteration goes unperceived; his clothes, but not his character, are the same on each side, whence comes the illusion of stability. Thus we are denied the pleasures of the spectators at the Carnival—and we are cheated at the same time.

The Strategy of Reform

A self-control that appears only in crises brought on by its absence is a poor sort of self-control indeed. It is comparable to the personal

[2] *Aubrey's Brief Lives,* edited by Oliver Lawson Dick (London, Secker and Warburg, 1949), p. 126.

discipline of a man who guards his body well while he convalesces from heart attacks only to lead a hard and irregular life between them. We all recognize this folly in a man and most of us—except those who seek to gather figs from thistles—condemn it. In a government, however, we do not so often recognize and, even recognizing, do not so often condemn. But erratic discipline in our institutional life is just as debilitating as it is in personal life. I will not have written in vain if from this book a few more people learn to recognize and condemn this governmental folly, this jumpiness, this uneven tempo of governing. But to condemn the folly of either man or nation is unavailing if the condemnation be not followed with practical advice. And so this great and final question: What can we do to compensate for our erratic self-control?

How difficult, though, is the strategy of reform. In one direction it verges to utopianism, in the other to inconsequential tinkering. In the one case reformers become chiliasts, awaiting the millennium as soon as their plans are executed. In the other, they become faddists, about as useful in politics as the inventors of perpetual motion machines in physics. In either case, however, they are ineffectual. Utopians waste energy in planning what will never be applied and even their criticism of the *status quo* is irrelevant, for it proceeds from entirely unrelated premises. Faddists, on the other hand, waste their energy on trifles. Indeed both faddists and utopians become unwitting conservatives: By their defection from the party of practical reform they make the conservative balance heavier.

That these hazards of reform exist is not, however, the danger, but that they are so easily overlooked. It is easy enough to recognize the utopianism of, for example, the Socialist Labor party or Technocracy, both descendants in the bend sinister line of great utopias, the one by Marx out of Daniel De Leon, the other by Veblen out of Howard Scott. It is, on the other hand, equally easy to recognize the faddism of, for example, the Greenback party, now a decadent survival of a trifle favored in nineteenth century America. What are not so easy to recognize, however, are the fads and utopias sponsored by serious scholars. Unfortunately, there are many such delusive reforms, persistent will-o'-the-wisps in the tradition of American scholarship.

Consider two examples, proportional representation and parliamentary government, both of which have been urged (mistakenly) as roads to responsible government. One of the most persistent (and superficial) of the fads is P. R., to the propagating of which, even though now a somewhat dubious faith, men still devote their lives. It was invented in the nineteenth century as a defense of the aristocratic interest when universal suffrage seemed about to overrun it with an illiterate mass. To John Stuart Mill, the most influential of its adherents, it seemed a way by which "manual labourers and . . . employers of labour . . . should be . . . equally balanced, each influencing about an equal number of votes in Parliament." [3] With the triumph of universal suffrage, which made such balance impossible, P. R. lost its original justification. But it has still persistently attracted enthusiasts. In Europe, this is understandable, for there it serves as a way to maintain the *status quo* of parties in a multi-party system inherited from pre-democratic days. But in the United States it is at best a fad. In part, no doubt, it has attracted American scholars with an arithmetical bent who made a pastime of devising improvements (or rather complications) in proportional vote counting.[4] Aside from this mathematical hypnosis, however, it has attracted those who dream Rousseau's dream of perfect representation of all the interests of the community, of a government responsible to everybody, majority and minority alike. After much experience in both Europe and the United States, it is clear, however, that P. R. encourages splinter groups and thereby overrepresents minorities at the expense of majorities. (See Chapter 3.) In this way, then, it fails even to represent well, for representing everybody means representing nobody. But still some amount (fortunately declining) of misplaced enthusiasm is directed toward it. So preoccupied are its adherents with the technique of representation—which is only one part of the structure of popular government—that they continue to agitate for a device which not only fails to improve representation but even destroys popular government itself.

Consider also the hazard of utopias occasionally advocated by contemporary scholars, of which no better example exists than the idea of transplanting parliamentary government here. When, after the great crisis of the Civil War, Americans began to think more critically about their own institutions, some of them were seduced by the message of Bagehot's great work, *The English Constitution,* which he wrote in 1865–66 (revised, 1872) to persuade constitution-makers in Italy, Canada, and France to copy the "Cabinet Government" of England rather

---

[3] John Stuart Mill, *Considerations on Representative Government,* Chapter VI.
[4] On the arithmetical interests of the earliest advocates of P. R. see Clarence G. Hoag and George H. Hallet, *Proportional Representation* (New York, Macmillan, 1926), pp. 163–64, 175.

than the "Presidential Government" of the United States.[5] His analysis, epitomized by the following famous passage, had important repercussions in America: [6]

The English constitution, in a word, is framed on the principle of choosing a single sovereign authority, and making it good: The American, upon the principle of having many sovereign authorities, and hoping that their multitude may atone for their inferiority. The Americans now extol their institutions, and so defraud themselves of their due praise. But if they had not a genius for politics . . . the multiplicity of authorities in the American Constitution would long ago have brought it to a bad end. Sensible shareholders, I have heard a shrewd attorney say, can work *any* deed of settlement; and so the men of Massachusetts could, I believe, work *any* Constitution.

A few years later Woodrow Wilson adapted Bagehot's argument in light of a better knowledge of how American government really worked; and ever since scholars in a small but steady stream have proposed that we adopt either parliamentary government in its entirety or some portion of it which they think is its essential principle. While Wilson himself was far too sensible to propose that we adopt it simply because he thought Bagehot's argument was "clear-sighted," [7] while he wished instead to develop American government in its own way into "a straightforward thing of simple method, single, unstinted power, and clear responsibility," [8] the less sophisticated of his successors have thought we could reverse the whole tendency of our politics, making the President a figurehead and lodging sovereignty in a committee of Congress. Some of these writers have made incisive, practical critques of our representative system, for example, Thomas K. Finletter, a lawyer-turned-bureaucrat during World War II, who was shocked beyond measure by the mish-mash the Executive-Legislative conflict makes of our foreign policy and military strategy and by the opportunity it gives for pressure groups to wangle special privilege.[9] Unfortunately, however, they have marred their otherwise excellent critiques with utopian conclusions.

Utopians of any variety are wont to think there is but one road

---

[5] Walter Bagehot, *The English Constitution* (World's Classics ed., London, Oxford University Press, 1928), pp. 14, 311.
[6] *Ibid.*, p. 202.
[7] Woodrow Wilson, *Congressional Government* (Fifteenth edition, Boston, Houghton Mifflin, 1960), p. 310.
[8] *Ibid.*, pp. 332–33.
[9] Thomas K. Finletter, *Can Representative Government Do the Job?* (New York, Reynal and Hitchcock, 1945).

to salvation. And so it is in the case of the parliamentary government utopians: only one set of institutions can foster responsibility. In this they err; the town meeting, for example, once made for quite responsible government, although it is obviously no longer effective now that very few important functions of government are lodged in towns. Worse still, however, the utopians suppose that their utopia will work, when in fact it is a utopia in the exact sense, a noplace. And this for two reasons: First, cabinet government may once have been the secret of responsible government in England, but now it seems that the strong national leadership depends more on party discipline and the solidarity of the social classes that dominate the parties. And if the cabinet system is only a part of the method of responsible government in England, if it does not have the effects in reality which are attributed to it in theory, there is little point to transplanting it here. And second, even if the cabinet system did once have the effects the utopians attribute to it, it would still not be appropriate for constructing responsible government here. To adopt cabinet government would be to deny our tendency toward Presidential leadership, to revise our whole pattern of thought about government—and that, clearly, we cannot do. In England the gap between the separated powers was bridged by exalting the legislature, by reducing the old executive (i.e. the King) to a figurehead and replacing him with a legislative mayor of the palace (i.e. the prime minister). With one short exception, we have been attempting to bridge another way, by exalting the President above Congress. How could we possibly reverse that deep tendency in our constitutional life?

These are the twin hazards that reformers must avoid: Of the faddish tinkering we must remember that no particular device is by itself enough to transform our political society—life is too complex for that; of the utopias we must remember that no grandiose proposal to rewrite the Constitution is applicable—we cannot escape the history we inherit. Rather, in our search for a way to overcome our erratic self-control, we must recognize the complexity and immensity of our task, scorning the easy, oversimplified reform, and we must accept the American tradition, resisting the temptation to import the unimportable. Only thus can we avoid the monomania of faddists and utopians. Only thus can we follow Aristotle's good advice which is set at the head of this chapter.

Universal suffrage and Presidential leadership inside the two-party system are, if the analysis of the preceding chapters is even approximately correct, the American tendencies that can be exploited for the sake of more regular self-control. If we concentrate on these, we can perhaps avoid the hazards of reform. But how can we exploit them? Concerning suffrage there is nothing to add to what was suggested at the end of Chapter 2. The strategy of democrats ought always to be to take advantage of every political opportunity to work toward universal suffrage. It is a clear and simple program, though difficult indeed to carry through. Much more difficult, however, both in theory and application is the development of Presidential leadership, the problem to which we now turn.

Our Attitude Toward Political Parties: How Can It Be Transformed?

In Chapter 6 it was suggested that only the President could reconcile the separated powers, but that he was hampered in the doing of it by his inadequate leadership of his political party. In Chapter 8 this inadequacy was traced to its roots, the localism of political parties. The problem is, therefore, how to transform parties from things local, incoherent, and irresponsible into national, rationalized, and obedient servants of the people. Thus simply can the problem be stated in generalized terms; but it is very difficult to discover just what specific measures will solve it.

One specific measure is clearly necessary, however: a radical change in our attitudes toward political parties. We cannot make parties good servants if we are unwilling to trust them in their work. If we are determined to interpret their every action with cynical suspicion, we will probably get just what we expect, like the master who complains he is cheated by servants whom he treats with contempt. We need to nationalize our parties and to make them stronger; but this we cannot do if we fear their strength. We need to trust our parties and make them responsible; but this we cannot do if we consider them semi-criminal conspiracies.

Our attitude toward political parties is now a strange complex. We adhere to them, but we don't really trust them. We adhere to them, or at least most of us do, in election after election. Nearly eighty percent of the voters think of themselves as members of one of the major parties, so the public opinion pollsters say. And while the technique of opinion polling may be both infant and inexact, this particular conclusion can be checked by other, more objective methods. It is well known, for example, that particular election districts return majorities for the same party in a series of elections; and, assuming some continuity of voters' residence, it follows therefrom that most people adhere to one party for fairly long periods of time. (See, in this connection, the analysis of the continuity of party success made in Chapter 4 and a study of Bloomington, Illinois, in which it was found that twenty-five precincts out of thirty-four gave a plurality to the same party in every Presidential election from 1932 to 1944.[10]) But even though most of us identify ourselves with the same party during most of our voting life, it does not follow that we really trust it. Again, according to the pollsters, about two-thirds of the voters regularly say that they vote for the man rather than the party, claiming thereby an independence which they do not really exhibit. Why this discrepancy between what we do and what we say? Why do we treat our party attachments as if they were some secret sin practiced in the privacy of the voting booth? Is it not that we are ashamed of what we think are cabals existing only to mulct the public? Is it not that we are ashamed to acknowledge the intellectual leadership of politicians, who, as all the cartoons show, are predatory fat men, sometimes stupid, sometimes guileful, but always predatory?

Whence comes this distrust of something we find so necessary? Part of it, certainly, is a fair inference from actual circumstance. Whether there be a higher proportion of criminal types among politicians than among businessmen or lawyers, or whether the politicians' crimes are simply more publicized—as they should be in a democracy—I do not know. Surely, however, our journalistically drawn stereotype of a politician does emphasize the worst side of the political personality. And it is indeed true that politicians, who ought to be as much beyond suspicion as Caesar's wife, have sometimes been bad men, besmirching the whole trade with their filth. Part of this distrust is, however, inherited from pre-democratic days when faction was regarded as the first step toward rebellion and the primary political sin. (See Chapter 3.) But along with this traditional distrust, this foreboding of civil war, is a newer distrust based on a false interpretation of democratic ideals. Ever since Rousseau there has been a minor strain of democratic thought which holds that each citizen ought to participate equally with every other in democratic government. This extreme individualism is, of

[10] J. A. Kinneman and S. E. Shipley, "The Ecology of Pluralities in Presidential Elections," *American Sociological Review*, X (1945), p. 382–89.

course, appalled by the hierarchical form of parties and the division of labor it promotes between citizens who simply vote and citizens who organize the voting. One of the most influential of these quasi-anarchists was Moisei Ostrogorski, the Russo-French student of English and American parties, whose great book, *Democracy and the Organization of Political Parties,* was so often quoted as gospel by American progressives early in this century. In the conclusion of his book, the first systematic study of parties ever written, he recognized, reluctantly, that parties were necessary for the citizen "to facilitate the discharge of his political duties." But he also castigated them, saying: [11]

Instead of moulding opinion, the Caucus maimed it by forcing it into, and keeping it within, the groove of stereotyped parties. It crippled the character and the intelligence of the citizen. . . . Continually invoking this [fictional] majority . . . , it made external conformity the sole criterion which dispensed with private judgement and individual responsibility. Henceforth even a "yellow dog" had to be voted for, once he was put on the party ticket. . . . For the individual conscience, party piety substituted the discipline of the party. . . .

The widespread repetition of this point of view by those American progressives who hoped the direct primary, the initiative and referendum, and other similar devices would lead to the democratic millennium, certainly bred enough distrust to weaken the leadership of political parties. One cannot help sympathizing with the vision these democrats had of every hearthside a political salon, of every citizen a Tom Paine. But one regrets they did not also realize that government operates by a majority opinion, which is always a compromise patched together by parties. While the anti-party progressives taught a much-needed lesson, that parties ought to be as responsible as elected officials, they unfortunately taught it by breeding distrust of the one institution which can give us self-control.

Fortunately, Americans are now beginning to acquire a deeper understanding of the role of political parties—although the acquisition is still, unhappily, limited to a narrow circle of professional specialists. It is hopeful, however, that some scholars have gone beyond the naive distrust of Ostrogorski to a critical appreciation of both the necessity and the faults of our party system. Contrast the tone of the following

[11] M. Ostrogorski, *Democracy and the Organization of Political Parties,* translated by F. Clarke (New York, Macmillan, 1902, 2 vols.), II, pp. 566–67.

passage, taken from a 1950 report of the Committee on Political Parties of the American Political Science Association, with the polemic just quoted from Ostrogorski. While the report as a whole is sharply critical of the localism, the ineffectiveness, the irresponsibility of our party system, it still postulates that the system is an indispensable tool for democratic self-control: [12]

Throughout this report political parties are treated as indispensable instruments of government. That is to say, we proceed on the proposition that *popular government in a nation of more than 150 million people requires political parties which provide the electorate with a proper range of choice between alternatives of action.* The party system thus serves as the main device for bringing into continuing relationship those ideas about liberty, majority rule and leadership which Americans are largely taking for granted.

This is the difference: Ostrogorski, and all those scholars and journalists who reiterated his argument, wished to destroy parties in the name of democracy. Contemporary scholars, equally critical of party defects, recognize that they are democracy's most valued invention; hence they wish not to destroy them, but to make them good servants of the public weal.

Hopeful as is this change in the scholars' attitude, it remains unfortunately true that most voters distrust parties still. So the difficulty emerges: How can the expert understanding of scholars be passed on to citizens generally? How can it become an active political force?

In the propagation of this faith, the scholars themselves have both a power and a duty. Perhaps their word alone, rippling out in an ever-widening circle, can fertilize in citizens a sense of their civic need. To rely entirely on the influence of experts, however, displays a naive trust in the rationality of irrational mankind. For at least two generations scholars have understood that democracy needs parties and needs them strengthened and improved. This was the message of, for example, Woodrow Wilson, Frank Goodnow, and other outstanding American political writers at the end of the nineteenth century.[13] Their under-

---

[12] Committee on Political Parties of the American Political Science Association, *Toward a More Responsible Party System.* Copyright 1950 by the American Political Science Association, p. 15 (emphasis in original).

[13] See Woodrow Wilson, *op. cit.* and Frank J. Goodnow, *Politics and Administration* (New York, Macmillan, 1900). For some sensible remarks on this aspect of their thought, see Austin Ranney, "Toward a More Responsible Two-Party System: A Commentary," *American Political Science Review,* XLV (1951), pp. 488–99.

standing has been public domain ever since, but clearly it has not been much taken up. Even if the tuition of scholars were effective, however, it ripples out too slowly, impressing the next generation far more than this. Yet it is this generation that needs the understanding. It is our democracy today that may die from popular contempt. It is ours today that may be destroyed from without because we have not the strength within.

TENDENCIES TOWARD PARTY CENTRALIZATION

Still it is true that today a far larger proportion of American scholars than in the day of Wilson and Goodnow are interested in stronger, more responsible political parties. Perhaps the interest is now enough that scholars can make a substantial impression on the public, provided, of course, that the public is willing to listen to their message. But how willing is the public to listen? Are there any tendencies in American politics which will encourage the listening?

Fortunately there are such tendencies, not the least of which is the very complexity of our contemporary politics, a complexity which can hardly be understood without simplifying and rationalizing by party leaders. Of course, it is very easy to overestimate the complexity of real life in one's own time, especially by comparison with the history book's simplifications of life long ago. But that our contemporary politics is more complex than ever before is hardly to be denied. It is not so much that government is bigger, although that fact alone contributes something to the complexity. Rather it is that we have laid more and more responsibilities on it. In this age of optimism, when advances in scientific and social theory have taught us (often falsely) to believe that human ingenuity can conquer every obstacle to the good and easy life, we have come to expect that government, the greatest human institution, will do the conquering for us. The total environment, physical and social, once regarded as an uncontrollable given which men must suffer or at best to which they must adjust, is increasingly regarded as a variable which men can manipulate to their advantage. Quite understandably, this changed viewpoint has magnified the political problems of manipulation. It has made more problems in governing; and worse it has increased the number and significance of incompatibles in policy. In the field of public health, for example, from ancient times to the mid-nineteenth century, urban people expected at most a system of water supply and sewage disposal. Now we expect not only water, but clean water; and beyond that we expect government to control disease, minimizing if not eliminating it, or at least to set the conditions of controlling it, without, of course, bothering us too much about it when we are well. We nowadays expect government to make everybody literate, without, of course, spending too much money on the job. We expect that government will set the conditions for more and more intensive exploitation of natural resources, without, of course, depriving our descendants of their rightful heritage. We have come to expect also that government will set the conditions for perpetual prosperity and ever-expanding material ease, without, of course, taxing us too much or regulating business too severely. We expect that government will, even now that the Atlantic wall no longer protects us from jet bombers, maneuver us to military security, without, of course, turning too many of us into citizen-soldiers. Most amazing of all, some of us even expect that government can attain for us the blessings of perpetual peace, without, of course, sacrificing any of our national sovereignty.

One important consequence of this complexity, of these conflicting expectations from government, is that a coherent reconciliation of our inconsistent desires is for most of us very difficult. And in that difficulty we have but one place to turn for help. We are increasingly forced to rely on party leaders to systematize and rationalize our expectations for us. Pressure groups, the only conceivable competitors with parties in making the reconciliation, are inherently incapable of synthesizing a whole range of citizens' interests, for they are, by definition, organized around particular and partial interests. We turn to parties, therefore, and inevitably party allegiance must play a larger role in our political life.

Granting, however, that by the very complexity of politics today party leadership must play a greater role, it does not necessarily follow that the party leadership that plays it will be responsible and centralized. Just as conceivably, it may be divided up among a dozen coteries inside each party, as has usually been the case in the past. Yet there is in American life another and related tendency, driving us toward party centralization. The complexity of government which demands leadership in thought demands also centraliized leadership in action. If synthesizing the complexity of interests is difficult for the citizen, it is the more so for the party leaders who bear the heavy duty of synthesis. Nowadays politicians are being overwhelmed, just as the citizen has been already, by the difficulty of appropriate reconciliations of, for example, particular aspects of foreign policy with particular kinds of internal improvements, a reconciliation which must necessarily be made within the context of policies covering the whole range of governmental activity. Of course, the party in opposition need not worry unduly over this; it can neglect its own synthesis in order to snipe at the synthesis the party in power has made. But the party in power must make a budget and divide up governmental activities in a rational satisfaction of the interests on which its majority rests. The day-to-day urgency of this duty has in the last half-century driven the party in power to look more and more for centralized leadership, usually in the most convenient place, the Presidency. Throughout our history we have sought Presidential leadership in crises, though between them we have usually relaxed to a government of a half-dozen or so competing powers. Now, however, the search for Presidential leadership is much more frequent, possibly because in this complex society politics has more frequently assumed crisis proportion. World politics being what it is, an easily upset balance between peace and war, our economic system being what it is, an easily upset balance between inflation and depression, it seems certain that we will for a long time to come be living in an expanding spiral of crises. Can there be any doubt that perpetual crisis will in turn emphasize Presidential leadership of government and party?

Thus two tendencies, one working in voters, the other in politicians, seem certain to compel more definite responsibility in more centralized parties. The voters need party leadership to rationalize their expectations from government. The politicians, at least those of the party in power, need centralized leadership to create a coherent program.

But these two tendencies do not exhaust the diversity of American life. Who can doubt that, on the other hand, there still exist powerful centrifugal forces? Perhaps they are not so great as they were a hundred years ago when the theory of state sovereignty was so commonly advanced and the theory of the separation of powers uncontested. They are still very strong, however, so strong that a seemingly genuine popular fear of Presidential leadership produced the Twenty-second Amendment, so strong that a real popular preference for local leadership balked Roosevelt's "purge" in 1938. The centrifugal forces may not again lead to civil war or compel the kind of abdication of the national government that characterized the 1870's or 1880's; but surely they are strong enough to impede centralized and responsible leadership. Furthermore, there seems little immediate chance that the centrifugal tendencies will significantly weaken. They are based, as was suggested in Chapter 8, on the localism of our politics. And so long as local politicians control nominations to national offices—which will be so long as voters remain unwilling to trust their national party leaders—localism will discourage centralization. It is true, as was also suggested in Chapter 8, that the federalism which supports localism is dying, but it is also true that the death is extraordinarily protracted. Consequently, it is not possible to predict with any assurance the future course of American party life. Probably the centralizing tendencies are the stronger, but our grand-children may be dead before any sure evidence of their strength is dis-covered.

We Need a Greater Schoolmaster

The characteristic fallacy of historians and social scientists is the fancy that tendencies carry themselves out regardless of human intervention. Having abstracted the idea of a tendency from real events, having per-haps dignified the abstraction as a philosophy of history and called it an inevitable direction in the historical process, they unconsciously per-sonify it, attributing to it the human characteristics of will and self-direction. It was by this kind of unconscious personification that the classical economists made a secular deity out of Competition and the Marxists made one out of Materialist Dialectic. Yet historical tendencies are not real, at least apart from the people who believe in them. It may be true that conditions of society suggest to men with similar cultural backgrounds that they act one way in preference to another. The nature of Congress, for example, may discourage men from looking to it for leadership, while, on the other hand, the nature of the Presidency may suggest to men that they get leadership there. But it is still men who act, not political tendencies: The tendencies are realized only because men act on them. Whether the centralizing tendencies or the cen-trifugal ones will triumph in the long run depends, therefore, not so much on the inherent nature of the tendencies themselves as upon the action of men in the next few decades.

While men act within the conditions that they believe surround them, they do also have some freedom of choice when confronted with incon-sistent conditions or conflicting tendencies. They can choose wrongly. Thus, although the teaching of scholars and the tendencies toward centralization *might* lead to responsible parties, there are still enough conditions of centrifugality that the public may not demand responsible parties for a very long time.

Hence, besides scholars, we need a greater schoolmaster, one great enough to teach us all to trust our parties in conscious confidence that we can hold them responsible. And where shall we find a schoolmaster so persuasive, at once a wise man and a hero? He can be but one place in our democracy: in the White House.

Only heroes have what is the first requisite of mass persuasion: charisma, the gift of grace, or as Max Weber secularized the term, that: [14]

quality of an individual personality by virtue of which he is set apart from ordinary men and treated as endowed with supernatural, superhuman, or at least specifically exceptional powers or qualities.

The suggestion that we need heroes, charismatic heroes, often arouses fear in democratic hearts. One side of democratic theory—the side most often emphasized by democratic theorists in their polemics against competing systems—stresses restraints on the pride of high station. And because democracy is so often praised for its restraints on leaders, democrats sometimes find it difficult to appreciate their own need for creative heroes, men who, though restrained in the ordinary democratic ways, still have enough charisma to persuade their fellows to a faith in the democratic order. It is quite true, as democratic theorists so often point out, that leaders whose sole basis for their authority is their charisma, men like Savonarola or John Brown or Gandhi, are irresponsible; their only method of leading is to teach the ultimate political blasphemy: that they are God's chosen agents in whose interests all the traditional restraints on rulers must be swept away. Even worse are those whose gift of grace is believed to come from a class or a race or a nation. While politico-religious heroes are at least occasionally impelled to humble soul-searching, those whose charisma is secular are wholly unrestrained. A leader like Stalin or Hitler, for example, can force everyone to obey him, degrading all independent spirits until at the end of the terror

---

[14] Max Weber, *The Theory of Social and Economic Organization*, trans. by Talcott Parsons and A. M. Henderson (New York, Oxford University Press, 1947), p. 358. In his secularization of the word Weber transformed it from a divinely granted favor to a personality characteristic that exists because it is recognized by followers.

they, like Winston Smith, sob out their overwhelming love of Big Brother.

However repelled we are by the atrocities committed in the name of an irresponsible charisma, we cannot therefore deny our own need for creative leadership. All political doctrines—and democracy is no exception—are at base myths, that is, unprovable faiths resting on a series of unprovable propositions about men, society, and knowledge. Although the contents of political myths may differ, they have this in common: That they are faiths propagated by leaders whose authority rests on their teaching. Every religion needs its saints—indeed one may almost say that the content of a religion is the lives of its saints—and similarly every political theory needs its heroes. Saints and heroes serve to inculcate faith in the doctrine by which they themselves have lived. And democracy, as a political theory, needs its heroes too, charismatic leaders who persuade their followers to the democratic faith.

It goes almost without saying, however, that the charisma of democratic heroes differs from the charisma of, for example, fascist heroes: Their messages differ and hence their lives differ. The Christian saint differs from the Muslim because each embodies a different scale of values. The heroes of democracy must, by definition, therefore, embody the major democratic virtues. They must be humble and self-respecting, as those virtues were defined in Chapter 1. They must accept gladly the democratic principles of competing political parties and tolerance of dissent which were set forth in Chapter 3. So in fact it is with the great heroes the United States has already had, men whom most of us, regardless of party feeling, acknowledge as teachers of the democratic virtues, Washington, Jefferson, Jackson, Lincoln, Theodore Roosevelt, Wilson, and Franklin Roosevelt. They have never been military heroes, even when they have had some military experience. Rather, they have always been leaders of *one of two* competing parties; and, with the exception of Wilson, and possibly of Washington, they have been professional politicians within the democratic context all their adult lives. Except Washington, perhaps, they have been hated by some as deeply as they have been loved by others; yet, being both party leaders and humble men, they have never questioned their enemies' right to condemn them. Most important, these American heroes have always, while in office, had a clear program of democratic action. They have not, like Grant, for example, rested on laurels which they earlier won; they have rather been heroes because they led wisely and well as President, led us indeed toward their own expanded conception of the democratic life. Thus, while they have been restrained in the usual democratic ways (free elections and the two-party system), they have also been able to inculcate a faith in democratic institutions. Such schoolmasters are what our democracy needs today to overcome the separated powers and decentralized parties.

REFORMS FOR PRESIDENTIAL LEADERSHIP

All Presidents have an interest in nationalizing and strengthening political parties; hero Presidents have further the ability to do both. Consequently, the hope for more effective party government is not a vain dream, for, in some heroes at least, interest and power are joined.

All Presidents have both personal and official incentives to centralize party leadership in themselves. The Constitution charges them with the duty of suggesting and executing law. The electorate holds them responsible for much more: despite the separation of powers, despite even the popular acceptance of the check and balance verbalisms, the electorate still holds Presidents responsible for all of government. It is a curious oversimplification, this expectation that Presidents will control even those things over which they have no formal and very little informal power. If one starts from our constitutional theory, it is simply another evidence of the illogicality of men. But in the commonsense of democracy, it is wholly reasonable, for the President, the one official responsible to everybody, *ought* to equate power and duty, even if he does not. Indeed, our problem today is that our constitutional theory lags behind our democratic commonsense.

Because their responsibility to the people exceeds their power, Presidents are always frustrated, always aware that they will be judged by a standard they can never meet. Hence also their political interest, their interest in re-election and in party success, is to centralize power in themselves in order to rise to the electorate's expectation. What interferes with their interest is their inability to manage Congress; and that in turn depends on their inadequate control of their party. The only way, then, by which Presidents can hope to equalize their power with the electorate's interpretation of it is by attaining party leadership in Congress. The only way to attain it is to centralize it in themselves. And the only way they can centralize it in themselves is by teaching their fellow partisans to want and to trust a strong national party.

All Presidents have an interest in centralizing party leadership, but only the heroes can do it. Every act of the unheroic man is subjected to so much popular and Congressional scrutiny that he must spend all his energy compromising petty details of executive policy. He has no room left in his personality or program for constructive party leadership. Not so restricted is the President who speaks as one having authority. His leadership is welcomed because it is *his,* not because it is a compromise. He must compromise petty details too, but he can do more than that. People trust the hero, even if he was once just a politician; and the hero, if he deserves the trust, is able to transfer some of it from himself to his party. Ordinary Presidents are incapable of this constructive leadership. They, like most other politicians in a democracy, are obsessed—and properly so—with the question: "How will my action affect the next election?" But in their obsession they interpret it wrongly and narrowly: "Will the people tolerate this?" Terrified of their masters and fearing to provoke them, they answer no and thereby become donothings of the order of Buchanan, Grant, or Harding. These are like the servant who buried his talents; but the heroes are like him who multiplied the talent tenfold, for they interpret the democratic question broadly: "Can I show the people by the next election how useful, how essential is this new departure?" This is not the distinction so commonly made between politicians and statesmen. Rather it is a distinction between two kinds of politicians: those who bow always to the public opinion of the moment and those who in the self-confidence of their heroism pour public opinion into their own molds.

So far the argument involves a paradox: We say we need heroic Presidential leadership, yet we say we must have heroic Presidential leadership to get it. But it is not really a logical circle, equating an effect with a cause. Some Presidents like Washington or Jackson come to the Presidency heroes already. Others like Lincoln or Franklin Roosevelt acquire charisma in their first few months in office. So truly heroism can precede Presidential leadership and in turn make it heroic. The more important question is about the reasonableness of the hope, not the logic: Will we have a hero President, or a succession of hero Presidents, soon enough to save our democracy from contempt? Considering the rarity of folk heroes in the Presidency, men who at least in their time have made a strong party combination, we cannot predict when another will be forthcoming. But more men than the folk heores have charisma in office. Washington, Jefferson, Jackson, Lincoln, Wilson, Franklin

Roosevelt—these greatest of heroes continued to influence even after death by the shadow of their own heroic lives. But other Presidents, too, are temporary heroes, missing permanent hero-worship only because they failed to exploit the charisma they had. It is not too much to say that every elected President comes to office a hero. Even a President as incompetent as Grant now seems was during his lifetime accorded extraordinary hero-worship. The people made him a hero and refused to recognize his defects because they knew that the office he held demanded heroism. In other instances too, for example, William Henry Harrison, Zachary Taylor, and Dwight Eisenhower, the people have raised to office men whose chief virtue is that they once held a successful military command. Of course, there is no necessary connection between military success and heroic party leadership, but our people, aware of the necessity of hero Presidents, have seized on the one straw of evidence, however dubious, to accord charisma to otherwise unimpressive men. Even when Presidents have had in their backgrounds neither outstanding military nor outstanding partisan leadership, the people have still found ways to accord charisma. A President like Coolidge, who now seems so unexciting, was heroized for incidental attributes like Yankee taciturnity. Indeed, in office he possessed a kind of charisma, enough, surprisingly, to inspire Clarence Day to write a funeral tribute almost as touching as Walt Whitman's on Lincoln.[15] Of course, folk heroes in the Presidency are rare; but almost every President has some real ability to lead, else he would not be where he is. Therefore, the chance for charisma is not so rare as the self-confidence to use it. To the self-confidence scholars can, perhaps, make some contribution, teaching us to welcome heroes rather than to fear them, and thereby encouraging lesser heroes to use what charisma they have.

The hero President can teach us to welcome party centralization, but he can do so only by creation, not by mere preaching. He must actually centralize his own party, justifying it to his fellow partisans. The increase in effectiveness therefrom will in turn stimulate the opposition. Centralization of the one will be fed on the centralization of the other in spiraling series, so long as we have hero Presidents conscious of their interest in the power to govern. Hence the hero's duty to transform the reputation of parties involves also specific institutional innova-

---

[15] Clarence Day, *In the Green Mountain Country* (New Haven, Yale University Press, 1934).

tions aimed both at increasing the effectiveness of his own leadership and at centralizing his (and indirectly the other) political party.

The lore of political gadgetry contains many proposed innovations conducive to Presidential party leadership. For example, it is often said that the elimination of the electoral college would reduce one-party monopoly and thus encourage local political organization in both parties all over the country. Presumably, the increased degree of local party organization would give greater scope to Presidential leadership, but the argument of Chapter 8 makes it fairly clear that this expectation is illusory. Again, it is often said that a variety of gadgets to encourage responsible party government would promote Presidential leadership, although it is doubtful if any of the frequently proposed gadgets (e.g., closed primaries—closed, that is, to all but party members—mid-term party conventions, short party platforms, etc.) would have any significant effect on Presidential leadership. We must reject political gimmicks and ask the question directly.

PRESIDENTIAL PARTY LEADERSHIP

How can a President acquire leadership of his party? Some control he exercises because of his heroism alone. Possessed of charisma, he can appeal over the heads of recalcitrant Congressmen to those who recognize his grace. But charisma is not enough. Heroes cannot require the people to recognize it too often, lest some begin to suspect that it is not there. Instead, the hero must institutionalize some of his charisma so that, without demagoguery, he can regularly lead his congressional partisans. And how shall he institutionalize? The best method available is this: by developing further the methods with which Roosevelt experimented in the primary campaign of 1938.

Only the hero, fully conscious of what specific devices he himself can use, is able to decide when and how the experiment ought to be tried again. Even the armchair politician, however, can suggest possibilities. The central problem of party control is, of course, the opposition of those party recalcitrants who are well-entrenched in their home areas. Having decided which of the recalcitrants are most disrupting and most easily displaced, a courageous President might, a full two years before party primaries, pick out other residents of the areas, zealous supporters of his own, to run against the recalcitrants. He ought to encourage them to spend full time on the campaign for two years ahead of the elections.

While a President cannot himself be conversant with political circumstances in every state and Congressional district, his political lieutenants, perhaps the national chairman, perhaps his official assistants, can select both the districts and the President's candidates. Beyond simple encouragement, moreover, he ought to give them assistance in the organization of local party groups, to subsidize them—if need be—out of party funds, and, in general, to place himself and an expanded apparatus of the national committee behind their candidacies.

A President who proceeded thus, regularly from the very beginning of his tenure, could immeasurably strengthen his own position in Congress and his party. Some of the extreme recalcitrants he could successfully eliminate, others he could bring into line by the unspoken threat of similar elimination. It is possible that in two or three years the President could obtain enough party leadership to regularize his position. He could perhaps establish regular channels for a national party group—in which he would serve as *primus inter pares*—to approve party candidates in the primaries. He could perhaps establish central leadership in Congress of those party leaders thoroughly loyal to him. And from that position it would be easy enough to effect such other reforms as seemed necessary for responsible government: suffrage extension, Senate cloture and perhaps even revision of the Senate structure, elimination of the seniority system in Congress, control of the tenure of the Supreme Court, etc. In short, the separated powers could be brought together into an effective and responsible tool of the majority, brought together not just for the moment of crisis, but regularly for the whole process of government.

Thus applied, the technique of party centralization would affect only one party. In extended application, however, it would affect both. As here suggested, its first purpose would be to eliminate recalcitrants from districts and states certain to be carried by his own party; but it would, certainly, work just as well in those districts which hover between the parties. Were a great President to encourage and support his own, permanent, full-time candidates in perhaps twenty-five to fifty marginal districts held by the other party, he could probably transfer at least half of them to his side of the House. So it appears, at least, as we observe the primitive, unprofessional fashion in which congressional campaigns are organized by the losing party in many marginal districts. If he should succeed to a degree even approaching this, the minority party would certainly be impelled to copy as much as possible the nationalizing methods of the majority. And further, the next time the minority of the moment elected a President, it too would be prepared to develop the same kind of Presidential centralization.

What kind of President can do what I suggest? As a minimum requirement, he must have charisma. While Vice-Presidents who entered office of President accidentally and did not seek an election of their own (e.g., Tyler, Fillmore, Andrew Johnson, and Arthur) probably never had charisma, still the electorate seems willing to grant at least some charisma to any elected President, no matter how colorless and purposeless he seems to later generations. So we can be assured that all but accidental Presidents have the minimum requirement—and at least one of the accidental Presidents, Theodore Roosevelt seems to have acquired some charisma before he was elected on his own.

A second requirement is that the President want the power of office. Not all men want power and glory, but nearly every one who has been President has been the kind of person who thrives on these possessions. Twenty-two elected Presidents have survived their first term and thus been able to seek a second term. Of these only four (Polk, Pierce, Buchanan, Hayes) have refused to try for a second term, and of the four only one (Hayes) apparently would not have tried for a second term if the political circumstances were such that he could have done so. Even so superficially reluctant a President as Eisenhower who rejected attempts to nominate him in 1948, who complained throughout his Presidency about the difficulties of his office, and whose family was apparently reluctant to have him run in 1956, still showed very little hesitation in seeking a second term. Despite the fact that in the year prior to his decision to run again he had had both a serious heart attack and a serious abdominal operation, he decided to seek re-election. Clearly the lure of power and glory was great for him, as, I believe, it is for any man who seeks the office in the first place. So we can conclude that the second requirement will nearly always be filled—except when the Presidency is occupied by a former Vice-President who, like Chester Arthur, was apparently appalled at the demands of the job that had befallen him.

A third requirement, less frequently satisfied than the previous two, is that the President have a clear picture of the policy goals he wishes to use his power to achieve. This is where many Presidents have failed. They have wanted power, but they have not been certain what they wanted it for. And since they have not known this, they have not had a necessary incentive to develop the leadership they need to control their own parties.

Dwight Eisenhower is the most recent example of the purposeless President, although there have unfortunately been many others among elected Presidents—e.g., Harding, Benjamin Harrison, Grant, and Pierce. Eisenhower came to office a great hero because of his military record, which had indeed been heroic. He called his first campaign a crusade in reminiscence of the title of his war memoirs, *Crusade in Europe*. But the purpose of the crusade was unclear: Perhaps it was to eliminate isolationists from the Republican party; perhaps it was to eliminate corruption of the sort found all too frequently in Truman's second administration; perhaps, as he later suggested, it was to reduce national expenditures; but clearly he was not firmly committed to any one of these goals, for, as President, he did not try to eliminate isolationists from the party, he did not in fact eliminate corruption in the office of the President, and, except for a brief period in 1958, he did not try seriously to alter the upward trend of national expenditures. In short, the crusade was without content, which is apparently what Eisenhower himself intended. According to Neustadt, Eisenhower had a picture of his office somewhat reminiscent of Washington's: that the President was a moderator of strife, of partisan conflict, not a leader in developing party ideology; that the President was a remote center of patriotism, not a mobilizer of opinion for new forms of public policy; and that the President was a hero who stood above party.[16] Naturally, with this view of his office there is no reason for a President to develop party leadership. If, as Eisenhower did, he substantially accepts the domestic policy he inherits (in this case from Franklin Roosevelt) and the foreign policy he inherits (in this case from Harry Truman), then his only function as President is to smooth over crises as they arise. This Eisenhower did, with, in his public image, an imperturbable calm— the Suez crisis, the Little Rock crisis, the Lebanon crisis, etc. But since he did not wish to lead for something new in public policy, he lacked the incentive to lead his party and thus effectively foreclosed for himself the possibility of achieving Presidential centralization of power.

Of recent Presidents, the three who most clearly wished to lead *for* something, who most clearly had a set of policy goals they wished to accomplish, were Franklin Roosevelt, Harry Truman, and John Ken-

[16] Richard Neustadt, *Presidential Power* (New York, John Wiley and Sons, 1960), pp. 152–80.

nedy. They meet our third requirement of an ideological commitment and hence they could be Presidents who tried to centralize their parties in themselves. All three took an active part in party affairs, seeking constantly to improve their own control of lesser party members.

Finally, a fourth requirement is that those who meet the third requirement also have a sense of being schoolmasters to the nation. This is more than an ideological commitment—it is a conviction that they must impress their own commitment on the nation. If a President is to lead, he must be convinced that *his* leadership is necessary, that he has some unique value in himself to inspire others. Among recent Presidents only Franklin Roosevelt and John Kennedy have satisfied this requirement.

So, I conclude, only occasionally do Presidents occur who meet the four requirements—who possess charisma, who want power, who have an ideological conviction, and who wish to impress their conviction on others. Nevertheless, about one third of our Presidents have met these requirements, and these are the kind who, if they come in the future, may conceivably acquire genuine party leadership and thus improve the working of our total political system.

DEMOCRATIC HEROES

Possibly this picture, sketched here, of *our* St. George slaying *our* dragon will seem unattractive to many good democrats. Secular sceptics as they are, they believe not in such saints nor understand mankind's need for such inspiration; they fear that underneath the helmet will hide the face of a Casear or a Napoleon. Unable to distinguish between the white and black knights, they prefer the customary conflicts of ambition, half-democratic as they are, to a matured democratic responsibility which is hard for them to imagine. One cannot, however, contemptuously dismiss their fears: Despots are real enough in the twentieth century. Fortunately, we have had neither Hitlers nor Boulangers here; but we have had our narrow escapes, local demagogues with national ambitions and military heroes yearning for the scepter as well as the sword. But a hero President is not a Caesar and we need not fear he will be. And this for two reasons: American heroes, particularly the heroes in public life, have in the past always been good men, essentially humble; we can, therefore, reasonably expect that they will be so in the future. Further, we have a variety of institutional devices, not the least of which is the party system itself, which serve to inhibit dictatorial ambitions; therefore, our heroes, or at least our political heroes who necessarily operate inside our two-party structure, cannot metamorphose to tyrants.

Americans have always insisted that their heroes be chivalrously devoted to the pursuit of an ideal. They have acknowledged charisma only in heroes who are essentially honest, who are self-respecting but not prideful, who place patriotic service above personal glory. They have not, of course, required that their heroes be Galahads, perfectly pure; but with a realistic appreciation of human nature, they have required that their heroes' sins be venial, that their only pride be a zeal for service. A quotation from the concluding chapter of Dixon Wecter's study of American heroes sets forth precisely our standards in heroism: [17]

The sort of man whom Americans admire, trust, and are willing to follow can be sketched with a few lines. . . . At the basic level he must be self-respecting, decent, honorable, with a sense of fair play; no Machiavelli nor Mussolini need apply. . . . An able man must not glory in his cleverness. By our standards one is sometimes allowed to "put over a fast one"—Benjamin Franklin and Abraham Lincoln did, repeatedly—but he must not appear to relish the coup for its own sake. Art must conceal art. Jefferson understood this restraint just a little better than does his disciple Franklin Roosevelt. A clodhopper politician like Huey Long . . . did not understand it at all. Long's scornful assertion that he could buy votes in his Legislature "like sacks of potatoes," to the country at large was . . . bad politics. Uncle Sam allows his favorites to be shrewd in a good cause, but there must be no avowal of cynicism in principle. . . . The backwoods has a certain admiration for rustic rascality, and the metropolis loves a flippant wisecrack—but in America at large there is a pretty strong prejudice against the wise guy.

Vanity or personal arrogance in any form is taboo. The dandy in public life—accepted more tolerantly in the England of Disraeli or Lord Curzon—is disliked by Americans. . . . The arrogance of caste is equally deadly in American hero-worship. Hancock, Jay, Gouverneur Morris were snobs who never won the sway, with even a seasoning of popular admiration, that some Tory statesmen have enjoyed in England. The public can never forget that Hamilton once exclaimed, "Your people, sir, is a great beast." . . . [and] have repaid his scorn with neglect. . . .

[17] Dixon Wecter, *The Hero in America.* Copyright 1941 by Charles Scribner's Sons, pp. 482–87.

What then in the final analysis do Washington, Franklin, Jefferson, Jackson, Lincoln, and in a provisional verdict Wilson and the Roosevelts have in common? . . .

All of them, the people believe, loved America more deeply than any selfish consideration. The hero as made in America is a man who has the power and yet does not abuse it. He is the practical demonstration of romantic democracy. Washington is the most sublime because, after winning our freedom, he refused a crown, military dictatorship, and every personal reward. Lee is the grandest because he did what he thought was his duty, failed under heartbreaking odds, and then with gentleness did his best to repair all hate and malice. Lincoln is most appealing because, in the conduct of that same desperate war which gave him the power of a czar, he never forgot his love for the common people of North and South.

This sketch of our heroes suggests the surest guarantee we have that our St. George will not turn to attack us once he has slain the dragon. The American tradition has so far—and it is unlikely it will suddenly change—heroized virtues and personalities that are colorful but essentially modest, forceful but essentially humble. If *we* make him, he will be a St. George; and if he is St. George, he cannot be Caesar. It is true that we admire the noble assurance of Washington and the cheerful self-confidence, even arrogance, of Franklin Roosevelt. These are virtues, we believe, because they renew our courage in moments of despair. But though these traits verge to the authoritarian personality, we know that we can safely admire them because they are not accompanied by a lust for dominion or a glory-hunting willfulness. And on the other side, the American tradition has always refused to admit to hero status men who exact servility as their personal due or in the name of the social class they represent. So deeply do Americans admire the democratic virtue of self-respect, so genuinely horrified are they at any valid evidence of pride, that no President can expect his charisma to be acknowledged unless he is really a trustworthy man.

In this, the age of dictatorships, the specter of Caesarism is so terrifying, however, that some good democrats still fear the hero President, even though they may admit that the American commonsense has heretofore selected its heroes uncommonly well. There are other safeguards, however, institutional ones, which should allay this dread. For one thing, there is the constitutional provision for impeachment, which has been used once and can be used again. Consider what would probably happen in the unlikely event that Americans misjudged a hero until it was too late. A President who sought to go beyond the traditional bounds of our politics, who sought for example, not to lead Congress but to ignore it, would very likely provoke these two reactions: He would, on the one hand, probably alienate many of his partisans in Congress and, on the other, probably bring on himself a process of impeachment. Whether convicted or not, he would thereby certainly lose much of his charisma and with that most of his power to govern. The impeachment process may seem to some so much rusted by disuse that it cannot be used again. But what seems atrophied to the private citizen seems well nourished and healthy to Presidents in office. Even one so self-assured as Franklin Roosevelt paused, at the very height of his power just after he had been elected for a third time, to worry lest an accidental encounter between American and German warships lead to his impeachment.[18]

Impeachment is a last resort, however, not likely to be necessary except for Presidents like Johnson who never—except in defeat—approached heroic stature. For the heroic Presidents, the really useful controls are the two-party system itself, the fact of opposition, and the heroes' leadership of one of the parties. Constructive leadership in a functioning two-party system can never go outside the traditional political bounds. The party leader remains leader simply because in primaries, mid-term elections, and elections in Presidential years his leadership is re-endorsed by the people. Since other men than himself have to be endorsed, part of the endorsement has to be in terms of the leader's platform and program as well as in terms of the spell cast by his personality. Furthermore, the existence of the minority opposition, always eager to welcome all the people the President offends, always hoping to recruit a majority from the rebellious, constantly reminds him that he must play fair according to the democratic rules.

Even assuming that a President were repeatedly re-endorsed in elections, even assuming that, Odysseus-like, he stuffed his partisans' ears so that they could not hear the sirens of the minority, still his leadership would be an uncertain possession. He can expect his congressional partisans to follow him only so long as they have a prospect of being re-elected with his aid. When that prospect is befogged, some at least of his partisans will desert him, whenever, for example, he throws away his charisma in a tyrannical move or, more obviously, whenever he nears the end of his second term. This is what the Twenty-

[18] Robert Sherwood, *Roosevelt and Hopkins: An Intimate History* (New York, Harper & Brothers, 1948), p. 295.

second Amendment assures: That the President's party leadership will collapse entirely midway in his second term. Congressmen will certainly ignore him then, as so many Presidents complained they were ignored when the two-term tradition was in force and when, hence, a President could never be expected to give his congressional partisans aid in the elections at the end of his second term. (The Amendment has also a secondary effect in that it will encourage—much more than the tradition ever did—Presidents in their second term to ignore the essential democratic question: "How will this act affect the next election?" Thus, paradoxically, it will actually encourage the kind of arbitrary action it was intended to prevent.) Even if the somewhat dubious protection of this Amendment did not exist, however, it must be remembered that charisma is unstable, changing quickly with circumstance. And this, in a two-party system, is the essential guarantee that great men will not abuse power.

Hence we ought not be misled by the fear of tyranny. We ought to recognize that a hero President's control of his party is the surest, safest way to democratic self-control. It is the way to self-control first for the majority of the moment, and, because majorities are shifting, for the whole people. Indeed it is the only way that the separation of powers can be brought together democratically.

St. George or Caesar

We are in our era about to reach a crossroads in democratic development, a crossroads at which we have a choice between responsible government and tyranny, between St. George and Caesar. The separated powers, so far as they make government impotent, are what may bring our democracy into popular contempt. And once they have brought it there, as they did for example in Germany in the 1920's, the only cure for impotence will be a tyrant, strong enough to bring the separated powers together unconstitutionally. This is what democrats want at all costs to avoid. And how can they avoid it? One method, now occasionally suggested, is the Roman, constitutionally established dictatorship. Rousseau, for example, argued that in times of crisis a dictator ought to be granted power to do anything, except make permanent laws. And some contemporary American scholars, pondering the sickness of our separated powers, have argued the same thing. "No sacrifice is too great for our democracy," concludes one proposal for a regularized reliance on temporary dictatorship, "least of all the temporary sacrifice of democracy itself." [19] But constitutional dictatorship has unfortunate precedents which suggest that it is not much different from dictatorship full-fledged. Was not the end of the Roman Republic the dictatorship of the triumvirs? Did not Robespierre imagine himself the dictator of Rousseau? Proponents of constitutional dictatorship may indeed be riding the wave of the future, but it is a wave which will engulf them as well as us. There is yet another way to avoid the tyrant, one which does not involve even the temporary sacrifice of democratic forms. This is the method briefly set out in this chapter. A strong government, one which is strong all the time, capped by a strong President, either a hero or one who has inherited a hero's inventions, and a responsible government, responsible in the ordinary partisan ways—this is how we can avoid dictatorship, either constitutional or permanent. And thereby will be declared an extra dividend. Government will become truly an extension of our own faculties, truly an institution for popular self-control, truly a method of creating self-respect for everybody.

The Struggle for Democracy in the United States

One major assumption beneath the argument of this study is that government can make men good. Like Aristotle, I believe that men are political beings, that felicity in persons is the same as felicity in the state, that, indeed, good constitutions make good men. The definition of democracy set forth in Chapter 1—self-respect for everybody to be obtained by responsible government—assumes just that. Self-respect is a virtue—the highest one in the democratic order—and it is attained by the conquest of evil in private and public life. Good men, therefore, are made when a democratic constitution disciplines their propensity to pride, when it will not let them disfigure their souls with servility, when it encourages them to express their fullest dignity and manhood.

Many would deny, however, that virtue is made politically, would assert instead that virtue must be sought in private, only by isolated, non-political men. Of course, men can and do strive for virtue in their own private ways. But those who emphasize the private path, entirely excluding the public, overlook this one thing: Virtues, observed outside

[19] Clinton L. Rossiter, *Constitutional Dictatorship* (Princeton, Princeton University Press, 1948), p. 314.

man, are indeed words which can, perhaps must, be communicated in private ways; but virtue, observed inside man, is naught but a series of habits of thought and action. And how do men make their habits? Some few they perhaps make for themselves by conscious self-direction. But more of them are made for us, so that we adopt them unconsciously as we grow up into society. These prepared habits are what we call "institutions," habits depersonalized by the fact that so many people follow them, habits depersonalized even more by being written down in laws and constitutions. Political institutions, then, are habits magnified. But, although the habits may seem at the same time to be dehumanized, we ought not to conclude therefrom that institutions are inhuman too, that they have no direct effect on human life. Whether one man or many follow them they still affect action and have still thereby a moral significance. "We cannot suppose," said Plato arguing this same point, "that States are made out of 'oak and rock' and not out of the human natures which are in them." Hence it follows that the goodness or badness of men is in some way controlled by the goodness or badness of their government.

Democrats, who have chosen self-respect as their highest good, are quite justified, therefore, in seeking it through political forms. But they should not expect to find it easily. Not so long ago democrats believed that their devices, once set in motion, would work as surely and as automatically as an electronic brain. But we today know that they do not. Pride and special privilege are human, and the malicious cleverness that serves them is more skillful far than the tricks with which we have hitherto tried to root them out. Things spiritual that we love are got hold of only by persistent devotion and untiring struggle. Even faith and endurance, however, are not enough, for the best faith in the world is impotent without knowledge and the greatest endurance is wasted without skill. The chapters foregoing have set forth, so far as possible, the knowledge faith needs of the ideals it is devoted to. They have tried as well to explain the skills endurance needs for the making of good habits. America can, let us hope and believe, acquire the habits of self-control, enough perhaps to avoid a depression or to win a war, enough perhaps even to recognize the worthiness of every man. With rational faith and instructed endurance, clearly aware of the hardships it involves, American democrats ought to persist in the struggle.

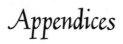

Appendices

Appendix to
Chapter 1

PERICLES' FUNERAL ORATION [1]

(Athens, circa 431 B.C.)

(35) Most of those who have stood in this place before me have commended the institution of this closing address. It is good, they have felt, that solemn words should be spoken over our fallen soldiers. I do not share this feeling. Acts deserve acts, not words, in their honour, and to me a burial at the State's charges, such as you see before you, would have appeared sufficient. Our sense of the deserts of a number of our fellow-citizens should not depend upon the felicity of one man's speech. Moreover, it is very hard for a speaker to be appropriate when many of his hearers will scarce believe that he is truthful. For those who have known and loved the dead may think his words scant justice to the memories they would hear honoured: while those who do not know will occasionally, from jealousy, suspect me of overstatement when they hear of any feat beyond their own powers. For it is only human for men not to bear praise of others beyond the point at which they still feel that they can rival their exploits. Transgress that boundary and they are jealous and distrustful. But since the wisdom of our ancestors enacted this law I too must submit and try to suit as best I can the wishes and feelings of every member of this gathering.

(36) My first words shall be for our ancestors; for it is both just to them and seemly that on an occasion such as this our tribute of memory should be paid them. For, dwelling always in this country, generation after generation, in unchanging and unbroken succession, they have handed it down to us free by their exertions. So they are worthy of our praises; and still more so are our fathers. For they enlarged the ancestral patrimony by the Empire which we hold to-day and delivered it, not without labour, into

---

[1] From Thucydides *History*, II 35–46, translated by Alfred E. Zimmern in *The Greek Commonwealth*, pp. 196–204.

the hands of our own generation; while it is we ourselves, those of us who are now in middle life, who consolidated our power throughout the greater part of the Empire and secured the city's complete independence both in war and peace. Of the battles which we and our fathers fought, whether in the winning of our power abroad or in bravely withstanding the warfare of barbarian or Greek at home, I do not wish to say more: they are too familiar to you all. I wish rather to set forth the spirit in which we faced them, and the constitution and manners with which we rose to greatness, and to pass from them to the dead; for I think it not unfitting that these things should be called to mind at to-day's solemnity, and expedient too that the whole gathering of citizens and strangers should listen to them.

(37) For our government is not copied from those of our neighbours: we are an example to them rather than they to us. Our constitution is named a democracy, because it is in the hands not of the few but of the many. But our laws secure equal justice for all in their private disputes, and our public opinion welcomes and honours talent in every branch of achievement, not for any sectional reason but on grounds of excellence alone. And as we give free play to all in our public life, so we carry the same spirit into our daily relations with one another. We have no black looks or angry words for our neighbour if he enjoys himself in his own way, and we abstain from the little acts of churlishness which, though they leave no mark, yet cause annoyance to whoso notes them. Open and friendly in our private intercourse, in our public acts we keep strictly within the control of law. We acknowledge the restraint of reverence; we are obedient to whomsoever is set in authority, and to the laws, more especially to those which offer protection to the oppressed and those unwritten ordinances whose transgression brings admitted shame. (38) Yet ours is no work-a-day city only. No other provides so many recreations for the spirit— contests and sacrifices all the year round, and beauty in our public buildings to cheer the heart and delight the eye day by day. Moreover, the city is so large and powerful that all the wealth of all the world flows in to her, so that our own Attic products seem no more homelike to us than the fruits of the labours of other nations.

(39) Our military training too is different from our opponents'. The gates of our city are flung open to the world. We practise no periodical deportations, nor do we prevent our visitors from observing or discovering what an enemy might usefully apply to his own purposes. For our trust is not in the devices of material equipment, but in our own good spirits for battle.

So too with education. They toil from early boyhood in a laborious pursuit after courage, while we, free to live and wander as we please, march out none the less to face the self-same dangers. Here is the proof of my words.

When the Spartans advance into our country, they do not come alone but with all their allies; but when we invade our neighbours we have little difficulty as a rule, even on foreign soil, in defeating men who are fighting for their own homes. Moreover, no enemy has ever met us in full strength, for we have our navy to attend to, and our soldiers are sent on service to many scattered possessions; but if they chance to encounter some portion of our forces and defeat a few of us, they boast that they have driven back our whole army, or, if they are defeated, that the victors were in full strength. Indeed, if we choose to face danger with an easy mind rather than after a rigorous training, and to trust rather in native manliness than in state-made courage, the advantage lies with us; for we are spared all the weariness of practising for future hardships, and when we find ourselves amongst them we are as brave as our plodding rivals. Here as elsewhere, then, the city sets an example which is deserving of admiration. (40) We are lovers of beauty without extravagance, and lovers of wisdom without unmanliness. Wealth to us is not mere material for vainglory but an opportunity for achievement; and poverty we think it no disgrace to acknowledge but a real degradation to make no effort to overcome. Our citizens attend both to public and private duties, and do not allow absorption in their own various affairs to interfere with their knowledge of the city's. We differ from other states in regarding the man who holds aloof from public life not as 'quiet' but as useless; we decide or debate, carefully and in person, all matters of policy, holding, not that words and deeds go ill together, but that acts are foredoomed to failure when undertaken undiscussed. For we are noted for being at once most adventurous in action and most reflective beforehand. Other men are bold in ignorance, while reflection will stop their onset. But the bravest are surely those who have the clearest vision of what is before them, glory and danger alike, and yet notwithstanding go out to meet it. In doing good, too, we are the exact opposite of the rest of mankind. We secure our friends not by accepting favours but by doing them. And so we are naturally more firm in our attachments: for we are anxious, as creditors, to cement by kind offices our relation towards our friends. If they do not respond with the same warmness it is because they feel that their services will not be given spontaneously but only as the repayment of a debt. We are alone among mankind in doing men benefits, not on calculation of self-interest, but in the fearless confidence of freedom. (41) In a word I claim that our city as a whole is an education to Greece, and that her members yield to none, man by man, for independence of spirit, many-sidedness of attainment, and complete self-reliance in limbs and brain.

That this is no vainglorious phrase but actual fact that supremacy which our manners have won us itself bears testimony. No other city of the present day goes out to her ordeal greater than ever men dreamed; no other is so powerful that the invader feels no bitterness when he suffers at her hands, and her subjects no shame at the indignity of their dependence. Great indeed are the symbols and witnesses of our supremacy, at which posterity, as all mankind to-day, will be astonished. We need no Homer or other man of words to praise us; for such give pleasure for a moment, but the truth will put to shame their imaginings of our deeds. For our pioneers have forced a way into every sea and every land, establishing among all mankind, in punishment or beneficence, eternal memorials of their settlement.

Such then is the city for whom, lest they should lose her, the men whom we celebrate died a soldier's death: and it is but natural that all of us, who survive them, should wish to spend ourselves in her service. (42) That, indeed, is why I have spent many words upon the city. I wished to show that we have more at stake than men who have no such inheritance, and to support my praise of the dead by making clear to you what they have done. For if I have chanted the glories of the city it was these men and their like who set hand to array her. With them, as with few among Greeks, words cannot magnify the deeds that they have done. Such an end as we have here seems indeed to show us what a good life is, from its first signs of power to its final consummation. For even where life's previous record showed faults and failures it is just to weigh the last brave hour of devotion against them all. There they wiped out evil with good and did the city more service as soldiers than they did her harm in private life. There no hearts grew faint because they loved riches more than honour; none shirked the issue in the poor man's dreams of wealth. All these they put aside to strike a blow for the city. Counting the quest to avenge her honour as the most glorious of all ventures, and leaving Hope, the uncertain goddess, to send them what she would, they faced the foe as they drew near him in the strength of their own manhood; and when the shock of battle came, they chose rather to suffer the uttermost than to win life by weakness. So their memory has escaped the reproaches of men's lips, but they bore instead on their bodies the marks of men's hands, and in a moment of time, at the climax of their lives, were rapt away from a world filled, for their dying eyes, not with terror but with glory.

(43) Such were the men who lie here and such the city that inspired them. We survivors may pray to be spared their bitter hour, but must disdain to meet the foe with a spirit less triumphant. Let us draw strength, not merely from twice-told arguments—how fair and noble a thing it is to show courage in battle—but from the busy spectacle of our great city's life as we have it before us day by day, falling in love with her as we see her, and remembering that all this greatness she owes to men with the fighter's daring, the wise man's understanding of his duty, and the good man's self-

discipline in its performance—to men who, if they failed in any ordeal, disdained to deprive the city of their services, but sacrificed their lives as the best offering on her behalf. So they gave their bodies to the commonwealth and received, each for his own memory, praise that will never die, and with it the grandest of all sepulchres, not that in which their mortal bones are laid, but a home in the minds of men, where their glory remains fresh to stir to speech or action as the occasion comes by. For the whole earth is the sepulchre of famous men; and their story is not graven only on stone over their native earth, but lives on far away, without visible symbol, woven into the stuff of other men's lives. For you now it remains to rival what they have done and, knowing the secret of happiness to be freedom and the secret of freedom a brave heart, not idly to stand aside from the enemy's onset. For it is not the poor and luckless, as having no hope of prosperity, who have most cause to reckon death as little loss, but those for whom fortune may yet keep reversal in store and who would feel the change most if trouble befell them. Moreover, weakly to decline the trial is more painful to a man of spirit than death coming sudden and unperceived in the hour of strength and enthusiasm.

(44) Therefore I do not mourn with the parents of the dead who are here with us. I will rather comfort them. For they know that they have been born into a world of manifold chances and that he is to be accounted happy to whom the best lot falls—the best sorrow, such as is yours to-day, or the best death, such as fell to these, for whom life and happiness were cut to the self-same measure. I know it is not easy to give you comfort. I know how often in the joy of others you will have reminders of what was once your own, and how men feel sorrow, not for the loss of what they have never tested, but when something that has grown dear to them has been snatched away. But you must keep a brave heart in the hope of other children, those who are still of age to bear them. For the newcomers will help you to forget the gap in your own circle, and will help the city to fill up the ranks of its workers and its soldiers. For no man is fitted to give fair and honest advice in council if he has not, like his fellows, a family at stake in the hour of the city's danger. To you who are past the age of vigour I would say: count the long years of happiness so much gain to set off against the brief space that yet remains, and let your burden be lightened by the glory of the dead. For the love of honour alone is not staled by age, and it is by honour, not, as some say, by gold, that the helpless end of life is cheered.

(45) I turn to those amongst you who are children or brothers of the fallen, for whom I foresee a mighty contest with the memory of the dead. Their praise is in all men's mouths, and hardly, even for supremest heroism, will you be adjudged to have achieved, not the same but a little

less than they. For the living have the jealousy of rivals to contend with, but the dead are honoured with unchallenged admiration.

If I must also speak a word to those who are now in widowhood on the powers and duties of women, I will cast all my advice into one brief sentence. Great will be your glory if you do not lower the nature that is within you—hers greatest of all whose praise or blame is least bruited on the lips of men.

(46) I have spoken such words as I had to say according as the law prescribes, and the graveside offerings to the dead have been duly made. Henceforward the city will take charge of their children till manhood: such is the crown and benefit she holds out to the dead and to their kin for the trials they have undergone for her. For where the prize is highest, there, too, are the best citizens to contend for it.

And now, when you have finished your lamentation, let each of you depart.

THE AGREEMENT OF THE PEOPLE

[Putney (now in London), 1648]

An Agreement of the People for a firm and present peace upon grounds of common right.

Having by our late labours and hazards made it appear to the world at how high a rate we value our just freedom, and God having so far owned our cause as to deliver the enemies thereof into our hands, we do now hold ourselves bound in mutual duty to each other to take the best care we can for the future to avoid both the danger of returning into a slavish condition and the chargeable remedy of another war; for, as it cannot be imagined that so many of our countrymen would have opposed us in this quarrel if they had understood their own good, so may we safely promise to ourselves that, when our common rights and liberties shall be cleared, their endeavours will be disappointed that seek to make themselves our masters. Since, therefore, our former oppressions and scarce-yet-ended troubles have been occasioned, either by want of frequent national meetings in Council, or by rendering those meetings ineffectual, we are fully agreed and resolved to provide that hereafter our representatives be neither left to an uncertainty for the time nor made useless to the ends for which they are intended. In order whereunto we declare:—

I

That the people of England, being at this day very unequally distributed by Counties, Cities, and Boroughs for the election of their deputies in

Parliament, ought to be more indifferently proportioned according to the number of Inhabitants; The circumstances whereof for number, place, and manner are to be set down before the end of this present Parliament.

II

That, to prevent the many inconveniences apparently arising from the long continuance of the same persons in authority, this present Parliament be dissolved upon the last day of September which shall be in the year of our Lord 1648.

III

That the people do, of course, choose themselves a Parliament once in two years, viz. upon the first Thursday in every 2d March, after the manner as shall be prescribed before the end of this Parliament, to begin to sit upon the first Thursday in April following, at Westminster or such other place as shall be appointed from time to time by the preceding Representatives, and to continue till the last day of September then next ensuing, and no longer.

IV

That the power of this, and all future Representatives of this Nation, is inferior only to theirs who choose them, and doth extend, without the consent or concurrence of any other person or persons, to the erecting and abolishing of offices and courts, to the appointing, removing, and calling to account magistrates and officers of all degrees, to the making war and peace, to the treating with foreign States, and, generally, to whatsoever is not expressly or impliedly reserved by the represented to themselves:

Which are as followeth,

1. That matters of religion and the ways of God's worship are not at all entrusted by us to any human power, because therein we cannot remit or exceed a title of what our consciences dictate to be the mind of God without wilful sin: nevertheless the public way of instructing the nation (so it be not compulsive) is referred to their discretion.

2. That the matter of impresting and constraining any of us to serve in the wars is against our freedom; and therefore we do not allow it in our Representatives; the rather, because money (the sinews of war), being always at that disposal, they can never want numbers of men apt enough to engage in any just cause.

3. That after the dissolution of this present Parliament, no person be at any time questioned for anything said or done in reference to the late public differences, otherwise than in execution of the judgments of the present Representatives or House of Commons.

4. That in all laws made or to be made every person may be bound alike, and that no tenure, estate, charter, degree, birth, or place do confer any exemption from the ordinary course of legal proceedings whereunto others are subjected.

5. That as the laws ought to be equal, so they must be good, and not evidently destructive to the safety and well-being of the people.

These things we declare to be our native rights, and therefore are agreed and resolved to maintain them with our utmost possibilities against all opposition whatsoever; being compelled thereunto not only by the examples of our ancestors, whose blood was often spent in vain for the recovery of their freedoms, suffering themselves through fraudulent accommodations to be still deluded of the fruit of their victories, but also by our own woeful experience, who, having long expected and dearly earned the establishment of these certain rules of government, are yet made to depend for the settlement of our peace and freedom upon him that intended our bondage and brought a cruel war upon us.

THE DECLARATION OF INDEPENDENCE

(Philadelphia, 1776)

The unanimous Declaration of the thirteen united States of America

When in the Course of human events, it becomes necessary for one people to dissolve the political bands, which have connected them with another, and to assume among the powers of the earth, the separate and equal station to which the Laws of Nature and of Nature's God entitle them, a decent respect to the opinions of mankind requires that they should declare the causes which impel them to the separation.—We hold these truths to be self-evident, that all men are created equal, that they are endowed by their Creator with certain unalienable Rights, that among these are Life, Liberty and the pursuit of Happiness.—That to secure these rights, Governments are instituted among Men, deriving their just powers from the consent of the governed.—That whenever any Form of Government becomes destructive of these ends, it is the Right of the People to alter or to abolish it, and to institute new Government, laying its foundation on such principles and organizing its powers in such form, as to them shall seem most likely to effect their Safety and Happiness. Prudence, indeed, will dictate that

Governments long established should not be changed for light and transient causes; and accordingly all experience hath shewn, that mankind are more disposed to suffer, while evils are sufferable, than to right themselves by abolishing the forms to which they are accustomed. But when a long train of abuses and usurpations, pursuing invariably the same Object evinces a design to reduce them under absolute Despotism, it is their right, it is their duty, to throw off such Government, and to provide new Guards for their future security.—Such has been the patient sufferance of these Colonies; and such is now the necessity which constrains them to alter their former Systems of Government. The history of the present King of Great Britain is a history of repeated injuries and usurpations, all having in direct object the establishment of an absolute Tyranny over these States. To prove this, let Facts be submitted to a candid world.—He has refused his Assent to Laws, the most wholesome and necessary for the public good.—He has forbidden his Governors to pass Laws of immediate and pressing importance; unless suspended in their operation till his Assent should be obtained; and when so suspended, he has utterly neglected to attend to them.—He has refused to pass other Laws for the accommodation of large districts of people, unless those people would relinquish the right of Representation in the Legislature, a right inestimable to them and formidable to tyrants only.— He has called together legislative bodies at places unusual, uncomfortable, and distant from the depository of their public Records, for the sole purpose of fatiguing them into compliance with his measures.—He has dissolved Representative Houses repeatedly, for opposing with manly firmness his invasions on the rights of the people.—He has refused for a long time, after such dissolutions, to cause others to be elected; whereby the Legislative powers, incapable of Annihilation, have returned to the People at large for their exercise; the State remaining in the meantime exposed to all the dangers of invasion from without, and convulsions within.—He has endeavoured to prevent the population of these States; for that purpose obstructing the Laws for Naturalization of Foreigners; refusing to pass others to encourage their migrations hither, and raising the conditions of new Appropriations of Lands.—He has obstructed the Administration of Justice, by refusing his Assent to Laws for establishing Judiciary powers.—He has made Judges dependent on his Will alone, for the tenure of their offices, and the amount and payment of their salaries.—He has erected a multitude of New Offices, and sent hither swarms of Officers to harass our people, and eat out their substance.—He has kept among us, in times of peace, Standing Armies without the Consent of our legislatures.—He has affected to render the Military independent of and superior to the Civil power.—He has combined with others to subject us to a jurisdiction foreign to our constitution, and unacknowledged by our laws; giving his Assent to their Acts of pretended Legislation.—For quartering large bodies of armed troops among us:—For protecting them, by a mock Trial, from punishment for any Murders which they should commit on the Inhabitants of these States:—For cutting off our Trade with all parts of the world:—For imposing Taxes on us without our Consent:—For depriving us in many cases, of the benefits of Trial by Jury:—For transporting us beyond Seas to be tried for pretended offenses:—For abolishing the free System of English Laws in a neighboring Province, establishing therein an Arbitrary government, and enlarging its Boundaries so as to render it at once an example and fit instrument for introducing the same absolute rule into these Colonies:—For taking away our Charters, abolishing our most valuable Laws, and altering fundamentally the Forms of our Governments:—For suspending our own Legislatures, and declaring themselves invested with power to legislate for us in all cases whatsoever.—He has abdicated Government here, by declaring us out of his Protection and waging War against us.—He has plundered our seas, ravaged our Coasts, burnt our towns, and destroyed the lives of our people.—He is at this time transporting large Armies of foreign Mercenaries to compleat the works of death, desolation and tyranny, already begun with circumstances of Cruelty & perfidy scarcely paralleled in the most barbarous ages, and totally unworthy the Head of a civilized nation.—He has constrained our fellow Citizens taken Captive on the high Seas to bear Arms against their Country, to become the executioners of their friends and Brethren, or to fall themselves by their Hands.—He has excited domestic insurrections amongst us, and has endeavoured to bring on the inhabitants of our frontiers, the merciless Indian Savages, whose known rule of warfare, is an undistinguished destruction of all ages, sexes and conditions. In every stage of these Oppressions We have Petitioned for Redress in the most humble terms: Our repeated Petitions have been answered only by repeated injury. A Prince whose character is thus marked by every act which may define a Tyrant, is unfit to be the ruler of a free people. Nor have We been wanting in attentions to our British brethren. We have warned them from time to time of attempts by their legislature to extend an unwarrantable jurisdiction over us. We have reminded them of the circumstances of our emigration and settlement here. We have appealed to their native justice and magnanimity, and we have conjured them by the ties of our common kindred to disavow these usurpations, which would inevitably interrupt our connections and correspondence. They too have been deaf to the voice of justice and of consanguinity. We must, therefore, acquiesce in the necessity, which denounces our Separation, and hold them, as we hold the rest of mankind, Enemies in War, in Peace Friends.—

We, therefore, the Representatives of the united States of America, in General Congress, Assembled, appealing to the Supreme Judge of the world for the rectitude of our intentions do, in the Name, and by Authority of the good People of these Colonies, solemnly publish and declare, That these United Colonies are, and of Right ought to be Free and Independent States; that they are Absolved from all Allegiance to the British Crown, and that all political connection between them and the State of Great Britain, is and ought to be totally dissolved; and that as Free and Independent States, they have full Power to levy War, conclude Peace, contract Alliances, establish Commerce, and to do all other Acts and Things which Independent States may of right do.—And for the support of this Declaration, with a firm reliance on the protection of divine Providence, we mutually pledge to each other our Lives, our Fortunes and our sacred Honor.

DECLARATION OF
THE RIGHTS OF MAN AND CITIZEN

(Versailles, 1789)

The representatives of the French people, organized in National Assembly, considering that ignorance, forgetfulness or contempt of the rights of man are the sole causes of the public miseries and of the corruption of governments, have resolved to set forth in a solemn declaration the natural, inalienable, and sacred rights of man, in order that this declaration, being ever present to all the members of the social body, may unceasingly remind them of their rights and their duties: in order that the acts of the legislative power and those of the executive power may be each moment compared with the aim of every political institution and thereby may be more respected; and in order that the demands of the citizens, grounded henceforth upon simple and incontestable principles, may always take the direction of maintaining the constitution and the welfare of all.

In consequence, the National Assembly recognizes and declares, in the presence and under the auspices of the Supreme Being, the following rights of man and citizen.

1. Men are born and remain free and equal in rights. Social distinctions can be based only upon public utility.

2. The aim of every political association is the preservation of the natural and imprescriptible rights of man. These rights are liberty, property, security, and resistance to oppression.

3. The source of all sovereignty is essentially in the nation; no body, no individual can exercise authority that does not proceed from it in plain terms.

4. Liberty consists in the power to do anything that does not injure others; accordingly, the exercise of the natural rights of each man has for its only limits those that secure to the other members of society the enjoyment of these same rights. These limits can be determined only by law.

5. The law has the right to forbid only such actions are are injurious to

society. Nothing can be forbidden that is not interdicted by the law and no one can be constrained to do that which it does not order.

6. Law is the expression of the general will. All citizens have the right to take part personally or by their representatives in its formation. It must be the same for all, whether it protects or punishes. All citizens being equal in its eyes, are equally eligible to all public dignities, places, and employments, according to their capacities, and without other distinction than that of their virtues and their talents.

7. No man can be accused, arrested, or detained except in the cases determined by the law and according to the forms that it has prescribed. Those who procure, expedite, execute, or cause to be executed arbitrary orders ought to be punished; but every citizen summoned or seized in virtue of the law ought to render instant obedience; he makes himself guilty by resistance.

8. The law ought to establish only penalties that are strictly and obviously necessary and no one can be punished except in virtue of a law established and promulgated prior to the offence and legally applied.

9. Every man being presumed innocent until he has been pronounced guilty, if it is thought indispensable to arrest him, all severity that may not be necessary to secure his person ought to be strictly suppressed by law.

10. No one ought to be disturbed on account of his opinions, even religious, provided their manifestation does not derange the public order established by law.

11. The free communication of ideas and opinions is one of the most precious of the rights of man; every citizen then can freely speak, write, and print, subject to responsibility for the abuse of this freedom in the cases determined by law.

12. The guarantee of the rights of man and citizen requires a public force; this force then is instituted for the advantage of all and not for the personal benefit of those to whom it is entrusted.

13. For the maintenance of the public force and for the expenses of administration a general tax is indispensable; it ought to be equally apportioned among all the citizens according to their means.

14. All the citizens have the right to ascertain, by themselves or by their representatives, the necessity of the public tax, to consent to it freely, to follow the employment of it, and to determine the quota, the assessment, the collection, and the duration of it.

15. Society has the right to call for an account from every public agent of its administration.

16. Any society in which the guarantee of the rights is not secured or the separation of powers not determined has no constitution at all.

17. Property being a sacred and inviolable right, no one can be de-

prived of it unless a legally established public necessity evidently demands it, under the condition of a just and prior indemnity.

THE GETTYSBURG ADDRESS

(Gettysburg, Pennsylvania, 1863)

Fourscore and seven years ago, our fathers brought forth upon this continent a new nation, conceived in liberty and dedicated to the proposition that all men are created equal.

Now we are engaged in a great civil war, testing whether that nation—or any nation, so conceived and so dedicated—can long endure.

We are met on a great battlefield of that war. We have come to dedicate a portion of it as the final resting place of those who have given their lives that that nation might live.

It is altogether fitting and proper that we should do this.

But, in a larger sense, we cannot dedicate, we cannot consecrate, we cannot hallow, this ground. The brave men, living and dead, who struggled here, have consecrated it, far above our poor power to add or to detract.

The world will very little note nor long remember what we say here; but it can never forget what they did here.

It is for us, the living, rather, to be dedicated, here, to the unfinished work that they have thus far so nobly carried on. It is rather for us to be here dedicated to the great task remaining before us; that from these honored dead we take increased devotion to that cause for which they here gave the last full measure of devotion; that we here highly resolve that these dead shall not have died in vain; that the nation shall, under God, have a new birth of freedom and that government of the people, by the people, for the people, shall not perish from the earth.

Appendix to
Chapter 5

HOW A BILL BECOMES LAW:
CONCISE SUMMARY OF
LEGISLATIVE PROCEDURE

1. Legislative action is the approval of bills and resolutions. About 14,000 propositions are offered in each Congress in the form of:

(a) public bills, for general legislation affecting classes of people;

(b) private bills, for legislation affecting named persons or organizations;

(c) joint resolutions, for unusual legislative problems such as correcting errors, abrogating treaties, and proposing Constitutional amendments. Behind many bills lies a long history of agitation and planning by pressure groups and government agencies. Most of the important bills are suggested by the President in special messages or in his annual State of the Union or budget messages, but only Congressmen may actually introduce bills. The abundance of bills reflects not only the complexity of our social problems but also the fact that government agencies, pressure groups, and Congressmen themselves consider bills an excellent propaganda device. Few Congressmen refuse to introduce any bill because, even if they disapprove of it, they can label it "by request," thus absolving themselves of personal responsibility.

2. Committees decide which bills each house MAY consider. There are twenty standing (i.e., permanent) committees in the House and fifteen in the Senate, each with jurisdiction over specific areas of legislation such as foreign affairs or appropriations. The presiding officer refers all bills to them (or sometimes to select—i.e., temporary—committees) by a usually automatic, precedent-following process, although in the Senate occasionally and in the House rarely he may be overruled on appeal to the floor. Committees "pigeonhole" most bills; but important bills they may study carefully, usually by holding hearings at which interested parties are invited to testify. In executive (i.e., secret) session, committees decide whether or not to propose amendments, to report bills to the house, and to recommend favorable action.

If a committee holds up a bill which other members want to vote on, it can be discharged from consideration of the bill by a majority vote in the Senate (a rarely used power because Senate committees seldom obstruct) and in the House by a motion to discharge which is in order only after 218 out of 435 Representatives have signed a petition for it. Certain other devices, such as unanimous consent, suspension of the rules, special orders, etc.—described in item 3 following—are also available to discharge House committees; but they are even more difficult to use than a discharge petition. So great is the committee power over bills that all these devices together are seldom successful more than ten times in a Congress in either house.

3. Party and committee leaders and rules determine which bills each house WILL consider. In both houses bills go on calendars in the order reported; but, since calendars are inordinately crowded, devices are necessary to select among the bills for floor consideration. In the Senate, bills either are considered immediately when reported or are taken up out of their calendar order by special orders of business, in both cases usually on the agreement of party and committee leaders. Only Mondays are devoted to the consideration of bills in calendar order. The crowding of the House calendar is partly compensated for by dividing it up into several parts, some of which have specific days set aside for them: (a) a "Union Calendar" for money bills, (b) a "House Calendar" for non-money, public bills, (c) a "Private Calendar," and (d) a "Consent Calendar" for probably non-controversial bills transferred from the House and Union calendars. Four days per month are set aside for calling up and, if no member objects, considering immediately bills at the head of the latter two calendars. Both party caucuses keep careful watch on the consent calendars by means of an "Objectors Committee"; but even so about 75 percent of the bills which pass the House are called up in this way and promptly passed. Important controversial bills are brought to the floor by one of the following motions which are listed in order of the frequency of their use:

(a) Special orders (or "rules"): These are proposed only by the Rules Committee and, being highly privileged business by House rules, are voted upon whenever the Committee reports them. They usually provide for a specific time for consideration of the bill and set limits on debate, points of order, and the number and kind of amendments. Most important bills, other than revenue and appropriations bills, reach the floor in this way.

(b) Privileged matters: Certain committees are permitted by the rules to move at almost any time that the House goes into Committee of the Whole to consider its bills. Most general appropriations and revenue bills are brought up this way, although sometimes they too are granted a special order in order to limit debate, amendments, etc.

(c) Calendar Wednesday: The rules provide that on Wednesday the role of committees be called so that chairmen may move immediate consideration of one of their bills from the House or Union calendars. The call is so often dispensed with, however, that some committees are not called for an entire Congress.

(d) Suspension of rules: A motion to suspend the rules to consider a bill immediately is in order two days per month and requires a two-thirds vote of the members voting—a motion too difficult to be used often.

(e) Atrophied methods: The call of committees during the "morning hour" at which committee chairmen may move consideration of bills from the House calendar is now in practice superseded by Calendar Wednesday; motions to consider by unanimous consent are now superseded by the consent calendars, except in emergency situations; the calendar order itself is now usually superseded by all the methods here described.

4. Procedure on the floor is an amalgam of devices invented by past majorities to force action and devices invented by past minorities to obstruct action. In the Senate rules dilatory devices predominate, in the House, expediting ones. So complex has floor procedure become in a century and a half of rules development—Hinds' and Cannon's *Precedents of the House of Representatives* is eight fat volumes—that every bill is piloted through each house by a "manager" (who is often the chairman of the committee which has reported the bill). In the House the manager is entitled to prior recognition for all motions to expedite the bill; he controls half the time allotted for debate and handles the bill on the floor. In the Senate his position is less formalized, but none the less essential for action. In both houses the managers are almost always members of the conference committees.

House procedure, action elements: Since legislative action is the final passage of bills and resolutions, all devices which bring them quickly to a final vote are expediting in effect.

(a) One of the oldest devices for speed is the Committee of the Whole in which the House opinion on bills and amendments can be quickly determined. The Committee, which is simply the members meeting in the chamber with a Chairman instead of a Speaker presiding, debates and reads for amendment all bills authorizing expenditures, appropriating money, raising revenue, etc. In Committee, a quorum is only 100 as against 218 in the House; votes are taken by tellers rather than by roll calls; many motions sometimes dilatory (e.g. to adjourn, to lay on the table, to refer, etc.) are not in order; and debate on amendments is limited to one five-minute speech for and one against.

(b) The best way to obstruct is to prevent a vote on final passage and the best way to prevent a vote is to debate interminably. Limitations on debate are, therefore, the basic assurance against successful obstruction.

Rule XIV prohibits members speaking for more than an hour on any one question; and in fact members rarely speak that long. Most special orders limit debate to two or four or eight hours, granting time to the manager of the bill and the leader of the opposition to it, who in turn yield it to their supporters in five- or ten-minute driblets. The motion for the previous question (i.e. that the question under discussion be voted on) is very frequently used because it can be adopted by a simple majority of those voting. It has the effect of cutting off all further debate except for forty minutes when there has been no debate on the main question.

(c) The Speaker's control of debate, that is, his power to rule dilatory motions out of order and his power to ask "For what purpose does the member rise?" before recognizing a member, is, in the hands of a strong Speaker, an effective means of overcoming obstruction.

(d) Other important methods for forcing action have already been described: the consent calendars, the rule on privileged bills, special orders, discharge petitions, the informal system of bill "managers," etc.

House procedure, dilatory elements: Although House rules encourage action, they also encourage obstruction enough that minorities can often exact important concessions or even sometimes force a dispirited majority to pass on to other business.

(a) The most important obstruction occurs in committees. Their power to refuse to report bills and the Rules Committee's power to refuse to report special orders are necessary devices to winnow the politically feasible from the infeasible; but when committees are not truly representative of the opinion of the whole House, these powers turn into obstructionist devices. The House has unsuccessfully tried to meet Committee obstruction with the discharge petition and the rule of the 81st Congress (not readopted in the 82nd Congress) to permit committee chairmen as well as the Rules Committee to call up special orders.

(b) The fact that obstruction on the floor is less important today than formerly is simply evidence that committee obstruction has superseded it on most bills. But floor obstruction is still possible by means of roll calls and quorum calls. These are based on the constitutional provisions that one-fifth of the members present may demand a roll call and that a majority of each house shall constitute a quorum to do business. Both provisions are conducive to democratic government and the electoral responsibility of Congressmen; but both can also be distorted for obstruction. The worst abuses of quorum counts were eliminated in the 1890's when it was established that the Speaker may refuse to count a quorum when the point of no quorum is obviously dilatory and that he can count as present all those within sight even when they do not answer. Still the pressure of committee business, errands for constituents, etc. is so great that poor attendance makes perpetual opportunity for alert obstructionists and perpetual headaches for majority floor leaders. House voting is not, of course, intrinsically dilatory. Voice voting, the most frequently used method, takes but a few minutes. Standing votes (i.e. a "division") and teller votes (i.e. by walking between tellers who count the number on each side) are almost as expeditious. But the "yeas and nays" (a roll call) take about an hour. Were bills voted on only three times, as in the Elizabethan House of Commons, roll calls could not be obstructive. But in the last 300 years minorities have multiplied occasions to vote with stubborn fertility. Now every bill is voted on at least five times; and with important amendments a really controversial bill may be voted upon as many as fifteen times.

Senate procedure: Senate rules are notorious all over the world for encouraging the filibuster, an instrument so effective that other dilatory devices are seldom used in the Senate. Committee obstruction is rare; and procedural obstruction usually occurs only as an adjunct to the filibuster, even though bills go through about the same voting stages in the Senate as the House (except for votes on the previous question, a motion not recognized in Senate rules). Talking for days to prevent a vote or to force a compromise is possible only because the provisions for cloture are difficult to apply. Up to 1917 there were no limitations at all on debate; from 1917 to 1949 debate could be closed by two-thirds of those voting, although it was actually so closed only four times; in 1949 a new rule provided for closing debate only by two-thirds of the whole Senate, thus making cloture almost impossible. In 1961, the cloture rule of 1917–49 was readopted. The measure of the Senate's procrastination is the fact that the House, for all its larger size and unwieldy procedure, ordinarily passes about 25 percent more bills per session than the Senate. The Senate is able to act at all only by a tacit agreement to expedite bills by all ways except limitations on debate. In fact, most bills passed by the Senate go through the unanimous consent procedure, which holds debate to a minimum.

5. Conference committees decide the final provisions of bills. After a bill passes one house, it goes through substantially the same procedure in the other, where most controversial bills at least are amended. Customarily today, the originating house perfunctorily disagrees with the amendments and asks the amending house for a conference. The two presiding officers appoint a conference committee, usually three from each house and usually including the two managers of the bill (most often the chairmen of the committees which reported the bill) and the two leaders of the opposition to the points in disagreement (usually the ranking minority members of the same committees). The conference committee can only compromise differences; it cannot change parts of the bill on which both houses agree. Even so, very often it can radically alter the tenor of a bill. When standing committees in the two houses have been working on the same legislative problem, it is quite common for the Senate, for example, to strike out all after the enacting clause of a House bill and to substitute for it the contents of a similar Senate bill. In such case, the conference committee may actually write a new bill. While occasionally one house may refuse to pass a bill reported back by a conference committee and may insist on another conference, usually the committee compromises are the final shape of legislation.

6. **The President acts as a third house of the legislature.** While he has, of course, formally suggested most important bills and often informally participated in the management of them, he does not enter the actual legislative process until both houses have passed a bill in exactly the same form. In current practice, when he receives the enrolled bill (i.e., printed on parchment and signed by the Speaker and the Vice-President), the Budget Bureau collects for him opinions on whether or not he ought to sign it from all executive departments concerned. He may then act in one of three ways: (a) He may sign the bill, in which case it becomes law. (b) He may return it to the house in which it originated with his objections (the "veto" message), in which case it can become law only when repassed in both houses by two-thirds of the members voting. (c) He may neither sign nor object, in which case, if Congress is in session on the tenth day, excepting Sundays, after he received the bill, it becomes law, but, if Congress has adjourned, the bill fails by "pocket veto." In a few cases, the President has appended his interpretation of a bill to the copy which he signs; but it is uncertain whether his interpretation is binding law or not.

Constitution
of the United States

We the people of the United States, in order to form a more perfect union, establish justice, insure domestic tranquillity, provide for the common defense, promote the general welfare, and secure the blessings of liberty to ourselves and our posterity, do ordain and establish this Constitution for the United States of America.

ARTICLE I
Section 1
All legislative powers herein granted shall be vested in a Congress of the United States, which shall consist of a Senate and House of Representatives.

Section 2
1. The House of Representatives shall be composed of members chosen every second year by the people of the several States, and the electors in each State shall have the qualifications requisite for electors of the most numerous branch of the State legislature.

2. No person shall be a representative who shall not have attained to the age of twenty-five years, and been seven years a citizen of the United States, and who shall not, when elected, be an inhabitant of that State in which he shall be chosen.

3. Representatives and direct taxes [1] shall be apportioned among the several States which may be included within this Union, according to their respective numbers, which shall be determined by adding to the whole number of free persons, including those bound to service for a term of years, and excluding Indians not taxed, three-fifths of all other persons.[2] The actual enumeration shall be made within three years after the first meeting of the Congress of the United States, and within every subsequent

[1] See the Sixteenth Amendment, p. 378.
[2] Party superseded by the Fourteenth Amendment. (See p. 377.)

term of ten years, in such manner as they shall by law direct. The number of representatives shall not exceed one for every thirty thousand, but each State shall have at least one representative; and until such enumeration shall be made, the State of New Hampshire shall be entitled to choose three, Massachusetts eight, Rhode Island and Providence Plantations one, Connecticut five, New York six, New Jersey four, Pennsylvania eight, Delaware one, Maryland six, Virginia ten, North Carolina five, South Carolina five, and Georgia three.

4. When vacancies happen in the representation from any State, the executive authority thereof shall issue writs of election to fill such vacancies.

5. The House of Representatives shall choose their speaker and other officers; and shall have the sole power of impeachment.

Section 3

1. The Senate of the United States shall be composed of two senators from each State, chosen by the legislature thereof,[3] for six years; and each senator shall have one vote.

2. Immediately after they shall be assembled in consequence of the first election, they shall be divided as equally as may be into three classes. The seats of the senators of the first class shall be vacated at the expiration of the second year, of the second class at the expiration of the fourth year, and of the third class at the expiration of the sixth year, so that one-third may be chosen every second year; and if vacancies happen by resignation, or otherwise, during the recess of the legislature of any State, the executive thereof may make temporary appointments until the next meeting of the legislature, which shall then fill such vacancies.[4]

3. No person shall be a senator who shall not have attained to the age of thirty years, and been nine years a citizen of the United States, and who shall not, when elected, be an inhabitant of that State for which he shall be chosen.

4. The Vice President of the United States shall be President of the Senate, but shall have no vote, unless they be equally divided.

5. The Senate shall choose their other officers, and also a president *pro tempore,* in the absence of the Vice President, or when he shall exercise the office of President of the United States.

6. The Senate shall have the sole power to try all impeachments. When sitting for that purpose, they shall be on oath or affirmation. When the President of the United States is tried, the chief justice shall preside: and no person shall be convicted without the concurrence of two-thirds of the members present.

[3] See the Seventeenth Amendment, p. 379.
[4] See the Seventeenth Amendment, p. 379.

7. Judgment in cases of impeachment shall not extend further than to removal from office, and disqualifications to hold and enjoy any office of honor, trust or profit under the United States: but the party convicted shall nevertheless be liable and subject to indictment, trial, judgment and punishment, according to law.

Section 4

1. The times, places, and manner of holding elections for senators and representatives, shall be prescribed in each State by the legislature thereof; but the Congress may at any time by law make or alter such regulations, except as to the places of choosing senators.

2. The Congress shall assemble at least once in every year, and such meeting shall be on the first Monday in December, unless they shall by law appoint a different day.

Section 5

1. Each House shall be the judge of the elections, returns and qualifications of its own members and a majority of each shall constitute a quorum to do business; but a smaller number may adjourn from day to day, and may be authorized to compel the attendance of absent members, in such manner, and under such penalties as each House may provide.

2. Each House may determine the rules of its proceedings, punish its members for disorderly behavior, and, with the concurrence of two-thirds, expel a member.

3. Each House shall keep a journal of its proceedings, and from time to time publish the same, excepting such parts as may in their judgment require secrecy; and the yeas and nays of the members of either House on any question shall, at the desire of one-fifth of those present, be entered on the journal.

4. Neither House, during the session of Congress, shall, without the consent of the other, adjourn for more than three days, nor to any other place than that in which the two Houses shall be sitting.

Section 6

1. The senators and representatives shall receive a compensation for their services, to be ascertained by law, and paid out of the Treasury of the United States. They shall in all cases, except treason, felony and breach of the peace, be privileged from arrest during their attendance at the session of their respective Houses, and in going to and returning from the same; and for any speech or debate in either House, they shall not be questioned in any other place.

2. No senator or representative shall, during the time for which he was elected, be appointed to any civil office under the authority of the United

States, which shall have been created, or the emoluments whereof shall have been increased during such time, and no person holding any office under the United States shall be a member of either House during his continuance in office.

Section 7

1. All bills for raising revenue shall originate in the House of Representatives; but the Senate may propose or concur with amendments as on other bills.

2. Every bill which shall have passed the House of Representatives and the Senate, shall, before it become a law, be presented to the President of the United States; if he approve he shall sign it, but if not he shall return it, with his objections to that House in which it shall have originated, who shall enter the objections at large on their journal, and proceed to reconsider it. If after such reconsideration two thirds of that House shall agree to pass the bill, it shall be sent, together with the objections, to the other House, by which it shall likewise be reconsidered, and if approved by two thirds of that House, it shall become a law. But in all such cases the votes of both Houses shall be determined by yeas and nays, and the names of the persons voting for and against the bill shall be entered on the journal of each House respectively. If any bill shall not be returned by the President within ten days (Sundays excepted) after it shall have been presented to him, the same shall be a law, in like manner as if he had signed it, unless the Congress by their adjournment prevent its return, in which case it shall not be a law.

3. Every order, resolution, or vote to which the concurrence of the Senate and House of Representatives may be necessary (except on a question of adjournment) shall be presented to the President of the United States; and before the same shall take effect, shall be approved by him, or being disapproved by him, shall be repassed by two thirds of the Senate and House of Representatives, according to the rules and limitations prescribed in the case of a bill.

Section 8

1. The Congress shall have the power to lay and collect taxes, duties, imposts, and excises, to pay the debts and provide for the common defense and general welfare of the United States; but all duties, imposts, and excises shall be uniform throughout the United States;

2. To borrow money on the credit of the United States;

3. To regulate commerce with foreign nations, and among the several States, and with the Indian tribes;

4. To establish an uniform rule of naturalization, and uniform laws on the subject of bankruptcies throughout the United States;

5. To coin money, regulate the value thereof, and of foreign coin, and fix the standard of weights and measures;

6. To provide for the punishment of counterfeiting the securities and current coin of the United States;

7. To establish post offices and post roads;

8. To promote the progress of science and useful arts, by securing for limited times to authors and inventors the exclusive right to their respective writings and discoveries;

9. To constitute tribunals inferior to the Supreme Court;

10. To define and punish piracies and felonies committed on the high seas, and offenses against the law of nations;

11. To declare war, grant letters of marque and reprisal, and make rules concerning captures on land and water;

12. To raise and support armies, but no appropriation of money to that use shall be for a longer term than two years;

13. To provide and maintain a navy;

14. To make rules for the government and regulation of the land and naval forces;

15. To provide for calling forth the militia to execute the laws of the Union, suppress insurrections and repel invasions;

16. To provide for organizing, arming, and disciplining the militia, and for governing such part of them as may be employed in the service of the United States, reserving to the States respectively the appointment of the officers, and the authority of training the militia according to the discipline prescribed by Congress;

17. To exercise exclusive legislation in all cases whatsoever, over such district (not exceeding ten miles square) as may, by cession of particular States, and the acceptance of Congress, become the seat of the government of the United States, and to exercise like authority over all places purchased by the consent of the legislature of the State in which the same shall be, for the erection of forts, magazines, arsenals, dockyards, and other needful buildings; and

18. To make all laws which shall be necessary and proper for carrying into execution the foregoing powers, and all other powers vested by this Constitution in the government of the United States, or in any department or officer thereof.

Section 9

1. The migration or importation of such persons as any of the States now existing shall think proper to admit, shall not be prohibited by the Congress prior to the year one thousand eight hundred and eight, but a tax or duty may be imposed on such importation, not exceeding ten dollars for each person.

2. The privilege of the writ of *habeas corpus* shall not be suspended, unless when in cases of rebellion or invasion the public safety may require it.

3. No bill of attainder or *ex post facto* law shall be passed.

4. No capitation, or other direct, tax shall be laid, unless in proportion to the census or enumeration hereinbefore directed to be taken.[5]

5. No tax or duty shall be laid on articles exported from any State.

6. No preference shall be given by any regulation of commerce or revenue to the ports of one State over those of another: nor shall vessels bound to, or from, one State be obliged to enter, clear, or pay duties in another.

7. No money shall be drawn from the treasury, but in consequence of appropriations, made by law; and a regular statement and account of the receipts and expenditures of all public money shall be published from time to time.

8. No title of nobility shall be granted by the United States: and no person holding any office or profit or trust under them, shall, without the consent of the Congress, accept of any present, emolument, office, or title, of any kind whatever, from any king, prince, or foreign State.

Section 10

1. No State shall enter into any treaty, alliance, or confederation; grant letters of marque and reprisal; coin money; emit bills of credit; make anything but gold and silver coin a tender in payment of debts; pass any bill of attainder, *ex post facto* law, or law impairing the obligation of contracts, or grant any title of nobility.

2. No State shall, without the consent of the Congress, lay any imposts or duties on imports or exports, except what may be absolutely necessary for executing its inspection laws: and the net produce of all duties and imposts laid by any State on imports or exports, shall be of the use of the treasury of the United States; and all such laws shall be subject to the revision and control of the Congress.

3. No State shall, without the consent of Congress, lay any duty of tonnage, keep troops, or ships of war in time of peace, enter into any agreement or compact with another State, or with a foreign power, or engage in war, unless actually invaded, or in such imminent danger as will not admit of delay.

ARTICLE II
Section 1

1. The executive power shall be vested in a President of the United States of America. He shall hold his office during the term of four years, and, to-

[5] See the Sixteenth Amendment, p. 378.

gether with the Vice President, chosen for the same term, be elected, as follows: [6]

2. Each State shall appoint, in such manner as the legislature thereof may direct, a number of electors, equal to the whole number of senators and representatives to which the State may be entitled in the Congress: but no senator or representative, or person holding an office of trust or profit under the United States, shall be appointed an elector.

The electors shall meet in their respective States, and vote by ballot for two persons, of whom one at least shall not be an inhabitant of the same State with themselves. And they shall make a list of all the persons voted for, and of the number of votes for each; which list they shall sign and certify, and transmit sealed to the seat of the government of the United States, directed to the president of the Senate. The president of the Senate shall, in the presence of the Senate and House of Representatives, open all certificates, and the votes shall then be counted. The person having the greatest number of votes shall be the President, if such number be a majority of the whole number of electors appointed; and if there be more than one who have such majority, and have an equal number of votes, then the House of Representatives shall immediately choose by ballot one of them for President; and if no person have a majority, then from the five highest on the list the said House shall in like manner choose the President. But in choosing the President, the votes shall be taken by States, the representation from each State having one vote; a quorum for this purpose shall consist of a member or members from two thirds of the States, and a majority of all the States shall be necessary to a choice. In every case, after the choice of the President, the person having the greatest number of votes of the electors shall be the Vice President. But if there should remain two or more who have equal votes, the Senate shall choose from them by ballot the Vice President. [7]

3. The Congress may determine the time of choosing the electors, and the day on which they shall give their votes; which day shall be the same throughout the United States.

4. No person except a natural born citizen, or a citizen of the United States, at the time of the adoption of this Constitution, shall be eligible to the office of President; neither shall any person be eligible to that office who shall not have attained to the age of thirty-five years, and been fourteen years a resident within the United States.

5. In case of the removal of the President from office, or of his death, resignation, or inability to discharge the powers and duties of the said office, the same shall devolve on the Vice President, and the Congress may by law

[6] See the Twenty-second Amendment, p. 381.
[7] Superseded by the Twelfth Amendment, p. 376.

provide for the case of removal, death, resignation, or inability, both of the President and Vice Prseident, declaring what officer shall then act as President, and such officer shall act accordingly, until the disability be removed, or a President shall be elected.[8]

6. The President shall, at stated times, receive for his services a compensation, which shall neither be increased nor diminished during the period for which he shall have been elected, and he shall not receive within that period any other emolument from the United States, or any of them.

7. Before he enter on the execution of his office, he shall take the following oath or affirmation:—"I do solemnly swear (or affirm) that I will faithfully execute the office of President of the United States, and will to the best of my ability, preserve, protect and defend the Constitution of the United States."

Section 2

1. The President shall be commander in chief of the army and navy of the United States, and of the militia of the several States, when called into the actual service of the United States; he may require the opinion, in writing, of the principal officer in each of the executive departments, upon any subject relating to the duties of their respective offices, and he shall have power to grant reprieves and pardons for offenses against the United States, except in cases of impeachment.

2. He shall have power, by and with the advice and consent of the Senate, to make treaties, provided two thirds of the senators present concur; and he shall nominate, and by and with the advice and consent of the Senate, shall appoint ambassadors, other public ministers and consuls, judges of the Supreme Court, and all other officers of the United States, whose appointments are not herein otherwise provided for, and which shall be established by law; but the Congress may by law vest the appointment of such inferior officers, as they think proper, in the President alone, in the courts of law, or in the heads of departments.

3. The President shall have power to fill up all vacancies that may happen during the recess of the Senate, by granting commissions which shall expire at the end of their next session.

Section 3

1. He shall from time to time give to the Congress information of the state of the Union, and recommend to their consideration such measures as he shall judge necessary and expedient; he may, on extraordinary occasions, convene both Houses, or either of them, and in case of disagreement between them with respect to the time of adjournment, he may adjourn

[8] See the Twentieth Amendment, p. 379.

them to such time as he shall think proper; he shall receive ambassadors and other public ministers; he shall take care that the laws be faithfully executed, and shall commission all the officers of the United States.

Section 4

The President, Vice President, and all civil officers of the United States, shall be removed from office on impeachment for, and conviction of, treason, bribery, or other high crimes and misdemeanors.

ARTICLE III
Section 1

The Judicial power of the United States shall be vested in one Supreme Court, and in such inferior courts as the Congress may from time to time ordain and establish. The judges, both of the Supreme and inferior courts, shall hold their offices during good behavior, and shall, at stated times, receive for their services, a compensation, which shall not be diminished during their continuance in office.

Section 2

1. The Judicial power shall extend to all cases, in law and equity, arising under this Constitution, the laws of the United States, and treaties made, or which shall be made, under their authority;—to all cases affecting ambassadors, other public ministers and consuls;—to all cases of admiralty and maritime jurisdiction;—to controversies to which the United States shall be a party;—to controversies between two or more States;—between a state and citizens of another State; [9]—between citizens of different States,—between citizens of the same State claiming lands under grants of different States, and between a State, or the citizens thereof, and foreign States, citizens or subjects.

2. In all cases affecting ambassadors, other public ministers and consuls, and those in which a State shall be party, the Supreme Court shall have original jurisdiction. In all the other cases before mentioned, the Supreme Court shall have appellate jurisdiction, both as to law and to fact, with such exceptions, and under such regulations as the Congress shall make.

3. The trial of all crimes, except in cases of impeachment, shall be by jury; and such trial shall be held in the State where the said crimes shall have been committed; but when not committed within any State, the trial shall at such place or places as the Congress may by law have directed.

Section 3

1. Treason against the United States shall consist only in levying war against them, or in adhering to their enemies, giving them aid and com-

[9] See the Eleventh Amendment, p. 376.

fort. No person shall be convicted of treason unless on the testimony of two witnesses to the same overt act, or on confession in open court.

2. The Congress shall have power to declare the punishment of treason, but no attainder of treason shall work corruption of blood, or forfeiture except during the life of the person attained.

ARTICLE IV
Section 1

Full faith and credit shall be given in each State to the public acts, records, and judicial proceedings of every other State. And the Congress may by general laws prescribe the manner in which acts, records and proceedings shall be proved, and the effect thereof.

Section 2

1. The citizens of each State shall be entitled to all privileges and immunities of citizens in the several States.

2. A person charged in any State with treason, felony, or other crime, who shall flee from justice, and be found in another State, shall on demand of the executive authority of the State from which he fled, be delivered up to be removed to the State having jurisdiction of the crime.

3. No person held to service or labor in one State under the laws thereof, escaping into another, shall, in consequence of any law or regulation therein, be discharged from such service or labor, but shall be delivered up on claim of the party to whom such service or labor may be due.

Section 3

1. New States may be admitted by the Congress into this Union; but no new State shall be formed or erected within the jurisdiction of any other State; nor any State be formed by the junction of two or more States, or parts of States, without the consent of the legislatures of the States concerned as well as of the Congress.

2. The Congress shall have power to dispose of and make all needful rules and regulations respecting the territory or other property belonging to the United States; and nothing in this Constitution shall be so construed as to prejudice any claims of the United States, or of any particular State.

Section 4

The United States shall guarantee to every State in this Union a republican form of government, and shall protect each of them against invasion; and on application of the legislature, or of the executive (when the legislature cannot be convened) against domestic violence.

ARTICLE V

The Congress, whenever two-thirds of both Houses shall deem it necessary, shall propose amendments to this Constitution, or, on the application of the legislatures of two-thirds of the several States, shall call a convention for proposing amendments, which, in either case, shall be valid to all intents and purposes, as part of this Constitution when ratified by the legislatures of three-fourths of the several States, or by conventions in three-fourths thereof, as the one or the other mode of ratification may be proposed by the Congress; Provided that no amendment which may be made prior to the year one thousand eight hundred and eight shall in any manner affect the first and fourth clauses in the ninth section of the first article; and that no State, without its consent, shall be deprived of its equal suffrage in the Senate.

ARTICLE VI

1. All debts contracted, and engagements entered into, before the adoption of this Constitution, shall be as valid against the United States under this Constitution, as under the Confederation.

2. This Constitution, and the laws of the United States which shall be made in pursuance thereof; and all treaties made, or which shall be made, under the authority of the United States, shall be the supreme law of the land; and the Judges in every State shall be bound thereby, anything in the Constitution or laws of any State to the contrary notwithstanding.

3. The senators and representatives before mentioned, and the members of the several State legislatures, and all executive and judicial officers, both of the United States and of the several States, shall be bound by oath or affirmation to support this Constitution; but no religious test shall ever be required as a qualification to any office or public trust under the United States.

ARTICLE VII

The ratification of the conventions of nine States shall be sufficient for the establishment of this Constitution between the States so ratifying the same.

Done in Convention by the unanimous consent of the States present the seventeenth day of September in the year of our Lord one thousand seven hundred and eighty-seven, and of the independence of the United States of America the twelfth. In witness whereof we have hereunto subscribed our names.

[Names omitted]

Articles in addition to, and amendment of, the Constitution of the United States of America, proposed by Congress, and ratified by the legislatures of the several States pursuant to the fifth article of the original Constitution.

ARTICLE I [10]

Congress shall make no law respecting an establishment of religion, or prohibiting the free exercise thereof; or abridging the freedom of speech, or of the press; or the right of the people peaceably to assemble, and to petition the government for a redress of grievances.

ARTICLE II

A well regulated militia, being necessary to the security of a free State, the right of the people to keep and bear arms shall not be infringed.

ARTICLE III

No soldier shall, in time of peace, be quartered in any house, without the consent of the owner, nor in time of war, but in a manner to be prescribed by law.

ARTICLE IV

The right of the people to be secure in their persons, houses, papers, and effects against unreasonable searches and seizures, shall not be violated, and no warrants shall issue, but upon probable cause, supported by oath or affirmation, and particularly describing the place to be searched, and the persons or things to be seized.

ARTICLE V

No person shall be held to answer for a capital, or otherwise infamous crime, unless on a presentment or indictment of a grand jury, except in cases arising in the land or naval forces, or in the militia, when in actual service in time of war or public danger; nor shall any person be subject for the same offense to be twice put in jeopardy of life or limb; nor shall be compelled in any criminal case to be a witness against himself, nor be deprived of life, liberty, or property, without due process of law; nor shall private property be taken for public use without just compensation.

ARTICLE VI

In all criminal prosecutions, the accused shall enjoy the right to a speedy and public trial, by an impartial jury of the State and district wherein the crime shall have been committed, which district shall have been previously

[10] The first ten amendments were adopted in 1791.

ascertained by law, and to be informed of the nature and cause of the accusation; to be confronted with the witnesses against him; to have compulsory process for obtaining witnesses in his favor, and to have the assistance of counsel for his defense.

ARTICLE VII

In suits at common law, where the value in controversy shall exceed twenty dollars, the right of trial by jury shall be preserved, and no fact tried by a jury shall be otherwise re-examined in any court of the United States, than according to the rules of the common law.

ARTICLE VIII

Excessive bail shall not be required, nor excessive fines imposed, nor cruel and unusual punishments inflicted.

ARTICLE IX

The enumeration of the Constitution of certain rights shall not be construed to deny or disparage others retained by the people.

ARTICLE X

The powers not delegated to the United States by the Constitution, nor prohibited by it to the States, are reserved to the States respectively, or to the people.

ARTICLE XI [11]

The judicial power of the United States shall not be construed to extend to any suit in law or equity, commenced or prosecuted against one of the United States by citizens of another State, or by citizens or subjects of any foreign State.

ARTICLE XII [12]

The electors shall meet in their respective States, and vote by ballot for President and Vice President, one of whom, at least, shall not be an inhabitant of the same State with themselves; they shall name in their ballots the person voted for as President, and in distinct ballots, the person voted for as Vice President, and they shall make distinct lists of all persons voted for as President and of all persons voted for as Vice President, and of the number of votes for each, which lists they shall sign and certify, and transmit sealed to the seat of the government of the United States, directed to the President of the Senate;—The President of the Senate shall, in the presence

[11] Adopted in 1798.
[12] Adopted in 1804.

of the Senate and House of Representatives, open all the certificates and the votes shall then be counted;—The person having the greatest number of votes for President, shall be the President, if such number be a majority of the whole number of electors appointed; and if no person have such majority, then from the persons having the highest numbers not exceeding three on the list of those voted for as President, the House of Representatives shall choose immediately, by ballot, the President. But in choosing the President, the votes shall be taken by States, the representation from each State having one vote; a quorum for this purpose shall consist of a member or members from two thirds of the States, and a majority of all the States shall be necessary to a choice. And if the House of Representatives shall not choose a President whenever the right of choice shall devolve upon them, before the fourth day of March next following, then the Vice President shall act as President, as in the case of the death or other constitutional disability of the President. The person having the greatest number of votes as Vice President shall be the Vice President, if such number be a majority of the whole number of electors appointed, and if no person have a majority, then from the two highest numbers on the list, the Senate shall choose the Vice President; a quorum for the purpose shall consist of two thirds of the whole number of Senators, and a majority of the whole number shall be necessary to a choice. But no person constitutionally ineligible to the office of President shall be eligible to that of Vice President of the United States.

ARTICLE XIII [13]

1. Neither slavery nor involuntary servitude, except as punishment for crime whereof the party shall have been duly convicted, shall exist within the United States, or any place subject to their jurisdiction.

2. Congress shall have power to enforce this article by appropriate legislation.

ARTICLE XIV [14]

1. All persons born or naturalized in the United States, and subject to the jurisdiction thereof, are citizens of the United States and of the State wherein they reside. No State shall make or enforce any law which shall abridge the privileges or immunities of citizens of the United States; nor shall any State deprive any persons of life, liberty, or property, without due process of law; nor deny to any person within its jurisdiction the equal protection of the laws.

2. Representatives shall be apportioned among the several States according to their respective numbers, counting the whole number of persons in

[13] Adopted in 1865.
[14] Adopted in 1868.

each State, excluding Indians not taxed. But when the right to vote at any election for the choice of electors for President and Vice President of the United States, representatives in Congress, the executive and judicial officers of a State, or the members of the legislature thereof, is denied to any of the male inhabitants of such State, being twenty-one years of age, and citizens of the United States, or in any way abridged, except for participation in rebellion, or other crime, the basis of representation therein shall be reduced in the proportion which the number of such male citizens shall bear to the whole number of male citizens twenty-one years of age in such State.

3. No person shall be a senator or representative in Congress, or elector of President and Vice President, or hold any office, civil or military, under the United States, or under any State, who, having previously taken an oath, as a member of Congress, or as an officer of the United States, or as a member of any State legislature, or as an executive or judicial officer of any State, to support the Constitution of the United States, shall have engaged in insurrection or rebellion against the same, or given aid or comfort to the enemies thereof. But Congress may by a vote of two-thirds of each House, remove such disability.

4. The validity of the public debt of the United States, authorized by law, including debts incurred for payment of pensions and bounties for services in suppressing insurrection or rebellion, shall not be questioned. But neither the United States nor any State shall assume or pay any debt or obligation incurred in aid of insurrection or rebellion against the United States, or any claim for the loss or emancipation of any slave; but all such debts, obligations, and claims shall be held illegal and void.

5. The Congress shall have power to enforce, by appropriate legislation, the provisions of this article.

ARTICLE XV [15]
Section 1

The right of citizens of the United States to vote shall not be denied or abridged by the United States or by any State on account of race, color, or previous condition of servitude.

Section 2

The Congress shall have power to enforce this article by appropriate legislation.

ARTICLE XVI [16]

The Congress shall have power to lay and collect taxes on incomes, from whatever source derived, without apportionment among the several States, and without regard to any census or enumeration.

[15] Adopted in 1870.
[16] Passed in 1909; proclaimed in 1913.

ARTICLE XVII [17]

The Senate of the United States shall be composed of two senators from each state, elected by the people thereof, for six years; and each senator shall have one vote. The electors in each State shall have the qualifications requisite for electors of the most numerous branch of the State legislature.

When vacancies happen in the representation of any State in the Senate, the executive authority of such State shall issue writs of election to fill such vacancies: *Provided,* That the legislature of any State may empower the executive thereof to make temporary appointments until the people fill the vacancies by election as the legislature may direct.

This amendment shall not be so constructed as to affect the election or term of any senator chosen before it becomes valid as part of the Constitution.

ARTICLE XVIII [Repealed by 21st Amendment] [18]

After one year from the ratification of this article, the manufacture, sale, or transportation of intoxicating liquors within, the importation thereof into, or the exportation thereof from the United States and all territory subject to the jurisdiction thereof for beverage purposes is hereby prohibited.

The Congress and the several States shall have concurrent power to enforce this article by appropriate legislation.

This article shall be inoperative unless it shall have been ratified as an amendment to the Constitution by the legislatures of the several States, as provided in the Constitution, within seven years from the date of the submission hereof to the states by Congress.

ARTICLE XIX [19]

The right of citizens of the United States to vote shall not be denied or abridged by the United States or by any State on account of sex.

The Congress shall have power by appropriate legislation to enforce the provisions of this article.

ARTICLE XX [20]
Section 1

The terms of the President and Vice President shall end at noon on the 20th day of January, and the terms of Senators and Representatives at noon on the 3d day of January, of the years in which such terms would have

---

[17] Passed 1912, in lieu of paragraph one, section 3, Article I, of the Constitution and so much of paragraph two of the same section as relates to the filling of vacancies; proclaimed 1913.

[18] Submitted by Congress, 1917; proclaimed, 1919.

[19] Proposed in 1919, adopted in 1920.

[20] Proposed in 1932, adopted in 1933.

ended if this article had not been ratified; and the terms of their successors shall then begin.

Section 2

The Congress shall assemble at least once in every year, and such meeting shall begin at noon on the 3d day of January, unless they shall by law appoint a different day.

Section 3

If, at the time fixed for the beginning of the term of the President, the President elect shall have died, the Vice President elect shall become President. If a President shall not have been chosen before the time fixed for the beginning of his term, or if the President elect shall have failed to qualify, then the Vice President elect shall act as President until a President shall have qualified; and the Congress may by law provide for the case wherein neither a President elect nor a Vice President elect shall have qualified, declaring who shall then act as President, or the manner in which one who is to act shall be selected, and such person shall act accordingly until a President or Vice President shall have qualified.

Section 4

The Congress may by law provide for the case of the death of any of the persons from whom the House of Representatives may choose a President whenever the right of choice shall have devolved upon them, and for the case of the death of any of the persons from whom the Senate may choose a Vice President whenever the right of choice shall have devolved upon them.

Section 5

Sections 1 and 2 shall take effect on the 15th day of October following the ratification of this article.

Section 6

This article shall be inoperative unless it shall have been ratified as an amendment to the Constitution by the legislatures of three-fourths of the several States within seven years from the date of its submission.

ARTICLE XXI [21]

Section 1

The eighteenth article of amendment to the Constitution of the United States is hereby repealed.

[21] Adopted in 1933.

Section 2

The transportation or importation into any state, territory, or possession of the United States for delivery or use therein of intoxicating liquors, in violation of the laws thereof, is hereby prohibited.

Section 3

This article shall be inoperative unless it shall have been ratified as an amendment to the Constitution by convention in the several States, as provided in the Constitution, within seven years from the date of the submission hereof to the States by the Congress.

ARTICLE XXII [22]
Section 1

No person shall be elected to the office of President more than twice, and no person who has held the office of President, or acted as President for more than two years of a term to which some other person was elected President, shall be elected to the office of the President more than once.

Section 2

But this Article shall not apply to any person holding the office of President when this Article was proposed by the Congress, and shall not prevent any person who may be holding the office of President, or acting as President, during the term within which this Article becomes operative from holding office of President or acting as President during the remainder of such term.

ARTICLE XXIII [23]

1. The District constituting the seat of Government of the United States shall appoint in such manner as the Congess may direct:

A number of electors of President and Vice President equal to the whole number of Senators and Representatives in Congress to which the District would be entitled if it were a State, but in no event more than the least populous state; they shall be in addition to those appointed by the states, but they shall be considered, for the purposes of the election of President and Vice President, to be electors appointed by a state; and they shall meet in the District and perform such duties as provided by the twelfth article of amendment.

2. The Congress shall have power to enforce this article by appropriate legislation.

[22] Proposed in 1947, adopted in 1951.
[23] Adopted in 1961.

ARTICLE XXIV [24]

Section 1

The right of citizens of the United States to vote in any primary or other election for President or Vice President, for electors for President or Vice President, or for Senator or Representative in Congress, shall not be denied or abridged by the United States or any State by reason of failure to pay any poll tax or other tax.

Section 2

The Congress shall have power to enforce this article by appropriate legislation.

[24] Adopted in 1964.

Suggestions
for Further Reading

So vast is the number of books and articles about subjects touched on in this book that it is not possible to print an adequate bibliography here. For the sake, however, of those readers whose first experience with systematic discussion of American government comes with this book, I have compiled a list of suggestions for further reading. So that it might be genuinely helpful, the list has been kept brief, including no more books than the serious beginning student might reasonably be expected to read. Furthermore, it is limited to those books which seem to be genuinely penetrating and original arguments; it avoids so far as possible derivative studies and mere compilations of so-called fact. Perhaps more accurately, this is a list of books which I have found especially helpful in my own thinking about the subject. It does not pretend to be anything more than that.

General Treatises: The beginning student can, I believe, get a deeper appreciation of our system of government from a half-dozen or so great treatises produced at different stages of our historical development than from many times that number of specialized monographs produced today. Fortunately for that purpose, at least once a generation since 1788 someone has written a thoughtful study of American constitutional forms, one with so broad a sweep that it helps greatly in understanding American government today. The first such is *The Federalist Papers* (now available in many convenient editions), written by Alexander Hamilton, James Madison, and John Jay as propaganda for the Constitution during the campaign over its adoption in New York. It remains the great rationalization of our constitutional forms and ought to be thoroughly mastered by anyone who wishes to understand just what they were intended to be. During the 1830's, Alexis De Tocqueville traveled through the United States and then wrote *Democracy in America;* the most recent edition is edited by Phillips Bradley (New York, Knopf, 1945, 2 vols.). De Tocqueville was a sensitive observer and a many-sided thinker, and hence his book is still of great value today for the study of the methods and problems of our democracy; but the reader ought always to remember that he wrote it because he believed democracy was the wave of the future and because he was not certain he liked the direction the wave was carrying him. Although Walter Bagehot's study, *The English Constitution* (published in 1867 and often reprinted) is accurately described by its title, it proceeds by constant (and invidious) comparison with American government; the comparisons contribute much to an understanding of the features of American government which Bagehot thought were unique. Just as *The Federalist Papers* were the primary statement of the traditional rationale of our political forms, *The English Constitution* is the primary statement of a more critical appreciation of them; and for that reason alone it ought to be read by the contemporary student. Most of what Bagehot had to say, however, can be got from Woodrow Wilson, *Congressional Government* (Boston, Houghton Mifflin, 1885), which has the merit of Bagehot's theory combined with a clear exposition of the way the national government really worked in the early 1880's. The disadvantage of Wilson's book is that time soon passed it by, that Presidential leadership soon superseded Congressional government. Although James Bryce, *The American Commonwealth* (New York, Macmillan, 1888, 2 vols. revised 1893–95, 1910, 1914) is regarded as a great classic, it is, perhaps, too conventionally encyclopedic; it does contain, however, one of the first good systematic treatments of our party politics, a subject which had seldom been discussed up to that time. A more penetrating discussion of the theoretical problems of our party politics during roughly the same period is to be found in Frank Goodnow, *Politics and Administration* (New York, Macmillan, 1900). *The Spirit of American Government* (New York, Macmillan, 1908) by J. Allen Smith, an aggressive exposition of the Progressive viewpoint, contains many revealing observations about every aspect of American government. D. W. Brogan, *Government of the People* (New York, Harpers, 1933), is an excellent survey of our constitutional forms and party politics written by a sympathetic Englishman on the eve of the New Deal. It is almost exactly one hundred years later than *Democracy in America* and has almost as much of the same virtue, that is, clear analysis by a foreigner after close study of American life. Of recent treatises, the two best—very different in their points of view— seem to me to be Harold Laski, *The American Democracy* (New York, Viking Press, 1948), and William Mitchell, *The American Polity* (Glencoe, Ill., The Free Press, 1962).

Chapter 1: The meaning of the word *democracy* is much discussed, although, unfortunately, seldom very thoughtfully. Some of the most worthwhile comments on this difficult subject are scattered through all the general treatises heretofore mentioned. The definition set forth in this chapter is the end-product of a line of thought which was initiated by A. D. Lindsay, *The Modern Democratic State* (London, Oxford University Press, 1943), vol. I, Ernest Barker, *Reflections on Government* (London, Oxford University Press, 1942), and Carl Becker, *Modern Democracy* (New Haven, Yale University Press, 1941). Much of the best discussion with which I am familiar of the formal definition of democracy is in the pamphlet, *What Is Democracy?* (London, National Peace Council, circa 1946), reprinting articles from the *Manchester Guardian* by A. D. Lindsay, Salvador de Madariaga, Harold Laski, Bertrand Russell, and D. W. Brogan. Excellent recent discussions of democracy are Robert Dahl, *A Preface to Democratic Theory* (Chicago, University of Chicago Press, 1956), Anthony Downs, *An Economic Theory of Democracy* (New York, Harper and Bros., 1957), and Thomas L. Thorson, *The Logic of Democracy* (New York, Holt, Rinehart and Winston, 1962). The background and significance of the five documents here used for the definition—and of many others in similar vein—is well explained in *Great Expressions of Human Rights*, edited by R. M. MacIver (New York, Institute for Religious and Social Studies, Harper, 1950), although no effort is made in the series of essays to extract an essential meaning from the several documents together.

Chapter 2: Most discussions of suffrage are, unfortunately, entirely technical, taking for granted the theory of democracy and the relation of democracy and suffrage. There are, however, several books which, although technical, do escape from the simple recitation of fact. The best of these are the reports for 1961 and 1962 of the United States Commission on Civil Rights, which may be compared with the older report of the President's Committee on Civil Rights, *To Secure These Rights* (Washington, Government Printing Office, 1947). Harold Gosnell, *Democracy: The Threshold of Freedom* (New York, Ronald Press, 1948), is a good systematic analysis of American suffrage within an adequate theoretical framework, while Dudley C. McGovney, *The American Suffrage Medley* (Chicago, University of Chicago Press, 1949), is especially interesting for its argument for the nationalization of suffrage laws. On voting behavior generally, by far the best work is: Angus Campbell, Philip E. Converse, Warren E. Miller, and Donald E. Stokes, *The American Voter* (New York, John Wiley and Sons, 1960).

Chapter 3: There are two complementary methods of studying our political parties: One is the systematic analysis of party forms and the interplay of parties, pressure groups, and public policy. The other is historical description of party action in particular localities. Three very good books of the first sort are Pendleton Herring, *The Politics of Democracy* (New York, Farrar and Rinehart, 1940), which is generally naturalistic in its philosophical framework, E. E. Schattschneider, *Party Government* (New York, Farrar and Rinehart, 1942), which is somewhat more critical of party forms and looks toward a renovation of party structure, and David Truman,

The Governmental Process (New York, Knopf, 1951), which represents the interest-group approach to politics. V. O. Key, Jr., *Southern Politics in State and Nation* (New York, Knopf, 1949), is a magnificent description and analysis of the eleven states of the old Confederacy, and his work *American State Politics* (New York, Knopf, 1956) is the best general study of politics in the states. Paul Lazarsfeld, Bernard Berelson, and Hazel Gaudet, *The People's Choice: How the Voter Makes Up His Mind in a Presidential Campaign* (2nd ed., New York, Columbia University Press, 1948), is an intensive analysis by public opinion polling methods of one Ohio county in one election year, while Bernard Berleson, Paul Lazarsfeld, and William McPhee, *Voting* (Chicago, University of Chicago Press, 1954), is a similar analysis of Elmira, New York. Other informative studies of local politics are James Q. Wilson, *The Amateur Democrat* (Chicago, University of Chicago Press, 1962), and Robert Dahl, *Who Governs?* (New Haven, Yale University Press, 1961). For a bibliography of such materials, see William H. Riker, *The Study of Local Politics* (New York, Random House, 1958).

Concerning civil liberties, which are touched on in this chapter, the books referred to under Chapter 1 all have intelligent discussions, as also do the reports of the United States Commission on Civil Rights (listed under Chapter 2). The classic discussion of a particular civil liberty is Zechariah Craffee, *Free Speech in the United States* (rev. ed., Cambridge, Mass., Harvard University Press, 1941). A good recent survey of civil rights is Paul G. Kauper, *Civil Liberties and the Constitution* (Ann Arbor, University of Michigan Press, 1962), while a critical study of recent Supreme Court decisions is to be found in Walter Berns, *Freedom, Virtue, and the First Amendment* (Baton Rouge, Louisiana State University Press, 1957). In the last thirty years, however, most of the profound discussion of civil liberties has been worked into opinions of the Supreme Court, printed in the *United States Reports*. The casebooks listed under Chapter 7 serve as a good introduction to this vast storehouse of ideas.

Chapter 4: Nearly all the contemporary discussion of the making of the Constitution depends on Max Farrand, *The Records of the Federal Convention of 1787* (New Haven, Yale University Press, vols. I–III, 1911, vol. IV, 1937). Although these four fat volumes may seem somewhat forbidding to the beginning student, there is no better way to understand the Convention than to follow—by means of the index—a few particular subjects through the *Records*. Jonathan Elliot, ed., *Debates in the Several State Conventions on the Adoption of the Federal Constitution* (2nd ed., Washington, printed by the author, 1836–45, 5 vols.), is harder than Farrand for the beginning student to use, but some of the debates recorded in it are very informative, especially those in Virginia. And, of course, no study of the framing of the Constitution can go very far without a knowledge of *The Federalist Papers* (listed above under General Treatises). Charles Warren, *The Making of the Constitution* (Boston, Little, Brown, 1928) is a comprehensive, day-by-day account of the Convention based on Farrand's *Records*. In sharp contrast to Warren, who treats the Convention traditionally, is Charles Beard, *An Economic Interpretation of the Constitution of the United States* (New York, Macmillan, 1913), which is debunking and realistic in turn. A critical revision of Beard's theory is to be found in Robert E. Brown, *Charles Beard and the Constitution* (Princeton, Princeton University Press, 1956). A recent and well-written account, influenced by Beard but leaning toward the traditional interpretation, is Carl Van Doren, *The Great Rehearsal* (New York, Viking Press, 1948). The political condition of the states just prior to the Convention, a subject too often neglected or only cursorily treated in discussions of the Convention itself, is very well handled in Allan Nevins, *The American States During and After the Revolution, 1775–1789* (2nd ed., New York, Macmillan, 1927).

Chapter 5: The not very successful movement during the last decade for reassertion of Congressional power has inspired a number of studies of Congress, two of which are really outstanding: Roland Young, *This Is Congress* (2nd ed., New York, Knopf, 1946), and Bertram M. Gross, *The Legislative Struggle* (New York, McGraw-Hill, 1953). The former is especially good on the structure of Congress, while the latter is especially good in its analysis of Congress' operation. Standing back of these, perhaps as their model, is Woodrow Wilson's great study, *Congressional Government* (listed above under General Treatises). Among the more specialized studies of recent years, several deserve mention: Donald Matthews, *U. S. Senators and Their World* (Chapel Hill, University of North Carolina Press, 1960), is the definitive study of the Senate. Stephen K. Bailey, *Congress Makes a Law: The Story Behind the Employment Act of 1946* (New York, Columbia University Press, 1950), and Raymond A. Bauer, Ithiel de Sola Pool, and Lewis Anthony Dexter, *American Business and Public Policy: The Politics of Foreign Aid* (New York, Atherton, 1963), are two excellent and detailed case studies of legislation; Arthur MacMahon, "Congressional Oversight of Administration: The Power of the Purse," *Political Science Quarterly,* LV (1943), 161–190, 380–414, is an excellent brief summary of financial procedure, while David Truman, *The Congressional Party* (New York, John Wiley, 1959), is an excellent study of political parties in Congress. Finally, one should mention the highly perceptive work of a Congressman: Clem Miller, *Member of the House,* edited by John W. Baker (New York, Scribner's, 1962).

Chapter 6: The outstanding work on the Presidency, one which is generally in accord with the emphasis of this chapter, is Richard E. Neustadt, *Presidential Power* (New York, John Wiley and Sons, 1960). Two other outstanding general treatises are: Edward S. Corwin, *The President: Office and Powers* (rev. ed., New York, New York University Press, 1941), which emphasizes the legal structure of the office, and Pendleton Herring, *Presidential Leadership* (New York, Farrar and Rinehart, 1940), which emphasizes the political operation of it. The relation of the President to the administrative system is well treated in the reports of the two national committees on administrative reform: The President's Committee on Administrative Management, *Administrative Management in the Government of the United States* (Washington, Government Printing Office, 1937), and Commission of the Organization of the Executive Branch of the Government (popularly known as the Hoover Commission), *Concluding Report,* House Document #97, Eightieth Congress. Of course, most textbooks on public administration deal extensively with this subject; the most attractive of them for the beginning student is, I think, Charles Hyneman, *Bureaucracy in a Democracy* (New York, Harpers, 1950).

Undoubtedly the best way to understand the role of the President is to understand Presidents themselves. Unfortunately the occupants of the office have seldom had either the leisure of retirement to write extensively or the inclination to speak frankly about their life and work. However, two Presidents have left extraordinarily valuable autobiographical accounts, *Polk: The Diary of a President, 1845–1849,* edited by Milo Quaife (Chicago, McClurg, 1910, 4 vols.), and Theodore Roosevelt, *Autobiography* (New York, Charles Scribner's, 1920). But although Presidents themselves have been reticent, many good biographers and historians have been attracted to the study of them. Out of a very large number of good studies, I recommend the following for the beginning student: Leonard White's two books, *The Federalists: A Study in Administrative History* (New York, Macmillan, 1948) and *The Jeffersonians: A study in Administrative History, 1801–1829* (New York, Macmillan, 1951), because they are by a man who understands administration; Claude Bowers, *Jefferson in Power* (Boston, Houghton Mifflin, 1936), because it is by a man who understands party politics; Arthur M. Schlesinger, Jr., *The Age of Jackson* (Boston, Little, Brown, 1945), because it is by a man who understands the role of party politics and Presidential leadership in the whole society: Carl Sandburg, *Abraham Lincoln: The War Years* (New York, Harcourt, Brace, 1939, 4 vols.), because it is by a man who understands American heroes and hero-worship; Henry Pringle, *Theodore Roosevelt* (New York, Harcourt, Brace, 1931), because it is by a man who understands the politicians' personality; and Robert Sherwood, *Roosevelt and Hopkins* (New York, Harpers, 1948), Frances Perkins, *The Roosevelt I Knew* (New York, Viking Press, 1946), and Rexford Tugwell, *The Democratic Roosevelt* (New York, Doubleday, 1957), because all three authors taken together understand the most recent of our hero Presidents.

Chapter 7: The role of the Supreme Court has been well studied by scholars. Of the analytical works, two by Glendon Schubert are unquestionably the most revealing: *Quantitative Analysis of Judicial Behavior* (Glencoe, Ill., The Free Press, 1959), and *Constitutional Politics* (New York, Holt, Rinehart and Winston, 1960). Of the historical works, Charles Warren, *The Supreme Court in United States History* (rev. ed., Boston, Little, Brown, 1926, 2 vols.), is instinctively Federalist in bias, while Charles Grove Haines, *The Role of the Supreme Court in American Government and Politics, 1789–1835* (Berkeley, Calif., University of California Press, 1944) is frankly Jeffersonian. The Court's action during the early New Deal of course occasioned a vast literary debate, of which Robert H. Jackson, *The Struggle for Judicial Supremacy* (New York, Knopf, 1941), and Charles P. Curtis, *Lions Under the Throne* (Boston, Houghton Mifflin, 1947), seem to be among the most thoughtful. Ever since Albert Beveridge wrote his monumental *Life of John Marshall* (Boston, Houghton Mifflin, 1916), judicial biography has been a popular field. Among the best and most useful of these books are Charles Fairman, *Mr. Justice Miller and the Supreme Court, 1862–1890* (Cambridge, Mass., Harvard University Press, 1939), Max Lerner, *The Mind and Faith of Mr. Justice Holmes: His Speeches, Essays, Letters, and Judicial Opinions Selected and Edited with an Introduction and Commentary* (Boston, Little, Brown, 1943), and Alpheus Mason, *Brandeis: A Free Man's Life* (New York, Viking Press, 1946). Possibly the best way, however, for the student to understand the Supreme Court is to read judicial opinions. While the *United States Reports* are quite cumbersome for the beginner, there are a number of good casebooks designed for beginning students: Wallace Mendelson, *The Constitution and the Supreme Court* (New York, Dodd Mead, 1959), and Rocco J. Tresolini, *American Constitutional Law* (New York, Macmillan, 1965). Both have excellent introductory notes and comment.

Chapter 8: Important as federalism is in American politics, it has seldom been discussed theoretically, although there are many monographs on technical problems. Inasmuch as the relations between the national government and the states have been a continuing concern for the Supreme Court, the books listed under Chapter 7 are perhaps the best source of material, both theoretical and technical, available today. About the only general studies available are William H. Riker, *Federalism* (Boston, Little, Brown, 1964), and Arthur W. MacMahon, ed., *Federalism: Mature and Emergent* (New York, Doubleday, 1955). For the portion of this chapter that deals with political parties, the list of books under Chapter 3 should be consulted.

Chapter 9: In addition to the materials listed under Chapter 6, two books extensively cited in the text should be recommended here: Committee on Political Parties of the American Political Science Association, *Toward a More Responsible Party System* (New York, Rinehart, 1950), and Dixon Wecter, *The Hero in America* (New York, Charles Scribner's, 1941).

Index